Analyzing Variation in Language

in Language

Papers from the Second Colloquium
on New Ways of Analyzing Variation

Ralph W. Fasold
Roger W. Shuy

Editors

Georgetown University Press, Washington, D.C. 20057

Library of Congress Cataloging in Publication Data

Colloquium on New Ways of Analyzing Variation, 2d,
    Georgetown University, 1973.
    Analyzing variation in language.

    1. Language and languages--Variation--Congresses.
2. Languages in contact--Congresses. 3. Sign lan-
guage--Congresses. I. Fasold, Ralph W. II. Shuy,
Roger W. III. Title.
P120.C6 1973   401.   75-15973
ISBN 0-87840-207-1

International Standard Book Number: 0-87840-207-1

CONTENTS

VARIATION THEORY

VARIATION IN GRAMMAR

APPLICATIONS OF VARIATION STUDIES

PREFACE

An increasing number of linguists become aware that a fully adequate linguistic theory must account for the variation that is apparent
in language. Variation has come to be studied from numerous perspectives. In October 1973, the Second Annual Colloquium on New
Ways of Analyzing Variation (N-WAV) at Georgetown University provided a forum for linguists interested in variation in language.

The present volume contains twenty papers selected from those
presented at the conference. The topics of these papers represent
the different perspectives in which variation is approached. A number
of them represent efforts to analyze and develop the theoretical framework proposed by William Labov and the variation theorists who have
followed him. But while most of the work in this framework has dealt
with phonology and surface syntax, other scholars have begun to investigate variation at deeper syntactic levels, in semantics, and in
the conventions of language use. Investigations of these types are
also to be found in this collection, as well as studies of variation
growing out of language-contact situations and of variation in the sign
language used by the deaf. One contribution suggests ways in which
the study of variation can be applied.

This collection is a companion volume to New Ways of Analyzing
Variation in English edited by Charles-James Bailey and Roger Shuy,
which contains papers from the first N-WAV colloquium.

R. W. S.
R. W. F.

VARIED OBJECTIONS
TO VARIOUS VARIABLE RULES

FRANK ANSHEN

State University of New York

Introduction.   A casual and perhaps incomplete count reveals that the data on deletion of que by French-Canadian speakers in Montreal has been analyzed according to five different conceptions of how to handle variable data: once by G. Sankoff (1973), once by Cedergren and D. Sankoff (1973), once by Bickerton (1973), and twice in the same paper by Berdan (1973a). Labov's data on copula deletion in Black English also has been treated from a variety of views: first by Labov (1969), then by Bickerton (1971), Cedergren and Sankoff (1973), and Berdan (1973a). Clearly it is difficult to take seriously the study of language variation if all that its practitioners can say is that there are several possible analyses, any of which may be true. Unfortunately it is not true that we can choose between these alternative analyses simply on the basis of how well they describe the que and copula data. If it were, then the proponents of the various incorrect proposals could be shown the error of their ways and peace would reign over the land. It is the purpose of this paper to investigate the various claims entailed by these various analyses with the aim of supporting some, refuting some, and identifying those which are still up for grabs and how they might be supported or refuted. It is hoped that this will permit those of us studying linguistic variation to concentrate our energies on questions of fact rather than ideology.

The proposals

The most basic division among proposals puts Bickerton on one side with Labov, Cedergren, the Sankoffs, and Berdan on the other.

1

All of the latter use models which accept as fact that variation is inherent in certain grammatical rules. That is, they believe that associated with certain rules are a set of probabilities describing the probability of application of that rule in various environments. In contrast, Bickerton believes that variation is more apparent than real, an artifact of the fact that groups rather than individuals are the unit of analysis. He feels that it is possible to order the environments of apparently variable rules from 1 to N so that for individuals any use of a given variant in environment K implies categorical use of that variant in environment K - 1 and any absence of that variant in environment j implies categorical absence of that variant in environment j + 1. This implies that an individual can be variable in at most one environment per rule.

Berdan is distinct from the other proponents of variable rules in that he feels that the probability of a rule applying is determined by the environment as a whole. The others break the environment down to its component parts and assign probabilities to each part. In Labov's original work (Labov 1969) he proposes an additive model of combining the probabilities of each part of the environment; more recently he, Cedergren, and the Sankoffs have favored a multiplicative model.

Deciding from data

In a recent paper, David Sankoff and Pascal Rousseau (1973) attacked Bickerton's (1973) reanalysis, by implicational rules, of the Montreal que data, in which Bickerton showed, to his own satisfaction, that implicational rules gave a more adequate account of the data than did variable rules. What Sankoff and Rousseau did was to use probability estimates based on the observed frequencies of usage by the sixteen speakers in the sample to computer-simulate que deletion for new sets of persons with the same sociological characteristics as the original people for the same number of instances for the same environments. They found that in over 1000 simulations, the most likely result was that the data which emerged was just as susceptible to implicational analysis, i.e. had the same number of violations of the implicational principle above as the original data. From this they concluded that the scaleability of the Montreal data is predicted by variable rules and the experiment gives no reason to prefer implicational analysis. This is correct and not too surprising. If variable rules are constructed from observed data which scale with N exceptions and then one uses these rules to have a computer generate new data sets, then it is reasonable that the new data sets will tend to be scaleable with N exceptions. What they do not add is that the experiment also gives no reason to prefer variable analysis if implicational analysis also predicts variable analysis. In fact it is one of Bickerton's major points that variable analysis usually is done on groups and the implicational nature of individual performance is thus concealed. To illustrate, consider the following oversimplified example. Given three people, person A has a variant categorically absent in environments 1 and 2, person B has the variable categorically in environment 1 and lacks it categorically in environment 2, and person C has the variant categorically in both environments. If the three are considered as a group, then a variable rule will be needed which gives a probability of occurrence of the variable of 2/3 in environment 1 and 1/3 in environment 2. This rule would work for the group but would be unrevealing for the individuals. In general, if implicational analysis is true for individuals then it will predict a variable analysis for groups. This leaves us in the not too happy position of variable rules predicting observed implicational rules and vice versa.

There is another area in which Bickerton's claims are more vulnerable to direct disproof by data. Bickerton (1971:476 and, implicitly, 1973:31) claims that variation can occur for individuals in at most one environment at a time with respect to a given rule. Table 1 shows the number of people with various combinations of categorical [r] absence and variable (there was no categorical) [r] presences in pertinent environments for black speakers in Hillsborough, North Carolina. If Bickerton is correct, only the two rows marked with a star should represent patterns which are actually used; in fact only twelve of sixty-seven speakers follow these patterns. Bickerton's (1973:31) own display of lects for Montreal speakers with respect to que deletion shows that nine of the sixteen speakers, that is, more than half, are variable in more than one environment. In this regard it is important to note that Bickerton's empirical base for claim that only one environment per person may be variable is two studies with relatively scant data. The Montreal data mentioned above averages only 3.2 potential instances of que per person per environment. His original study of complementizer choice in Guyana considered twenty-six speakers in three environments, but of the seventy-eight potential environments for individuals twenty-two were empty and thus unable to contribute to variation and overall the average is less than three instances of the complementizer per environment per person. Further, 78 percent of the variable cells are found in the speech of the half of the informants with the most occurrence of complementizers. On the other hand, the Hillsborough data, with its large number of variable cells, averages about thirty cases of possible [r] use per person per environment. It is not reasonable that the number of variable cells should increase as the number of

TABLE 1.   Patterns of PVR presence by environment for black speakers in Hillsborough, North Carolina.

Front vowel	Central vowel	Back vowel	ə̆	Number of people
*−	−	−	−	5
−	−	−	+	3
−	−	+	−	1
−	−	+	+	0
−	+	−	−	1
−	+	−	+	0
−	+	+	−	1
−	+	+	+	1
*+	−	−	−	7
+	−	−	+	1
+	−	+	−	2
+	−	+	+	8
+	+	−	−	4
+	+	−	+	3
+	+	+	−	5
+	+	+	+	25

+ = some PVR presence but not categorical presence
− = PVR absence
* = predicted by Bickerton

instances per cell increases. Each new instance can increase but not decrease the number of variable cells.

Group minds and such

It has been suggested by Bickerton (1971, 1973) that variable rules are unlikely in that they require the human mind to do some very unlikely things. He says an individual must know his target percentages for a variable in various environments, he must keep track of the number of times he has used a given variant in a given environment, and must calculate the new rate he must use in the future to make his usage conform to his target usage. But even here his problems do not end; he must also keep track of what other members of the groups of which he is a member are doing so that he can make his proper contribution to the group averages. He must do this even if he is out of contact with the other members. Bickerton argues that it is unlikely that a real person could do all this counting and calculating all the time and even more unlikely that he would have command of some psychic power that informed him of usage of other people whom he can neither hear nor see.

Bickerton is right that it is very unlikely that real people have these capacities, but wrong in stating that they are necessary for the operation of variable rules. Clearly, what a variable rule states is that in a given situation a given person, better still, an arbitrary member of certain social groupings, has a given probability of using a given variant. These probabilities are estimated from observed data. If this is true then nobody needs to count or calculate anything. The laws of probability will automatically make everything work out right. As a simple illustration of this, some students flipped coins fifty times each; the results are given in Table 2.

TABLE 2. Percentage of heads tossed by students with presumably honest coins.

No. of tosses		10	20	30	40	50	
Person	1	30	45	50	48	50	
	2	40	35	46	48	46	
	3	30	45	50	53	58	
	4	70	60	53	58	60	
	5	70	55	44	48	48	
	6	60	45	50	45	46	
	7	50	25	30	38	36	
	8	60	55	60	55	52	
	9	40	35	37	43	40	
	10	60	50	47	50	46	
	11	40	40	43	45	40	
Group average		50	45	47	47	47	

Note that there is a strong tendency for both the individual and the entire group to approach 50 percent heads. This is despite the fact that a coin cannot even remember what it, itself, has done, much less keep track of what other coins have done. The same conclusion is reached a different way by calculating the probability of having between 40 and 60 percent heads after a given number of tosses. After one toss it is 0, after ten it is 0.656, and after twenty-five it is .770. Again the actual total is increasingly likely to approach the number predicted by the rule as the number of instances increases. This is still without hypothesizing that the coins remember or count anything.

Finally, one must respond to Bickerton's claim that variable rules cannot work for groups the same way as to the man who proved that bumblebees cannot fly. Groups of speakers do differ from other groups of speakers by the percentage of use of certain variants and

such results are reproducible with different samples from the same
group. Wolfram's (1973) study of copula deletion in Mississippi
blacks and whites is the most recent study showing that significant
differences between groups must be expressed as differences in frequency rather than in categorical rules, but almost all major works
in sociolinguistics since Labov's (1963) Martha's Vineyard study
show the same thing.

There is still one possible question: how does an individual learn
and know the probabilities of variants occurring in various environments? The answer is that he does not need to know this in the same
way he needs to know the English passive rule. Kiparsky (1969:603-
610) suggested and my own work with general conditions on copula
deletion (Anshen 1972b) supports a claim that the effect of variable
rules is largely predictable from linguistic universal. If we know
that final /t/ and /d/ are being variably deleted we would certainly
expect that this process would be more likely where the next word
begins with a consonant than when it begins with a vowel and more
frequent where the deleted item does not contain grammatical information. Similarly, I have shown that if copulas are being optionally
deleted, the process is more likely before an adjective than a NP,
though admittedly the reason for this latter fact is more obscure
(that is, I don't know it) than the reason for the former. Under this
interpretation the effect of various constraints is predictable although
their relative power may not be. This surely simplifies the task of
the child learning the language.

Micro- and macro-linguistics

One result of dealing with linguistic variation is that one must consider seriously the relationship between individual and group linguistic behavior. One never seems to find the 'ideal speaker-hearer
in the perfectly homogeneous speech community' and it becomes increasingly obvious that 'my dialect' is not a platonic ideal from which
others may vary only at their own risk. Individuals may and do act
linguistically in ways which are not reflected by group data. Berdan
(1973a) has shown that for a sample of Los Angeles school children,
individual behavior and group behavior do not match. Similarly,
Levine and Crockett (1967) showed that the high status group of
white speakers is disproportionately made up of extremely high and
extremely low users of post-vocalic r. When the means for groups
are considered, the higher PVR users balance the low PVR users
and the mean use of PVR for the group does not differ significantly
from other groups.

Bickerson (1973) proposes to deal with this problem by assigning
grammars to individuals and assigning to the group the set of possible

individual grammars. Berdan (1973a) takes a somewhat similar
position. He assumes that sociologically determined groups within
the community share grammatical rules and that these rules are a
subset of the rules for the community as a whole. The more orthodox proponents of variable rules (Labov, Cedergren, and the Sankoffs)
do not deal with this problem explicitly but they are exploring the extent to which variable rules written for individuals reflect rules
written for the group.

I would suggest that our lives as linguists would be happier if we
recognized, as do economists, that individual behavior is interesting
and important to study, that group behavior is interesting and important to study, and that the latter may not be a direct reflection of
the former. Anshen (1972a) and Wolfram (1973) both show that there
are differences between black and white speakers in southern towns
when considered as groups. But both of these studies show differences
in relative frequencies of rule application, rather than the presence of
different rules. Further, though these differences are quite pronounced
for groups, they do not hold for all individuals. Thus, for both studies
it is possible to find individual black and white speakers whose relative frequencies are the reverse of those for whites and blacks considered in groups. Similar conclusions can be found for differences
between men's and women's speech (see Trudgill 1972 and the references cited there), and, indeed, in most sociolinguistic studies from
Labov's Martha's Vineyard paper to the present. Clearly there are
interesting linguistic differences between groups which do not hold
for all possible pairs of individuals picked from the groups.

It is with the utmost trepidation that I risk contributing to the jargon
explosion; nonetheless I think it will be helpful if we recognize two
areas within the study of linguistic variation: microlinguistics, which
is concerned with the determination of the constraints on individual
grammars, and macrolinguistics, which is concerned with the linguistic behavior of groups.

Explanatory adequacy

Bickerton (1973:28) attacks variable rules in general and Cedergren
and Sankoff's rules in particular as being mere displaying devices,
i.e. simply a rearrangement of the data, while, he states, implicational rules are explanatory, that is, based upon a theory of language change which predicts the form the data must take. In the
main he is right, although that 'mere' deserves further attention.
Cedergren and Sankoff type variable rules make few assumptions about
the form of the data and therefore it is difficult even to make up data
which would refute variable rules, whereas not only can one imagine
data which would refute Bickerton's rules, but the real data presented

above seem to contradict part of Bickerton's claims. Explanatory rules are good things, they incorporate our theories of human language into linguistic statements and they are subject to disproof. However, it is about time that somebody spoke up for the virtues of data-displaying devices. Many statistical operations including means, medians, and modes are data displaying rather than explanatory devices. Like variable rules, they merely rearrange the data in a form more easy to perceive. Nonetheless, they make it possible to draw conclusions which were not obvious from the raw data and thus to facilitate explanations. See for example Labov (1966) or for that matter almost any recent work in sociolinguistics. The problems which arise in generative grammar when one begins to take the simplicity metric seriously, should make us consider the advantages of recording our statements about the nature of language in a section called 'conclusions' rather than attempting to build them into the rules we write.

The spread of variable rules

There is one implicit claim in Cedergren-Sankoff type variable rules which contrasts interestingly with Bickerton's. Cedergren-Sankoff rules assign positive probability of occurrence of linguistic variants to almost all environments, apparently claiming that variable rules apply, though unequally in all relevant environments, and expand by a general increase in probability of occurrence in all environments. Bickerton, on the other hand, agreeing with Bailey explicitly, asserts that variable rules apply at first in only one environment and expand by adding new environments.

This is, indeed, a substantive question of the nature of linguistic change. Unfortunately it is not easy to answer. The problem arises because it is not easy to tell if an observed non-occurrence of a given variant is the result of a very small probability of rule application or if it is a result of the rule simply not applying in that environment. As pointed out above, the number of non-zero cells increases as the number of instances per cell increases; this is in accordance with the Cedergren-Sankoff prediction, but Table 1 shows that there may be a fair number of zero cells left even with a relatively large number of instances per cell, although it is not clear here how many cases are enough. Another possible way to choose between the claims would be to suggest that if rules expand by adding environments in a certain order, there should be a tendency for percentage of use in adjacently ordered environments to correlate more closely than in non-adjacent environments. Under the Cedergren-Sankoff proposal there would be no reason to assume this. Table 3 shows little clear tendency for the prediction from the Bickerton model to be true, but the results are hardly conclusive.

TABLE 3. Correlation coefficients for percentage of PVR use between environments for black speaker in Hillsborough, North Carolina.

	Front vowel	Central vowel	Back vowel	ə̆
Front	–	.685	.398	.656
Central	.685	–	.505	.711
Back	.398	.505	–	.713
ə̆	.656	.711	.713	–

Unfortunately, I am unable to devise any more conclusive tests. I am also haunted by the thought that the world may be inhabited by two types of people, those who acquire linguistic rules by the Bickerton method and those who use the Cedergren-Sankoff method.

REFERENCES

Anshen, Frank. 1972a. The statistical bases for the existence of Black English. Florida FL Reporter.
_____. 1972b. General constraints on copula deletion. Mimeographed.
Berdan, Robert. 1973a. Probability and variable rules: A formal interpretation. Paper delivered at the Summer Meeting of the Linguistic Society of America, Ann Arbor, Michigan.
_____. 1973b. The use of linguistically determined groups in sociolinguistics. SWRL Educational Research and Development.
Bickerton, Derek. 1971. Inherent variation and variable rules. Foundations of Language 7:452-492.
_____. 1973. Quantitative versus dynamic paradigms: The case of Montreal que. In: New ways of analyzing variation in English. Edited by C. J. Bailey and R. Shuy. Washington, D.C., Georgetown University Press. 23-43.
Cedergren, Henrietta and David Sankoff. 1973. Variable rules: Performance as a statistical reflection of competence. Mimeographed.
Kiparsky, Paul. 1969. Historical linguistics. In: A survey of linguistic science. Edited by William O. Dingwall. College Park, University of Maryland.
Labov, William. 1963. The social motivation of a sound change. Word 19:273-309.
_____. 1966. The social stratification of English in New York City. Arlington, Virginia, Center for Applied Linguistics.

Labov, William. 1969. Contraction, deletion, and inherent variation of the English copula. Language 45:715-767.

Levine, Lewis and Harry Crockett. 1966. Speech variation in a Piedmont community. In: Explorations in sociolinguistics. Edited by Stanley Lieberson. The Hague, Mouton & Co. 124-151.

Sankoff, David and Pascale Rousseau. MS. A method for assessing variable rule and implicational scale analysis of linguistic variation. To appear. Proceedings of the International Conference on Computers in the Humanities. Edited by C. Mitchell. Edinburgh University Press.

Sankoff, Gillian. 1972. A quantitative paradigm for the study of communicative competence. Mimeographed.

Trudgill, Peter. 1972. Sex, covert prestige and linguistic change in the urban British English of Norwich. Language in Society 1:179-195.

Wolfram, Walter. 1973. The relationship of southern white speech to vernacular Black English: Copula deletion and 'invariant be'. Mimeographed.

THE NECESSITY OF VARIABLE RULES

ROBERT BERDAN

SWRL Educational Research and Development

Since Labov (Labov et al. 1968) first introduced the notion of variable rules there have been several examples of the way in which they account for the data of sociolinguistics (e. g. Fasold 1972). There have also been significant advances in understanding the way variable rules operate, most notably the papers by Cedergren and the Sankoffs (e. g. Cedergren & Sankoff 1974). Wolfram (1973) presented arguments for the adequacy of variable rules. This paper expands on Wolfram's presentation to argue that variable rules are an essential component of any notion of linguistic competence that attempts to explain linguistic knowledge in a real-world context.

There is no argument that variation exists in speech. Variation has always been noted by careful observers of real speech. The argument is: does variation exist in language, given the traditional distinctions drawn between speech and language? More recently, variation has been assumed to be part of performance. The question becomes: can there be a meaningful notion of competence that excludes variation?

Wolfram (1973) observed that if one assumes that inherent variation does not exist, its existence can never be proven by linguistic data. Any putative instance of observed inherent variation can always be discounted as failure to observe some categorical conditioning environment. This has the form of the classical argument from ignorance: one does not know that all inherent variation will not ultimately be proven to be categorically determined. Such arguments are never very strong.

There is another equally unsatisfying argument. If one assumes that inherent variation does exist, it can never be proven by linguistic data that it does not. Demonstrating that some putative instance of inherent variation is in fact categorically conditioned by some exotic environment can disprove only that particular instance as inherent variation. It can never disprove the notion of inherent variation itself. These arguments do little to advance an understanding of variation. To pursue them is to be reduced to a shouting match of 'I like my assumptions better than yours.'

Code switching

The existence of inherent variation has been challenged from another direction. Rather than arguing that variation results from unidentified influences, this is an argument which suggests that it results from alternation among grammars, i.e. code switching. That there is code switching among bi-linguals is well-established. But recently, publications such as Dillard's (1972) work on Black English seem to argue that what has in the past been identified as inherent variation is better described as code switching. The notion of code switching implies that there is some set of rules underlying the code that may be observed to covary.

Figure 1 is a display of runs of realizations against word count. The word count is from the conversation of a black kindergarten girl from Los Angeles.[1] A run is a sequence of instances of one realization of a variable, with no intervening instances of another realization of that variable. Symbols above the zero line represent instances of a standard realization, symbols below the line represent a nonstandard realization. Vertical distance from the center line at any point in the text represents the length of a run of realizations without variation for that feature. Slope of the line reflects the density of the variable in the text. A switch from standard to nonstandard realizations, or nonstandard to standard, is shown by a line crossing the horizontal axis.

At about word 430 the girl begins to tell a rather intense story in which she claims initially that her dog and cat were shot. Later she reveals that the shot was medicine from the veterinarian as treatment for the dog, who had been run over by a car. The story continues through word 620. At that point she begins a recitation of 'Eenie, meanie, minee, moe.' This extends about to word 782.

Throughout the story and the recitation of the familiar jingle, the five variables in Figure 1 have almost exclusively nonstandard realizations. By word 800 she begins to count and to spell, or at least recite letters of the alphabet. These are school tasks and the distribution of the realizations changes markedly.

This is the type of phenomenon that is usually referred to as code switching. In this instance it is a style shift. But if this nearly simultaneous switching of linguistically distinct processes from

FIGURE 1. Runs by word count

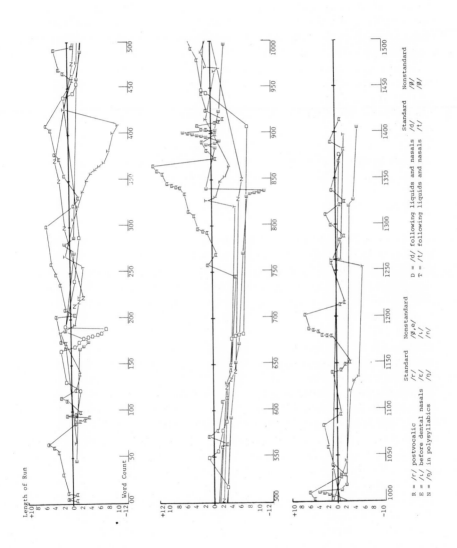

nonstandard to standard is code switching, then the situation in the first 400 words of the conversation is markedly different. There different features are observed to switch simultaneously, but in different directions. In that part of the text the five features do not covary. There are no instances of simultaneous switching of all features. Nor is there any hierarchical arrangement among features, as posited by DeCamp (1971) for sets of related codes. What there appears to be is the independent cooccurrence of randomly distributed realizations.

If this were code switching it would constitute counter-evidence to the DeCamp notion of hierarchies of codes. However, to call this code switching is to make the term synonymous with what has been called inherent variation: independent alternations among surface forms with none of the external cues associated with code switching. The fact that this is so very different from what is usually meant by code switching, that there are no predictable relationships among the 'codes', argues rather that this is not code switching at all.

Randomness

Another type of argument accepts the notion of inherent variation, but contends that the variation is random and therefore not properly described by rules in a grammar (Gobel and Kypriotaki 1973). However, this position represents a misapprehension of the notion of randomness.

It is possible to subject the data in Figure 1 to a runs analysis (Siegel 1956). One way to determine whether the realizations of some variable are randomly distributed is to count the number of runs and calculate the probability of that number occurring by chance. There are established statistical procedures for determining the number of runs to be expected in a random distribution. If the observed number of runs is greater or less than the expected, one can reject the hypothesis that the variants are randomly distributed throughout the text. Table 1 gives the probabilities associated with the number of runs observed for each of the five variables in Figure 1. None of the distributions of the variables is significantly different from chance. [2]

There is a certain imprecise but useful sense in which 'random' and 'probabilistically determined' mean essentially the same thing. To describe variation as random does not preclude describing it as 'probabilistically determined'. It is in fact the randomness of the distribution of realizations summarized in Table 1 that allows formulation of statements for the probability of any particular realization.

Variation does exist in speech. It is not just a reflex of some code switch, nor have there yet been discovered categorical explanations

TABLE 1. Runs analysis for five phonological variables

Variable	No. std.	No. nst.	Runs	Probability
/r/	67	43	43	.037
/ɛ/	14	29	13	.015
/ŋ/	4	10	4	> .05
/d/	7	24	11	.652
/t/	9	34	15	.912

within a single code. The variation is, however, random and amenable to description in probabilistic terms. From this it does not
automatically follow that the facts of variation merit incorporation
into the grammar.

It is true that the variation in Table 1 can be described as a set
of percentages. But no motivation has been presented here for including those percentages in the grammar. They are the simple
consequence of the application of an arithmetic operation to this
particular corpus spoken by this particular speaker within some
particular time-frame. To the extent that the variable rule claims
nothing more, its detractors are quite right in excluding the variable
rule from the provenience of the competence grammar. However,
there are sociolinguistic data that do argue strongly for the necessity
of incorporating variable rules into the grammar.

Patterns across time

Successive samples of speech from a single individual show that
patterns of variation are constant across time. To minimize the
enormous amount of work involved in transcription and analysis of
casual conversation, Legum and Coots (1971) explored the possibility of analyzing some sample of the available corpus. Transcripts
of the Los Angeles Child Language Survey data (Legum et al. 1971)
were divided into ten equal segments on the basis of word count.
Analysis of variance for 23 high-frequency variables on 11 transcripts
failed to show interaction between segment and realization.[3] From
this it was concluded that a sample from any segment would produce
essentially the same results as analysis of the entire text.

This means that although alternation between realizations for any
variable was random, there were no significant differences in relative
frequency as one moved through time from segment to segment of the
transcript.

In a study of plurals used by first and sixth grade black children in
Los Angeles, responses were compared across two interviews separated by several months of time. When the samples were matched for
phonological characteristics of the final consonants of the nouns, two

observations could be made. First, there were no changes between studies in the relationships among the relative frequencies for the different allomorphs of the plural morpheme. Secondly, there were virtually no significant changes in the absolute relative frequencies for any allomorph for any child.

The 'transcript segment study' and the repeated plural study show that although variation is random, for the individual the rate of variation does not vary significantly across time; in one instance it is throughout the duration of extended discourse and in the other instance it is constant between two interviews separated by several months.

This constancy argues that relative frequencies and the resulting variable rules are not simply descriptive of some corpus; they have predictive value as well. Frequency statements derived from one sample predict the rate of occurrence of realizations in other samples. In moving from describing a sample to making predictions about the population from which the sample is drawn, the notion of probability is introduced. In associating variable rules with statements of probability rather than relative frequencies, Cedergren and Sankoff (1974) have made explicit an important property of the variable rule. The variable rule, with its integral statement of probability of application, becomes the ideal device for making linguistic generalizations about the random or probabilistic distribution of realizations of linguistic variables.

Variable rules with statements of probability have predictive value for the individual. That does not preclude their being totally idiosyncratic on the one hand, or a product of some universal constraint on human behavior on the other.

Language acquisition

However, there have been other observations of regularities in variation. Consider the case of language acquisition. Language is a discontinuous phenomenon; it is learned anew by each generation. We posit for the child a Language Acquisition Device that enables him to sort through the linguistic data of his environment, make appropriate generalizations, and establish a grammar.

G. Sankoff (1973), in an interesting paper discussing syntactic variation, studied the use of a future marker by New Guinean speakers of Tok Pisin. She found that placement of the marker was best described by a variable rule, with rate of application conditioned by syntactic environment. Although both parents and their children applied the rule variably, Sankoff found no differences across generations. This suggests that when the child acquired the rule for placing the future marker, he also acquired a knowledge of the probabilistic influence of syntactic environments on its application.

If one admits variable rules in the competence grammar, this is readily accounted for by the existing mechanisms posited for language acquisition. The alternative which dismisses variation as 'vagaries of performance' puts one in the uncomfortable position of explaining how the child who acquires not only significant generalizations about his language, but also 'random' performance errors, ever makes any significant generalizations in the first place.

Cross-generation studies have, in general, not been looking for constancy in variation, and the evidence is limited. That, however, is a reflection on the paradigm of sociolinguistic research, not necessarily a reflection of the facts of language. Should future studies find more cases of cross-generational uniformity in variation, the acquisition argument will become much more important.

Socialization

Language acquisition is not the only place to look for nonidiosyncratic variation. There are many studies indicating that persons who undergo a similar socialization process are similar with respect to certain kinds of linguistic variation. Studies that only report mean rates of variation for groups provide no evidence for this argument. Irrespective of how the group is constituted or how linguistically divergent the individuals in it are, they will be described by some mean rate of variation. Rather, the evidence comes from statements like those in Labov (1970:53) concerning consonant cluster reduction:

(a) There are no speakers who never have these clusters; nor are there any who always preserve them; it is a case of inherent variation in NNE.

(b) For every speaker and every group, the second consonant is absent more often when the following word begins with a consonant than when it begins with a vowel.

The similarity among groups mentioned by Labov is of course a consequence of the similarity among individuals, all exhibiting variation, but each having the same pattern of variation. Wolfram (1973) and Fasold (1972), reporting independent studies in different cities, found the same pattern to hold.

Unlike Sankoff's acquisition data where children evidenced the same patterns of variation as their parents, the individuals in these studies have in all likelihood never heard or heard of the individuals in the other studies. Nonetheless, they are in possession of a single cultural artifact: a pattern of language variation. The phenomenon is readily explained if indeed one is willing to posit the pattern of variation as a fact of the language. Then the distribution of the pattern is simply a result of the socialization mechanism by which we can say that they all speak the same language. If patterns of variation exist as part of that cultural institution language, then they are difficult to exclude from what linguists describe as competence.

Universals

There is a counter argument, one suggested by Kiparsky (1971) and elaborated on by Fraser (1972). It could be that the regularities in patterns of variation have nothing to do with particular linguistic rules, or even language particular grammars. Rather, they may result from universal properties of language: tendencies toward CVCV syllable patterns, and tendencies to avoid sequences of stressed or sequences of unstressed syllables, for example.

A possible candidate for these universal principles would be that a phonetic sequence is deleted less often if it is a morphological marker than if it is not. The three studies mentioned above of consonant cluster simplification found that, in addition to the influence of following environment, dental consonants were deleted less often when they marked past tense than when they were part of a single lexical item. Cedergren (1973) reported similar effect of morphemic status on the deletion of word final D and N in Spanish. However, she found medial D in past participles and final R in infinitives to be deleted more often than in similar monomorphemic contexts. In other words, morphological content cannot be considered a language-universal inhibiting influence on consonant deletion.

Besides such possible universals that do not hold, there are also observed instances of variation that cannot result from any universal principles. If a principle were truly universal it must apply to all speakers alike. However, there are cases where patterns of variation are different for different groups of people.

For many black children, deletion of the third person agreement marker is conditioned by whether the verb takes the regular morpheme or irregular form, as with <u>do/does</u> and <u>have/has</u>. Among children in a low income Los Angeles school, the non-use of inflection was more probable with irregular verbs, less probable with regular verbs. Exactly the opposite relationship held for children in a middle income black neighborhood. For these children the probability that agreement did not occur was greater for regular verbs than for irregular verbs (Berdan 1973a).

Although variation is not idiosyncratic, it is not necessarily universal. There are some conditioning factors that are not universal across different language situations. There are also some patterns of variation that are not universal across different social groups.

These facts suggest that variation cannot be described only as universal. It must be language, and grammar, specific.

The general principles Fraser proposes do not necessarily preclude the influence of specific environments on the probability of rule application. The effect of this is not to argue against the incorporation of probabilistic statements into the grammar, only to suggest that the situation is more complex than had been reported.

Style and dialect

A theory of language that disallows probabilistic statements cannot account for the uniformity of patterns of variation across generations and across social groups. It also cannot account for differences in patterns that individuals produce and perceive.

Much of style shift is not shift from categorical use of a rule to categorical non-use of a rule; rather, it is shift in the rate of application of the rule. Labov (1966) found a consistent pattern across individuals and across phonological features: the more formal the context, the greater the probability of standard realizations of phonological variables. If probability statements are part of the grammar, then style shifts may be viewed as a regular, grammatical process. On the other hand, a theory that does not recognize relative frequencies as meaningful data cannot even observe that these style shifts are taking place.

Failure to accept probability statements as meaningful data has also compounded the problem of dialect definition and the recognition of dialect differences. The 'check-list' approach to dialect definition (e.g. McDavid 1967) historically has been quite distinct from the tradition of generative grammar. Nonetheless, they share the inability to recognize gradient differences. Williamson (1971) catalogs surface structures that have been reported as typical of Black English, and cites parallel structures used by southern Anglos. She concludes that the features are neither 'black nor white, but American'.

Anshen (1972) points out that those who argue that there are no ethnic dialect differences must still account for the accuracy with which ethnic differences in dialect are perceived. He cites a study by Bryden (1968) in which Anglo and black listeners from Charlottesville, Virginia, perceived the race of other Anglo and black speakers with 84 percent accuracy. The speakers, from a range of social and educational backgrounds, read a passage of only sixteen-second duration. Other studies have also shown high degrees of accuracy in ethnic identification. Stroud (1956) found that listeners were 93 percent accurate in distinguishing the recorded voices of Anglo speakers from those of black speakers.

Bryden found no categorical differences between the Anglo and black speakers in his study. But he did find significant differences in what he called 'number of phonetic errors' and 'number of mis-articulated phonemes'. The study also showed high correlation between perceived race and number of 'errors'. In other words, there was a high correlation between perceived race and rate of non-standard usage. Correlation does not imply causation, but the observed correlates were perception and variable use of nonstandard realizations, not categorical use of realizations.

Anshen examined the distribution of realizations of two phonetic variables, /r/ and /ŋ/, among Anglo and black informants. Both Anglos and blacks used standard and nonstandard forms of each. However, the rates of nonstandard realizations were differentially distributed through the populations. The differences, always in the same direction, were significant among men, and among women, at each educational level, and in each age group. This consistent pattern of differences would be readily explained as dialect difference, if probability were part of the grammar.

The distinction between competence and performance has been supported by showing that some characteristics of speech, such as memory limitations on center embeddings or long sentences, are not properly part of the grammar. They are better treated as some general limitation on cognitive processing. If probability functions are likewise explicable outside the grammar, one must speculate on what that explanation could be. Racial differences in the physical characteristics of the vocal apparatus have been suggested in the past (Wiggam 1949) to explain dialect differences. Hopefully, advances in application of the scientific method have put that notion to rest. The alternatives are cognitive differences or cultural differences (excluding language, of course). There is absolutely no evidence whatsoever to suggest that the propensity to pronounce /n/ rather than /ŋ/ is associated with any racially differentiated cognitive mechanism, if such did exist. Cultural differences do exist. But the a priori exclusion of language as an explanation of differences in speech, in deference to unrelated areas of culture, is indefensible. If the probabilistic nature of a rule is a fact of competence, then the differences noted by Anshen follow from differences in the distribution of grammars among Anglo and Black populations.

Language change

There are systematic, nonidiosyncratic differences in language among social groups. There are also differences among age groups. The New Guinean situation reported by Sankoff (1973), with no difference between generations, is the exception, not the rule, in cross-generation studies of language variation. And, although Sankoff found no difference across generations in the syntax of the future marker, she did find differences in stress.

Languages do change. Linguists have debated for decades whether those changes are gradual or instantaneous. Since Labov's (1963) pioneering work on Martha's Vineyard there have been a number of studies looking at language across apparent time, that is, across age groups. What has been found has rarely been categorical innovation or extinction of some form. Rather there have been changes in the relative proportions of variant realizations.

In New York, Labov (1966) found that the probability a person used retroflection of preconsonantal /r/ varied inversely with the age of the informant: younger informants were more likely to use retroflection than older informants. Cedergren (1973) observed language change in a different framework. Rather than the spread of a rule throughout a population, she observed that younger informants applied a rule for lenition of CH in Panamanian Spanish at a higher rate than did older speakers.

A grammar that disallows statements of probability can recognize three synchronic states: a grammar prior to the innovation, a grammar with the innovating form and the preexisting form in 'free variation', and a later grammar with only the innovating form. The observed dynamic process is describable only as static grammars. The problem has been stated lucidly by Weinreich, Labov, and Herzog (1968). If the grammar allows probability, then what is observed to be change in language can in fact be described as change in grammars. That change is gradual ceases to be a problem for the historical linguist; it is rather the type of change the grammar predicts.

Bailey (1971, 1972), responding largely to the problems of describing language change, created what he calls the 'dynamic' model of grammar, distinct from former 'static' models. However, incorporation of probability into the competence grammar is not without consequences, consequences that have been largely overlooked by those who discuss variable rules.

Problems

A grammar, as traditionally conceived, is a device capable of generating all and only the sentences of a language. It makes no claims whatsoever about the relative frequencies with which any rules are applied. 'Sentences' of the language are implicitly assumed to be 'sentence types', not 'sentence tokens' or utterance tokens. That is, two languages are not different simply because one contains two tokens of some sentence and another language contains three tokens of the same sentence. A grammar is not defined by some corpus, but by what the hypothetical idealized speaker-hearer would accept as sentences of his language.

The probabilities of rule application, on the other hand, are computed by observing the relative frequencies of variant realizations in some corpus, or speech sample. If the corpus contains repeated tokens of a single sentence type, and the tokens contain a realization being studied, then the relative frequency of the realization is based on data undefined in the generative grammar. The resulting probability statements must also be undefined in the generative grammar. If variable rules and probability statements are to become part of the competence grammar, there needs to be serious rethinking of the way in which language is defined and of the definition of the grammar that accounts for language.

Evaluation of grammars

The incorporation of variable rules into the grammar makes the grammar more powerful. That is not necessarily desirable. But the increased power is justifiable in terms of the increased range of language phenomena for which the grammar can account.

It also makes different claims about language behavior. The orthodox grammar claims that language behavior is either categorical or outside the scope of grammatical description. The probabilistic grammar recognizes that much of language behavior is probabilistically determined and must be explained in probabilistic terms.

Variable rules not only make the grammar more powerful, they make the grammar more strong; they increase the ability of the theory to evaluate competing grammars. For example, there are several proposals in literature for accounting for the facts of English inflectional morphology. One proposal, by Luelsdorff (1969) suggests that the underlying form of the plural morpheme is syllabic [əz]. The rules that provide for contraction of the singular copula is also provide for the reduction of this plural morpheme before nonstrident consonants and vowels. An alternative proposal by Hoard and Sloat (1971) has an underlying consonant with a rule of epenthesis to give the inflectional morpheme the proper phonetic shape.

The facts of variation provide evidence for choosing between these analyses for Black English. For many children the plurals of ghost and desk alternate between ghos and ghoses, and des and desses, respectively. In the Luelsdorff grammar we hypothesize that ghoses and desses result from deleting the final consonant by the consonant cluster simplification rule, thus bleeding the contraction rule.

Luelsdorff grammar
    Underlying   ghost#əz
    Cluster simplification   ghos #əz
    Nonconsonant deletion   N. A.

For the Hoard and Sloat grammar we hypothesize that consonant cluster simplification occurs and feeds the epenthesis rule. Either grammar will account for the facts.

Hoard and Sloat grammar
    Underlying   ghost#z
    Cluster simplification   ghos #z
    Epenthesis   ghos #əz

But these children are no exception to the pattern found in eastern cities for consonant cluster reduction: consonants delete less often when followed by a vowel than when followed by a consonant. Many of the same children who have dusses as the third person singular of dust have dusting in the progressive. If we chose the Luelsdorff grammar, the underlying schwa inhibits consonant deletion. The rate of consonant cluster simplification followed by vowels is insufficient to account for the rate at which dusses and ghoses occur. Thus, we have to posit a special case of consonant cluster simplification for consonants followed by inflectional morphemes. Any supposed generalizations that the Luelsdorff grammar would provide, are lost.

On the other hand, the Hoard and Sloat grammar posits an underlying form that makes consonant cluster simplification most probable: cluster followed by a consonant. The variable rule that simplifies clusters in this environment is sufficient to account for these facts of inflectional morphology. In this way, the use of probabilities provides evidence for choosing among alternate grammars.

Another case in which the facts of probability offer evidence is the deletion of the copula in Black English. Labov (1969) has proposed that the deletion is essentially a phonological process. Others claim it is grammatical. The phonological explanation exploits rules that are needed elsewhere in the grammar to delete final consonants; the siblant of contracted is and the /r/ of contracted are. The question to be asked is: are the patterns of deletion of phonologically distinct is and are more similar than either of those patterns to the respective noncopula consonant deletion rules? If so, there is good reason to believe the deletion is syntactic. If not, the phonological deletion argument is much stronger.

Conclusions

Variation with respect to the individual is truly random. Variation with respect to different features of the grammar is independent, it is not code switching. Because variation is random, its rate can be observed in a speech sample and predicted for the language. Patterns of variation are not idiosyncratic; they can be observed across generations. Children do not only acquire the form of a rule, they acquire the probability of its use. Patterns of variation are observed to co-occur with other linguistic entities; they are language and dialect specific, not universal. Changes in probabilities provide the mechanism for gradual language change. Incorporating probability into the grammar not only provides a framework for explaining language variation; it facilitates the description of language acquisition, language change, and the delineation of languages and dialects. The facts of variation and variable rules provide the grammar a strong mechanism for determining among alternate solutions to grammatical problems.

The grammar is a theoretical construct that attempts to provide an explanation for the phenomenon of human language. Sociolinguists in the past decade have amassed a large body of facts that argues that language is in part probabilistic. The grammar must attempt to explain those facts. The variable, or probabilistic, rule provides the grammar the necessary mechanism to account for the facts of variation.

NOTES

1. These data are from a transcript summarized and tabulated in Legum et al. (1971).
2. The [I, ɛ] variation before nasals, which would be significant at 0.05, reflects a lexical bias.
3. One interaction was significant. That was for post-consonantal /r/. However, there were virtually no realizations of [ə] or [∅]. This means that the interaction was not between segment of the transcript and realizations of the variable, but between segment and density of the variable.

REFERENCES

Anshen, Frank. 1972. Some statistical bases for the existence of Black English. Florida FL Reporter 10.19-20.
Bailey, C.-J.N. 1971. Trying to talk in the new paradigm. Papers in Linguistics 4.312-338.

Bailey, C.-J.N. 1972. The integration of linguistic theory: Internal reconstruction and the comparative method in descriptive analysis. In: Linguistic change and generative theory. Edited by R. Stockwell and R. Macaulay. Bloomington, Indiana University Press. 22-31.

_____ and Shuy, R. W., eds. 1973. New ways of analyzing variation in English. Washington, D.C., Georgetown University Press.

Berdan, R. 1973a. The use of linguistically determined groups in socio-linguistic research. Professional Paper 26, Southwest Regional Laboratory.

_____. 1973b. Probability and variable rules: A formal interpretation. Paper read at the Summer LSA Meeting, Ann Arbor.

Bryden, James D. 1968. An acoustic and social dialect analysis of perceptual variables in listener identification and rating of Negro speakers. Charlottesville, University of Virginia. ERIC No. ED 022 186.

Cedergren, Henrietta. 1973. On the nature of variable constraints. In: Bailey and Shuy (1973). 13-22.

_____ and Sankoff, David. 1974. Variable rules: Performance as a statistical reflection of competence. Language 50.333-355.

DeCamp, David. 1971. Toward a generative analysis of a post-creole speech continuum. In: Pidginization and creolization of languages. Edited by Dell Hymes. Cambridge, University Press. 349-370.

Dillard, J. L. 1972. Black English: Its history and usage in the United States. New York, Random House.

Fasold, Ralph W. 1972. Tense marking in Black English. Washington, D.C., Center for Applied Linguistics.

Fraser, Bruce. 1972. Optional rules in grammar. In: Georgetown University Round Table on Languages and Linguistics (GURT) 1972. Edited by R. W. Shuy. Washington, D.C., Georgetown University Press. 1-16.

Gobel, E. C., and Kypriotaki, L. 1973. Mouses and mices: A study in grammatical variation. Paper presented at the Summer LSA Meeting, Ann Arbor.

Hoard, J. and Sloat, C. 1971. The inflectional morphology of English. Glossa 5:1.47-56.

Kiparsky, Paul. 1971. Historical linguistics. In: A survey of linguistic science. Edited by William O. Dingwell. College Park, University of Maryland. 576-649.

Labov, W. 1963. The social motivation of a sound change. Word 19.273-309.

_____. 1966. The social stratification of English in New York City. Washington, D.C., Center for Applied Linguistics.

Labov, W. 1969. Contraction, deletion, and inherent variability of the English copula. Language 45:4. 715-762.

_____. 1970. The study of language in its social context. Studium Generale 23. 30-87.

_____, P. Cohen, C. Robins, and J. Lewis. 1968. A study of the non-standard English of Negro and Puerto Rican speakers in New York City. Final Report, Cooperative Research Project 3288, 2 vols. Washington, D. C., Office of Education.

Legum, S. E. and Coots, J. 1971. Transcript homogeneity study. Technical Note No. TN2-71-40, November 23, 1971. Southwest Regional Laboratory.

Legum, S. E., C. Pfaff, G. Tinnie, M. Nicholas, and W. Riley. 1971. The speech of young Black children in Los Angeles. TR 33. Southwest Regional Laboratory.

Luelsdorff, P. A. 1969. On the phonology of English inflection. Glossa 3:1. 39-48.

McDavid, Raven I. 1967. A checklist of significant features for discriminating social dialects. In: Dimensions of dialect. Edited by E. Evertts. Champaign, Illinois, N. C. T. E. 7-10.

Sankoff, Gillian. 1973. Above and beyond phonology in variable rules. In: Bailey and Shuy (1973). 44-61.

Siegel, Sidney. 1956. Nonparametric statistics for the behavioral sciences. New York, McGraw-Hill.

Stroud, R. 1956. A study of the relation between social differences of White and Negro high school students of Dayton, Ohio. Unpublished Master's Thesis, Bowling Green State University.

Weinreich, U., W. Labov, and M. Herzog. 1968. Empirical foundations for a theory of language change. In: Directions for historical linguistics. Edited by W. P. Lehmann and Y. Malkiel. Austin, University of Texas Press. 97-195.

Wiggam, Albert E. 1949. Let's explore your mind. Cleveland Plain Dealer, July 3, 1949. Cited by R. I. McDavid and V. G. McDavid. 1951. The relationship of the speech of American Negroes to the speech of American Whites. American Speech 26. 3-17.

Williamson, Juanita. 1971. A look at Black English. Crisis 169-185.

Wolfram, Walt. 1973. On what basis variable rules? In: Bailey and Shuy (1973). 1-12.

THE BAILEY WAVE MODEL:
A DYNAMIC QUANTITATIVE PARADIGM

RALPH W. FASOLD

Georgetown University

For some time there has been a controversy among variation theorists on the relative merits of theories of variation which include variable rules versus theories which do not. The most eloquent and thorough arguments against variable rules have been mounted by Derek Bickerton (1971, 1973). In his arguments, Bickerton appeals to what he calls the Bailey Wave Model which he believes is superior as a model for understanding variation and change to variable rule analysis of either the classical Labov (1969) type or the newer quantitative Cedergren-Sankoff type (Cedergren and D. Sankoff MS, G. Sankoff MS). [1] I will attempt to show here that the model actually proposed by Bailey incorporates variable rules and is superior to Bickerton's modification of the Bailey model for the understanding of both variation and change.

We may begin by making explicit three conditions imposed on variation theory by Bickerton and compare them with the conditions Bailey himself actually endorses. Bickerton's conditions are the following:

1. Variation is to be understood basically in terms of a three-valued implicational scale. This condition implies that quantitatively measurable degrees of variation are not linguistically significant and therefore variable rules have no place in linguistic theory.

2. Language changes as speakers abandon a rule in favor of a very similar rule in which more specific constraints in old rules are lost leaving more general constraints in the newer rule.

3. No lect may have variation in more than one environment, and variable environments must occur between an environment in which the rule operates categorically and one in which the rule does not operate at all, on an implicational scale.

The corresponding conditions on what I take to be the model actually proposed by Bailey are the following:

4. Variation is to be understood basically in terms of a multi-valued implicational scale. This implies that the model is theoretically open to the incorporation of either the classical or quantitative variable rule and that quantitatively measurable degrees of variation are linguistically significant.

5. Language changes as speakers increase output frequency of a rule in heavier environments first, then in progressively lighter environments. In cases of rule inhibition, language changes as speakers decrease output frequency in lighter environments first, then in progressively heavier environments. [2]

6. A lect may show variation in any or all environments provided it does not show variation in an environment heavier than one in which the rule involved shows categorical operation, nor in an environment lighter than one in which it shows no operation, and provided that output frequency in heavier environments exceeds output frequency in lighter environments. [3]

Conditions 1 through 6 cannot be fully understood without further explanation of certain crucial terms used in their definitions. First, it must be made clear what we mean by three-valued (Condition 1) and multi-valued (Condition 4) implicational scales. There are actually, in effect, three kinds of implicational scales that appear in the literature; two-valued, three-valued, and multi-valued scales. A two-valued scale requires that only the presence or absence of a phenomenon be recognized. This is usually done by interpreting variable and categorical presence as presence and categorical absence as absence. Sometimes it is necessary to set thresholds such that a frequency above a certain value counts as presence and a frequency below that value counts as absence (Stolz and Bills 1968). A three-valued scale distinguishes categorical presence, categorical absence, and variable presence. Variable presence, often symbolized by X, appears only between categorical presence and categorical absence on a chart of well-scaled data. A frequency chart, from which variable rules are typically written, can be viewed as a multi-valued implicational scale in which significance is attached to the degree of variability rather than simply to the existence of variability along with categorical presence and absence. A frequency, or multi-valued implicational chart makes stronger predictions about how data will appear than does a three-valued implicational chart which, in turn, makes stronger claims than does a two-valued chart.

This discussion is badly in need of illustration at this point. Labov's treatment of negative concord (Labov 1972:130-196) provides us with example data. The rule is fairly complicated, but it is not necessary for our purposes to understand the syntactic details of the rule. The rule incorporates a copy of a negative element in an indeterminate to the right in the sentence, or, if there is no indeterminate, in the verb. The rule is variable and is more likely to operate if an indeterminate is present. If the original negative and the position in which the copy is made are clause-mates (i.e. there is no intervening sentence boundary) the rule is also favored. The favoring effect of the indeterminate (the α constraint) is stronger than the favoring effect of the absence of the sentence boundary (the β constraint). Labov's rule, modified to fit the classical variable rule format, appears below:

$$(1) \quad [_S W[+NEG]X \; \beta \; (-[_S)Y \; \left\{ \begin{array}{c} \alpha([+INDET]) \\ Vb \end{array} \right\} \; Z_S]$$

1	2	3	4	5	6	7
1	2	3	4	5	(2)+6	7

In Labov et al. (1968:277) we find some of the data on which Rule (1) is based. The data for the case in which neither of the favoring constraints (absence of sentence boundary and presence of an indeterminate) occurs is missing because of the extreme rarity with which the rule operates under these conditions. The frequency data for the remaining three environments is given in Table 1.

TABLE 1. Frequency (multi-valued implicational) chart for negative concord in three environments.

Indet, Same Clause α, β	Indet,~ Same Clause α	Vb, Same Clause β
.98	.35	.09
.81	.25	.00
.00	.00	.00

The three rows of figures represent three lects. The top row is from adolescent Vernacular Black English in New York City, the second row represents speakers of a New York City white nonstandard lect, and the bottom row is standard English. It would be easy to display the data in Table 1 as a two-valued implicational chart, simply by calling any degree of operation of the rule, 1, and categorical nonapplication, 0. This is done in Table 2. To make finer discriminations than are made in Table 2, but not so fine as in Table 1, we can convert Table 1 into a three-valued implicational chart. This can be done by setting thresholds; say, anything above 90 percent counts as 1, or categorical application, anything below 10 percent counts as 0, or non-application and anything between is symbolized by X, standing for variable application. The result is Table 3.

TABLE 2. Two-valued implicational chart for negative concord in three environments.

Indet, Same Clause α,β	Indet, ~ Same Clause α	Vb, Same Clause β
1	1	1
1	1	0
0	0	0

TABLE 3. Three-valued implicational chart for negative concord in three environments.

Indet, Same Clause α, β	Indet, ~ Same Clause α	Vb, Same Clause β
1	X	0
X	X	0
0	0	0

Theoretically, then, Rule (1) makes predictions, depending on the interpretation placed on it, to which Tables 1, 2, and 3 all conform. Given that the presence of both alpha and beta is the most favored, or 'heaviest' environment, alpha alone is the second heaviest, beta alone is the third, and the non-occurrence of both alpha and beta is the lightest environment, the following four predictions are made.

1. The lects defined by Table 4, and no others, are possible (two-valued interpretation).

2. If a lect has categorical, variable, and zero outputs of Rule (1) in various environments, it will only have variable outputs in lighter environments than those in which it has categorical output and in heavier environments than those in which it has zero output. That is, X's only occur between 1's and 0's (three-valued interpretation).

3. If the rule has an output in more than one environment, it will have a higher frequency output in a heavier environment than in a lighter one (multi-valued interpretation).

4. Except in cases of reweightings, rule inhibiting, and stagnant rules (Fasold 1973), the rule will operate in the heaviest environment earliest in time and spread to successively lighter environments as time passes (dynamic interpretation).

The two-valued, three-valued, and multi-valued interpretations make progressively more stringent claims and each implies the claims of the preceding interpretation. The dynamic interpretation relates variable rules to linguistic change and is not directly related to the first three interpretations.

TABLE 4. Lects predicted by Rule (1) under the two-valued interpretation. VBE = Vernacular Black English; WNS = White Nonstandard English; SE = Standard English.

Rule operates in environment of:				Example sentence in lightest environment allowed in lect:	Identity of speakers:
α,β	α	β	Neither		
1	1	1	1	Nobody didn't know it didn't rain.	VBE, deep South WNS
1	1	1	0	Nobody didn't do it.	'WNS$_2$', a relatively rare white nonstandard lect
1	1	0	0	He didn't do it, neither.	'WNS$_1$', a common white nonstandard lect
1	0	0	0	He didn't do nothing.	Not attested
0	0	0	0	--	SE

Beyond understanding the various types of implicational patterns, we need definitions of the terms 'constraint', 'environment', and 'weighting'. A 'constraint' is an individual factor which serves to promote the operation of a variable rule. Taking Rule (1) as an example, the two constraints are ([+INDET]) and (~[$_S$), the last indicating the absence (~) of a sentence boundary. An 'environment' is the total combination of constraints that are present at the time of a given operation of the rule. The column headings in Tables 1 through 3 designate three of the four possible environments for the operation of Rule (1). 'Weighting' refers to the relative degree to which various constraints and environments favor the operation of a variable rule. Constraints, in a classical variable rule, are weighted in order of the Greek letters associated with them. An alpha constraint is heavier weighted than a beta constraint, and so on. [4] Environment weights are determined by calculations based on combinations of weighted constraints. The more favoring constraints that are present and the higher their weighting, the heavier the environment. The environments for Rule (1) designated by the column headings in Tables 1 through 3 are ordered from heaviest to lightest, reading from left to right. The lightest environment of any variable rule, the one which does not appear in Tables 1 through 3, is the environment in which none of the favoring constraints appear. [5]

In the remainder of the article, I wish to deal with two objections to variable rule analysis raised by Bickerton. In Bickerton (1971), part of the reason for rejecting variable rule analysis in favor of his three-valued implicational scale based theory was that procedures for writing variable rules do not allow spurious constraints to be distinguished from real ones. We shall attempt to show that Bickerton has failed to demonstrate this weakness in variable rule theory, and that, in any case, the same weakness is inherent in two- and three-valued implicational analyses. Bickerton (1973) argues that the variable rule analysis of the deletion of que in Montreal French proposed by Gillian Sankoff (MS) obscures the facts of language change which are revealed by Bickerton's version of three-valued implicational analysis. It will be our contention that the Bailey Wave Model, including a variable rule of que-deletion, accounts for the dynamic facts of language change far more elegantly than does Bickerton's proposal.

We do not intend to spend any time on the most-raised objection to variable rule analysis, that is, that the multi-valued interpretation leads to claims which are too strong to be psychologically real, an objection also raised in Bickerton (1971). It seems that it should be obvious that people can do what they do do and there is so much data that actually does conform to the multi-valued interpretation that it is clear that it must be accounted for by linguistic theory.

The problem of spurious constraints in variable rules has already been discussed in Wolfram (1973), and I shall conclude by endorsing the same solution Wolfram proposed. In his insightful discussion of the tu and fu variants of the for-to complementizer in Guyanese Creole, Bickerton attempts to discredit variable rule analysis by showing that almost any old posited constraint set will produce good cross-product data but reveals nothing of interest, linguistically. The three constraints he tries for the Guyanese rule are, first, the presence of formatives between the complementizer and its dominating verb (symbolized FM in Figures 1 through 4), second, whether or not the preceding segment is voiced (symbolized V), and third, whether or not the subject of the dominating verb is a pronoun (symbolized P). His claim is that all three of these constraints are wrong, even though they produce cross-products that are as good as those in Labov's discussion of contraction and deletion in American English (Labov 1969). It turns out that the first two constraints (the one about intervening formatives and the one about preceding voicing) in a sense follow from the real constraints he finds in his brilliant analysis of the Guyanese Creole case. The third constraint, the one about the pronoun subject, is completely spurious and was chosen specifically because Bickerton thought it would not be a constraint.

To begin with, it is not true that his spurious constraints produce displays that are as good as Labov's. To show this, I have reproduced his four cross-product charts, one for each of the three social

classes and one for the whole group, and one of the two displays from
Labov (1969) with which he compares them.[6]

FIGURE 1.   Ordering of constraints, all classes (Bickerton 1971:
469).

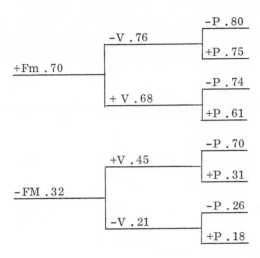

FIGURE 2.   Ordering of constraints, Class A (Bickerton 1971:469).

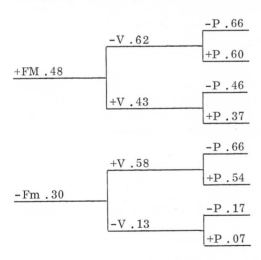

FIGURE 3. Ordering of constraints, Class B (Bickerton 1971:469).

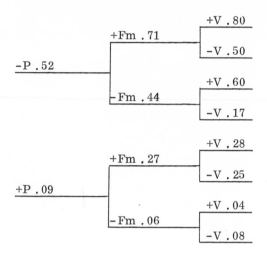

FIGURE 4. Ordering of constraints, Class C (Bickerton 1971:469).

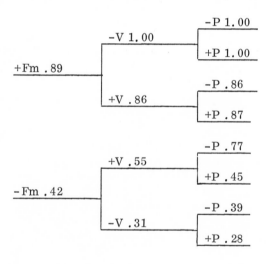

FIGURE 5. Ordering of constraints on deletion (adapted from
Labov 1969:749).

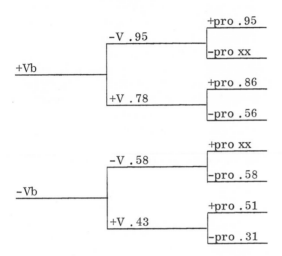

The symbol Vb in Figure 5 means a verb follows the consonant subject
to deletion, V means the preceding word ends in a vowel, and pro
means the subject of the construction is a pronoun. The display is not
at complete as Bickerton's because two of the logically conceivable
combinations do not exist. Except for it which requires special treatment with respect to the deletion, there are no subject case pronouns
which do not end in a vowel.

Ideally, in such displays, the frequency of numbers should show a
steady decrease from the top of the display to the bottom, with no
figure higher than the one above it. Of this Bickerton (1971:469) says
'Neither Labov's results nor ours conform perfectly with the ideal,
but there is little to choose between the two sets of actual figures.'
Actually there are important differences between them and Bickerton's
come off second best. To begin with, no variable rule writer worth
his salt would even begin to write a rule from the data in Figures 1,
2, or 4. To see why this is so, examine the signs associated with
the feature V in these figures. Within +Fm, -V outranks +V. Within
-Fm, +V outranks -V. This amounts to a claim that the absence of
voicing favors the rule just in case there are intervening formatives,
but the presence of voicing favors selection of fu if there are no
intervening formatives. In the first place, there is no plausible
reason why the presence or absence of intervening formatives should
have the slightest influence on the effect of the voicing of the preceding word. But there is a more serious objection. If we relax the
claims of variable rule analysis to allow Bickerton's procedure, it
would be very difficult to find a set of data involving only two

constraints which could not be claimed to be valid. If the crucial cross-products come out in the wrong order, simply reverse the sign of the second-order constraint and everything fits. If the theory is relaxed to that extent, it would be impossible to write a variable rule with just two constraints which would convince anyone, because there would be no way to show that you had the wrong hierarchy. Variable rule analysis entails the claim that any constraint which favors a rule favors it under all combinations of other constraints. This claim should be maintained. If it is maintained, and the results come out as they do in Figures 1, 2, and 4, the conclusion is forced that you haven't found the correct constraints, which Bickerton would agree is ultimately the right conclusion.

Supposing, however, that we have only the data for Class B in Figure 3. Here there are no reversals of signs. Unlike the other three figures, Figure 3 requires the preceding pronoun to be the first-order constraint instead of the third. This is no problem, as Bickerton correctly points out, since the theory allows for reordering of constraints by different subgroups of speakers. But examination of Figure 3 shows that two figures are out of order; there is a .17 between a .60 and a .28, and there is a .04 between a .25 and a .08. But there is a disorder also in Figure 5 from Labov's work; a .58 appears between a .56 and a .51. All of these are an embarrassment for variable rule theory. But random factors will always intervene when real speech data, extracted from tape-recorded data by human phoneticians, are used. As a result, it is common practice to 'forgive' slight disorders in numbers if the main pattern is good. But one should not be too 'forgiving' if he wishes to maintain credibility. It is my own rule of thumb that one should worry a little about wrong orderings involving discrepancies of 5 percent or less and that discrepancies of a larger magnitude demand an explicit explanation beyond an appeal to the vagaries of data handling. A discrepancy of 11 percent, as in the case of the .17 above the .28, should make the analyst extremely suspicious of his putative constraints. The presence of an additional discrepancy, even if a small one, in the same set of data can only increase the suspicion. In this case, these suspicions are well-grounded; we simply are not looking at the correct constraints on the selection of fu. In Labov's data, we are being asked to 'forgive' only one discrepancy and that one is only off by 2 percent.

I think it is fair to say that Bickerton's attempt to show that spurious constraints conform to variable rule theory as well as real ones, fails. Even if he had succeeded, is there a better way to handle variation? His solution is to use the correct constraints, which cannot help but improve the situation, and to analyze them according to his conception of the Bailey Wave Model which meets Conditions 1, 2, and 3 rather than Conditions 4, 5, and 6. The question becomes

'Does this model succeed any better at distinguishing spurious and real constraints than the variable rule approach does?' On the face of it, it would seem that spurious constraints could more easily get through the three-valued interpretation than the multi-valued one since the three-valued model makes weaker demands of the data. And the answer, in fact, is affirmative, there are spurious constraints that meet the requirements of the three-valued model.

Table 5 is one example, taken from the work of Carolyn Kessler which appears as an annex to Fasold (1972). The data conform equally well to the two-valued interpretation since no group deletes the plural morpheme categorically in any environment (as it stands, it is technically a three-valued chart in which the third value--categorical deletion--happens not to occur). Kessler's implicational scale is as neat a one as anyone could hope to see, and as unlikely as Bickerton's, one would have thought, to be the result of chance. Yet it suffers

TABLE 5. Implicational chart for plural morpheme deletion in Washington, D. C., Black English in four environments (from Kessler 1972:235).

Class	C#_##(V)	C#_##C	V#_ ##	V#_##V	V#_##C
Upper middle	X	0	0	0	0
Lower middle	X	X	0	0	0
Upper working	X	X	X	0	0
Lower working	X	X	X	X	0

from one serious defect. The constraint ordering which it indicates cannot possibly be the right one. The preceding environments are plausible; a preceding consonant favors deletion more than a preceding vowel. But the following environments are surely incorrect. Table 5 forces the conclusion that a following vowel favors deletion more than a following consonant. This is contrary to everything we know about constraints on consonantal deletion rules and is extremely implausible phonetically as well. If this were not bad enough, the pause environment--where neither a vowel nor a consonant occurs-- does not appear between the vocalic and consonantal environments where pause environments are expected to appear, but actually appears to favor deletion more than either of them. It is clear that the sort of analysis that Bickerton relies on is as susceptible to giving neat results with wrong constraints as he would have us believe the use of variable rule analysis is. [7]

If neat results cannot be relied upon to give us correct answers, what can? The answer is to be found in Wolfram (1973)--replication. We must come to realize what scholars in the social sciences have known for a long time; that impressive results from one analysis can be accepted only tentatively until they are replicated by another set of data. Fortunately, two of the cases we have discussed have been subject to replication attempts, at least partially. The deletion rule of Labov has been tested with other sets of data by Wolfram (1969) in Detroit, by Pfaff (1971) in Los Angeles, by me in an unpublished study of a group of Detroit and Washington speakers, and by Wolfram again recently with a group of white Mississippi speakers (Wolfram forth-coming). In every case, Labov's contention that a preceding pronoun and a following verb favor deletion has been confirmed. Unfortunately, none of the replication studies attempted to show that the absence of a preceding vowel favors deletion nor have any of them attempted to hierarchize the constraints by cross-product analysis. In Wolfram's most recent study (Wolfram 1974), data are provided from which it can be calculated that a following verb outranks a preceding pronoun as a constraint favoring deletion.

Kessler's results have likewise been subject to numerous repli-cating attempts with dismal success. Working with the speech of black children in Texas, Linda Sobin (n. d.) very carefully followed Kessler's analytical methods and was disappointed when she was unable to replicate her results. In Wolfram's Detroit study (1969), in the study of Labov and his colleagues in New York City (1968) and in a study of another group of black and Puerto Rican adolescents in New York reported in Wolfram 1971) there is no hint of a following vowel favoring plural deletion more than a following consonant or of a pause favoring deletion more than both.

Obviously, a certain amount of doubt must accompany arguments, regardless of the type of implicational analysis employed, which are based on a single study. The task of replication is not a needless waste of time, but an essential part of the process of theory develop-ment. Of course, the point about the need for replication applies equally well to the next section of this paper which will also be based on only one set of data.

In Sankoff (MS), the rule for que-deletion in Montreal French is used as an illustrative case for the use of quantitative variable rules. Sankoff is primarily interested in accounting for the facts of syn-chronic variation and does not attempt any sort of dynamic interpre-tation of her data. Bickerton, as always, is basically interested in how any theory stacks up as a theory of language change and, in Bickerton (1973), argues that Sankoff's analysis obscures the facts of change while his theory reveals them. Bailey (1973) has con-vincingly shown that it is reasonable to demand of a theory that it account for both synchronically observed variation and linguistic change, so it is legitimate for Bickerton to examine Sankoff's presen-tation with a view to testing how it accounts for change. It will be the contention of the remainder of the article that slight modifications of

Sankoff's approach make it possible for her analysis to fit into the
Bailey Wave Model and account for language change in a way superior
to Bickerton's proposal.

The constraints on que-deletion presented in Sankoff (MS) are:
(1) a preceding sibilant favors deletion more than (2) a preceding
non-sibilant consonant which in turn favors deletion more than (3) a
preceding vowel. Similarly, as it turns out, (4) a following sibilant
favors deletion more than (5) a following non-sibilant consonant which
favors it more than (6) a vowel. Using Sankoff's cover symbols S for
sibilant, C for non-sibilant consonant, and V for vowel, the constraints
combine to allow nine possible environments, viz., S_S, S_C, S_V,
C_S, C_C, C_V, V_S, V_C, and V_V.

In preparation for developing a theory meeting Condition 2, Bickerton correctly observes that the S constraint, both in the preceding environment and in the following one, is the most specific constraint.
The C constraint, in both parts of the environment, represents a re-
laxation of the S constraint to the extent that the presence of a consonant is still required, but it need not be specifically a sibilant. Since
the V constraint implies the C and S constraint (in the sense that no
speaker will delete que either preceding or following V unless he or
she also deletes it preceding or following C and S, at least ideally),
the V constraint actually represents the elimination of both C and S
as constraints. That is, deleting in the V environments means that
both constraints about consonants have been relaxed.

The environment in which deletion is most likely to take place is
in the S_S environment. This environment ideally implies all the
other environments and is the heaviest (under the dynamic interpretation, the oldest) environment. The rule Bickerton proposes for
speakers who delete only in the heaviest environment (the most conservative speakers) is Rule (2):

$$(2) \quad que \rightarrow (\emptyset)/ \begin{bmatrix} (+cor) \\ (+strd) \\ (-syll) \end{bmatrix} \underline{\quad} \begin{bmatrix} (+cor) \\ (+strd) \\ (-syll) \end{bmatrix}$$

Bickerton uses the feature [-syll] to indicate consonants and [+strd]
to designate sibilants. Since all English sibilants are also [+cor],
this feature is also included.[8] But Sankoff's cover symbols do not
allow a reanalysis, Bickerton observes, to deal with the feature
[+cor], although he would like to be able to. Since this is true, for
the purposes of reanalyzing Sankoff's data, the rule might just as
well be Rule (2'):

$$(2') \quad que \rightarrow (\emptyset)/ \begin{bmatrix} (+strd) \\ (-syll) \end{bmatrix} \underline{\quad} \begin{bmatrix} (+strd) \\ (-syll) \end{bmatrix}$$

The implicational scale that Bickerton develops from Sankoff's data indicates that the next-heaviest environment is C_S. Speakers who delete in this environment as well as in S_S would have Rule (3):

$$(3) \quad que \longrightarrow (\emptyset) \, / \quad [(-syll)] \underline{\quad} \begin{bmatrix} (+strd) \\ (-syll) \end{bmatrix}$$

The rule states that que can be deleted after any consonant, whether or not it is a sibilant, but only before a sibilant. Speakers who delete in C_S as well as S_S are said to have given up Rule (2') in favor of Rule (3), thus conforming to Condition 2. So far, so good.

The next environment which would appear on an implicational scale based on Sankoff's data would be S_C. According to Bickerton's interpretation of Bailey's theory the only way a speaker could delete in S_C without going on to delete in C_C as well would be for such speakers to retain Rule (3) and to add yet another que-deletion rule, namely Rule (4):

$$(4) \quad que \longrightarrow (\emptyset) \, / \begin{bmatrix} (+strd) \\ (-syll) \end{bmatrix} \underline{\quad} [(-syll)]$$

Aside from the fact that such speakers would, in Bickerton's view, have to have two rules for deleting que, Rule (4) would require the restoration of a constraint that had been lost in a temporally earlier state in the development of que-deletion in the language, namely, [+strd] in the preceding environment. But this would certainly violate Condition 2, a corollary to which would specify that once a constraint is lost, it is lost forever. One possible development which would conform to Condition 2 would be for the next most advanced set of speakers to drop the constraint [+strd] from Rule (3), giving Rule (5):

$$(5) \quad que \longrightarrow (\emptyset) \, / \, [(-syll)] \underline{\quad} [(-syll)]$$

Of course, Rule (5) specifies the C_C environment. Hence Bickerton's analysis would require that there be no speakers who delete in S_C who do not also delete in C_C. At this point, Bickerton is vindicated. There are, in fact, no speakers in Sankoff's data who delete in S-C without also deleting in C_C.[9]

Thus far, Bickerton's analysis has been quite successful. True, it requires a separate que-deletion rule for each lect, but the rule sequence fits Condition 2 and the lect which would delete in S-C but not in C_C--a lect which would, for Bickerton, require both Rule (3) and Rule (4), violating Condition 2--appears not to exist.

But things are not quite so neat from here on. Following the same procedures, one would expect that the next lect would drop the constraint [-syll] from either the preceding or following environment and delete in either V_C or C_V. The next simplification would then be to drop the remaining [-syll] constraint and allow deletion in V_V. It would indeed have been a striking confirmation of Bickerton's way of doing things if the remaining speakers in Sankoff's data deleted in either V_C or C_V (but not both) or in V_V. This would require that there be no speakers who stopped deleting at the C_S, V_S, or S_V stages. But unfortunately there are representatives of all three types of speakers in the data. To account for any of them would seem to require the objectionable restitution (if Condition 2 is to be salvaged) of the [+strd] constraint after it had been lost in moving from Rule (2') to Rule (3) in the preceding environment, and in moving from Rule (3) to Rule (5) in the following environment.

Bickerton's solution is to propose that there be diverse simplification paths after Rule (3). In moving from Rule (3) to Rule (5), of course, the [+strd] constraint was lost in the following environment. But, Bickerton points out that the theory does not predict just what constraints are lost, just so long as an additional constraint is lost and none which have already been lost be restored. Rule (3) could equally well have been simplified by the loss of the [-syll] constraint from the preceding environment giving Rule (6):

(6) que $\longrightarrow$ (∅) / _____ $\begin{bmatrix} (+strd) \\ (-syll) \end{bmatrix}$

Such speakers, in addition to deleting in S_S, would also delete in V_S. His proposal is that the progress of que-deletion followed two paths, some speakers simplifying Rule (3) by dropping it in favor of Rule (5); others by replacing it with Rule (6). Either Rule (5)--by dropping the preceding [-syll] constraint--or Rule (6)--by dropping the [+strd] constraint--can then be simplified to Rule (7):

(7) que $\longrightarrow$ (∅) / _____ [(-syll)]

Speakers with Rule (7) delete, in addition to the environments in which speakers with Rules (2') through (6) delete, in V_C. The final rule in the sequence would be Rule (8) in which all constraints are lost and que becomes freely deletable:

(8) que $\longrightarrow$ (∅) / _____

This corresponds to the V_V environment of Sankoff's paper. [10]

To recapitulate, the temporal progress of que-deletion for Bickerton would correspond to the following sequence of rules:

que —→ (∅)

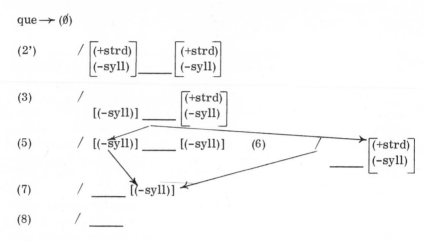

(2')   / $\begin{bmatrix} (+strd) \\ (-syll) \end{bmatrix}$ ____ $\begin{bmatrix} (+strd) \\ (-syll) \end{bmatrix}$

(3)   / $[(-syll)]$ ____ $\begin{bmatrix} (+strd) \\ (-syll) \end{bmatrix}$

(5)   / $[(-syll)]$ ____ $[(-syll)]$ (6)   / ____ $\begin{bmatrix} (+strd) \\ (-syll) \end{bmatrix}$

(7)   / ____ $[(-syll)]$

(8)   / ____

Notice that the relationship among the rules is such that each succeeding rule differs from the preceding one by the loss of a single constraint and that each succeeding rule automatically generates the output of the preceding rule plus outputs in new environments. Thus the rules, in the nature of the case, create an implicational scale. Speakers with Rule (3) can delete que in the same environments as speakers with Rule (2') plus some more. Being able to delete in the environment of Rule (3) implies that the speaker can also delete in the Rule (2') environment, but not the reverse. The same relationship holds throughout the sequence.

In Bickerton (1973) there is an overall three-valued implicational scale showing the types of output for all sixteen of Sankoff's informants in the nine environments. This scale is presented in modified and simplified form here as Table 6.[11] Table 6, however, is really not the clearest way to see what Bickerton's theory is claiming. Part of the reason for this is that Sankoff's environments are not relevant to Bickerton's rules throughout. For example, Table 6 shows both the C_C and S_C environments covered by Rule (5). The reason for this is that once the [+strd] constraint is lost in Rule (3) in the preceding environment, it can never again be relevant to subsequent rules. For Bickerton, there is no point in observing deletion in S_C. By the time Rule (5) has come into the language, a preceding sibilant is theoretically just another consonant. Therefore, the columns headed by C_C and S-C ought to be a single column headed C_C where C means, not a non-sibilant consonant, but any consonant, sibilant or not. Similarly, the left-most three environments ought to be a single column headed V_V. Once it is possible to delete before a vowel, in Bickerton's theory, the preceding environment is no longer relevant. Since deletion after V implies deletion after C and S, the V_V designation would be appropriate for the first three columns.

TABLE 6. Three-valued implicational scale of Sankoff's que data with environments covered by Bickerton's rules indicated. 1 = categorical deletion; X = variable deletion; 0 = no deletion. Apparent deviations are ringed.

Rule:	(8)			(7)		(5)		(3)	(2')
				(6)	(7)				
Environment:	C_V	V_V	S_V	V_S	V_C	C_C	S_C	C_S	S_X
Speaker: 12	0	0	0	0	0	0	0	–	0
16	0	0	0	0	0	–	–	①	0
15	0	0	–	0	–	0	–	0	X
10	0	0	–	0	–	①	0	0	–
1	①	–	–	⊗	0	0	–	–	–
11	0	0	–	0	⊗	0	0	X	–
9	0	0	⊗	0	0	0	0	X	1
6	0	0	0	⊗	0	–	0	X	1
13	0	0	⊗	0	0	⊗	0	X	1
14	0	0	0	⊗	⊗	0	0	X	1
4	0	⊗	⊗	⊗	0	0	–	X	1
8	0	0	–	0	0	–	–	1	1
3	0	⊗	①	⊗	0	–	–	1	–
5	0	0	0	0	X	1	1	⊗	–
7	0	0	0	X	⊗	1	–	1	1
2	0	–	0	X	1	–	–	1	1

The overlap of Rules (6) and (7) with respect to the V_S and V_C environments reveals another reason why Table 6 is not the most felicitous display of the results of Rules (2') through 8. There is a split rule in the rule sequence after Rule (3), with some speakers acquiring Rule (5) and others Rule (6). Those who move from Rule (3) to Rule (6) should delete next in V_C, the environment governed by Rule (7). But those who acquire Rule (5) after Rule (3) forever after render the distinction between following sibilants and non-sibilant consonants meaningless. For them, Rule (7) covers both V_S and V-C under a column headed V_C where C includes sibilants and non-sibilants. All of these environmental revisions are made necessary, ultimately, by the maintenance of Condition 2.

To really show how Bickerton's system works and how well or poorly the data conform to it, it is necessary to construct two three-valued implicational charts, one for each routing. Further, the environments should be revised to reflect what is relevant to Bickerton's analysis rather than Sankoff's. This is done in Tables 7 and 8.

TABLE 7. Three-valued implicational scale of Sankoff's que data for those speakers who have adopted or may adopt Rule (5) in the temporal progress of que-deletion.

Rule:	(8)	(7)	(5)	(3)	(2')
Environment:	V—V	V—C	C—C	C—S	S—S
Speaker: 12	0	0	0	–	0
16	0	0	–	①	0
15	0	0	0	0	X
10	0	0	⊗	0	1
11	0	⊗	0	X	1
9	⊗	0	0	X	1
13	⊗	0	⊛	X	1
8	0	0	–	1	1
5	0	X	1	⊗	–
7	0	X	1	1	1
2	0	X	–	1	1

Note: Symbols used as in Table 6, except that double-ringed deviations, are cells that would not be deviant if Condition 3 were replaced by Condition 6.

TABLE 8. Three-valued implicational scale of Sankoff's que data for those speakers who have adopted or may adopt Rule (6) in the temporal progress of que-deletion.

Rule:	(8)	(7)	(6)	(3)	(2')
Environment:	V—V	V—C	V—S	C—S	S—S
Speaker: 12	0	0	0	–	0
16	0	0	0	①	0
15	0	–	0	0	X
10	0	①	0	0	–
11	0	⊗	0	X	–
9	⊗	0	0	X	1
6	0	0	⊛	X	1
4	⊗	0	⊛	X	1
14	0	⊛	⊛	X	1
8	0	0	0	1	1
3	⊗	0	X	1	–
1	①	0	X	–	–

Note: Symbols used as in Table 7.

Before going to discuss Tables 7 and 8, a few words on the mechanics of their construction are in order. Speakers 12, 16, 15, 10, 11, and 9 have not advanced beyond Rule (3) and so appear on both Table 7 and Table 8, since they may follow either pattern. Speakers 2, 5, 7, and 13 appear on Table 7 since they appear to have acquired Rule (5) rather than Rule (6). These are the speakers Bickerton (1973:39) says have his equivalent of Rule (5), except that I have added Speaker 13. While he or she is not clearly an example of a lect with Rule (5) for Bickerton, when his error in copying from Sankoff's table is corrected, Speaker 13 fits better in Table 7 than in Table 8. Speakers 6, 4, 14, 8, 3, and 1 have acquired Rule (6) and therefore appear in Table 8. These are the speakers said by Bickerton to have acquired the equivalent of Rule (6), except for Speaker 13 who, as has been explained, we assume fits rather in Table 7.

Following Bickerton's reasoning, Sankoff's environments have been conflated in Tables 7 and 8 in the following manner:

In Table 7:
 Sankoff's C_V, V_V, and S_V are conflated as V_V.
 Sankoff's V_S and V_C are conflated as V_C.
 Sankoff's C_C and S_C are conflated as C_C.
 Sankoff's C_S and S_S are unchanged.

In Table 8:
 Sankoff's C_V, V_V, and S_V are conflated as V_V.
 Sankoff's V_C, C_C, and S_C are conflated as V_C.
 Sankoff's V_S, C_S, and S_S are unchanged.

Table 9 shows how the contents--X, -, 0, or 1--of the conflated environments are determined from the data in Table 6. That these procedures are reasonable will become clear upon reflection.

TABLE 9. Procedures for determining cell contents of conflated environments in Tables 7 and 8.

If original environments contained:	Conflated environment contains:
All dashes	–
All 0's, or 0's and dashes	0
All 1's, or 1's and dashes	1
At least one 1 and one 0	X
At least one X	X

With Table 7 and Table 8, we are in a position to see how well the two proposed patterns of change fit the data. Sankoff's data are plagued with numerous examples of empty and sparsely populated cells, so that the chances of finding very neat patterns under any theory are not too good. However, we shall use the same data with the same problems to test Bickerton's model and the actual Bailey Wave Model.

The most common way to test the fit of data to an implicational model is to calculate 'percent scalability'. This is a simple calculation in which the number of cells in a table such as Table 6, 7, or 8 which conform to the theory are divided by the total number of cells in the table. Calculating percent scalability for Table 7, we find that it is 87.3 percent scalable. In his original proposal of the scaling technique, Guttman claimed that 'in practice, 85 percent perfect scales or better have been used as efficient approximations to perfect scales' (Guttman 1944:150). The scalability of Table 7 thus falls in a range that Guttman would have accepted. If we relax Condition 3, that only one variable cell may appear in each row, replacing it with Condition 6 which allows any number of variable cells as long as they are not out of position, then the double-ringed variable cell for Speaker 13 in the C_C environment becomes non-deviant. With one fewer deviation, the data in Table 7 become 89.1 percent scalable.

Moving to Table 8, we find that when we insist on Condition 3, the data are 81.6 percent scalable. Thus they do not achieve the level that Guttman found acceptable. However, replacing the unnecessarily stringent Condition 3 with Condition 6 allows us to consider the four double-ringed cells in Table 8 non-deviant and raises the scalability figure to 88.3 percent. While we do not take percent scalability too seriously as a measure of the success of an implicational theory, it does provide a 'rough and ready' measure for those not skilled in more sophisticated statistical techniques.

Now we are prepared to look at what the Bailey Wave Model, as a quantitative dynamic paradigm, would predict about Sankoff's data and to see how well the data conform. The differences between the Bickerton and Bailey models can be seen best by comparing Conditions 1 through 3 with Conditions 4 through 6. Condition 1 limits Bickerton's interpretation to a three-valued scale in which relative frequencies must be taken into consideration. We have already discussed the differences between Condition 3 and Condition 6 and shown how Bickerton's model would fit his data better if he abandoned Condition 3 in favor of Condition 6.

Perhaps the most crucial differences between the two models are the differences between Conditions 2 and 5. As we have seen, Condition 2 calls for a series of rules, presumably temporally ordered, in which successive rules drop constraints from previous rules. In the Bailey model, the wave moves from heavier to lighter environments. To see how this works, we must convert Sankoff's data into the classical variable rule format. Theoretically, we should be able to work directly from Sankoff's quantitative variable rule by observing the gradations among constraint probabilities, but unfortunately, in writing the rule, she coded 'sibilant' and 'consonant' as mutually exclusive constraints rather than maximizing cross-product comparisons by coding 'sibilant' as a subcategory of 'consonant'. However, it is easy to see from her raw data how the constraints are hierarchized. The classical variable rule would be:

$$\text{que} \rightarrow (\emptyset)/ \begin{vmatrix} \delta(+\text{strd}) \\ \gamma(+\text{cons}) \end{vmatrix} \underline{\qquad} \begin{vmatrix} \beta(+\text{strd}) \\ \alpha(+\text{cons}) \end{vmatrix}$$

Mechanical application of the environment weighting calculus (Bailey 1973, Fasold 1974) would predict that que-deletion would spread successively through the various environments in the following order:

$$\begin{bmatrix} +\text{strd} \\ +\text{cons} \end{bmatrix} \underline{\qquad} \begin{bmatrix} +\text{strd} \\ +\text{cons} \end{bmatrix}$$

$$\begin{bmatrix} -\text{strd} \\ +\text{cons} \end{bmatrix} \underline{\qquad} \begin{bmatrix} +\text{strd} \\ +\text{cons} \end{bmatrix}$$

$$\begin{bmatrix} +\text{strd} \\ -\text{cons} \end{bmatrix} \underline{\qquad} \begin{bmatrix} +\text{strd} \\ +\text{cons} \end{bmatrix}$$

$$\begin{bmatrix} -\text{strd} \\ -\text{cons} \end{bmatrix} \underline{\qquad} \begin{bmatrix} +\text{strd} \\ +\text{cons} \end{bmatrix}$$

$$\begin{bmatrix} +\text{strd} \\ +\text{cons} \end{bmatrix} \underline{\qquad} \begin{bmatrix} -\text{strd} \\ +\text{cons} \end{bmatrix}$$

$$\begin{bmatrix} -\text{strd} \\ +\text{cons} \end{bmatrix} \underline{\qquad} \begin{bmatrix} -\text{strd} \\ +\text{cons} \end{bmatrix}$$

$$\begin{bmatrix} +\text{strd} \\ -\text{cons} \end{bmatrix} \underline{\qquad} \begin{bmatrix} -\text{strd} \\ +\text{cons} \end{bmatrix}$$

$$\begin{bmatrix} -\text{strd} \\ -\text{cons} \end{bmatrix} \underline{\qquad} \begin{bmatrix} -\text{strd} \\ +\text{cons} \end{bmatrix}$$

$$\begin{bmatrix} +\text{strd} \\ +\text{cons} \end{bmatrix} \underline{\qquad} \begin{bmatrix} +\text{strd} \\ -\text{cons} \end{bmatrix}$$

$$\begin{bmatrix} -\text{strd} \\ +\text{cons} \end{bmatrix} \underline{\qquad} \begin{bmatrix} +\text{strd} \\ -\text{cons} \end{bmatrix}$$

$$\begin{bmatrix} +strd \\ -cons \end{bmatrix} \quad \underline{\quad\quad} \quad \begin{bmatrix} +strd \\ -cons \end{bmatrix}$$

$$\begin{bmatrix} -strd \\ -cons \end{bmatrix} \quad \underline{\quad\quad} \quad \begin{bmatrix} +strd \\ -cons \end{bmatrix}$$

$$\begin{bmatrix} +strd \\ +cons \end{bmatrix} \quad \underline{\quad\quad} \quad \begin{bmatrix} -strd \\ -cons \end{bmatrix}$$

$$\begin{bmatrix} -strd \\ +cons \end{bmatrix} \quad \underline{\quad\quad} \quad \begin{bmatrix} -strd \\ -cons \end{bmatrix}$$

$$\begin{bmatrix} +strd \\ -cons \end{bmatrix} \quad \underline{\quad\quad} \quad \begin{bmatrix} -strd \\ -cons \end{bmatrix}$$

$$\begin{bmatrix} -strd \\ -cons \end{bmatrix} \quad \underline{\quad\quad} \quad \begin{bmatrix} -strd \\ -cons \end{bmatrix}$$

But this mechanical application of the calculus is only valid when all combinations of the constraints are possible. In our case, combinations specifying [+strd] and [-cons] are not possible, since there are no strident non-consonants. Eliminating the seven environments calling for [+strd] and [-cons] either in the preceding or following environments, we are left with a sequence of nine environments which correspond to Sankoff's environments. These appear in Table 10. Notice that the sequence in Table 10 allows features which have become minus in earlier environments to become plus again in later environments. No doubt Bickerton would object that there is no way feature values can be restored once they have disappeared. But, like old-fashioned love songs, there's "no need in bringin' 'em back, 'cause they've never really gone". In the model we are discussing, change does not spread only by the loss of constraining features but, more finely, under conditions of lesser and lesser favorability. Using Anshen's term (Anshen MS), the variable constraints should be viewed as more or less strong 'mental urges' toward deletion ('mental urges' is a term I find convenient, although not to be taken too seriously). When the most and strongest constraints ('urges') are present, the deletion rule will first occur and always occur with the greatest frequency. The rule takes hold and moves toward categoricality by becoming operative, then operating at even greater frequencies, under combinations of successively fewer and weaker constraints.

Of course, ultimately, the constraints do drop out of the rule, but not quite so quickly as in Bickerton's proposal. Under the dynamic interpretation, the Bailey Wave Model predicts the following sequence of rules.

TABLE 10. Successive environments for que-deletion according to the Bailey Wave Model.

Environments in features		Environments in Sankoff's cover symbols
$\begin{bmatrix} +strd \\ +cons \end{bmatrix}$ ____ $\begin{bmatrix} +strd \\ +cons \end{bmatrix}$		S_S
$\begin{bmatrix} -strd \\ +cons \end{bmatrix}$ ____ $\begin{bmatrix} +strd \\ +cons \end{bmatrix}$		C_S
$\begin{bmatrix} -strd \\ -strd \end{bmatrix}$ ____ $\begin{bmatrix} +strd \\ +cons \end{bmatrix}$		V_S
$\begin{bmatrix} +strd \\ +cons \end{bmatrix}$ ____ $\begin{bmatrix} -strd \\ +cons \end{bmatrix}$		S_C
$\begin{bmatrix} -strd \\ +cons \end{bmatrix}$ ____ $\begin{bmatrix} -strd \\ +cons \end{bmatrix}$		C_C
$\begin{bmatrix} -strd \\ -cons \end{bmatrix}$ ____ $\begin{bmatrix} -strd \\ +cons \end{bmatrix}$		V_C
$\begin{bmatrix} +strd \\ +cons \end{bmatrix}$ ____ $\begin{bmatrix} -strd \\ -cons \end{bmatrix}$		S_V
$\begin{bmatrix} -strd \\ +cons \end{bmatrix}$ ____ $\begin{bmatrix} -strd \\ -cons \end{bmatrix}$		C_V
$\begin{bmatrix} -strd \\ -cons \end{bmatrix}$ ____ $\begin{bmatrix} -strd \\ -cons \end{bmatrix}$		V_V

Stage 1. que $\rightarrow (\emptyset) / \begin{bmatrix} +strd \\ +cons \end{bmatrix}$ _____ $\begin{bmatrix} +strd \\ +cons \end{bmatrix}$

At the beginning, que is deleted only in the most favorable environment. Deletion is variable (indicated by the parentheses around $\emptyset$) and presumably operates at very low frequencies.

Stage 2. que $\rightarrow (\emptyset) / \begin{bmatrix} \alpha(+strd) \\ +cons \end{bmatrix}$ _____ $\begin{bmatrix} +strd \\ +cons \end{bmatrix}$

At Stage 2, deletion begins to occur in C_S as well as S_S. Now, [+strd] is not essential in the preceding environment, but the rule operates more frequently if it is present. Hence, the designation [α(+strd)].

Stage 3.   que → (∅)/ $\begin{bmatrix} β(+strd) \\ α(+cons) \end{bmatrix}$ _____ $\begin{bmatrix} +strd \\ +cons \end{bmatrix}$

Now the rule begins to operate in V_S as well as the two preceding environments. The rule operates most frequently if both [+strd] and [+cons] are present in the preceding environment, and more frequently if [+cons] is present than if neither constraint is present. Of course, [+strd] cannot occur without [+cons].

Stage 4.   que → (∅)/ $\begin{bmatrix} γ(+strd) \\ β(+cons) \end{bmatrix}$ _____ $\begin{bmatrix} α(+strd) \\ +cons \end{bmatrix}$

At Stage 4, the rule still operates only before consonants, but the consonant need no longer be [+strd]. Naturally, the rule is more favored if it is than if it is not. The rule now moves all the way down to the V_C environment. But under the two-valued implicational interpretation, the rule predicts that there may be a lect in which deletion is possible in S_C, but not in C_C or V_C, a lect which allows deletion in S_C and C_C, but not in V_C, and one which allows deletion in all three environments. There are not three separate rules for these lects, but they are predicted from the general theory nonetheless.

Stage 5.   que → $\begin{bmatrix} δ(+strd) \\ γ(+cons) \end{bmatrix}$ _____ $\begin{bmatrix} β(+strd) \\ α(+cons) \end{bmatrix}$

The Stage 5 rule is the rule given earlier and allows variable deletion all the way down to V_V. Again, the two-valued interpretation can use the rule to predict the lect in which deletion is allowed in S_V but not C_V and V_V, in S_V and C_V but not V_V, and in all three environments. For that matter, the Stage 5 rule predicts all the lects predicted by the rules of Stages 1 through 4, as well.

The next few stages call for 'knockouts' in the stronger environments. First, que-deletion is obligatory in S_S. Later, it becomes obligatory in C_S. There are no separate rules for these stages, but again they are predicted, this time by the three-valued interpretation which distinguishes obligatory and variable application. When the rule becomes categorical in V_S, it is categorical whenever a strident consonant follows. Therefore, the feature [+strd] gets the 'knockout' symbol, *.[12] Now the rule takes the form:

$$\text{que} \rightarrow (\emptyset) \; / \; \begin{bmatrix} \gamma(\text{+strd}) \\ \beta(\text{+cons}) \end{bmatrix} \underline{\quad\quad} \begin{bmatrix} *(\text{+strd}) \\ \alpha(\text{+cons}) \end{bmatrix}$$

This rule says that if que is followed by a strident segment, the rule is categorical. If a strident segment does not follow, both progress and relative frequencies are determined by the relative weightings of the remaining environments.

The rule does not change until it becomes categorical in V_C, but the theory predicts that it first becomes categorical in S_C, then in C_C. When it becomes categorical in V_C, it is categorical before any consonant. The feature [+cons] becomes 'knockout' in the following environment and [+strd] is no longer relevant and drops out. It is only at this stage that a feature actually drops out of the rule.

$$\text{que} \rightarrow (\emptyset) \; / \; \begin{bmatrix} \beta(\text{+strd}) \\ \alpha(\text{+cons}) \end{bmatrix} \underline{\quad\quad} [*\text{+cons)}]$$

When the rule becomes categorical in S_V, it is categorical following a strident segment regardless of what follows, and the preceding [+strd] becomes 'knockout'.

$$\text{que} \rightarrow (\emptyset) \; / \; \begin{bmatrix} *(\text{strd}) \\ \alpha(\text{+cons}) \end{bmatrix} \underline{\quad\quad} [*(\text{+cons)}]$$

Next, the rule reaches categoricality in C_V, that is, after any consonant. Now [+cons] in the preceding environment is 'knockout' and [+strd] is irrelevant.

$$\text{que} \rightarrow (\emptyset) \; / \; \underline{\quad\quad} [*(\text{+cons)}]$$

At both of these stages, the rule is categorical when que is in the presence of either 'knockout' constraint and variable otherwise.

When the rule becomes categorical in V_V, it is fully categorical. The rule is:

$$\text{que} \rightarrow \emptyset$$

and the grammar of relative clause formation is wide open to restructuring. [13]

Although only the stages outlined here are possible, not all of them need occur. The rule can begin at a stage later than Stage 1, it may skip stages, but it may not move backwards or go through stages not designated above. [14]

Returning to the Sankoff data, we may observe how well it conforms to the predictions of the Bailey Wave Model. We do this using

Table 11. Each cell of Table 11 contains the number of deleted que over the total number of observed que constructions in the upper left hand corner in fraction form, and the decimal equivalent in the lower right hand corner. As with Bickerton's scales, the scale in Table 11 is far from perfect. The percent scalability is 89.6 percent, which compares very favorably with the scalability of Tables 7 and 8. [15] This level is achieved in spite of the fact that in Table 11, of two cells showing variability, the one to the right must show a higher value than one to the left. Bickerton's three-valued scales, if Condition 3 is relaxed, require only that variable cells not appear to the right of categorical cells or to the left of zero cells. Two neighboring variable cells meeting those requirements would be non-deviant regardless of their frequency values.

Obviously, we are making no claim for the superiority of the Bailey Wave Model based on the fact that Table 11 scales are fractionally better than the best interpretation of Tables 7 or 8. Our claim is based on more basic principles. We have demonstrated that Sankoff's data scale as well under the requirements of multivalued implicational scaling as they do under the less stringent requirements of three-valued analysis. Furthermore, the data are equally well scalable using the environments ordered to express the fine-grained stages of change predicted by the Bailey Wave Model as they do when ordered into conflated environments reflecting the grosser change stages allowed by Bickerton.

But there is another reason to prefer the Bailey theory. Table 11 reveals that many of Sankoff's cells are sparsely populated indeed. With more data on each speaker there is every reason to expect that many of 0/1, 0/2, and 0/3 zero cells will become variable as will many of the 1/1, 2/2, and 3/3 categorical ones. A look at the variable cells in Table 11, deviant or non-deviant, shows that, considering cells that have, say, five or more que constructions, there is a tendency for higher frequency levels to occur toward the left of the table than to the right, exactly as the Bailey Wave Model would predict. There is every reason to expect that as more data were collected and more cells became variable this trend would continue, quite likely making many of the apparently deviant cells in Table 11 non-deviant in the final analysis. Bickerton, on the other hand, depends heavily on a number of crucially located zero and categorical cells, many of them very sparsely populated. It would not take too many cases in which some of these became variable with increasing amounts of data to make a hopeless shambles of Bickerton's arguments. If, for instance, three-fourths of the cells in Tables 7 or 8 became variable, Bickerton's argument would very likely be destroyed, especially if he insists on Condition 3. Every single cell in Table 11 could become variable without damaging the Bailey model predictions, as long as the relative frequency values conformed to Condition 6. In short, the

TABLE 11. Multi-valued implicational table of Sankoff's que-deletion value according to the Bailey Wave Model. Environments become progressively heavier from left to right. Deviant cells are circled.

Environments

Speaker	V_V	C_V	S_V	V_C	C_C	S_C	V_S	C_S	S_S
12	0/1 .00	0/1 .00	0/3 .00	0/8 .00	0/1 .00	0/3 .00	0/5 .00	----	0/3 .00
16	0/15 .00	0/5 .00	0/2 .00	0/2 .00	----	----	0/9 .00	1/1 1.00	0/1 .00
10	0/2 .00	0/1 .00	----	----	1/1 1.00	0/2 .00	0/7 .00	0/1 .00	----
15	0/6 .00	0/2 .00	----	----	0/3 .00	----	0/5 .00	0/2 .00	2/3 .67
11	0/3 .00	0/2 .00	----	1/3 .33	0/3 .00	0/1 .00	0/4 .00	1/2 .50	----
9	0/10 .00	0/5 .00	1/7 .14	0/1 .00	0/1 .00	0/1 .00	0/9 .00	1/4 .25	1/1 1.00
13	0/10 .00	0/1 .00	1/12 .08	0/4 .00	1/2 .50	0/3 .00	0/3 .00	6/7 .86	8/8 1.00
6	0/15 .00	0/2 .00	0/3 .00	0/7 .00	----	0/1 .00	5/16 .31	1/3 .33	5/5 1.00
14	0/11 .00	0/1 .00	0/1 .00	1/10 .10	0/1 .00	0/1 .00	1/4 .25	3/5 .60	3/3 1.00
4	1/3 .33	0/3 .00	2/5 .40	0/1 .00	0/1 .00	----	1/2 .50	4/5 .80	7/7 1.00
1	----	0/3 .00	----	0/1 .00	0/1 .00	----	3/4 .75	----	----
8	0/11 .00	0/2 .00	----	0/5 .00	----	----	0/3 .00	2/2 1.00	1/1 1.00
3	1/4 .25	0/2 .00	1/1 1.00	0/2 .00	----	----	1/4 .25	4/4 1.00	----
2	0/1 .00	----	0/1 .00	3/3 1.00	----	----	4/5 .80	3/3 1.00	4/4 1.00
7	0/5 .00	0/4 .00	0/2 .00	1/3 .33	1/1 1.00	----	6/8 .75	8/8 1.00	2/2 1.00
5	0/6 .00	0/2 .00	0/1 .00	2/5 .40	1/1 1.00	1/1 1.00	0/3 .00	1/2 .50	----

probable increase in the number of variable cells with the accumulation of additional data can scarcely help but weaken the Bickerton
model. There is good reason to hope that increased data--and increased variability--would strengthen the Bailey interpretation. [16]

There is no reason to suppose that quantitative models incorporating variable rules are incapable of handling the dynamic aspects
of language change. In fact, the dynamic quantitative Bailey Wave
Model appears to be very successful at it indeed.

NOTES

1. While there are profound differences between classical and
quantitative variable rules, our discussion applies to either type.
Our arguments here will defend what is common to both and the
differences between them will not be emphasized.

2. Although a complete explanation must wait until later in the
article, Condition 5 predicts the loss of constraints ultimately in the
same order as does Condition 2, but allows account to be taken of
change at a much more finely grained level.

The terms 'heavy' and 'light' mean more and less favorable to the
operation of the rule, respectively. These and other terms are defined in more detail beginning on p. 31.

3. Bickerton's Condition 3 is implicit in all his work, but is never
made explicit nor is it justified. Condition 3 is not really essential
to Bickerton's major arguments and could be replaced with Condition
6 minus the second provision without changing anything essential in
his theory. Condition 3 is certainly not part of the most recent version of the Bailey Wave Model, since, in a prepublication version of
Bailey forthcoming, he at one point says exactly the opposite:
'[Principle] (16) All the environments of a rule become variable before the oldest becomes categorical'. Far from allowing only one
environment to remain variable before the next becomes categorical
Principle 16 requires all environments to become variable before
any become categorical. However, on the next page, Bailey relaxes
Principle 16, bringing it into conformity with Condition 6.

It is interesting to speculate on the reason why Bickerton should
have assumed Condition 3 while Bailey at least temporarily proposes
Principle 16. The difference between Condition 3 and Principle 16 is
that Condition 3 predicts very rapid change in which a heavier environment has a chance to become variable. Principle 16 predicts very
slow changes in which all environments dawdle along at variable
stages before the most advanced one becomes categorical. The reason for the differences in approaches of the two linguists is that
Bickerton argues on the basis of data from creole languages in the
early stages of decreolization while Bailey looks primarily at data

on languages not involved in decreolization. It may well be that decreolizing languages typically or always undergo changes so rapid that they conform to Condition 3, while languages not involved in decreolization usually change slowly enough to conform to Principle 16. Condition 6 is neutral with respect to rapidity of change and situations conforming both to Condition 3 and to Principle 16 are a fortiori in conformity with Condition 6.

4. In a quantitative variable rule, constraint weighting may be determined by ranking in numerical order the probabilities associated with each constraint. In Bailey's format for a classical variable rule, numbers replace Greek letters with higher numbers indicating heavier weighted constraints than lower ones.

5. Bailey proposed a method for calculating environment weight in Bailey forthcoming which was revised in Fasold 1974.

6. I have not reproduced the other one, Labov's (1969:740) display of the constraints on contraction, because of complications in that display (Labov's Figure 12). In that display, the third order constraint when a following verb is present, the presence of a following gonna, is irrelevant when a following verb is present. Furthermore, following verb and preceding vowel, which appear to be first and second order constraints, respectively, in Labov's Figure 12 turn out both to be first order constraints. In addition, there are mathematical errors in the numbers presented in Figure 12. A full explanation of all this would take us too far afield.

7. Kessler's table does not meet Condition 3, which specifies that there be only one variable environment in each row of the chart. It is not clear to me how failing to meet this requirement is in any way related to the fact that the environments are incorrectly ordered.

8. The distinctive features we refer to are [cor(onal)], [syll(abic)], [str(i)d(ent)], and [cons(onantal)].

9. It will be our ultimate contention that Bailey's wave model does not actually require that C_C be the next lighter environment after C_S and that it is an accident that Sankoff did not find any speakers who delete in S_C but not in C_C. This claim would be falsified if further study continued to show that there are no such speakers. Finding such speakers would, of course, falsify Bickerton's claim.

10. There would be one further step, that is when Rule (8) changes status from a variable (optional) rule to a categorical one. If and when this were to happen, it would have profound repercussions in the grammar of relative clause formation in Montreal French.

11. In transferring Sankoff's data to his format, Bickerton made a number of errors, so that his table is not quite accurate. In constructing Table 6, I have corrected these errors. Fortunately, the errors are not crucial to his argument. Except for two speakers, correcting the errors has no effect at all on their placement or

deviance. Speaker 13, however, whom Bickerton has as an example of his Lect II (Bickerton 1973:31) with two deviations is actually an example of Lect IV, with the same two deviations. Speaker 5 is not a perfect example of Lect X, as Bickerton's table would lead the reader to believe, but has a deviation (variable deletion in C_S) and there are no data for the S_S environment where Bickerton shows categorical deletion.

12. Ordinarily, one would expect that an alpha constraint would become the 'knockout' constraint first. Since there are no strident non-consonants, [+strd] becomes 'knockout' first, in this case.

13. The progress of the rule according to the Bailey Wave Model including the classical variable rule would follow the pattern outlined here, given the notational conventions of the variable rule as so far developed. The weakness is that not all stages are reflected in rule form, although all are predictable from the Stage 5 rule. The unevenness of what is expressible in rule form could be remedied in one of two ways. First, conventions could be added which would allow all stages to be reflected in rule form. Alternatively, we could dispense with all but the Stage 5 rule, allow it to generate all possible lects metatheoretically, and add the particular lect specification to the rule for a speaker of any given lect. For example:

$$\text{que} \quad (\emptyset) \: / \: \begin{bmatrix} \delta(\text{+strd}) \\ \gamma\,(\text{+cons}) \end{bmatrix} \underline{\qquad} \begin{bmatrix} \beta(\text{+strd}) \\ \alpha(\text{+cons}) \end{bmatrix} \quad \text{(Lect 5)}$$

The latter alternative has a certain appeal, since it implies that a speaker 'knows' where the rule has been, where it is going (if, indeed, it does not stagnate) and where he himself is in the progress of the rule.

14. Except in cases of rule inhibition, in which cases, the rule moves only backwards through the stages.

15. The fact that the line outlining (non-deviant) categorical cells is coterminus in spots with the line delineating (non-deviant) variable cells does not indicate deviance, as long as the categorical cell line does not extend beyond the variable cell line.

16. A very similar point is made in Anshen (1974) this volume.

REFERENCES

Anshen, Frank S. MS. Bickerton, Labov, and inherent variability. Stony Brook, State University of New York at Stony Brook.
_____. 1975. Varied objections to various variable rules. In: Analyzing variation in language: Papers from the second colloqium on new ways of analyzing variation. Edited by Roger W. Shuy and Ralph W. Fasold. Washington, D. C., Georgetown University Press.

Bailey, Charles-James N. 1973. Variation and linguistic theory. Arlington, Virginia, Center for Applied Linguistics.

_____ and Roger W. Shuy, eds. 1973. New ways of analyzing variation in English. Washington, D. C., Georgetown University Press.

Bickerton, Derek. 1971. Inherent variability and variable rules. Foundations of Language 7:457-492.

_____. 1973. Quantitative versus dynamic paradigms: The case of Montreal que. In: Bailey and Shuy (1973). 23-44.

Cedergren, Henrietta J. and David Sankoff. 1974. Variable rules: Performance as a statistical reflection of competence. Language 50:333-355.

Fasold, Ralph W. 1972. Tense marking in Black English: A linguistic and social analysis. Arlington, Virginia, Center for Applied Linguistics.

_____. 1973. The concept of 'Earlier-Later': More or less correct. In: Bailey and Shuy (1973). 183-197.

_____. 1974. Baileying out Bailey. The Lectological Newsletter 2. 1:3-6.

Guttman, Louis. 1944. A basis for scaling qualitative data. American Sociological Review 9, 139-150.

Kessler, Carolyn. 1972. Noun plural absence. Annex to Fasold (1972). 223-238.

Labov, William. 1969. Contraction, deletion, and inherent variability of the English copula. Language 45. 715-762.

_____. 1972. Language in the inner city. Philadelphia, University of Pennsylvania Press.

_____, Paul Cohen, Clarence Robins, and John Lewis. 1968. A study of the non-standard English of Negro and Puerto Rican speakers in New York City, Vol. 1. Final Report, Cooperative Research Project 3288, U. S. Office of Education. (ERIC ED 028 423).

Pfaff, Carol. 1971. Historical and structural aspects of sociolinguistic variation: The copula in black English. Inglewood, California, Southwest Regional Laboratory Technical Report 37.

Sankoff, Gillian. MS. A quantitative paradigm for the study of communicative competence. (Revised version).

Stolz, Walter and Garland Bills. 1968. An investigation of the standard-nonstandard dimension of Central Texas English. Final Report to the U. S. Office of Economic Opportunity. (Austin, Child Development Evaluation and Research Center, University of Texas).

Sobin, Linda L. n. d. Noun plural marker deletion in the speech of black children. Austin, Penn-Texas Working Papers in Sociolinguistics, No. 4.

Wolfram, Walter A. 1969. A sociolinguistic description of Detroit
Negro speech. Washington, D. C., Center for Applied Linguistics.
_____. 1971. Overlapping influence in the English of second gener-
ation Puerto Rican teenagers in Harlem. Final Report, Office of
Education Grant No. 3-70-0033(508). Washington, D. C., Center
for Applied Linguistics.
_____. 1973. On what basis variable rules? In: Bailey and Shuy
(1973). 1-12.
_____. 1974. The relationship of White Southern speech to vernacu-
lar Black English: Copula deletion and invariant be. Language
50:498-527.

USE AND APPLICATIONS OF THE
CEDERGREN-SANKOFF VARIABLE RULE PROGRAM

GREGORY R. GUY

University of Pennsylvania

A number of recent and forthcoming articles and papers have
dealt with variation in terms of what has been called a 'quantitative
paradigm' (G. Sankoff, in press). This approach to variation assumes
that variability is inherent in language and that it is describable by
means of a probabilistic or variable rule component in the grammar.
The theoretical framework for this approach is perhaps best set
forth in G. Sankoff (in press) and Cedergren and D. Sankoff (to appear).

But in addition to their theoretical contributions, these scholars
have also developed a practical method for estimating those underlying probabilities by which the quantitative paradigm accounts for
observed variation. That method is the Cedergren/Sankoff variable
rule program. It is a versatile and mathematically sophisticated tool
which will enable linguists to handle larger bodies of data and study
variation with greater precision than ever before. It has already been
applied to a number of problems in phonology and syntax with great
success. It is potentially applicable to all types of linguistic problems, including historical ones.

The program is, of course, based on the concept of the variable
rule. Essentially, any problem in variation that can be conceptualized
or formalized as a variable rule is amenable to treatment with this
computer program. Some linguists, of course, question the validity
of the variable rule and the quantitative paradigm and prefer to
formalize their treatment of linguistic variation in other ways. It
is not my purpose to treat those theoretical issues here. This paper
is intended, rather, as an introduction to, and an overview of, one
major analytical procedure in the quantitative paradigm. The program

is only a tool of analysis, and a useful discovery procedure. It is not itself a theoretical issue.

Any analysis using the variable rule program will involve the formulation of a tentative variable rule, which may be understood as a hypothesis about a given problem in variation. The general form of the variable rule, taken from Cedergren and D. Sankoff (to appear), is shown in (1).

(1) General Form of a Variable Rule

$$x \quad <y>/ \quad \begin{Bmatrix} \text{[fea A]} \\ \text{[fea B]} \\ \text{[fea C]} \\ \cdot \\ \cdot \end{Bmatrix} \begin{Bmatrix} \text{[fea I]} \\ \text{[fea J]} \\ \cdot \\ \cdot \end{Bmatrix} \begin{Bmatrix} \text{[fea P]} \\ \text{[fea Q]} \\ \text{[fea R]} \\ \cdot \\ \cdot \end{Bmatrix} \quad \text{[fea V]}$$

(1) is read as: 'X is variably rewritten as Y, variably conditioned by features A, B, C, etc. in the preceding environment, features I, J, etc. co-occurring, and features P, Q, R, etc. in the following environment, and invariably conditioned by a feature V.' Each of the conditioning factors is considered to have an underlying probability that the rule will apply associated with it. The rule as a whole has an 'input probability' associated with it, that is, the probability that the rule will apply regardless of its environment. (This can alternatively be stated as the probability that the rule will apply even in the most disfavored environments.) For any particular occurrence of the variable, the probability of rule application is obtained by multiplying together the input probability and the probabilities of all the factors which occur in the environment of the given token of the variable. Examples of this calculation are given in (2).

(2) Sample Calculations of the Probability of Rule Application in Specific Environments

(2a) Prob. of $x \rightarrow y$ / [fea A] _____ [fea P] = $P_o \times P_A \times P_I \times P_P$
[fea I]

(2b) Prob. of $x \rightarrow y$ / [fea B] _____ [fea R] = $P_o \times P_B \times P_J \times P_R$
[fea J]
(P_o = input probability)

(There is an alternative model in which the probabilities are added rather than multiplied.)[1] Ultimately, given a large number of occurrences of the variable in a variety of environments, these underlying probabilities will be reflected in the speech of an individual or a community as statistically observable fluctuations in the relative frequencies of the different variants.

The linguist who is studying variation, however, must proceed in the opposite direction. He begins with a set of statistical observations about the frequencies of the different variants in different environments, and on the basis of those observations must discern which factors promote the application of the rule, hinder it, or are irrelevant to it, as well as what the order of importance of the various factors is. In other words, one wishes not only to be able to establish whether, for example, feature A has an effect on the rule, but also to determine if that effect is greater or lesser than the effects of features B, C, J. P, etc. Until now linguists have approached this problem through elaborate tabular displays and comparison of cross-products. A much better way of dealing with it, however, is to determine in some way the values of those underlying probabilities. There are several mathematical procedures available which do exactly that. A variety of computer programs incorporating these procedures have been used to deal with similar problems in other social sciences for some time. The Cedergren/Sankoff program uses one such procedure, called the 'Maximum Likelihood' method, to determine a unique set of underlying probabilities for a given body of observations.[2] It also calculates a Chi-square value measuring how well those probabilities fit the observed statistical frequencies. These capabilities make it an excellent tool for the analysis of variation and the testing of linguistic hypotheses.

The first step in using this program in solving a problem in variation is to define the variable. This includes identifying all the possible variants and making an initial decision about what is to be considered the underlying form. The program is designed to handle binary variables, i.e. those with only two variants. This is the situation with any standard variable or optional rewrite rule with one input and one output. In any given case the rule either applies, in which case the output value of the rule is realized, or does not apply, in which case the input value is realized. A case with more than two variants can still be handled with this program by using several (possibly ordered) rules to describe them and several computer runs to analyze them. Thus the aspiration and deletion of /s/ in some dialects of Spanish, which is discussed in Cedergren's paper (1973) in the first NWAVE volume, can be treated as two successive rules, namely s→<h>, and then h →<∅>.[3] Independent evidence for the second rule--H-deletion--has been found by Longmire (personal communication) in Venezuelan Spanish, where all /h/'s, not just those derived from /s/, are subject to variable deletion. Similarly, Labov has analyzed the three variants of the English copula, full, contracted, and deleted, as resulting from two successive rules, one of contraction and the next of deletion (Labov 1969). To describe the phonological process in detail requires many more than two rules; in principle the variable rule program is applicable to every rule for which there is some surface indication.

After the variable has been clearly defined, the investigator must formulate an initial hypothesis about what sort of conditioning he expects to find, what environmental factors are possibly relevant to the rule. This decision should be based both on linguistic theory and an inspection of the data. It is important to note that one is not bound to a single theory, a single hypothesis about a given problem. Any number of theories can be tested with considerable ease by using this program, as is demonstrated by Griffin, Guy, and Sag (1973).

Next, in order to render one's hypotheses about relevant constraints intelligible to the program, one must devise a coding system. To each conditioning factor which one wishes to examine there is assigned a unique single-character code. It is best to choose these codes mnemonically because it facilitates interpreting the output. Available as code symbols are all the letters, numbers, and other characters on the IBM keypunch machine keyboard. However, no more than twenty factors may be analyzed on a single run of the computer. This limitation is built into the program because processing time increases almost geometrically with the number of factors, and because few linguistic rules show more than twenty constraints. For these reasons it is best not to try to be totally thorough in one's initial approach to a problem. One should first examine the grossest effects, the highest-order constraints, and then after that, the finer structures.

The conditioning factors are grouped into factor groups according to the positions where they occur in the environment of the variable. Thus phonological conditioning might require one factor group for the preceding segment, one for the following segment, one for the stress pattern, etc., and grammatical conditioning might involve a factor group for the type of sentence subject, the type of clause, or whether a certain transformation has applied. The factors in a given group must be mutually exclusive (i.e., none of them may wholly or partially include another) and must represent an exhaustive list of all possibilities for that group. For example, one would not set up a factor group for the following segment and then code only consonants while ignoring all vowels.

One important and useful aspect of this program should be noted here. The social distribution of a linguistic variable can be analyzed by including social factors in the coding system in the same fashion as linguistic ones. This must be done very carefully, of course, as the program operates on the assumption that the conditioning factors are independent and non-interactive, which is a valid assumption for most linguistic constraints but not necessarily for social ones. [4] Other methods of multivariate analysis may prove more appropriate for the treatment of some sociolinguistic problems. This program appears to be quite applicable to many sociolinguistic questions, and has already proven its usefulness in a number of studies, which are cited below. An estimate of its applicability in any given case can be made by closely examining the Chi-square measure.

By coding social factors in this way one can examine variation by age, social class, sex, style, geographical background, setting of the speech event, or even individual by individual, with a high degree of precision and great cross-rule and cross-investigation comparability of results. These constraints are handled exactly like the purely linguistic ones. Thus to examine a rule which shows social stratification, one might simply add to the coding system a factor group for the social class of the speaker, e.g. (1, 2, 3, 4); to examine sex differences, the factor group (M, F) could be used. Then each token of the variable would be coded for these factors as well as for any others which were being examined.

This brings us to the step of actually transcribing and coding the data. Usually the source of the data will be tapes of people talking, although for historical problems other sources, such as texts (and even dictionaries) may be used. Extracting the data from the tapes is a painstaking job of listening to the tapes and writing down every occurrence or potential occurrence of the variable together with an appropriate amount of context. What constitutes an 'appropriate amount' will vary with the problem. For a phonological variable it may be one or a few words, while for a syntactic problem a whole sentence or several sentences might be necessary.

In a large-scale investigation, a number of transcribers may be required. In this case it is essential to conduct reliability tests in order to measure the consistency of the different transcribers and make sure that every transcriber is coding the same thing in the same way. One approach to this problem is to prepare several test tapes, have each person transcribe them separately, and then compare the results. This gives control over the content and difficulty of the reliability test, and enables one to identify easily both overall problems of transcription and individual problems of transcribers. Furthermore, such tapes can be kept and the tests re-administered in longitudinal studies to see if the transcribers are changing their judgments as time goes on. In this way we researchers can hope to obtain some measure of 'inter-subjective objectivity' about their judgments.

Once the data have been transcribed in this way, the next step is to prepare a chart such as (3) containing a cell for all the possible

environments for which the coding system provides. The data are
coded onto this chart by noting for each token of the variable, in the
appropriate cell, a symbol signifying whether or not the rule has
applied.

(3) Example of a Coding Chart (-t/d deletion)

GRAM. STATUS		M		A		P	
Prec. Seg.		R	S	R	S	R	S
Fol. Seg.	K						
	G						
	L						
	V						
	Q						

These data are then summarized for computer input on punch
cards. There is one data card for each filled cell on the chart, indicating for that cell the number of tokens where the rule did not apply,
the total number of tokens in the cell, and the factor codes which
describe the cell. The format for the data cards is described in
documentation available with the program. Other data cards specify
the factors and factor groups for each run. Empty cells are just ignored. At this point begins the most important task, namely interpreting the results which are returned, understanding and explaining
their significance, and perhaps re-evaluating the coding system or
the linguistic hypothesis used.

So far this discussion has focussed mainly on how to use the program. Now it is necessary to examine what kinds of problems it has
been and can be applied to.

Most of the initial applications were in the area of phonology.
Cedergren's paper (1973) in the first NWAVE volume, for example,
dealt with two problems in Spanish phonology, namely /s/-aspiration
and /č/-lenition. At the University of Pennsylvania the program has
been applied to several problems in English phonology, such as the
simplification of final consonant clusters, the de-velarization of final
/ɪŋ/, and the vocalization of /r/ in New York City which is described
by Labov (1966).

At the borderline between phonology and syntax are such problems
as the well-known case of que-deletion in Canadian French (treated
in numerous articles by D. Sankoff, G. Sankoff, Cedergren, Bickerton, and others)[5] and also the contraction and deletion of English
copula. Variable rules of these types show both phonological and
grammatical (and sometimes lexical) conditioning.

Purely in the field of syntax, the program has been applied by
Sag (MS) to English complementizer-THAT deletion, which is

conditioned by such factors as position of the THAT in the clause, the type of clause, and in the case of post-verbal-THAT, lexical conditioning by the specific verb, such as 'figure that . . .', 'think that . . .', etc. G. Sankoff's (1973) paper treated BAI-placement in Tok Pisin, a transformation which is conditioned by type of subject NP. That paper in general demonstrates how the variable rule concept is applicable at linguistic levels 'above and beyond' the phonological.

Many of these have been sociolinguistic variables. As was noted above, some types of sociolinguistic conditioning may require other methods of mathematical analysis, such as are currently used in sociology. The program has proved useful in examining differentiation by sex and social class in the case of Montreal que; by ethnic group, age, and social class in the case of New York City /r/; by social class and race in the case of English Copula-Deletion; and by age, social class, and geographic origin in the case of Panamanian /s/-aspiration. Another sociolinguistic problem to which Brian Head is currently applying the program is the case of personal pronouns in Brazilian Portuguese. The situation there is that while the traditional distinction between informal and formal pronouns for second person is maintained in the nominative and vocative positions, it is highly variable in genitive, dative, and accusative positions (B. Head, personal communication). Thus while a student may address a professor directly as Vossa Excelencia, he may also in the same conversation refer to the man's house as a tua casa without being the least disrespectful. This variation also shows complex conditioning according to the nature of the social relationships involved.

One important new application of the variable rule program is being developed by I. Condax at the University of Hawaii. She is using the program on a historical problem in Chinese phonology. Some words which are attested as containing a medial /u/ at an earlier stage of the language have lost it without a trace, others retain it in its original form, and a third group has lost it but shows some trace of its original presence. In applying the program, Condax is approaching this as a sort of diachronic variable rule. This problem is an especially excellent site for the study of variation because medial /u/ deletion still exists as a sociolinguistic variable rule in modern Cantonese. Thus we have the opportunity to study and compare synchronic and diachronic variation quantitatively using a single unified formalism. This will enable us to, as Condax (personal communication) puts it, 'attack the question of what best explains historical residue, be it lexical diffusion, competing rules, competing grammars, or inherent variability as a constant in language.'

There are still a few difficulties with this approach. The data base for a historical study is of necessity very different from one for a synchronic study of the modern state of affairs. Condax's main source of information on the earlier stages of the language will be such materials as the Dictionary on Computer, developed by Wang and his associates, while the modern language will be surveyed through standard sociolinguistic techniques. It is felt, however, that these are not insurmountable obstacles to this approach.

Another important use of this program has been in testing distinctive feature theory. Simplification of final consonant clusters in English, of which -t/d deletion is an example, is highly conditioned by whether the following segment is a consonant or a vowel. A consonant favors the rule and a vowel disfavors it. This has been demonstrated in a number of studies by Wolfram (1969), Labov et al. (1968), Fasold (1972), etc., and has been confirmed by analysis with the variable rule program. Chomsky and Halle's distinctive feature theory, however, postulates the two binary features $\pm$ consonantal, $\pm$ vocalic, thereby generating a four-way distinction of consonants, glides, liquids and vowels, as is illustrated in (4).

(4)

	−voc	+voc
+cons	K consonants	L liquids
−cons	G glides	V vowels

From our earlier observations we would expect that the features [+cons], [−voc] should favor the rule and [−cons], [+voc] should disfavor it. Therefore, the variable rule probabilities for glides and liquids, which each contain one favoring and one disfavoring feature, should fall between the figures for consonants and vowels, which represent the extreme cases. The stronger claim that might be made on the basis of this distinctive feature analysis, would be that the value for V should equal the product of the values for G and L. This claim is too strong to be very useful at present, given limitations on sample size, the possibilities of chance fluctuation, the possibility of other unexamined phonological factors having an effect, etc. Using this analysis we have coded data on over a dozen speakers. Although the overall picture is still clouded due to the relative rarity of data on glides and liquids as against that on consonants and vowels, the results we have obtained generally tend to confirm the prediction of distinctive feature theory. As is shown in (5) seven speakers have the values for both G and L falling between the values for K and V, four speakers have one of them falling between K and V, and only two have neither G nor L between K and V.

(5) Distribution of G and L Values Relative to the Interval K-V.

	Both inside the interval	One inside the interval	Neither inside the interval
Number of speakers	7	4	2

Furthermore, we find G or L outside the interval K-V primarily for those speakers from whom we obtained very few tokens with following glide or liquid. The individuals whose data is most reliable in terms of quantity fall in the first column in Figure (5). Some sample figures from these individuals are shown in (6).

(6) Examples of probability of application of -t/d deletion rule by following environments.

Speaker No.	K	L	G	V
1	1.0	.392	.381	.180
2	1.0	.872	.896	.786
3	1.0	.764	.764	.207

The results that would run most counter to distinctive feature theory would be figures for G which were about equal to those for V and figures for L approximating those for K. This would indicate that perhaps only a single binary feature, rather than two, was required to adequately describe the situation. As the numbers in (6) indicate, this does not seem to be occurring. In any case, this example should serve to illustrate how the program can be used to empirically approach certain theoretical questions.

Many other applications of the Cedergren-Sankoff program are waiting only to be discovered. Even so, this is only one program, designed for one type of problem. Others are now being developed to attack other types of problems. For example, the paper in this volume by Hindle and Sag mentions two new programs to aid in the construction of syntactic squishes. The computerization of data handling alone will enable linguists to greatly increase the scope of their studies and the size of their data sets and hence, their reliability. These are healthy and necessary steps toward a more empirical linguistic science.

NOTES

1. For further discussion, see Cedergren and D. Sankoff (to appear in Language).

68 / GREGORY R. GUY

2. Cedergren and D. Sankoff.
3. For this analysis I am indebted to B. Jean Longmire of
Georgetown University.
4. See Cedergren and D. Sankoff for further discussion of this
point.
5. Cedergren and D. Sankoff; G. Sankoff (in press); Bickerton
(1973); D. Sankoff, paper at LSA summer meeting 1973; Berdan,
paper at LSA summer meeting 1973, etc.

REFERENCES

Bailey, Charles-James W. and Roger W. Shuy, eds. 1973. New
ways of analyzing variation in English. Washington, D.C.,
Georgetown University Press.
Berdan, Robert. Probability and variable rules: A formal interpre-
tation. Paper at the LSA Summer Meeting, 1973.
Bickerton, Derek. 1971. Inherent variability and variable rules.
Foundations of Language 7.457-92.
_____. 1973. Quantitative versus dynamic paradigms: The case of
Montreal que. In: Bailey and Shuy (1973). 23-43.
Cedergren, Henrietta. 1973. On the nature of variable constraints.
In: Bailey and Shuy (1973). 13-24.
_____ and David Sankoff. 1974. Variable rules: Performance as a
statistical reflection of competence. Language 30:333-355.
Fasold, Ralph. 1972. Tense marking in Black English. Arlington,
Virginia, Center for Applied Linguistics.
Griffin, Peg, Gregory Guy, and Ivan Sag. 1973. Variable analysis
of variable data. University of Michigan Papers in Linguistics,
1:2 (November, 1973).
Labov, William. 1966. The social stratification of English in New
York City. Washington, D.C., Center for Applied Linguistics.
_____. 1969. Contraction, deletion, and inherent variability of the
English copula. Language 45:715-762.
_____, Paul Cohen, Clarence Robins, and John Lewis. 1968. A
study of the nonstandard English of Negro and Puerto Rican
speakers in New York City. U.S. Office of Education, Cooperative Research Report No. 3288.
Sankoff, David. 1973. Choosing between variable rules and implicational scales. Paper at the LSA Summer Meeting, 1973.
Sankoff, Gillian. 1973. Above and beyond phonology in variable
rules. In: Bailey and Shuy (1973). 44-61.
_____. (in press). A quantitative paradigm for the study of com-
municative competence. Paper prepared for the Conference on
the Ethnography of Speaking, Austin, Texas.

Wolfram, Walt. 1969. A sociolinguistic description of Detroit Negro
speech. Washington, D. C., Center for Applied Linguistics.
_____. 1973. On what basis variable rules. In: Bailey and Shuy
(1973). 1-12.

VARIABLE CONSTRAINTS
AND RULE RELATIONS

WALT WOLFRAM

Federal City College and Center for Applied Linguistics

The formulation of new theoretical paradigms must be seen in terms of several stages. Initially, there is the claim that the theoretical model can handle data not dealt with in earlier models or account for it in some systematic way not afforded by a previous model. At this point, there appears to be a giant step in the formulation of the paradigm. Once this giant step is taken, however, a number of small steps (not all forward) follow. These are the so-called 'mopping-up' operations. Quite rightly, Kuhn (1962:24) has observed that lots of what we call mopping-up operations are directed to force nature into a preformed and inflexible box that the paradigm supplies. But there are also, as a part of authentic mopping-up operations, the necessary considerations of sorts of phenomena which the giant step may have leaped over in its initial formulation. Mopping-up operations, then, become important in order to see the full implications of the paradigmatic leap. Without either maximizing the contribution of so-called 'variable-rule theory' or minimizing my own janitorial role, I would like to consider this paper as a type of mop-up operation. [1] One must be fully aware that in mopping-up, we may find that we discover more dirt under the rug than we thought existed in our clean paradigm. But at least if we know where the dirt is, we can always try cleaning it up with a different solution.

In this paper, we shall be looking at how variable constraints may affect rule relationships. In order to look at this matter, it is of course necessary to accept fundamental notions concerning structured variability (cf. Wolfram 1973a). We can then start out with the acceptance of the notion that there are independent linguistic constraints

70

on variability which must be included in the formal account of non-categorical rules. At the very least, I am claiming that as part of a speaker's competence in his language, he has knowledge of variable rules, the linguistic factors favoring rule operation, and the hierarchical order in which these factors are ranked. (The acceptance of stronger claims, as put forth by Cedergren and Sankoff (1974), does not appear to affect the following discussion in any significant way.)
I am further claiming that at least some of the hierarchical ordering of the constraints on variable rules are language particular in that they do not necessarily derive from some universal principle of constraint hierarchies (cf. Wolfram 1973a:8-10).

Since we shall also be discussing rule ordering to some extent, it is necessary to accept here the notion that the rules of, at least, phonology are ordered with respect to each other. It is further necessary to accept the notion of some extrinsic rule ordering (cf. Koutsoudas 1972, Campbell 1973, Bailey 1973) although most of the discussion pertaining to rule ordering may apply equally to a position which only allows ordering which derives from universal principles.

In the discussion that follows, we will look at two aspects of rule relationships and how they may or may not be affected by considerations of variable constraints. The general question I am interested in is the extent to which variable constraints may provide formal motivation (i. e. a 'discovery procedure', if you will) in the consideration of rule separation and collapsing, and rule ordering. Do considerations of variability serve as a principled basis in the consideration of rule relations, and if so, under what sorts of conditions ?
I am concerned here with elucidating and illustrating how variable rules reveals that, in some cases, a principle has been followed, either explicitly or implicitly, to arrive at the 'correct' solution.
In other cases, the failure to apply a principle has resulted in a faulty analysis. The intent of this paper then, is to elucidate general principles of rule relationships affected by variable constraints and to illustrate them.

Rule separation and collapsing

The first claim that I would like to make is that considerations of variable constraints may provide a principled basis for combining or separating linguistic processes. Now where there are other types of 'conventional' motivations which can operate to provide a principled basis for separating or collapsing processes, the variability of variable constraints is, at best, simply confirmation. But I would like to go one step further and maintain that in the absence of other types of conventional motivations, variable constraints may be independently powerful enough to provide a principled basis for considering processes

as distinct or identical. An examination of certain types of variable
constraints, in fact, turns out to be the deciding factor in the resolution of different analyses of the same phenomenon. Several cases can
be cited to demonstrate this capability of variable constraints.

The case of post-consonantal and post-vocalic t, d deletion.

To illustrate how variable constraints can provide formal motivation for treating linguistic processes as unitary or disparate, we
can first look at the case of word-final alveolar stop deletion which
takes place in at least Vernacular Black English and Puerto Rican
English in East Harlem, among other English lects. In these lects,
there is a process(es) in which final post-vocalic and post-consonantal
alveolar stops may be deleted. That is, we have items such as tes',
buzz', rabbi', and rapi' for test, buzzed, rabbit, and rapid respectively. [2] Although Labov, et al. (1968), and I have both described the
same type of phenomenon, we have arrived at conclusions which are
somewhat different. (For a complete discussion of our differences,
see Fasold 1972:58-60, 76-82.) In Labov's et al. analysis, both post-
vocalic and post-consonantal alveolar stop deletion are considered to
be part of the same rule. That is, there is only one rule which affects final t and d whether they are the final member of a consonant
cluster or following a vowel. Labov (1972:111) has formulated the
rule as follows:

$$[\text{-cont}] \rightarrow <\emptyset> \ / \ <\text{+cons}> \ <\emptyset> \underline{\quad} \#\# \ <\text{-syl}> \quad ^{3}$$

As formulated by Labov, there are three ordered constraints on the
operation of this rule: (1) deletable t, d preceded by a consonant,
(2) deletable t, d followed by a non-vowel, and (3) deletable t, d
preceded by a non-morpheme boundary. Unmistakenly, Labov's
rule is written to include post-vocalic and post-consonantal t, d.
A version of this rule, with a more extended hierarchy of constraints, is followed by Fasold (1972:98). Both of these treatments,
then, differ from my earlier account in which post-vocalic t, d deletion and post-consonantal t, d deletion were considered to be a
part of different processes. Although we then argued for the analysis
on other grounds in that description, a reopening of this issue in our
more recent study of Puerto Rican English in New York City has
demonstrated how the examination of the constraint hierarchy can be
utilized to resolve this matter. In the account that follows, we will
illustrate with data from Puerto Rican English, but a comparison of
these speakers with Vernacular Black English speakers who were a
part of the study indicates that the same arguments are operative in
the resolution of this question in Black English as well.

If post-consonantal and post-vocalic t̲, d̲ deletion were to be considered as a part of the same process, we would expect that independent tabulations of t̲, d̲ deletion would show that the constraint hierarchies are isomorphic. With the exception of the post-consonantal/
vocalic environments, which may be a variable constraint in itself
incorporated into the hierarchy, the constraint hierarchy should match
whether post-consonantal or post-vocalic t̲, d̲ is the input for the deletion process. If it does not, then the generalization of the rule is
inadequate and the environments for the rule must be considered at
least disjunctive if not part of a separate rule. If an independent
tabulation of these two potentially separate processes indicates isomorphic hierarchies, this may provide, in the absence of other types
of formal motivation to separate them, a principled basis for considering them as part of the same general process. If, on the other
hand, our independent tabulation turns up a genuinely different hierarchy of constraints, then the generalization of the rule must be considered as inaccurate. (By genuinely different, we here mean to
exclude differences which are artifacts of unreliable tabulation such
as different categorization of linguistic categories, inadequate numbers of tokens, etc.) With this in mind, let us compare what happens
when the constraints for post-vocalic and post-consonantal t̲, d̲ are
tabulated separately. This is done in the versions of the rule given
by Shiels (1972) and Wolfram (1973). Shiels has tabulated the totals
for post-consonantal t̲, d̲ deletion and Wolfram has tabulated the results for post-vocalic t̲, d̲. Shiels' rule for post-consonantal stop
deletion is as follows:

$$
\begin{bmatrix} -\text{voc} \\ +\text{cons} \\ -\text{cont} \\ \alpha\text{voice} \end{bmatrix} \longrightarrow (\emptyset) \Big/ \begin{bmatrix} +\text{cons} \\ \alpha\text{voice} \\ \Delta\,(+\text{cont}) \end{bmatrix} \Gamma\ (\text{-\#})\underline{\quad}\begin{matrix} A([+\text{cons}]) \\ B([-\text{seg}]) \end{matrix}
$$

(Shiels 1972: 237)

In Wolfram's analysis of variable constraints for post-vocalic t̲, d̲
deletion, using the same sample as Shiels, the rule is written as:

$$
\begin{bmatrix} -\text{cont} \\ +\text{ant} \\ +\text{cor} \\ -\text{nas} \end{bmatrix} \longrightarrow (\emptyset) \Big/ \begin{bmatrix} V \\ \Gamma\text{-stress} \end{bmatrix} \Delta\ \text{-\#} \begin{bmatrix} \underline{\quad} \\ B+\text{vd} \\ E-\text{PAST} \end{bmatrix} \#\#A\text{-}V
$$

(Wolfram 1973: 146)

The ordered constraints for post-consonantal t̲, d̲ deletion are then:
1. deletable consonant followed by consonant.
2. deletable consonant followed by pause.
3. deletable consonant preceded by non-morpheme boundary.
4. deletable consonant preceded by continuant consonant.
The constraints for post-vocalic t̲, d̲ deletion are ordered as follows:
1. deletable consonant followed by non-vowel.
2. deletable consonant is voiced.
3. deletable consonant in an unstressed syllable.
4. deletable consonant preceded by non-morpheme boundary.
5. deletable consonant part of derived adjective.

As we stated previously, we would expect the two hierarchies not to differ in any significant ways, if both aspects of this process were handled by one general rule. Obviously, there are some parallels, such as the first order effect of the following non-vowel. But the hierarchies also appear to differ in non-trivial ways. Perhaps the most important difference is the constraint of voicing which operates on the post-vocalic deletable consonant but not on post-consonantal consonants. Independent of considering post-vocalic t̲, d̲ deletion, studies of final consonant deletion (e.g. Labov et al 1968, Wolfram 1969, Fasold 1972, Shiels 1972) have not shown voicing of the deletable stop to be a significant constraint on variability.[4] But quite clearly, it is shown to be a high order constraint for post-vocalic t̲, d̲ deletion. It should also be noted that the constraint of grammatical inflection (i.e. following a morpheme boundary) is ordered lower in the hierarchy of constraints for post-vocalic t̲, d̲ deletion than it is for post-consonantal t̲, d̲ deletion. The effect of stress, which is ordered before a grammatical inflection, is not even mentioned by Shiels, and other studies (e.g. Fasold 1972) tend to find stress for post-consonantal t̲, d̲ deletion ordered below the constraint of grammatical inflection.

The solution, then, seems to be quite clear. The rules should be kept as distinct in some sense, since the more general version of the rule obscures crucial differences in the constraint hierarchies of post-consonantal t̲, d̲ deletion. Stated as a general process which includes both aspects of the t̲, d̲ deletion, the rule does not account in an adequate way for what actually takes place (i.e. it is observationally inadequate). It should, however, be noted here that the evidence taken from considering post-consonantal and post-vocalic t̲, d̲ deletion separately is based on an assumption that constraint effects will operate independent of each other. If we found that the effects worked synergistically or antagonistically, our evidence might be questioned, but at this point, there is little counter-evidence to the assumption of constraint independence (cf. Cedergren and Sankoff 1974).[5] Apart from the motivational principle which variable constraints can be shown to provide for separating or combining processes, there is an obvious tabulational principle which emerges from this simple case. If there is some question as to whether processes should be generalized or separated in a descriptive account of non-categorical rules, tabulations of variable frequency treating them separately should be undertaken. If the hierarchies differ based on this separate tabulation, then they should be considered disjunctive in some sense. If, however, the processes are not tabulated as potentially different, the disjunction may not be revealed. In my dispute with Labov and Fasold's version of the rule, the apparent failure to carry out this simple procedure seems to be the reason why they did not arrive at the correct solution.

One might point out that it is not necessarily procedurally expedient to consider the tabulations of the potential disjunctive set completely independently, since a simple tabulation of all the logical possibilities of the combination of constraints for the potential generalized process might reveal the disjunction. Although this is certainly true in some cases, this procedure may leave the analyst in a difficult position of having to distinguish between non-significant hypothesized constraints for a general process and a significant disjunction. In distinguishing this important difference, the more statistically sophisticated program of Cedergren and Sankoff (1973) is obviously heuristically superior to the traditional impressionistic basis for deciding this difference (cf. Cedergren 1973:17 for an illustration of detecting 'hidden linguistic constraints' which suggest this sort of rule disparity).

The case of ARE copula absence and post-vocalic $\underline{r}$ desulcalization

The second example of how variable constraints may provide motivation concerning rule relations comes from a recent examination of present tense copula absence in Southern white speech. It is generally recognized that in white Southern speech, as well as in Vernacular Black English, there is a process by which copula forms involving the contracted forms of ARE can be deleted (i.e. You're ugly → You ugly). Although there is general acceptance of this observation, there is some question as to the process(es) by which this deletion comes about. This has become particularly important in comparing copula deletion in Southern white speech with copula deletion in Vernacular Black English (cf. Wolfram forthcoming). The basic question seems to be whether copula absence is to be derived from a general 'auxiliary deletion' rule which operates on the $\underline{r}$ remaining after contraction or whether absence is derived through a process related to general Southern $\underline{r}$-lessness. Labov (1969) has presented an attractive alternative in which 're deletion is derived

through a process related to r̲ desulcalization (in his terminology,
'vocalization') and subsequent post-vocalic schwa loss. As Labov
has shown, these two rules are needed for reasons quite independent
of copula deletion (cf. Labov (1969:754) where items like po̲'̲ [po]
and do̲'̲ [do] are derived by first desulcalizing the r̲, giving [poə]
and [doə], and then removing the ə̲ by post-vocalic schwa deletion.
The summary of the operations which derive A̲R̲E̲ deletion are given
by Labov in the following paradigm. In this paradigm, the number
of Labov's original rules is specified in the parentheses following
each rule title.

(a) ## ăr ## weak word rule (2)
(b) ## ər ## vowel reduction (4)
(c) ## əə ## vocalization of r̲ (5)
(d) ## ə ## loss of post-vocalic ə̲ (6)
(e) ##   ## contraction (9)
(f) ##   ## auxiliary deletion

In the above paradigm of rules, the weak word rule (a) prepares
unstressed copula to undergo vowel reduction (b). At that point, the
desulcalization rule (c) operates on post-vocalic r̲ generally. The
final r̲ of A̲R̲E̲ is desulcalized by this general rule. Operating on the
output of desulcalization is a rule to delete the post-vocalic ə̲ which
results from desulcalization (d). As has been pointed out by the
above, this is a rule which is required in Southern white speech and
Vernacular Black English for reasons independent of copula absence.
The ə̲ remaining after the application of the post-vocalic schwa loss
rule is the original nucleus of A̲R̲E̲, and this is then removed by contraction (e). In effect, then contraction is equivalent to deletion for
A̲R̲E̲, and there is nothing left for the deletion rule (f) to operate on
with reference to A̲R̲E̲.

Although this analysis has been accepted by a number of scholars,
there are several problems that arise in choosing to account for deletion in this way. One of the most persuasive of these is based on
constraint effects. If copula deletion were derived from a process
of desulcalization and subsequent post-vocalic schwa loss, we would
expect that the constraints affecting r̲-lessness derived from copula
A̲R̲E̲ to match those which effect r̲-lessness from other sources,
with, of course, the exception of copula itself which may be a constraint. That is, if r̲ is affected by a following consonant, then we
would expect this constraint to obtain for both copula-derived and
non-copula derived r̲'s. With respect to r̲ desulcalization involving
non-copula r̲'s, we find that a following consonant heavily favors
desulcalization. The following rule, which may delete the remaining post-vocalic schwa shows no constraints to neutralize this effect.
If copula-derived r̲ were related to this process, we would expect

this process to also operate for these forms. But compare the figures given in Table 1, which compares r desulcalization for non-copula r's with deletion for copula ARE. These figures are taken from my recent study of copula deletion in white Southern speech (Wolfram 1974). For r derived from copula ARE, the figures are broken down according to the following syntactic environment, so that they can be compared independent of any skewing effect that the following syntactic environment may have on the figures. The tabulation only includes a following consonant across word boundary for the sake of comparability.

TABLE 1. Influence of following vowel and consonant (a) on ARE deletion and (b) on non-copula r desulcalization; Franklin County, Mississippi, whites.

(a) Deletion

Following phonological environment	Following syntactical environment									
	NP		PA/Loc		Vb-ing		gonna		Total	
	No. D/T	%D	No. D/T	%D	No. D/T	%D	No. D/T	%D	No. D/T	%D
___##V	2/5	20.0	47/88	53.4	8/12	66.7	NA		57/105	54.3
___##C	9/30	30.0	59/130	45.4	84/128	65.6	59/69	85.5	211/357	59.1

(b) Desulcalization

Following phonological environment	No. Des/T	% Des
___##V	30/100	30.0
___##C	54/100	54.0

Table 1 indicates that a following consonant does not favor deletion to any significant extent for ARE deletion. In fact, when the figures for gonna are excluded because of the possible skewing effect (since there are no possible examples of gonna, the most favorable syntactic environment for deletion, beginning with a vowel) there is actually more deletion when followed by a vowel. With or without gonna, however, the difference is not significant. The pattern for copula ARE clearly contrasts with the pattern found for non-copula r, where a following consonant significantly favors desulcalization. Based on this lack of isomorphy in a variable constraint, we conclude that the

two processes are disparate in some way. The evidence from constraint effects, then provides a principled basis for supporting the
disjunction of the processes.[6]

In many respects, the argument for separating post-vocalic and
post-consonantal t, d deletion and copula ARE and non-copula r
processes are quite similar. Our arguments in both cases are based
on differences in constraint effects and hierarchies. There is, however, a sense in which the argument for separating copula ARE deletion and other types of r-lessness is less direct in that it argues
from a 'carry-over' effect of variable rules in a feeding relationship.[7]
It will be recalled here that my argument for different constraint
effects for non-copula r-lessness and copula ARE deletion was based
on a comparison of the constraints for r desulcalization and copula
ARE absence. But desulcalization is only Step 1 on the process which
has been claimed to account for ARE copula absence, since it still
leaves the vestige of a schwa which must be deleted by post-vocalic
schwa deletion (e.g. [wɪə] 'we're, [yvə] 'you're', etc.). Since the
input of the second rule (i.e. post-vocalic schwa loss variable rule
feeds on the variable output of the first rule (i.e. desulcalization),
the argument is based on the observation that the second rule will
reveal the constraint effects of the first rule unless there is a constraint in the second rule which neutralizes this effect. If we have
more r' desulcalized when followed by a consonant in the first rule,
there will be more tokens in this environment which become the input
for the post-vocalic schwa deletion variable rule.

Suppose, for example, that we have 200 tokens available for desulcalization, 100 followed by a consonant and 100 followed by a
vowel. Of the 100 followed by a consonant, 80 are desulcalized; of
the 100 followed by a non-consonant, 40 are desulcalized. This rule
then feeds into the post-vocalic schwa loss rule. The schwa loss
rule can only operate on the 80 desulcalized r's followed by a consonant and the 40 desulcalized r's followed by a non-consonant. If
there is no neutralizing constraint found in this rule (and following
Labov's (1969) analysis, there is not), then we may expect that this
variable rule will operate on more items when followed by a consonant. The constraint effect of the previous rule will then be realized
in a variable rule which feeds off of it. This description is illustrated
by the following rules, which incorporate the choice of tokens into the
approximate rule:

$$1. \quad r \rightarrow (\text{ə}) \ / \ [+V] \underline{\quad} \#\# \ \begin{array}{l} 80/100 + C \\ 40/100 - C \end{array}$$

$$2. \quad \begin{array}{l} 40/80\underline{\quad} + C \\ 20/40\underline{\quad} - C \end{array} \ \text{ə} \rightarrow (\emptyset) \ / \ [+V] \underline{\quad} \#\#$$

The argument for separating non-copula r desulcalization and copula deletion then, must be considered by looking at the cumulative constraining effect of two rules in a feeding relationship. This observation extends the use of variable constraints as a principled basis for separating or generalizing rules slightly beyond that of the t, d deletion case.

Extended rules and variable constraints

The use of variable constraints as a basis for separating or combining rules is not, of course, unique to the cases we have illustrated in the previous description. What we have tried to demonstrate here, however, is that such evidence can, of itself, serve as a principled basis for separating or combining processes; it is not simply an ad hoc procedure that allows for a convenient fit between quantitative data and formal rules. As mentioned earlier, a search of the literature on variable rules reveals that arguments quite similar to the ones presented here have been put forth to justify a rule generalization or separation into different rules. One of the prominent cases that has come up in the literature concerns the use of variable constraints to motivate the distinction between 'extended processes' and separate rules. A process of the type X → Y → Z is considered to be extended and therefore to be distinguished from separate rules of the type X → Y and Y → Z.[8] Labov's discussion of contraction and deletion examines both alternatives (Labov's Case 4, where Z → Z → ∅; Case 1, where Z → Z and Z → ∅) and resolves the issue largely on the basis of variable constraints. There are two aspects of variable constraints which provide the basis for Labov's conclusion that deletion is an independent process operating on the output of contraction. One is the fact that some of the constraints in the preceding environments are different for the two processes. Thus, we find that a preceding vowel favors contraction and a preceding consonant favors deletion. This sort of motivation is similar to the type of principled basis for separating rules as discussed previously. The second motivation is based on the fact that the constraints for the following syntactic environment (NP, PA, Verb-ing, and gonna) although ordered identically for contraction and deletion, apply to both contraction and deletion. That is, the constraints apply twice, making the constraints for deletion more exaggerated than they are for contraction. If the constraints applied only once, deletion would presumably be a fixed proportion of contraction in each following syntactic environment. (Compare Figure 8b and 8c in Labov 1969:734 for a graphic representation of this difference in application.)

Without questioning the ultimate relationship of contraction and deletion (since there may be other types of very sound reasons for viewing them as separate), I would like to address myself to the matter of reapplication of variable constraints as a principled basis for distinguishing between extended processes and separate rules. In an extended rule with two variable inputs, it would not appear to be particularly unnatural to have the variable constraints apply twice. In the light of other types of identical features of such processes (e.g. conflated identical environment specifications), it is questionable whether this reapplication can provide the formal basis for separation. Is this reapplication attributed too much motivational power?

Although there are few cases of variable constraints applying to extended rules of this sort, there is one case from Labov et al., where a variable rule is applied to an extended rule of this type. This is found in the discussion of the rule which changes morpheme-initial underlying interdental fricatives first to affricates, and then to stops. Labov et al. have formalized this rule as follows:

$$
\begin{bmatrix}
+\text{cons} \\
-\text{voc} \\
+\text{diff} \\
-\text{grave} \\
-\text{strid}
\end{bmatrix}
\longrightarrow
([-\text{cont}] \; ([+\text{abr off}]))/ \# \underline{\hspace{2cm}} \atop \alpha \; \text{voiced}
$$

Labov et al. observed that there is one main constraint on the rule, namely voicing. This means that more voiced segments will become affricates and subsequently more will become stops than their voiceless counterparts. Assuming that the variable constraint only applies once to the two variable inputs, we will have a frequency distribution something like the following:

TABLE 2. Comparison of interdental fricatives → affricates → stops with one application of variable constraints.

With one application of the variable constraints to the two variable inputs, we should find that there are more voiced segments that become affricates than voiceless ones. Then taking a fixed proportion of both voiced and voiceless affricates to become stops, the end result will be both more voiced affricates and more voiced stops than the corresponding voiceless affricates and stops. But this is apparently not what actually happens since according to Labov et al. (1968: 96) there are ' a great many affricates for (th), (th-2) but that the prevailing form for the (dh) is the stop, (dh-3).' Since there are more voiceless affricates than voiced ones, I understand this to mean that the actual configuration is like Table 3 rather than Table 2.

TABLE 3. Comparison of interdental fricatives → affricates → stops with two applications of constraint effects.

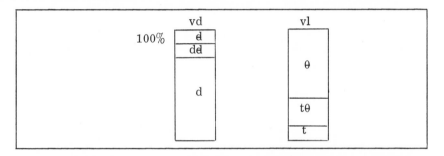

This figure, which represents the actual quantitative dimensions, can apparently be derived only from allowing the constraint effect of voicing to apply to both variable inputs of the rule. But it is noted that the rule is written as an extension type rule rather than two separate rules. How, then, do we deal with the lack of motivation provided by reapplying constraints in the one case (viz. the interdental fricatives) and the appeal to this same sort of reasoning in another case (viz. copula contraction and deletion) as a principled basis for rule separation? If we followed Labov's reasoning in the description of contraction and deletion, then the process for changing interdental fricatives to affricates and then stops must be considered as separate rules, with the effect of voicing as a constraint on each rule. But if we allow for the reapplication of constraints in an extended process, then there is no basis for arguing the separation of rules on these grounds in either case. The allowance of reapplication appears to be consonant with other identical aspects of extended processes (e.g. the conflated specified environment for application, identical constraint hierarchies) so that at this point we opt for latter solution. Further studies of variable constraints as they apply to processes considered extended on the basis of other types of 'conventional' evidence may reveal that we have underestimated the motivational powers of constraints, but it appears that counterevidence must be provided if the use of variable constraints in such cases is not to be considered ad hoc.

Variable constraints and rule ordering

In the previous discussion, we have only described the implications of variable constraints in terms of separating or combining processes. No mention has been made of the possible effect that constraints may have on rule ordering. The questions we want to ask with regard to rule ordering is what possible motivation variable constraints may provide for sequencing rules? Can variable constraints provide a type of principled basis for ordering which might be somewhat analogous to the type of motivation constraints may provide for rule separation?

We must first of all point out that from a purely quantitative standpoint, variable constraints do not appear to provide independent evidence for ordering related rules in only one particular sequence. The cumulative quantitative effect of two rules appears to be the same regardless of the order. For example, consider the case of the two rules needed to account for underlying //d// and //t// in Puerto Rican English. First of all, there is a rule which may delete word-final d̲ or t̲. This is the post-vocalic alveolar stop deletion rule which was discussed earlier in connection with the description of the effect of constraint hierarchies on rule separation and combining. Then there is another rule which changes underlying //d// to surface t̲. This means that both t̲ and ∅̸ may be the surface realizations of underlying //d//. For reasons elaborated elsewhere (Wolfram 1973), these rules must be kept separate. Both of the rules are variable, showing several different constraints favoring their operation. Without going into all the various constraints on their operation, let us look at some approximate overall variable relations. For every 100 tokens of underlying //d//, approximately 70 get realized ultimately as ∅̸ and 10 become t̲ in their surface realizations. Of the 100 tokens of underlying //t//, 20 get realized as ∅̸ and the remainder are unchanged. The graphic distribution of the ultimate surface realizations is shown in Table 4. Now let us suppose that the rule ordering for the two processes involved in the realization of these forms is first d̲, t̲ → ∅̸ and then d̲ → t̲. Placing the number of items affected into the rule input, we have the following:

1. $\left\{\begin{array}{l} 70/100 \text{ d} \\ 20/100 \text{ t} \end{array}\right\} \rightarrow (\emptyset)/ \ldots$

2. $10/30 \text{ d} \quad \rightarrow (t)/ \ldots$

TABLE 4. Graphic representation of surface forms for underlying //d// and //t// in Puerto Rican English.

	//d//	//t//
	t 10	Ø 20
	Ø 70	t 80
	d 20	

The output of the first rule allows only 30 d̠'s out of the original
tokens to become the output for the second process, and this process
operates to change 10 of the remaining d̠'s to t̠.

Now let us suppose that the order is the opposite; that is, the
proper ordering of these two variable rules is first d̠ → t̠ and then
d̠, t̠ → Ø. Placing our tokens again into the variable output of the
rule, we have:

1.   10/100 d → (t)/ . . .

2. $\begin{Bmatrix} 70/90 & d \\ 20/100 & t \end{Bmatrix}$ → (Ø)/ . . .

Although the variable input may be different for the two rules based
on how they are ordered, the end quantitative result of the application
of the two rules is the same. From a quantitative standpoint, it
really does not make any difference whether the totals of t̠ are added
to Ø and d̠, or Ø to d̠ and t̠. The individual rules may turn out to have
different application frequency values (e. g. 10 or 100 t̠'s for //d// is
very different from 10 out of 30), but the quantitative dimensions are
essentially neutral to the order, and can equally accommodate either
order.

Although the ultimate quantitative dimensions of two related variable rules will ultimately add up to the same cumulative output regardless of the way in which they are ordered, this is not to say that
the ordering of the rules cannot have a significant impact on the constraint effects. The significance of different ordering has been rather
dramatically illustrated by Labov (1969) in his discussion of the relations of contraction and deletion of the English copula. If we, for
the sake of discussion, assumed that contraction operated on the output of deletion, we would find that the constraints of the following
syntactic environment contraction would be illustrated by Figure 4a

FIGURE 4.

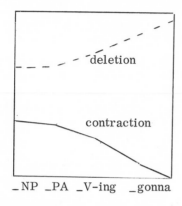 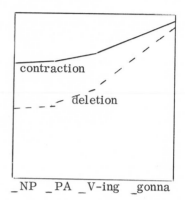

_NP _PA _V-ing _gonna   _NP _PA _V-ing _gonna

instead of the relationships of Figure 4b, which is the actual relationship of these rules. If the rules were sequenced so that deletion operated first and then contraction, the constraint hierarchies of contraction and deletion would be mirror images of each other. That is,
deletion would be favored by gonna, V-ing, PA, and NP in that order,
while for contraction the order would be NP, PA, V-ing, and gonna.
But if we ordered contraction before deletion as Labov has done (quite
correctly), the order would be gonna, V-ing, PA, and NP for both
contraction and deletion. The cumulative quantitative effect of the
two rules, however, might be the same regardless of the order (since
the variable inputs of the individual rules would simply have different
frequency values) but the constraint hierarchy would be quite different.
I am not here disputing Labov's ordering of contraction before deletion,
but simply pointing out that the motivation for this order cannot be
justified from the quantitative dimensions of the rules, since either
order can be accommodated by them.

At this point, it may be difficult to conceive of actual instances in
which constraint effects may allow only one ordering of rules, but it
seems reasonable to expect that further exploration of universal aspects of constraint effects and orders may provide a principled basis
for only one particular sequence of rules. In terms of the above case,
for example, we may find that there is universal prohibition of mirror
images in constraint hierarchies of related rules. If there were an
apparent option to order two rules with respect to each other and one
of the orderings allowed a mirror-image of hierarchical constraints,
then the constraint hierarchy might provide a basis for allowing only
one order.

One could conceive of other instances where a particular ordering
changed the effect of the constraints. Let us assume (and there
appears to be some basis for this assumption, cf. Wolfram 1973a)

that constraint effects are universal (i.e. particular environments will always have a particular effect on variability). Suppose we have a universal effect in which a following consonant always favored deletion of a consonant. In a particular language, we find that there is no type of 'conventional' motivation to order two rules with respect to each other. But ordering them in one sequence results in a non-consonant favoring deletion while ordering them in the other order reveals the consonant to favor deletion. If this were the case, the universal constraint effect would then provide evidence for ordering them only in one particular order. In this way, then, variable constraints could provide an independent basis for motivating a given order.

At this point, my comments on the effect that variable constraints may have on rule ordering consist of considerable speculation. A search of the literature turns up short in its attempt to substantiate claims about the formal evidence provided by variable constraints for particular orders. Several instances of supposed implication for rule ordering turn out to be inadequate.[9] This, of course, does not mean that there can be no such evidence, and we have speculated several possible types of evidence which might be relevant. But at this point, there are no cases in the variable rule literature which, to my knowledge, demonstrate convincingly that variable constraints can independently provide formal motivation for a particular rule ordering. Maybe this statement will provide an impetus for someone to provide counterevidence. That would be nice since I once read in an introductory textbook that that was what the advance of science was all about.[10]

NOTES

1. In defense of the dignity of mop-up operations, I simply quote here Kuhn's comment: 'Few people who are not actually practitioners realize how much mop-up work this sort of paradigm leaves to be done or quite how fascinating such work can prove in the execution' (1962:24). In several instances in the history of linguistic theory, I think the failure to undertake 'mop-up' operations has led to the ultimate dismissal of the theory, irrespective of its potential as a theoretical construct.

2. In my earlier study of alveolar stop deletion for Vernacular Black English (Wolfram 1969), I considered the relatively infrequent examples of post-vocalic t deletion, at least in some environments, to be due to performance factors rather than an integral part of the lect. This matter is still not quite resolved to my satisfaction, but in our discussion here we will consider t to be variably deleted as an authentic part of the lect.

3. The more recent version of this rule, while revised in conventions for its representation, does not essentially differ from the earlier version by Labov (1969:748). There is, however, correction of what apparently was a typographical error in the earlier version; namely, the omission of an 'in the absence of' sign to indicate that it is the non-grammatical boundary which favors the operation of the rule. In the earlier version, the preceding environment should read $\mathscr{f}$ (~ #) instead of $\mathscr{f}$ (#). However, in this version of the rule, the title t, d deletion is given but the designation of [-cont] as an input allows considerably more than t and d.

4. In an earlier version of the t, d deletion rule, Labov et al. (1968:136) did actually include voicing as a low order (fifth) constraint on deletion. Since the tabulational procedure is only given for the high order constraints, however, it is difficult to determine if this was due to the inclusion of post-vocalic t, d deletion along with post-consonantal deletion or an authentic low-order constraint for post-consonantal t, d deletion. At any rate, it is quite clear that if the two potentially different processes had been tabulated separately, the results would not have been isomorphic. Fasold's t, d deletion rule, which goes into considerably more detail for the constraints on post-consonantal stop deletion but does not actually include any tabulations of post-vocalic t, d deletion, does not include voicing even as a low-order constraint (cf. Fasold 1972:75-76).

5. Even if we were to find that some constraints did operate synergistically or antagonistically, it would not necessarily rule out such evidence, since there may be some principles of non-independent constraint operation (e.g. a constraint does not operate synergistically with all other constraints in the hierarchy of a given rule) by which we would differentiate them from apparent synergism.

6. In presenting my case for the separation of copula ARE deletion and non-copula r desulcalization and post-vocalic ə loss, there are two other arguments which would be sufficient to motivate this analysis independent of constraint effect (cf. Wolfram forthcoming). Interestingly, however, this was the first motivation which I became aware of, and the two other reasons became obvious after this argument was developed. In the absence of the other motivations, I would still maintain that the argument presented here is sufficient in itself.

7. Feeding relationship is here to be defined following Kiparsky (1968). That is, two rules, A and B, are functionally related so that the application of A creates representations to which B can apply. The application of A converts forms to which B cannot apply into forms to which B can then apply.

8. There are two basic differences between the extended process of the type X → Y → Z as opposed to the separate processes X → Y,

and Y → Z. In the former case, the environmental specification must be identical for the entire process while in the latter case, it may be different. Also, the former case only allows forms to change to Z which have been derived ultimately from X whereas in the latter case, a form not derived from X may become the input for Y → Z (e.g. A → Y, X → Y, Y → Z).

9. There are at least two cases in the literature on variable rules where constraints are suggested as providing formal motivation for rule ordering. One is my discussion on post-vocalic t, d deletion and its relation to the devoicing of d (Wolfram 1973:146). In this case, I simply failed to understand the frequency relations between related rules in terms of the second rule operating on the frequency output of the first rule. The second case is Labov's arguments for ordering deletion to operate on the output of the contraction rule. In this case, the argument is tautological. He first implies an ordered relationship in setting up his quantitative dimensions and then notes that 'deletion first and contraction second would not fit any of the quantitative results shown above for there is no reason for contraction of undeleted [əz] to be dependent upon the deletion of some other [əz]' (1969:733). In reality the quantitative dimensions are neutral to the ordering, and either order could theoretically result in the same cumulative effect. In both cases cited here, the order suggested is apparently the correct one, but for reasons unrelated to the variable constraints.

10. Extended discussions with Peg Griffin have been particularly helpful in the preparation of this paper. I am also grateful to Ralph W. Fasold and Tim Shopen for comments on an earlier draft. As always, I alone am responsible for remaining inadequacies.

REFERENCES

Bailey, Charles-James N. 1973. Variation resulting from different rule orderings in English phonology. In: New ways of analyzing variation in English. Edited by Charles-James N. Bailey and Roger W. Shuy. Washington, D.C., Georgetown University Press. 211-252.

Cedergren, Henrietta J. and David Sankoff. 1974. Variable rules: Performance as a statistical reflection of competence. Language 50:333-355.

Cedergren, Henrietta J. 1973. On the nature of variable constraints. In: Bailey and Shuy (1973). 13-22.

Campbell, Lyle. 1973. Extrinsic ordering lives. Indiana Linguistics Club Publications.

Fasold, Ralph W. 1972. Tense marking in Black English: A linguistic and social analysis. Arlington, Virginia, Center for Applied Linguistics.

Labov, William, Paul Cohen, Clarence Robins, and John Lewis. 1968. A study of the non-standard English of Negro and Puerto Rican speakers in New York City. USOE Final Report, Research Project Number 3288.

Labov, William. 1969. Contraction, deletion, and inherent variability of the English copula. Language 45:715-762.

_____. 1972. Language in the inner city: Studies in the Black English vernacular. Philadelphia, University of Pennsylvania Press.

Kiparsky, Paul. 1968. Linguistic universals and language change. In: Universals in linguistic theory. Edited by Emmon Bach and Robert T. Harms. New York, Holt, Rinehart and Winston. 171-204.

Koutsoudas, Andreas. 1972. The strict order fallacy. Language 48:88-96.

Kuhn, Thomas. 1962. The structure of scientific resolutions. Chicago, University of Chicago Press.

Sankoff, Gillian. MS. A quantitative paradigm for the study of communicative competence.

Shiels, Marie Eileen. 1972. Dialects in contact: A sociolinguistic analysis of four phonological variables of Puerto Rican English and Black English in Harlem. Unpublished Ph.D. dissertation, Georgetown University.

Wolfram, Walt. 1969. A sociolinguistic description of Detroit Negro speech. Washington, D.C., Center for Applied Linguistics.

_____. 1973. Sociolinguistic aspects of assimilation: Puerto Rican English in East Harlem. Arlington, Virginia, Center for Applied Linguistics.

_____. 1973a. On what basis variable rules? In: Bailey and Shuy (1973).

_____. 1974. The relationship of white Southern speech to vernacular Black English: Copula deletion and invariant be. Language 498-577.

SOME MORE ON ANYMORE

DONALD HINDLE AND IVAN SAG

University of Pennsylvania and MIT

1. Sentence (1) is a grammatical sentence in all dialects of English we know of.

(1) We don't eat fish anymore.

Ever since 1931, however, American linguists have recorded sentences like (2), which many speakers of English find bizarre and quite uninterpretable. [1]

(2) Anymore, we eat a lot of fish.

The usual hypothesis advanced about the grammars of those, primarily Mid-West, speakers who say sentences like (2) is that they have restructured anymore into a free-wheeling lexical item with the meaning of 'nowadays'.

This explanation has recently been shown to be unsatisfactory by Labov (1972), who observes that all English speakers balk at items like (3) and (4). [2]

(3) When would you rather live, 1920 or anymore?
(4) When was the best beer brewed? . . . Anymore.

Labov reasons as follows:

(5a) In Standard English a sentence of the form: 'X doesn't do Y anymore' presupposes that 'X used to do Y'.

(5b) In these 'positive' anymore dialects a complex semantic change has taken place creating a new lexical item any-more$_2$, which occurs only in positive sentences. Positive sentences of the form: 'X does Y anymore' assert that 'X didn't used to do Y.' Positive anymore speakers still have the old anymore in negative sentences, i.e. as a polarity alternant of still.[3]

Labov's analysis correctly accounts for the facts of (2). All speakers of this dialect agree that (2) means that we eat a lot of fish now, and implies that we didn't used to. Furthermore, the emergence in the Mid-West dialect of a second lexical item anymore$_2$, which 'fills a new grammatical category' and which is semantically different from anymore$_1$, is a reasonable hypothesis about why speakers of the standard dialect find sentences like (2) so uninterpretable.

Now the notions of presupposition and assertion are by no means clear. The literature abounds with counterexamples, unclear cases, and general confusion on these matters. The many criteria that have been proposed to test presuppositions vary somewhat from speaker to speaker and often fail to coincide. But it is generally agreed that presuppositions can be suspended whereas assertions cannot (cf. Horn 1972, Chapter 1). For example, (6), to revise a particularly hackneyed example,

(6) Mary has stopped beating her husband.

asserts itself (in the trivial sense that all sentences assert themselves). Therefore, if we try to suspend (6), we get a logical[4] contradiction as in (7).

(7) *Mary has stopped beating her husband, in fact, she may not have stopped beating him.

(6), however, presupposes something like (8):

(8) Mary has beaten her husband.

Therefore, suspending (8) will not produce a contradiction, as in (9).

(9) Mary has stopped beating her husband, in fact, she may never have beaten him.

Presuppositions, but not assertions, are suspendable.

Now let's return to the case of plain old negative anymore, as in (1). (1) has two relevant components of its meaning, which are roughly (10) and (11).

(10) We don't eat fish (now).
(11) We used to eat fish (at some time in the past).

Surely (1) asserts (10) and predictably, (12) is a contradiction for all speakers.

(12) *We don't eat fish anymore, in fact, we may eat fish now
      (=we may not eat fish now).

Conversely, speakers of all dialects accept sentence (13):

(13) We don't eat fish anymore, in fact, we may never have
      (eaten fish),

which shows that (11), which is suspendable, does in fact seem to be a presupposition, not an assertion, for all speakers.

Now let's consider the case of positive anymore. In this dialect, sentence (14) has the two meaning components (15) and (16).

(14) We eat a lot of fish anymore.
(15) We eat a lot of fish (now).
(16) We used to not eat a lot of fish (at some time in the past).

We have tried the suspension test with a number of positive anymore speakers, and found that the results were unanimous: (17) is a contradiction and (18) is not.

(17) *We eat a lot of fish anymore, in fact, we may not (now).
(18) We eat a lot of fish anymore, in fact, we may have always
      done so (=we may never have not done so).

In other words, (14) asserts (15) in this dialect and presupposes (16), in a manner quite parallel to negative anymore. If this dialect had really created a new anymore$_2$ that asserts the relevant component of the meaning instead of presupposing it, the (18) should be a contradiction, but it is not. Furthermore, as regards the other presupposition tests, e.g., the modal and conditional tests, the judgments are usually shaky for speakers of any dialect. But we have noticed that positive anymore speakers are pretty much equally shaky about contradictions that arise from negative anymore presupposition violations and those that arise from positive anymore.

What this suggests is that the semantics of positive anymore is quite like that of regular anymore, containing both an assertion about the present and what seems to be a presupposition about the past. This semantic sameness can be schematically illustrated as follows:

	ASSERTION	PRESUPPOSITION
X anymore:	eat fish now	~ASSERTION (time prior)
~X anymore:	~eat fish now	~ASSERTION (time prior)

Note additionally that if there were really two different anymore's, one for positive sentences and one for negatives, one would expect that for these speakers a question of the form: 'Do you eat fish anymore?' would be ambiguous, for anymore also occurs in questions pan-dialectally. We have tested this hypothesis, however, and found no such ambiguity.

If this is the case, then perhaps there are not two discrete anymore dialects, but rather a unique pan-dialectal anymore whose possible environments determine a continuum of anymore receptivity, with various speakers differing simply on how picky they are about the receptiveness of an environment. The totality of possible environments for anymore is surely not exhausted even by a list like (19).

(19a) We don't eat fish anymore.
(19b) Do you eat fish anymore?
(19c) We're reluctant to eat fish anymore.
(19d) I doubt that John eats fish anymore.
(19e) It's really hard for us to eat fish anymore.
(19f) I'm afraid to go out at night anymore.
(19g) It's impossible for John to eat fish anymore.
(19h) Fish is all we eat anymore.
(19i) It's amazing that John eats fish anymore.
(19j) We hate to eat fish anymore.
(19k) They've scared us out of eating fish anymore.
(19l) It's dangerous to eat fish anymore.
(19m) All we eat anymore is fish.
(19n) Any neighborhood is dangerous to walk in anymore.
(19o) We've stopped eating fish anymore.
(19p) All we eat is fish anymore.
(19q) We only eat fish anymore.
(19r) We eat a lot of fish anymore.
(19s) Anymore, we eat a lot of fish.
(19t) Anymore, I never go to the movies.
(19u) Anymore, we eat fish.
(19v) We eat fish anymore.

Having been persuaded of the plausibility at least of these all being
the same <u>anymore,</u> the next step is to find out if there is any hierarchy of these environments. For if there are two discrete <u>anymore</u>
dialects, why should there be such a hierarchy. Restructuring,
though by no means a well-understood phenomenon, seems to be in-
herently discrete. If a hierarchy does exist, then this would be strong
evidence for a semantically constant pan-dialectal, syntactically
gradient account of <u>anymore.</u> But with the mere mention of pan-
dialectal syntactic gradience, we find ourselves already in the domain
of squishes.

2. Recall that a squish is a two-dimensional matrix containing
intuitional judgments about various sentences, as in (20).

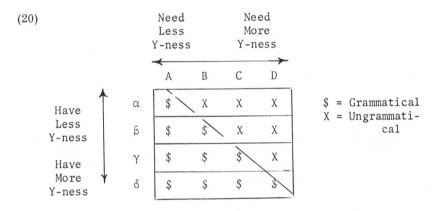

The Greek letters correspond to various linguistic forms, e. g. words
or strings of words, that possess some linguistic property to various
extents. Thus, the progression from α to δ might be a progression
from less nouny to more nouny, less stativey to more stativey, etc.
So associated with each item is a degree to which it possesses a
property Y (0.7 Nouny, 0.7 Stativey, etc.).
    The Roman letters across the top of the squish are various en-
vironments or syntactic frames in which the various items (the
Greek letters) might occur. These too are implicationally ordered,
the order being determined by how much of the property Y each frame
requires a form to have. Each cell in the squish is the sentence
formed by sticking a form (the Greek letter of that row) into a syntactic frame (the Roman letter of that column).
    The theory of squishes, by allowing variable possession of and
dependence upon a certain property, thus predicts that some forms
in some environments will be ungrammatical, i. e. when the Roman
letter needs more Y than the Greek letter has. Furthermore, since

both axes are linearly ordered, the theory of squishes makes the
additional prediction that the ungrammaticality will be systematic.
In the upper right-hand corner of (20), where there is more Y-
dependence and less Y-possession, the Greek into Roman substitution
will be ungrammatical. In the lower left-hand corner, where the
Romans require only the most meager amount of Y, and the Greeks
have an overabundance of it, the Greek form in the Roman frame will
be perfectly grammatical. Since the hierarchies on both axes are
strictly ordered, a roughly diagonal line can be drawn from upper
left to bottom right of (20), separating the grammatical sentences on
the left and below from the ungrammatical ones to the right and above.
Right around the line, of course, a sentence might have intermediate
grammaticality.

Now when Ross first started squishing, he hoped that they[5] would
be a means of encompassing the diverse intuitions of many, if not all,
speakers. Although the hierarchies on both axes were constant for
all speakers, the shape of the hazy judgment line might not always be
exactly diagonal. Thus speakers whose intuitional judgments looked
like any of those in (21) would be on the squish, so to speak, as would
be any speaker who categorically accepted or rejected all the sentences.

(21a)

	A	B	C	D
α	$	$	X	X
β	$	$	$	X
γ	$	$	$	$
δ	$	$	$	$

(21b)

	A	B	C	D
α	X	X	X	X
β	X	X	X	X
γ	X	X	X	X
δ	$	X	X	X

(21c)

	A	B	C	D
α	X	X	X	X
β	X	X	X	X
γ	$	X	X	X
δ	$	$	$	$

(21d)

	A	B	C	D
α	$	X	X	X
β	$	$	X	X
γ	$	$	X	X
δ	$	$	$	$

This hypothesis, that both hierarchies will be constant for all speakers, is the position taken in Ross (1972). Let's call it the STRONG SQUISH position.

Many weaker positions are possible, of course. One such hypothesis is that the frame hierarchy (the Romans) is constant for all speakers, but that the form hierarchy (the Greeks) may vary from speaker to speaker. This in fact is the position taken implicitly by Ross (1972 Linguistic Institute lectures) and explicitly in Sag (1973). Call this the WEAK SQUISH position. Under this theory intuitional judgments like those in (22) would all indicate co-squishhood.

(22a)

	A	B	C	D
α	X	X	X	X
β	$	X	X	X
γ	$	$	X	X
δ	$	$	$	X

(22b)

	A	B	C	D
α	X	X	X	X
β	$	X	X	X
γ	$	$	X	X
δ	$	X	X	X

≡

(22b')

	A	B	C	D
α	X	X	X	X
β	$	X	X	X
δ	$	X	X	X
γ	$	$	X	X

(22c)

	A	B	C	D
α	$	$	X	X
β	$	$	$	$
γ	X	X	X	X
δ	$	X	X	X

≡

(22c')

	A	B	C	D
γ	X	X	X	X
δ	$	X	X	X
α	$	$	X	X
β	$	$	$	$

But notice that if two speakers had different orderings of both hierarchies, they would be incompatible on either a STRONG or a WEAK
squish. (23a) and (23b), for example, are not squish-wise compatible
in either of the above theories.

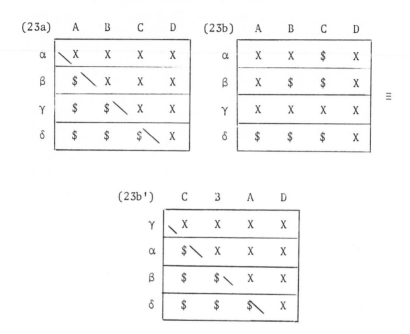

As Ross pursued his theory further, he found, much to his dismay,
that intuitional variation of the type shown in (23) frequently was in
fact the case. Neither Greek nor Roman hierarchies were pan-
dialectally constant. This forced Ross into an even weaker position,
namely, that co-squishhood holds among speakers as long as they
have some hierarchy of both the forms and the frames which is consistent with their judgments. Let's call this the ANY SQUISH position.

But alas, even this explanatorily impoverished position was too
strong, for subsequent work showed that hierarchies were sometimes
violated within a single speaker's judgment matrix. For instance,
Ross (1973) notes the following ill-behaved four-cell submatrix in his
Fake NP Squish:

(24)

	ACC -ing	CONJ RED
it (rain)	?*	??
there	✓	*

Raining <u>it</u>, judging from its behavior elsewhere in the squish, is a more bona fide NP than the <u>there</u> of THERE-<u>INSERTION</u>, i. e. <u>there</u> is a faker NP. Therefore, (25) should be better than or the same as (26).

(25) ?*It raining was a catastrophe. (ACC-<u>ing</u>)

(26) There being no more stagnant water must break your heart. (ACC-<u>ing</u>)

But Ross's judgments are as indicated. Furthermore, ACC-<u>ing</u> nominalizations are fussier elsewhere about the fakeness of an NP than CONJUNCTION REDUCTION is. Thus (26) should be worse than or the same as (27).

(27) *There were people in the garden, are dogs in the bushes, and will be muggers in the park. (CONJ.-RED.)

Again Ross's judgments are not in accord with his theory. Additionally he notes that this area of the squish is full of such inconsistencies for many speakers. He surmises that because of such wild hierarchical variation not only among speakers but also in the judgments of one single speaker, we can posit only common preferential tendencies as pan-dialectal phenomena. The squishes of the future are the confusion of the present, concludes Ross.

This is a sad conclusion, but it is quite evident that all three squish theories described above fail to meet even the level of observational adequacy, though certainly they are giant steps in the right direction.

Despite the apparent explanatory failure of squish theory to date, we proceeded with our investigation of <u>anymore</u> to see if there was some hierarchy of the possible environments that speakers might agree about. Our approach was to test a group of speakers first, and to see what hypothesis might be formed on the basis of the results of those tests.

3. The test sentences that we used are those that appear in (19a)-(19v). These twenty-two sentences were ordered arbitrarily and given in written form to thirty-six people, about half of whom were linguists. The informants were instructed to read the sentences and assign each one a rating on a five-point grammaticality scale. They were encouraged to make comparisons between the sentences rather

than judge each one in isolation. This gave us for each sentence a grammaticality rating relative to all the other sentences on the list.

Data of this sort demands very tedious analysis. Therefore, with the invaluable assistance of John Goldsmith, two computer programs were created to help do the analysis. The first of these is called SQUISH FINDER. This program takes pairs of speakers and looks for a common implicational hierarchy, comparing every possible sentence pair for every possible speaker pair. Finding even one preference reversal between a pair of speakers, that pair is labeled incompatible. If an overall ordering is possible to place two speakers on one continuum, the program will tell us so. [6]

SQUISH FINDER found no squish. In fact the program tells us that sixteen different orderings of the possible environments would be necessary to accommodate the thirty-six speakers. Clearly this data is not compatible with any theory of squishes mentioned above stronger than the ANY SQUISH theory. A squish hierarchy would have appeared only if most individuals were compatible with most others. We find exactly the reverse. Only a few speakers are compatible with many others. And these are precisely those at the extremes of the scale, that is, the speakers who either accept or reject almost all the sentences. A large number of speakers agree that sentences at one extreme are good, sentences at the other extreme are bad, but it appears that random variation exists in between. To find out this we needed a computer?

But the data is so random that we can't tell whether no series appears because none exists, or simply because our data is bad. At this point the results might lead one to conclude with the anti-intuitionist that in fact people don't know how they talk and that questionnaires like ours have no relation to how real people use anymore.

But before we discard the intuitions of thirty-six people, let's look once more at the data to see if some real information may be lurking there. A second computer program, PAIR COMPARE, was created, again the work of John Goldsmith, to check the implicational ordering of sentences. This program takes the intuitional ratings for any two sentences, call them A and B, and computes how many speakers rated A better than B, how many rated them as equal, and how many rated A as worse than B. This information can be summarized as in (28):

(28)   >   6
       A = 10 B
      <   5

which tells us that A was rated better than B by six speakers, equal by ten, and worse by five. We can define the 'preference factor' as the difference between the number of times A is rated better than B and the number of times it is rated worse. The preference factor for A over B in (28) is +1.

PAIR COMPARE shows a very weak ordering for the sentences in between the two extremes. For example, consider the results in (29).

(29) (19k) They've scared us out of eating fish anymore.
> 13
(19k) = 10 (19l)
< 10

(19l) It's dangerous to eat fish anymore.
> 12
(19l) = 13 (19m)
< 11

(19m) All we eat anymore is fish.
> 10
(19k) = 15 (19m)
< 11

(19k) is rated better than (19l) 13 times, equal to (19l) 10 times, and worse than (19l) 10 times. A slight preference for (19k) is revealed. The preference factor is +3 (19l) shows the following relation to (19m): better 12 times, equal 13 times, and worse 11 times. Here the preference factor for (19l) over (19m) is +1. Now consider the relation of (19k) to (19m). If the ordering (19k) > (19l) > (19m) is real, we would expect that (19k) would be preferred to (19m). In fact, we find that (19k) is better than (19m) 10 times, equal 15 times, and worse 11 times. (19m) is preferred to (19k) by a factor of +1! That is, though (19k) is generally better than (19l), and (19l) is generally better than (19m), (19k) is worse than (19m). The preference relation is intransitive and therefore not real. Between other sentences in the dubious zone the preferences are transitive, thus permitting a very weak tentative implicational ordering, but it is so weak that in no case is the preference factor for two adjacent sentences greater than +3. [7]

Thus PAIR COMPARE confirms the results of SQUISH FINDER showing no significant implicational ordering of the sentences in the dubious middle zone. But PAIR COMPARE further enables us to relate any two sentences from the list. We then decided to look at those sentences that had something in common. Three natural classes of environments (subsets of the anymore non-squish) were selected. These are sentences with controller subject or EQUI predicates as in (30), sentences (of unknown underlying structure) with all listed in (32), and thirdly sentences with sentential subject adjectives as in

(34). Any theory of syntax would claim that members of these groups had something in common.

The relative judgments for the EQUI predicate sentences appear in (31).

(30) (19c) We're reluctant to eat fish anymore.
    (19f) I'm afraid to go out at night anymore.
    (19j) We hate to eat fish anymore.
    (19k) They've scared us out of eating fish anymore.
    (19o) We've stopped eating fish anymore.

(31a) First order

$$
\begin{array}{ccccc}
& > 9 & > 12 & > 11 & > 20 \\
(19c) = 23 & (19f) = 20 & (19j) = 16 & (19k) = 15 & (19o) \\
& < 4 & < 3 & < 8 & < 1 \\
\text{Pref. Fac:} & \overline{5} & \overline{9} & \overline{3} & \overline{19}
\end{array}
$$

(31b) Second order

$$
\begin{array}{cccc}
& > 16 & > 20 & > 14 \\
(19c) = 16 & (19j) = 13 & (19o), \ \& \ (19f) = 19 & (19k) \\
& < 3 & < 2 & < 3 \\
\text{Pref. Fac:} & \overline{13} & \overline{18} & \overline{11}
\end{array}
$$

(31c) Third order

$$
\begin{array}{ccc}
& > 16 & > 24 \\
(19c) = 20 & (19k), \ \& \ (19f) = 12 & (19o) \\
& < 0 & < 0 \\
\text{Pref. Fac:} & \overline{16} & \overline{24}
\end{array}
$$

(31d) Fourth order

$$
\begin{array}{c}
> 27 \\
(19c) = 9 \ (19o) \\
< 0 \\
\text{Pref. Fac:} \ \overline{27}
\end{array}
$$

The first order preference factor between any two adjacent sentences in this subset is usually greater than and certainly at least equal to +3, which, you will recall, is the greatest preference factor for adjacent sentences in the tentative overall series. Furthermore the preference factor for any two non-adjacent sentences in this subset not only shows a transitive relationship, but also is greater than the preference factor of any adjacent sentences. As we make higher order comparisons the preference factors increase, and the number of speakers citing judgments contrary to the implicational preference tends toward zero. Thus, each of the second order preferences shown in (31b) show no more than three individuals disagreeing with the general preference. And the third and fourth order preferences in (31c) and (31d) show no deviations at all. In other words, the preference relations are indeed transitive. We can, therefore, conclude that the order of EQUI predicates shown in (30) is a real implicational order, with the sentences at the top better than those at the bottom.

Similar results are found for the three sentences containing <u>all</u> in (32).

(32)   (19h) Fish is all we eat anymore.
       (19m) All we eat anymore is fish.
       (19p) All we eat is fish anymore.

(33a) First order
$$> 13 \qquad > 22$$
$$(19h) = 20 \; (19m) = 12 \; (19p)$$
$$< \; 3 \qquad < \; 2$$

(33b) Second order
$$> 26$$
$$(19h) = 10 \; (19p)$$
$$< \; 0$$

Looking at (33), we see that 13 people found (19h) better than (19m), while only three found it worse. And 22 people find (19m) better than (19p); 26 individuals prefer (19h) to (19p) while none have the opposite preference. The implicational ordering again is undeniable.

The third subset in (34) with sentential subject adjectives shows similar preference relations (as shown in (35)), though somewhat less markedly.

(34)   (19e) It's really hard for us to eat fish anymore.
      (19g) It's impossible for John to eat fish anymore.
      (19i) It's amazing that John eats fish anymore.
      (19l) It's dangerous to eat fish anymore.
      (19n) Any neighborhood is dangerous to walk in anymore.

(35a) First order
$$> 10 \qquad > 10 \qquad > 14 \qquad > 18$$
$$(19e) = 18 \; (19g) = 20 \; (19i) = 16 \; (19l) = 12 \; (19n)$$
$$< \; 7 \qquad < \; 5 \qquad < \; 6 \qquad < \; 3$$

(35b) Second order
         > 13   > 19   > 16
       (19e) = 19 (19i) = 8 (19n), & (19g) = 14 (19l)
         < 4   < 6   < 6

(35c) Third order
         > 18   > 23
       (19e) = 16 (19l), & (19g) = 6 (19n)
         < 2   < 4

(35d) Fourth order
         > 22
       (19e) = 10 (19n)
         < 1

Here again, the deviations are inversely proportional to the order of comparison. There are indeed three consistent implicational sub-hierarchies, which don't seem to bear any systematic relationship to one another. Why should this be?

4. In the case of the all sentences in (32) some hypotheses come to mind. Notice that in (19h) and (19m) all and anymore are clausemates, whereas in (19p) they don't seem to be. This admittedly hard-to-defend fact (conjecture?) may be at the root of the worseness of (19p). Alternatively one might ponder whether (19p) has a lower acceptability for other reasons independent of the parameters, i.e. Y-haftigkeit, Y-süchtigkeit, which define the squish (-to be?).[8] That is, it seems to be a property of other adverbials that they resist the adverbial position of (19p). For example, many people find the sentences in (36) to be less acceptable paraphrases of their counterparts in (37).

(36a) All we eat is fish on Friday.
(36b) All we read was the Kāma Sūtra carefully.
(37a) All we eat on Friday is fish.
(37b) All we read carefully was the Kāma Sūtra.

If this is so, then an adequate theory of gradience will have to exceed in power the rather simplistic two-dimensional matrix model of squishes. Various surface frames may also have inherent gradient acceptability which must figure into the computation of the degree of acceptability of a particular sentence.

It's interesting to note that two-dimensionalism versus multi-dimensionalism of a quite analogous sort is a controversy that still rages among variationists and creolists (cf. Cedergren and Sankoff 1974, Bickerton 1971 and 1973, G. Sankoff 1973, and D. Sankoff 1973 just for a start). One could easily imagine a multi-dimensional theory of gradience that employed acceptability coefficients quite like the probability coefficients of Labov's variable rules. Thus, along with its haftigkeit coefficient and its süchtigkeit coefficient, a given cell of a squishoid matrix might also have a coefficient representing the contribution of some intersecting parameter, e.g. separation of an adverb from its clause. The total acceptability of a given cell might then be the product of all the acceptability coefficients (if they all ranged from, say, 0 to 1 as with probability coefficients).

Space prohibits further elaboration here. Suffice it to say that there are many different ways one might go about setting up a multi-dimensional theory of syntactic gradience.

As for the other sub-hierarchies, here there is little one can say except that a lot of further testing is necessary. For instance, in order to ascertain the actual incremental effect of the various properties of, say, the sentences in (30), such as type of complementation, EQUI triggered by matrix subject vs. matrix object, etc., one would have to know what the facts were in the case of other minimally different sentences like those in (38).

(38a) I'm afraid of eating fish anymore.
(38b) We're scared to eat fish anymore.
(38c) We hate eating fish anymore.
(38d) We've stopped them from eating fish anymore.

Minimal differences of this sort should produce changes in acceptability of a consistent kind. If they don't, then we are not dealing with independent events (in the sense of probability theory), and we might as well stop right now trying to construct any implicational theory of syntactic gradience.

But if acceptability is a composite function of various incremental factors, then the non-relationship of the various sub-hierarchies should come as no surprise. Why should a sentence like 'All we eat is fish anymore' be judged consistently better than or worse than one like 'We've stopped eating fish anymore'? It's sort of like comparing apples and oranges.

Recall, however, that syntactically unrelated constructions like these two are just the sort that have appeared across the top of most squishes. The hierarchical inconsistencies that have been noted in the study of squishes may be exactly parallel to the case of <u>anymore</u>. Searching for all-encompassing hierarchies, which was the downfall of the STRONG and the WEAK SQUISH positions, may be a misguided endeavor. The observed hierarchical irregularities may just be an epiphenomenon, a happenstance randomness which, when peeled away, reveals underlying regularity: the strict implicational series which obtain within syntactic natural classes.

So instead of looking for the neatly structured squish continua which result from two strictly ordered implicational hierarchies, perhaps the variationist should be looking for QUASI-CONTINUA as in (39) (leaving aside the question of multi-dimensionalism for the time being).

(39) Possible structure of a di-anchored quasi-continuum

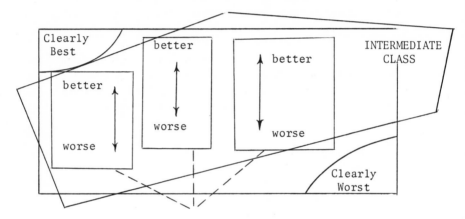

Syntactic 'Natural Classes'

If the facts of anymore are at all typical, then QUASI-CONTINUA like (39) should start showing up in future syntactic investigations. The clear cases, which are pan-dialectally preferred or disliked, and the intermediate set of natural sub-classes, which are internally hierarchical, are thus loci of gradient variation.

The 'clearly best' and 'clearly worst' subsets of the scale act as anchors, fixed points of reference. Thus this new theory (speculation?) of QUASI-CONTINUA still makes strong implicational claims like (40).

(40) No speaker will find a sentence in the 'clearly worst' anchor grammatical to degree n unless he also finds all intermediate cases grammatical to degree n.

Our anymore data in fact supports such a claim. What further relations might hold among the intermediate sub-classes will have to await further research.

Additionally, note that we've been dealing with what may someday become one row of a grandiose polarity semi-squish. Hopefully, the environmental sub-hierarchies for anymore will turn out to be the same as those for at all, budge, lift a finger, etc. In other words, we would hypothesize and pray that the at all EQUI predicate sub-hierarchy would come out like (41).

(41) We're reluctant to eat fish at all.   ↑ better
   We're afraid to eat fish at all.
   We hate to eat fish at all.
   They've scared us out of eating fish at all.
   We've stopped eating fish at all.   ↓ worse

If this turns out not to be the case, who knows where the theory will have to go? Maybe different parts of the squish will be controlled by different hierarchies. At the moment none of this is clear.

5. What is clear, however, is that even after the analysis into QUASI-CONTINUA, there remain a lot of individual deviations from the predicted implicational orders. Are these simply random errors, or is there some systematic basis for them?

Well, when we step back and look at the whole picture, we find that there is a large section of the continuum with no variation at all: the 'clearly worst' anchor. Twenty-six speakers are agreed in rejecting the same five worst sentences. This contrasts with the 'clearly best' anchor, where there is no such agreement. Even the two axiomatically grammatical sentences (19a) and (19b):

(19a) We don't eat fish anymore.
(19b) Do you eat fish anymore?

are given less than perfect ratings by eight speakers. In general, it appears that speakers incorrectly reject perfectly grammatical sentences, while they do not incorrectly accept ungrammatical sentences. That is, there is a bias to give sentences a lower rating than they deserve.

There is a good deal of anecdotal evidence to confirm this bias. For example, on several occasions we have heard one of our informants (a native of Colorado, heart of positive anymore country) saying sentences with preposed anymore similar to (19s), (19t), and (19u). However, on the grammaticality test he gave these three sentences ratings ranging from questionable to totally unacceptable. According to his intuitions, sentences with preposed anymore like the ones he actually says, are at best questionable.

We heard another woman say:

(42) I'm convinced anymore that that's the way it just is.

When later asked whether that sentence sounded like something she could say, she replied: 'I can't believe that I would say anything like that'. Clearly these two speakers' actual behavior is less conservative than their intuitional judgments. Furthermore, we know of no cases where a speaker rated an <u>anymore</u> sentence (or any other sentence, for that matter) as grammatical, and then was unable to interpret that sentence. [9]

From this a general methodological caveat may be formulated: BELIEVE AN 'OK' MORE THAN A '*'.

The general conservative tendency of intuitional judgments has the effect of pushing informants higher on the continuum. People simply talk systematically more liberally than they think they do. However, this does not mean that a speaker's intuitions reflect a non-existent dialect. Given the notion of a QUASI-CONTINUUM, we can now predict that the intuitional judgments of one speaker will reflect the actual behavior of a more conservative speaker, whose own intuitions will in turn reflect the behavior of an even more conservative speaker. The appropriate conclusion would seem to be that, while it is true that intuitional judgments do not precisely reflect the grammar of an individual, they do reflect that grammar indirectly.

6. So where does this leave us vis à vis <u>anymore</u>? Well, we've seen that there is no particular semantic evidence for setting up two different lexical items for sentences like those in (19). Secondly, given the notion of a QUASI-CONTINUUM, we've seen some hierarchical regularity in speakers' judgments about the intermediate cases. We might now look at the variation in terms of selectional restrictions.

The lexical entry for <u>anymore</u> for the most restricted <u>anymore</u> speakers would contain a selectional feature something like (43):

(43) [+[+negative] . . . ___]

The systematic variable is negativity, which seems to inhere gradiently in different ways in different types of lexical items (ergo the sub-hierarchies). The QUASI-CONTINUUM we have observed is simply the gradual erosion in various environments of this selectional feature.

One might still object that since some speakers are unable even to interpret extreme <u>anymore</u> sentences like (2):

(2) Anymore, we eat a lot of fish. ,

it is implausible to assume that <u>anymore</u> is a single lexico-semantic entity. Understanding a sentence that is deviant only in that it commits a single violation of a selectional restriction is no formidable task. Is this not what metaphor is all about?

Metaphor certainly makes use of such violations, but notice that these may be only of certain restricted types, typically involving movement within or across semantic fields. We don't know quite how to characterize this intuitive distinction, but somehow the feature of negativity is not involved in semantic fields in the same way as features like animateness, masculinity, abstractness, etc. Perhaps there is some gradient hierarchy of semantic feature types which corresponds to the degree of unintelligibility resulting from their violation.

Speculations aside, it is clear that violating the selectional feature in (43) can be sufficient grounds for uninterpretability. A clear example is the case of <u>at all</u>. For most speakers, <u>at all</u> is restricted to occur with negatives, as in (44).

(44) I don't like him at all.

But for some speakers, no such selectional restriction exists. <u>At all</u> can occur positively as in (45).

(45) I ignored it at all.

Some speakers confronted with (45) protest that a <u>didn't</u> was left out. Others interpret the <u>at all</u> as meaning 'somewhat'. In fact, it means something like 'a lot'. It is easy to see that <u>at all</u> does not have two distinct meanings in positive and negative environments. Rather, it has a single constant meaning in both environments, namely, intensification. The only change that has taken place is one of selectional restriction. This is the same kind of change we have found with <u>anymore</u>.[10]

Moreover, this type of change has happened before in English. Two examples are the adverbials <u>anyway</u> and <u>anyhow</u>. In American dialects, these exhibit no sensitivity to polarity. Both (46) and (47) are perfectly grammatical.

(46) I'm not going to do it anyhow.
(47) I'm going to do it anyhow.

However, in many British dialects <u>anyhow</u> is a polarity-sensitive item occurring only with negatives.[11] For example, (48)

(48) He couldn't do it anyhow.

is equivalent to There was no way he could do it.
The British dialects preserve an earlier stage in the English language, when anyhow was subject to the same polarity restrictions as any. Somewhere along the line both anyhow and anyway were lexicalized, and then lost their polarity-sensitivity.

Perhaps there is a general principle at work here: whereas there may be deeply rooted semantic reasons for the distribution of any (its distribution has remained essentially unaltered ever since Beowulf), once phrases with any are reanalyzed into single lexical items, the distributional restrictions that are dragged along are somewhat arbitrary semantically, and thus subject to erosion. How general such a principle may be we are not certain.

Be that as it may, anymore is but one example of a syntactic change common to English and other languages: the loss of polarity sensitivity. [12] This change has occurred perhaps to completion with anyway, in American dialects for anyhow, in some dialects for anymore, and in a few dialects for at all. We have as yet no direct evidence that anymore is presently undergoing change; it is not yet known what forces may be at work to stabilize its distribution. But given the history of the other any-words, we have here a rare opportunity for predictive historical linguistics: our grandchildren or great-grandchildren, whether they grow up in the Mid-West or not, will probably be unconstrained anymore speakers, as the 'clearly worst' anchor of the anymore QUASI-CONTINUUM fades into oblivion.

NOTES

We are greatly indebted to Mark Baltin, William Labov, Mark Liberman, and Laurel Taylor for valuable discussion and suggestions. Additionally we are in the debt of Peg Griffin for her insightful criticisms of our original manuscript. We hereby exculpate all the above from any errors that might remain.

1. See the references to various articles in American Speech cited by Klima (1964:283, fn. 13).

2. The argument is not clear however, for the syntactic discrepancies between nowadays and positive anymore do not necessarily invalidate the insightfulness of the original parallel. For their semantic parallelness, see Horn (1972, Chapter 1).

3. Notice that by this formulation the negativity test for presuppositions is rendered useless here.

4. The exact nature of this contradiction is not clear. It somehow involves the particular difficulties in changing one's mind in mid-sentence, and this may be extra-logical.

5. There seems to be a water shortage in our anaphoric ocean.

6. The output requires a considerable amount of interpretation, however, for squish-wise compatibility is not a transitive relation.

7. We are painfully aware that more sophisticated analytic techniques are necessary, and that our naivete in the manipulation of data may have obscured significant results. But, read on . . . .

8. Haftigkeit and süchtigkeit are Ross's terms for possession of and dependence on (respectively) a given syntactic property, e. g. nouniness.

9. Although conclusions of this type are harder to verify.

10. A quite analogous phenomenon seems to be going on in Japanese with the lexical item: <u>zenzen</u> 'at all', as was pointed out to us by Kazuko Inoue. In the standard dialect, sentences like (ia) and (ib) are acceptable, whereas (iia) and (iib), their exact counterparts, without the negative, are not.

(ia) John wa nihongo ga zenzen deki - na - i.
      John Topic Japanese Subject at all do can not Present
      'John cannot do well in Japanese at all'
(ib) ano kuruma wa zenzen hayaku-na-i.
      that car Topic at all fast not Present
      'That car is not fast at all'

(iia) John wa nihongo ga zenzen deki-ru.
       John Topic Japanese Subject at all can do
       'John can do very well in Japanese'
(iib) ano kuruma wa zenzen haya-i.
       That car Topic at all fast Present
       'That car is very fast'

Among younger Japanese speakers, however, the sentences in (ii) are starting to turn up. This is a point by point exact parallel of the case of positive <u>at all</u>.

11. As was first pointed out to us by Pat Wolfe.

12. For more on the universal nature of such changes, see Jespersen (1917).

REFERENCES

Bailey, C. -J. N., and R. Shuy, eds. 1973. New ways of analyzing variation in English. Washington, D. C., Georgetown University Press.
Bickerton, Derek. 1971. Inherent variability and variable rules. Foundations of Language 7. 457-92.

Bickerton, Derek. 1973. Quantitative versus dynamic paradigms:
The case of Montreal que. In: Bailey and Shuy (1973). 23-43.
Cedergren, Henrietta and David Sankoff. 1974. Variable rules:
Performance as a statistical reflection of competence.
Language 50:333-355.
Horn, Laurence. 1972. On the semantic properties of logical
operators in English. Unpublished Doctoral Thesis, University
of California, Los Angeles.
Jespersen, Otto. 1917. Negation in English and other languages.
Copenhagen.
Klima, Edward S. 1964. Negation in English. In: The structure of
language. Edited by J. Fodor and J. Katz. Englewood Cliffs,
New Jersey, Prentice-Hall. 246-323.
Labov, William. 1972. Where do grammars stop? In: Shuy (1972).
43-88.
Ross, John R. 1972. The category squish: Endstation Hauptwort.
In: Papers from the Eighth Regional Meeting of the Chicago
Linguistic Society. Edited by P. M. Peranteau, J. N. Levi, and
G. C. Phares. Chicago, Chicago Linguistic Society. 316-328.
Sag, Ivan A. 1973. On the state of progress on progressives and
statives. In: Bailey and Shuy (1973). 83-95.
Sankoff, David. 1973. Choosing between implicational scales and
variable rules. Paper presented at 1973 Summer Meeting of the
L. S. A.
Sankoff, Gillian. 1973. Above and beyond variable rules in phonology.
In: Bailey and Shuy (1973). 44-61.
Shuy, Roger, ed. 1972. Georgetown University Round Table on
Languages and Linguistics 1972. Washington, D. C., Georgetown
University Press.

SOME UNIVERSALS FOR QUANTIFIER SCOPE*

GEORGETTE IOUP

Graduate Center, City University of New York

> When two operators of the same sort occur, their order can
> be reversed. However, when two different operators occur,
> a reversal of their order will change the meaning of the ex-
> pression.
>
> (Reichenbach, Symbolic Logic, p. 101)

This quotation from Reichenbach is typical of the approach taken by
most logicians and linguists in their treatment of the relative scope of
quantifiers. Scope refers to the range of effect that a logical element,
such as a quantifier, has on the remaining members of an expression.
We speak of relative scope in reference to the interaction of two logical elements in a string where the domain of influence of one is affected by that of the other.

Where quantifiers are concerned, most linguists follow the views
of logicians and explain scope variation within a simple sentence on
the basis of the relative order of the quantifiers: the one which is
'leftmost' in the surface structure is interpreted with highest scope.
This paper puts forth the thesis that in natural language, order has
little to do with the determination of quantifier scope. First, the current linguistic treatments of quantifier scope will be examined and
their inadequacies presented. Many examples will be given from English and other languages where the scope assignment is opposite that
predicted by a left-right order hypothesis. Three factors will be
shown to interact to determine which quantifier has highest scope
within a clause. These are, in order of importance, the inherent
characteristics of the individual quantifiers, their grammatical function within the clause, and their location in a salient serial position

in the sentence. Evidence to support these claims is based on data
collected from a large number of languages. A hierarchy of grammatical functions is established resembling in many ways the principle of 'rank' recently proposed by Postal, [1] and Keenan's hierarchy
of accessible NP positions for relativization (Keenan 1972, 1974).
The concluding section of the paper will make some attempt to explain why quantifiers, unlike the other operators, are not influenced
by relative ordering arrangements in the surface structure of the
sentence.

One difficulty encountered in obtaining reliable responses in all
languages was the lack of clear intuitions on the precise interpretation
of sentences involving scope variation. In addition there seemed to be
a fair amount of dialect variation in this area. A method was developed
using a ranking scale to ascertain a relative degree of ambiguity.
Though there was individual variation, it was a matter of making all
judgments one degree higher or lower on the scale. The results then
are expressed in terms of relative position on the scale of ambiguity.

We must note here that linguists speak of two configurations at the
surface level for which quantifier scope relations can be defined: (1)
the two quantifiers in question may occur in different surface sentences,
one embedded within the other (two quantifiers which occur in different
conjuncts do not enter into scope relationships with each other), or (2)
the two quantifiers under consideration may be clause mates in the
same surface sentence. It is only the second class of quantifier interactions that we examine in this paper.

1. The current linguistic treatments

George Lakoff's definitive position on quantifier interpretation is
found in 'On Generative Semantics' (Lakoff 1971). In this article, he
iterates several times his belief that order alone accounts for scope
differences within a clause. In fact he expresses this belief in the
form of a derivational constraint which he suggests operates universally for all languages. There are two parts to the constraint, the
second of which pertains to quantifiers within a single S. Lakoff
(1971: 243) explains the constraint as follows:

If Q_1 commands Q_2 in surface structure but Q_2 doesn't command
Q_1, then Q_1 commands Q_2 in semantic representation. If, on
the other hand, Q_1 and Q_2 command each other in surface structure, then the leftmost quantifier commands the rightmost one
in semantic representation. If constraints 1 and 2 are reflec-
tions in grammar of perceptual strategies, then they would of
course be prime candidates for syntactic universals.

To summarize briefly, when quantifiers occur in different clauses at surface level, the one in the highest clause gets interpreted with widest scope; when both quantifiers are in the same clause, it is the leftmost one which is given largest scope by the semantics. [2]

His examples involve changes in order due to the application of the passive transformation. In the following set of sentences, he claims that each one is unambiguous and that the two are not synonymous.

(1) Many men read few books.

(2) Few books are read by many men.

In semantic interpretation the quantifier with highest scope would correspond to the one which is leftmost. All the speakers I have questioned find such sentences ambiguous, although giving each one a preferred reading. But a preferred reading must be accounted for as much as an unambiguous reading. It is necessary to investigate whether order alone can predict such preferences.

Lakoff rules out the possibility that grammatical function might have any effect on the determination of highest scope. He states, after discussing several examples:

It is important to note that the fact that one of the two quantifiers is in subject position in the sentences we have discussed
so far is simply an accident of the data we happened to have
looked at. The difference in the interpretation of quantifiers
has nothing whatever to do with the fact that in these examples
one quantifier is inside the VP while the other is outside the
VP. Only the left-right order within the clause matters
(p. 241).

He goes on to give two examples where the two quantified NP's occur as objects with their order reversed in the second sentence. He states emphatically that both sentences are unambiguous and differ in meaning exactly in that it is the leftmost quantifier in each sentence that is interpreted with highest scope, a difference I have difficulty perceiving. The following two sentences are used to illustrate his point.

(3) John talked to few girls about many problems.

(4) John talked about many problems to few girls.

But he chooses to use in his examples quantifiers which are diffi-cult to interpret in their own right, so that the reader is unsure what the exact interpretation of either sentence is. All his examples con-tain few and many as the two quantifiers which interact. Both of these are quantifiers which express relative size; thus the precision needed in interpretation to perceive the subtle distinctions caused by a change in scope is lacking due to the vagueness associated with these quantifiers. Once they are substituted by natural numbers, the reader can be more certain what meaning changes occur, if any.

(5) John talked to three girls about a problem.
(6) John talked about a problem to three girls.

Sentences (5) and (6) do not differ in meaning with regard to scope. If they can be construed at all as ambiguous, they are ambiguous in the same way. However, I and every informant questioned perceive the two of them as unambiguous and synonymous. In both sentences a problem has highest scope, and it is the same problem which is told to the three girls in both sentences.[3] Such sentences constitute counterexamples to Lakoff's theory.

Let us examine another linguistic treatment before proceeding with more extensive counterexamples. Jackendoff's position is presented within the interpretivist framework where logical relations in a sentence are not expressed in the deep structure, but are interpreted by the semantics directly from the derived structure (see Chomsky 1971). Like Lakoff, he defines the scope of a quantifier as that part of a sentence commanded by it and to the right of it. These relations are determined at the surface level by means of a 'modal projection rule', stated as follows:

Given a lexical item A whose semantic representation contains a modal operator M. If an NP is within the scope of A, it is optionally dependent on M in the modal structure, that is subject to C_m [where C_m means dependent on M]. If an NP is outside the scope of M, it is not dependent on M (Jackendoff 1972:293).

He then identifies three categories of scope--the third of which pertains to quantifiers. Type III scope 'consists of all material commanded by and to the right of the lexical item containing the operator' (Jackendoff 1972:292).

Unlike Lakoff, Jackendoff does not claim that all quantifiers on the left within a clause have highest scope. He only argues that ambiguities are possible when an NP occurs to the right of a quantifier. He does not limit the type of NP which can occur on the right, nor does he give examples of such ambiguities using proper names or definite descriptions. All his examples contain other quantified NP's or NP's introduced by the indefinite article, which he does not consider a quantifier. In essence it seems that all he is claiming is that ambiguities are possible when two quantifiers occur within the same clause; hardly a novel claim. He still ignores the difficult problem of predicting which reading will be preferred.

Sentences which Lakoff judges unambiguous, Jackendoff argues are ambiguous, judgments in accord with the preliminary data I have collected. But to other sentences which informants found equally ambiguous, Jackendoff assigns a single interpretation. He cites the following pair.

(7) $\begin{bmatrix} \text{Some} \\ \text{All} \\ \text{Five} \end{bmatrix}$ of the boys told me a story.

(8) A story was told to me by $\begin{bmatrix} \text{some} \\ \text{all} \\ \text{five} \end{bmatrix}$ of the boys.

Lakoff would claim that the pair was unambiguous and that each sentence differed in meaning. Jackendoff, on the other hand, claims that (7) is ambiguous, but (8) is not. This judgment of (8) accords with his theory since the indefinite article, which introduces the NP on the left, is not considered a quantifier. My data find (7) and (8) equally ambiguous but give them each a preferred reading. This ambiguity of (8) would constitute a counterexample to Jackendoff's hypothesis--for the only quantifier he recognizes in the sentence occurs to the right of the other NP, yet an ambiguity results. In working with the interpretation of logical elements a linguist must present more empirical evidence. Whole theories are built around a subjective interpretation of some sentence when the very interpretations are greatly disputed.

2. The inherent properties of quantifiers

Let us turn our attention to additional counterexamples where the quantifier on the right has highest scope. It seems that the type of quantifier used makes a difference. This fact is rarely considered by linguists, although Quine (1960) and Vendler (1967) have examined it from a logical perspective. The quantifiers each and every will always tend to have highest scope no matter where they occur in a sentence. This is more certain with each. In the following sentences each and every not only occur to the right of the second NP, but they occur in a prepositional phrase dependent on it. Yet the preferred (if not only) reading is the one where each or every has widest scope.

(9) I saw a picture of each child.
(10) She knows a solution to every problem.

(11) Ethel has a dress for every occasion.

When <u>all</u> is substituted for <u>each</u> or <u>every,</u> the preferred reading is one giving the indefinite highest scope, though the sentences are very ambiguous.

(12) I saw a picture of all the children.
(13) She knows a solution to all problems.
(14) Ethel has a dress for all occasions.

There seems to be a hierarchy of those quantifiers which tend to have highest scope regardless of the environment. At the top are the universal quantifiers with distributive properties. Then it seems to depend on the size of the set specified. The larger the set defined by the quantifier, the higher it will be in the hierarchy, and the greater its inclination toward highest scope when interacting with other quantifiers. The indefinite article and <u>some</u> followed by a singular NP are apparent exceptions to this generalization and have not been included in the hierarchy. These quantifiers, which will be referred to by the cover term Q_{sg}, seem to occur very high on the hierarchy, preceded only by <u>each</u> and <u>every</u>. However, the decision to assign them to that position is not yet supported by conclusive evidence; hence, their exclusion from the list. Table 1 indicates a tentative ordering of the most common quantifiers which quantify over plural sets (Q_{pl}).[4]

TABLE 1.

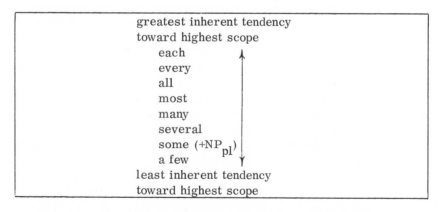

```
                greatest inherent tendency
                toward highest scope
                    each
                    every
                    all
                    most
                    many
                    several
                    some (+NP_pl)
                    a few
                least inherent tendency
                toward highest scope
```

The following sentences illustrate the proposed hierarchy.

(15) Joan gave a few handouts to some pedestrians.
(16) Joan gave a few handouts to several pedestrians.
(17) Joan gave a few handouts to many pedestrians.

(18) Joan gave a few handouts to all the pedestrians.
(19) Joan gave a few handouts to every pedestrian.

In sentence (15) it seems as if the total number of handouts are a few and each pedestrian received one. As the quantifiers get larger, the tendency is for one to interpret the sentences as if each pedestrian received more than one. With sentences (18) and (19) it becomes certain at once that each pedestrian received a few.

3. Grammatical function and relative scope

The inherent properties of the quantifiers are not the sole determinants of relative scope. The grammatical function of the quantified NP in question has much to do with it. Here again a hierarchy can be established. It goes from subject to indirect object to preposition object to direct object. It makes a difference whether the subject occupies that position at both the deep and surface levels. An NP which is subject at both levels will be highest in the hierarchy. Following it will be those NP's that are either deep or surface subject (following a passive T) but not both. All these will tend to have higher scope over the same quantifier in the indirect object or preposition object which in turn have higher scope over the same quantifier occurring in the direct object. In the last three cases, the objects occupy the same grammatical positions at both deep and surface levels. Table 2 specifies the hierarchy of grammatical relations (where $\geq$ reads 'greater tendency toward higher scope').

TABLE 2.

Deep & Surface Subj > Deep Subj/Surface Subj > Ind. Obj. > Prep. Obj. > Dir. Obj.

This hierarchy is very similar to the type of ranking Postal has done in connection with work on the function of the transformational cycle. He has stated that order is irrelevant in defining transformations. Grammatical relations, not word order, is the information needed to formulate the rules. This seems to be the case in assigning quantifier scope as well. The difference between his ranking and this one is the fact that the indirect and prepositional objects take precedence over the direct object in the hierarchy. It is also the case that a deep structure term which has been reassigned to a nonterm status at the surface level is included in the ranking. (Term indicates deep structure NP's which bear grammatical relations.)

Keenan (1972, 1974) establishes a similar order of the grammatical positions with greatest accessibility to relativization. It basically

follows the same order as Postal's and places the direct object before
the indirect and preposition objects. In his hierarchy the following
progression obtains: subject > direct object > indirect object > objects
of prepositions > possessives > objects of comparative particles.
Thus it is not strange that scope assignment should adhere to a similar
hierarchy of grammatical positions.

4. Levels of scope interpretation

Before looking at some examples which justify the above ordering
for quantifiers, let us examine the levels of interpretation which will
be used to evaluate the sentences. First, we must define more precisely what it means for a quantifier to be assigned higher scope.
This study employs the deep structure model formulated by Keenan
(1972). His deep structures distinguish between open sentences and
quantified sentences. Well-informed open sentences are those deep
structure sentences which have replaced any quantified noun phrase
(Q) by a pronominal index. Quantified sentences are formed by
combining Q with any well-formed S, provided that the pronominal
index on Q occurs free in S. The structure used to indicate that
some quantified noun phrase Q_i has higher scope than another Q_j is
shown in (20).

(20)

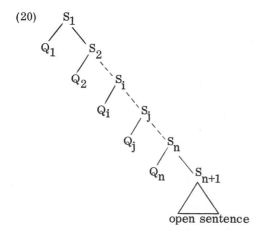

open sentence

or:

$$(Q_1(Q_2(\ldots\ldots Q_i(\ldots\ldots Q_j(\ldots\ldots Q_n(S_{n+1}))S_n\ldots\ldots)_{S_j}\ldots\ldots)_{S_i}\ldots\ldots)_{S_2})_{S_1}$$

Semantically Q_i has higher scope than Q_j means that the remainder of
the sentence dominated by the S node which immediately dominates Q_i

(and which contains Q_j) will be interpreted as an instance for every member of the set designated by Q_i. As an example consider the following sentence:

(21) All the women built a garage.

If in sentence (21) all the women is given highest scope, then the predicate built a garage applies to each of them in the interpretation and there can be as many garages as there are women. This interpretation which assigns the Q_{pl} higher scope will be referred to hereafter as an individual (I) interpretation. If, on the other hand, the quantified NP all the women is read with lower scope than a garage, then it will be contained in the predicate which is interpreted for each member of the set a garage (in this case just one member) which now has the higher scope. Each time the predicate applies, the set of women is referred to as a group. Looking back to sentence (21), we find that in this reading there will be just one instance of the predicate, for we have a single garage. Thus the women work collectively to build it. This interpretation, where the indefinite NP (Q_{sg}) is given highest scope, is referred to in the remainder of the paper as a collective (C) one.

Using these distinctions, we will outline a system to refer to degrees of ambiguity. This study defines five levels of ambiguity which will be referred to by the numbers assigned to them. A limited set of quantifiers will be used in the examples, since attention will be focused on differences not related to the individual properties of the quantifiers themselves. Each sentence will contain an existentially quantified NP introduced by the indefinite article if the language in question has one. The second quantifier it interacts with will be a Q_{pl}, usually a universal or the quantifier some followed by a semantically plural noun phrase.

There seems to be an ordered progression in the judgments of ambiguity ranging from completely unambiguous with an I-interpretation on the one end, to completely unambiguous with a C-interpretation on the other. The scale in Table 3 outlines the levels.

TABLE 3. Scale of ambiguity judgments.

Level 1 - Unambiguous: C-interpretation only
Level 2 - Ambiguous: C-interpretation preferred
Level 3 - Ambiguous: No preferred reading
Level 4 - Ambiguous: I-interpretation preferred
Level 5 - Unambiguous: I-interpretation only

When informants are uncertain about the interpretation of the
sentences asked them, it is always a hesitation between two contiguous levels. For example, if informants are not sure whether a
sentence is ambiguous or not, they will claim that if it is, it most
definitely has a preferred reading. Thus they might waiver between
levels 1 and 2, or levels 4 and 5. However, no informants were confused between levels 1 and 5, and no two informants in the same language gave judgments more than two levels away. When there are
differences between speakers, they are likely to be over more than
one example: all the sentences given to one informant will be judged
higher or lower on the scale than those of the other. Some people
tend to permit more logical ambiguities throughout the language than
others, and it has been my experience that people with linguistic
training fall in the former category.

5. Evidence from English supporting the Grammatical Relations
    Hierarchy

Now let us look at some evidence to support the claim that subjects take precedence over direct objects in scope assignments. The
judgments given the following sentences are my own. Any disagreement should not disrupt the pattern, but just move it up or down on the
scale. While each of the following sentences contains the same two
quantified NP's--one quantified by every and the other by the indefinite article, the deep and surface grammatical positions of the NP's
vary within them.

(22) Every girl took a chemistry course.
      Level 5 - I-only
(23) A chemistry course was taken by every girl.
      Level 4 - I-preferred
(24) Every chemistry course was taken by a girl.
      Level 4 - I-preferred
(25) A girl took every chemistry course.
      Level 2 - C-preferred

In (22) the universal is in both the deep and surface subject, in
(23) it is in just the deep subject, in (24) in just the surface subject
and in (25) it is neither deep nor surface subject--but the object at
both levels. The interpretations descend the ranking scale as the
universally quantified NP changes from subject to object position.
Clearly, order is not a contributing factor to the changes in interpretation. (22) and (24) have the same surface order of quantifiers,
but only (24) is ambiguous and permits a reading where the rightmost quantifier, Q_{sg}, has highest scope, i.e. a C-interpretation.

Again, the quantifiers in (23) and (25) have the same surface order, but (23) has a preferred I-interpretation, giving Q_{pl} highest scope, while (25) has a preferred C-interpretation which assigns Q_{sg} highest scope. Finally, (23) and (24) have opposite quantifier ordering but identical preferred and permitted readings.

Next we give examples to show that the indirect object position takes precedence over the direct object position. Here the order of the quantifiers is the same but their grammatical functions change.

(26) I told every child a story.
   Level 4 - I-preferred
(27) I told every story to a child.
   Level 2 - C-preferred

Reversing the order of the quantifiers in each of these sentences has little effect on its interpretation.

(26') I told a story to every child.
   Level 4 - I-preferred
(27') I told a child every story.
   Level 2 - C-preferred

Both (26) and (26') have a preferred reading in which a possibly different story is told to each child--an I-interpretation. In both cases it is the indirect object, every child, which has highest scope. The preferred readings in (27) and (27') are the same; collective interpretations. Here the indefinite article occurs with the indirect object rather than with the direct object as in (26) and (26'). Thus it is the indirect object again that receives highest scope on the preferred reading. We find that in all four sentences, though we have reversed the order of the quantifiers and interchanged their grammatical functions, the indirect object takes precedence throughout over the direct object.

The following pairs of sentences illustrate that a similar precedence relation obtains between the preposition object and the direct object.

(28) I had many conversations with a friend.
   Level 1 - C-only
(29) I had a conversation with many friends.
   Level 3 - Ambiguous
(30) Freddy hit many balls with a bat.
   Level 1 - C-only
(31) Freddy hit a ball with many bats.
   Level 3 - Ambiguous

In both pairs when the Q_{sg} occurs in the preposition object (28 and 30), it must necessarily receive highest scope, even though it is rightmost in the sentence. However, when this quantifier occurs in the direct object and the Q_{pl} is in the preposition object (29 and 31), the sentences become very ambiguous, and on one reading the Q_{sg}, which is leftmost in the sentence, gets assigned lower scope.

6. Data from other languages

The hierarchies of inherent characteristics and grammatical functions seem to work for other languages as well as English and so they are candidates for language universals. On the other hand, the hypothesis that relative order determines scope can be invalidated by numerous counterexamples from these same languages and so must be discounted as a universal possibility.

Twelve languages were examined besides English. They were, in the Indo-European family, Hindi, Greek, Iranian, Spanish, and Portuguese; two Semitic languages: Hebrew and Arabic; two African languages: Yoruba and Chiluba; and Tagalog, Japanese, and Turkish. They represent a variety of surface word orders. Eight of the languages have no indefinite article: Chiluba, Yoruba, Arabic, Hebrew, Turkish, Hindi, Tagalog and Japanese. Four of the languages have a single indefinite article: Greek, English, Spanish, and Portuguese. One language, Iranian, has two indefinite articles--yek, an unstressed form of the numeral 'one' which precedes the noun, and a suffix -i.

Informants were asked to translate the following six sentences into their native languages:

(32) John made some (a few) girls a cake.
(33) John made all the girls a cake.
(34) John made each girl a cake.
(35) Some (a few) girls made a cake.
(36) All the girls made a cake.
(37) Each girl made a cake.

The first three sentences have the Q_{pl} in the indirect object position; the last three place it in the subject position. In all six sentences Q_{sg} occurs in the direct object position.[5] After giving the translations, informants were asked whether any changes in word order were possible, and if so, what effect they had on the meaning of the sentence. The data given in response to this latter question constitute some of the most interesting data collected. It will be presented in a later section of the paper.

In order to ascertain how they interpreted the sentences, informants were asked whether the girls in each sentence acted or were acted upon as a group or individually. They were asked as well whether the other reading was equally possible, or possible at all. The responses were quite similar across languages and are presented in Table 4 and in Figures 1, 2, 3, and 4.

TABLE 4. Ambiguity level for quantifiers in different languages.

	Indirect Object			Subject		
	some	all	each	some	all	each
Level 1 C-Only	Greek English Spanish Portuguese Iranian Turkish Chiluba Yoruba Hindi Japanese Tagalog Hebrew Arabic	Portuguese Iranian-<u>yek</u> Chiluba Yoruba		English Iranian Yoruba Chiluba	Hindi	
Level 2 C-Preferred		Greek English Spanish Iranian-<u>i</u> Hebrew Arabic		Greek Spanish Portuguese Japanese Arabic Tagalog Turkish	Chiluba Hebrew Arabic	
Level 3 Ambiguous		Japanese Hindi Tagalog Turkish		Hebrew	Greek English Spanish Portuguese Iranian Japanese Yoruba Turkish	
Level 4 I-Preferred					Tagalog	
Level 5 I-Only		Tagalog Greek English Spanish Portuguese Iranian Turkish Chiluba Yoruba Hindi Japanese Hebrew Arabic				Tagalog Greek English Spanish Portuguese Iranian Turkish Chiluba Yoruba Hindi Japanese Hebrew Arabic

Table 4 shows the results for individual languages. Definite patterns can be perceived. Every language investigated had universal quantifiers equivalent to both <u>each</u> and <u>all</u>. There were never any differences in the way the universal quantifier with distributive properties was perceived. It always had widest scope and no other reading was permitted. This was the case no matter whether the distributive universal was in subject or indirect object position.

Comparing the quantifiers <u>some</u> (or <u>a few</u>) and <u>all</u> in any one language, one can observe a definite tendency to interpret <u>some girls</u> collectively more so than <u>all the girls</u>. The latter phrase permits many more ambiguous (level 3) scope interpretations, while a sentence containing <u>some</u> is interpreted only once in this way. With <u>some</u>, the readings normally refer to a particular cake which the girls relate to as a group.[6] The one exception occurred in Hebrew where the informants felt that either interpretation was equally possible when the quantifier <u>some</u> occurred in subject position. It is interesting that in all the languages examined, informants chose the same response when <u>some</u> occurred in an indirect object position. It is always a level 1 ambiguity rating which informants perceive; that is, the C-interpretation giving Q_{sg} higher scope is the only interpretation permitted for such a sentence.

FIGURE 1.   <u>Some</u> vs. <u>All</u>--total responses of both subject and indirect object.

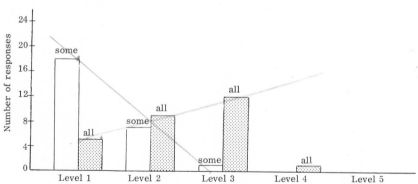

FIGURE 1. <u>Some</u> vs. <u>all</u>--total responses of both subject and indirect object

It is obvious that these data support the ranking of <u>each</u> before <u>all</u> and <u>some</u> in the hierarchy of inherent quantifier properties. <u>Each</u> is the only quantifier of the three that is consistently interpreted as having highest scope no matter what other parameters are present in the sentence. The data also support the conclusion that <u>some</u> is less distributive than <u>all</u>. This can easily be seen by looking at Figure 1. Figure 1 presents the distribution over the five possible interpretations of the combined subject and indirect object responses for <u>some</u> and <u>all</u> --a total of twenty-six responses for each quantifier. The largest number of responses for <u>some</u> occur at level 1, the level at which it can only be interpreted as having lower scope. The greatest concentration of responses for <u>all</u> are clustered around the center of the scale where scope interpretation is perceived as ambiguous. As the levels of interpretation progress from a C-interpretation to an I-interpretation, the number of responses for <u>all</u> increases, while the number for <u>some</u> decreases.

FIGURE 2. Subject vs. Indirect object--total responses for both <u>some</u> and <u>all</u>.

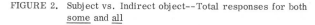

FIGURE 2. Subject vs. Indirect object--Total responses for both some and all

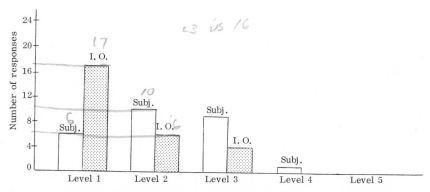

The data also support the hierarchy established for grammatical categories. Quantifiers in this sampling have a greater tendency to higher scope in a subject position than in an indirect object position. Figures 2, 3, and 4 present the results in support of this hypothesis. Figure 2 gives combined responses for <u>some</u> and <u>all</u>, while Figures 3 and 4 indicate the responses for the individual quantifiers. Note that the data for <u>each</u> are not included in these graphs since grammatical category made no difference in the interpretation of sentences containing this quantifier. The responses for the indirect object position, as shown in Figure 2, peak at the C-only level of interpretation and then taper off. The reverse is true of the subject position which is lower at the first level and then increases as the levels permit greater ambiguity. When the data are separated as to individual quantifiers, subject responses in both cases have heaviest concentration

FIGURE 3. All-subject vs. All-indirect object.

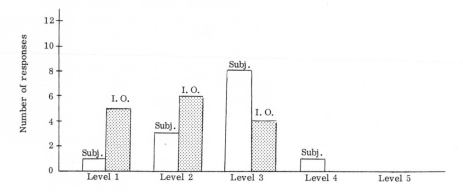

FIGURE 3. All-subject vs. All-indirect object

FIGURE 4. Some-subject vs. Some-indirect object.

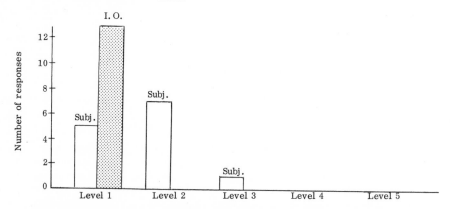

FIGURE 4. Some-subject vs. Some-indirect object

in the direction of individual interpretation, but indirect object responses in comparison are heavier at the collective interpretation
end of the graph. These data are depicted in Figures 3 and 4.

The evidence from the languages examined supports my hypothesis
that the parameters of relative scope assignment, where two quantifiers are concerned, are the inherent properties of the quantifiers
themselves and the grammatical function of the noun phrases which
contain them. I will now show evidence from these same languages
that left-right ordering cannot be a parameter of scope assignment
for quantifiers.

In Japanese word order is relatively free, although some patterns are more marked than others. As I understand it, virtually any noun can be topicalized and brought to the front of the sentence. [7] The following sentences show first the unmarked order, then two marked versions, first with indirect object topicalization and then with direct object topicalization. Listed below each sentence is the ambiguity level elicited from the informant.

(38a) Taro-wa nisannin-no onnanoko-ni keiki-o tsukuri-mashita.
       Taro a few-girl-for cake made.
       Level 1 - C-only
(38b) Nissanin-no onnanoko-ni Taro-wa keiki-o tsukuri-mashita.
       A few-girl-for Taro cake made.
       Level 4 - I-preferred
(38c) Keiki-o Taro-wa nisannin-no onnanoko-ni tsukuri-mashita.
       Cake Taro a few-girl-for made
       Level 1 - C-only

(38a) and (38b) have the same relative left-right ordering of quanti-fiers, yet the interpretations are very different. In sentence (38a), the unmarked version, though the noun phrase 'cake' is rightmost in the sentence, it is assigned highest scope on the only reading the sentence permits. In sentence (38b) focus is shifted to the indirect object which has been topicalized, and now this noun phrase has highest scope on the preferred reading. Again we must stress that the relative ordering of the quantifiers is the same in both sentences. It was not a change in relative order which reversed the scope assignment, but a change in the focus of attention. Sentence (38c) does have an opposite quantifier ordering from (38a). But the interpretation level remains constant. Here we are focusing on the direct object, but since it already had highest scope in the unmarked version, nothing changes.

Arabic and Hebrew offer even more striking counterexamples. In these languages topicalization is performed by placing the noun at the end of the sentence. And it is topicalization, not left-right ordering, which takes precedence in determining scope relations. In these examples, the (a) sentences are the unmarked versions and the (b) sentences have been topicalized.

(39) Arabic
(39a) Khabaz Hanna feteer li kol il binaat.
       Baked John cake for all the girls.
       Level 2 - C-preferred

(39b) Khabaz Hanna li kol il binaat feteer.
       Baked John for all the girls cake.
       Level 1 - C-only

(40)   Hebrew
(40a) Afa Jon ooga le kol ha banot.
       Baked John cake for all the girls.
       Level 2 - C-preferred
(40b) Afa Jon le kol ha banot ooga.
       Baked John for all the girls cake.
       Level 1 - C-only

Topicalization has the effect of putting the direct object, 'cake', to the right of the indirect object. However, the informants in both languages commented that placing 'cake' in sentence final position made it much stronger for a collective interpretation.

Iranian offers a similar phenomenon. Here the informants stated that although the direct object must always directly precede the verb, the indirect object could easily move to a sentence final position where it receives greater focus. As would be expected, it is also more likely in that position to be given highest scope. Again the (a) sentence represents the unmarked version.

(41a) Asghar baraie hamme doxhtar keki poxht.
       Asghar for all girls cake-a made.
       Level 2 - C-preferred
(41b) Asghar keki poxht baraie hamme doxhtarha.
       Asghar cake-a made for all girls.
       Level 4 - I-preferred

In Greek, [8] as in English, the direct and indirect objects can be interchanged, reversing the order of the two quantifiers--and there is no change in meaning. When the quantifier occurring in the indirect object is 'some', the direct object in both cases is given highest scope.

(42a) Giannos ekaine ena kaiki gai kapia koritsia.
       John made a cake for some girl.
       Level 1 - C-only
(42b) Giannos ekaine gai kapia koritsia ena kaiki.
       John made for some girls a cake.
       Level 1 - C-only

The normal word order in Hindi places the indirect object before the direct object. But it is the latter noun which is assigned highest scope when the indirect object is quantified by 'a few'.

(43) Ram ne kaiee ladkion ke liye mithaiee banaiee.
Ram a few girls for cake made.
Level 1 - C-only

Both the Greek and Hindi responses are predicted by the hierarchy
established above which assigns a low ranking to the quantifiers <u>some</u>
and <u>a few</u> in their chances of receiving highest scope.

The Malayo-Polynesian languages usually permit a sentence order
where the subject (sometimes referred to as the topic) is in the sentence final position. Tagalog is one such language. It is interesting
that the same relative ordering occurs when the two quantifiers are in
the direct, indirect object positions, as when they are in the subject,
object positions; yet there is a difference in ambiguity level. In both
cases the existentially quantified direct object occurs to the left.
When the universal 'all' is in the indirect object position, the sentence
is judged very ambiguous with either scope ordering acceptable. However, when this same quantifier is in the subject position, the informant assigned it an individual preferred reading.

(44a) Gumawa ng keik para sa lahat ng mga babae si Jose.
Made cake for all of (pl) girl Jose.
Level 3 - Ambiguous
(44b) Gumawa ng keik ang lahat ng mga babae.
Made cake all of (pl) girl.
Level 4 - I-preferred

Tagalog was the only language examined which gave sentence (44b)
a preferred individual interpretation. Yet it was the only language
where the subject (containing the universal) occurred after the direct
object. This judgment is exactly opposite that predicted by a theory
based on relative ordering. But the facts are accounted for by the
interaction of the two hierarchies previously outlined: the one ranking
individual quantifiers by their inherent tendency toward highest scope,
and the other ranking the grammatical positions in order of their
receptiveness to wider scope assignment.

Turkish word order is relatively free. Every sentence elicited
from the informant was capable of being transformed at the surface
level into another surface order. But in no case did a change in
linear order result in a change in interpretation. We will cite a few
typical examples.

(45a) Birkaç kız pasta yaptı.
       A few girl cake made.
       Level 2 - C-preferred
(45b) Pasta yaptı birkaç kız.
       Cake made a few girl
       Level 2 - C-preferred
(46a) Ahmet bütün kızlara pasta yaptı.
       Ahmet all girls-for cake made.
       Level 3 - Ambiguous
(46b) Bütün kızlara pasta yaptı Ahmet.
       All girls-for cake made Ahmet.
       Level 3 - Ambiguous
(46c) Pasta yaptı Ahmet bütün kızlara.
       Cake made Ahmet all girls-for.
       Level 3 - Ambiguous

The final evidence we offer comes from Yoruba. In this language clefting occurs by permuting a noun phrase to the beginning of the sentence and following it by the particle ni. Since this is not topicalization as we define it, there is no focusing of attention to cause a change in interpretation. The reversal of the left-right order of quantifiers does not alter the scope assignment.

(47a) Femi se işu-akara fun gbogbo awọn obinrin.
       Femi cooked loaf-bread for all (pl) girl.
       Level 1 - C-only
(47b) Fun gbogbo awọn obinrin ni Femi se işu-akara.
       For all (pl) girl Femi cooked loaf-bread.
       Level 1 - C-only

7. Grammatical function and sentential position

From the above data we can conclude that another sentential element belongs in the hierarchy of grammatical positions, this being the category of topic. One might question whether this is a legitimate grammatical category since in English there is no designated way to refer to the topic. But many languages do have a specific grammatical category for the topic. Some have argued that the sentential element usually considered the subject in Malayo-polynesial languages is actually a topic. We will revise the hierarchy presented earlier to include the topic position slightly ahead of the subject position. This decision is justified on the basis of the fact that in Japanese and Iranian, topicalization of the 'girls' noun phrase causes it to be given highest scope on the preferred reading (cf. sentences (38b) and (41b)). The same nouns in subject position do not give a level 4

rating, but only a level 2 or a level 3 (see Table 4). The revised list
appears in Table 5.

TABLE 5. Revised hierarchy of grammatical functions.

1. Topic
2. Deep and surface subject
3. Deep subject/surface subject
4. Indirect object
5. Preposition object
6. Direct object

One might speculate as to why the topic and subject are at the top
of the hierarchy. In all the languages examined, focus was accom-
plished by moving an element to either the front or the end of the sentence. In most languages these are also positions for the subject.
Exceptions are the Semitic languages, but in at least Hebrew and
Arabic this is changing in the colloquial language. It seems to me
that the explanation for why these two categories have greatest tendency to highest scope lies in the fact that they occur in very salient
positions in the sentential string. Sentences are uttered as ordered
series of elements and thus are subject to what is known as the serial
position effect. It has long been known in psychology that with an
ordered set of items, those at the beginning and at the end capture the
most attention and are retained the longest. This is due to what is
called the primacy and recency effect. Languages use these positions
to convey the most important information in the sentence. This is
why the element with higher scope will most likely be found at either
end of the sentence. English normally utilizes the subject-initial
position to convey important information. Thus the noun phrase with
highest scope can usually be found in the front of the sentence. This
is why linguists to date, who have built their theories around data
in English alone, have posited left-right order as the determining
factor in assigning scope. One need only look at a variety of languages to see that the left-most position is just a vehicle to convey
the important grammatical information.

8. Quantifiers as logical operators

The question which must now be given attention is why it is that
quantifiers are not affected by permutations which leave grammatical
relations intact while other operators are. A few examples will
suffice to show that the other operators, such as negation, modals,
and conjunction, are constrained by ordering arrangements. The

following pairs illustrate that a change in order causes a change in meaning.

(48)   NOT
(48a) Helen knows that Sally didn't arrive.
(48b) Helen didn't know that Sally arrived.

(49)   MODALS
(49a) Karen realized that Janice needed to make the finals.
(49b) Karen needed to realize that Janice made the finals.

(50)   CONJUNCTION
(50a) Squirrels and chipmunks or my neighbor's dogs are
       ruining my garden.
(50b) Squirrels or chipmunks and my neighbor's dogs are
       ruining my garden.

Quite clearly the (a) and (b) sentences differ in meaning. How can we account for the difference between these operators and quantifiers? It is my feeling that quantifiers differ from the other operators substantially and constitute a very special category of operators. One of the very basic ways they differ from most other operators is that they do not affect the specificity of indefinite nouns. Compare the following examples:

(51a) Anna didn't see a Bergman film.
(51b) Anna ought to see a Bergman film.
(51c) Did Anna see a Bergman film?
(51d) Every woman saw a Bergman film.

Sentences (51a) through (51c) are ambiguous between a specific, identifiable Bergman film and any random Bergman film. Sentence (51d) is ambiguous but in a very different way. In both of its interpretations the film is identifiable to the speaker. The difference between the two readings is whether we are talking about the same film that every woman saw or a different film for each one, that is, a collective vs. individual reading. Neither case affects the specificity of the indefinite noun phrase. In both interpretations of (51d), at least one Bergman film is presupposed to exist.

Another fact which distinguishes quantifiers from other logical operators is their mobility in a deep structure representation. The other operators must adhere to a strict ordering in the deep structure which mirrors that of the surface structure. They must occur in the immediate proximity of the predicate they appear with in the surface structure or they will be interpreted with a different scope than the sentence intends. Consider the following sentence:

(52) Master Bates wasn't surprised that Steven could resent that all presidents lie, cheat, steal and fornicate.

If one wished to represent it with a logical formula, or a semantically interpreted deep structure, they would have little choice as to where to place the operators within it--except for the universal quantifier. It can be placed indefinitely far from its clause in the underlying structure and will still find its way home, so to speak, at the surface level. This is so because it is the only operator which binds a variable and it must at the surface level occupy the position of that variable, no matter where it is located in the deep structure. (52a) depicts a class of possible underlying representations for (52), where the #'s indicate the different positions the quantifier could occupy. On the other hand, (52b), containing all the operators at the beginning of the formula, does not represent a possible logical structure for (52). Again, the notation used is that developed by Keenan (1972).

(52a) ($\forall$ presidents, x)(Master Bates, y) # $\sim$ (surprise y, fact
(Steven, z) # $\diamond$ (resent z, fact (# & # lie x, cheat x,
steal x, fornicate x)))

(52b) *(presidents, x)(Master Bates, y)(Steven, z) $\sim$ $\diamond$ &
(surprise y, fact (resent z, fact (lie x, cheat x, steal x,
fornicate, x)))

We have shown that quantifiers exhibit different properties from the other operators, namely, they are not constrained by linear ordering at the surface level, they do not affect the specificity of indefinite nouns, and they can be located indefinitely far from their predicates at the deep structure level. Why should this be the case? I believe there are two quite separate phenomena which account for this. The mobility of quantifiers in the underlying structure is accounted for by the index which accompanies them but no other operator. It guarantees identity with the proper variable indicating its relative position in the grammatical structure. The explanation for the other two differences is a bit more elusive. Quantifiers do not operate on the complete sentential formula in the same way the other operators do. They only specify the number of members in the sets referred to, and thus, the number of instances of the predicate. They do not alter the truth value of any predicate in the formula. Hence there is no reason they should affect the specificity of an indefinite noun. And because they do not affect the truth value of the other elements in the formula, their linear ordering in relation

to these elements should not affect interpretation. Quantifiers consistently occur in noun phrases. It seems that it is the grammatical
function, not the linear position, of the noun it accompanies that defines its domain. These ideas on an explanation are still quite specu-
lative, but this path seems worth further exploration.

9. Conclusion

To conclude, we have expounded three major points: different
quantifiers have differing probabilities of acquiring highest scope,
relative linear ordering at the surface level is not a parameter of
quantifier scope, and grammatical functions, both those at the deep
and those at the surface levels, are the relevant factors which determine the possible scope interpretations. Finally, we have noted that
in this latter respect quantifiers differ considerably from other operators.

NOTES

I wish to thank Emmon Bach, Ed Keenan, Lynette Hirschman,
Terry Langendoen, and Constantine Kaniklidis for reading an earlier
version of this paper and offering very valuable comments and suggestions.

1. These ideas were presented by Postal in a lecture entitled
'Grammatical relations in generative grammar' at Queens College
of the City University of New York, on April 5, 1973.

2. Though he admits to dialect variation in the interpretation of
sentences where quantifiers interact, he presents data for his dialect
alone. Without the use of rigorous psycholinguistic testing measures,
this is the only approach a linguist can take. However, Lakoff claims
that his dialect represents that of the majority of English speakers; a
claim he makes no attempt to substantiate. In fact, in questioning a
large number of both linguistically and non-linguistically trained
speakers, I have found none who share his dialect.

3. It is not specified whether the girls are in a group or not, but
this has nothing to do with the scope of the quantifiers. It is a question of whether the set of girls is interpreted by the semantics as one
set or as the individual members of it. Either way, the quantifier
NP, a problem, distributes over three girls in the interpretation.
This problem will not be dealt with here, but will be taken up at
length in my dissertation.

4. It must be noted that the quantifiers on this list are only the
unstressed variants. It is probably the case that another hierarchy
could be established for stressed quantifiers, or one showing the
interaction between stressed and unstressed occurrences.

5. In languages without an indefinite article, existentially quantified noun phrases are unmarked for number. A more accurate notation for Q_{sg} in these languages would be Q_u. However, for simplicity, the Q_{sg} designation is kept. The Q_{pl}'s in every language are followed by a semantically plural noun phrase whether the language indicates number syntactically on nouns or not. Semantically plural nouns are implied by the meaning of the Q_{pl}'s.

6. In languages without an indefinite article the number of cakes is unspecified. This remains so whether the set of girls is interpreted individually or collectively.

7. The notion of 'topic' used here is a very informal one. It is not used in the sense of 'old information', although it may serve this function in some of the languages. What we mean here by 'topic' is the element of the sentence on which attention is focused. No attempt is made to define the semantic import of this process of focusing attention.

8. The dialect of Greek used is that spoken on the island of Chios.

REFERENCES

Chomsky, Noam. 1971. Deep structure, surface structure, and semantic interpretation. In: Steinberg and Jakobovits (1971). 173-216.

Jackendoff, Ray S. 1972. Semantic interpretation in generative grammar. Cambridge, Massachusetts, The MIT Press.

Keenan, Edward L. 1972. On semantically based grammar. Linguistic Inquiry 3:413-461.

_____. 1974. Variation in universal grammar. [This volume, pp. 136-148].

Lakoff, George. 1971. On generative semantics. In: Steinberg and Jakobovits (1971). 132-296.

Quine, Willard V. O. 1960. Word and object. Cambridge, Massachusetts, The MIT Press.

Reichenbach, Hans. 1947. Elements of symbolic logic. New York, The Free Press.

Steinberg, D. and L. Jakobovits, eds. 1971. Semantics--An interdisciplinary reader in philosophy, linguistics, anthropology, and psychology. London, Cambridge University Press.

Vendler, Zeno. 1967. Linguistics in philosophy. Ithaca, New York, Cornell University Press.

VARIATION IN UNIVERSAL GRAMMAR

EDWARD L. KEENAN

King's College, Cambridge

0. If the study of universal grammar (UG) is conceived of loosely as the study of those properties which all natural languages (NLs) have, then it would appear that properties which vary from one NL to another are precisely those which cannot constitute universals. And narrowly construed this thesis is surely true. Yet I shall argue in this paper that the study of variation can provide universal generalizations about NLs--often, in fact, ones that could not be established on the basis of data from any single language.

In this paper I shall propose two such generalizations. The first is basically a syntactic constraint which any rule of relative clause formation (RCF) in any NL must obey. As an earlier form of this generalization was reported on in Keenan and Comrie (1972), I shall only summarize here the conclusions of that work without discussing in detail the evidence which supports it. The second generalization, whose discussion constitutes the major part of this paper, is a performance one based on, but independent of, the first generalization.

1. A syntactic constraint on relative clause formation (RCF)

In Keenan and Comrie (1972) the possibilities of relativizing on various noun phrase (NP) positions in a large range of NLs was investigated. It was found that NLs varied considerably with regard to which NPs could be relativized. But the variation was not random, as the relativizability of certain NP positions was not independent of that of others. Restricting ourselves to major or near major NP positions of main verbs, we can express these dependencies in the Case Hierarchy below:

136

CASE HIERARCHY (CH)

Subjects > Dir Obj > Ind Obj > Oblique > Genitive > Obj of Comparison

To understand the interpretation of the CH let me point out that I
am using a liberal, and semantically based, notion of relative clause
(RC). Roughly I am thinking of a RC as a syntactic means a language
uses to restrict the referents of a NP to those objects of which some
sentence is true (the sentence being expressed by the 'subordinate
clause' in surface). Thus a RC in English such as 'the boy who stole
the pig' can refer to any object which, one, is a boy, and two, is
such that the sentence 'he stole the pig' is true of him. Clearly many
NL will have two or more formally distinct means of forming RC. I
shall refer to such distinct means as relative clause forming (RCF)
strategies. For example, German has both a post-nominal and a
pre-nominal RCF strategy. We can say 'the man who is working in
his study' either by der Mann, der in seinem Büro arbeitet or der in
seinem Büro arbeitende Mann.
   Now suppose a NL has a RCF strategy that works on subjects of
main verbs, as in, e.g. 'the boy who stole the pig', where boy is the
subject of steal. That same strategy may or may not also work on
direct objects. If it doesn't then it will also fail to work on any of
the positions lower on the CH than the direct object position. And
indeed some NL (e.g. Tagalog, Malagasy) can relativize only on
subjects. On the other hand, if that RCF strategy works on subjects
and direct objects then, once again, it either may or may not work
on indirect objects. If not, then it also fails to work on any of the
NP positions lower than Ind Obj on the CH. And again, there are
NLs with RCF strategies that work only on subjects and direct objects (Shona, Finnish [prenominal strategy]). And similarly, for
each of the other positions on the CH we have found NL which can
relativize continuously from subjects through that position but no
farther using the same strategy.
   These facts can be generalized (Bernard Comrie, personal communication) to establish the following universal constraint on RCF:

THE CASE ORDERING CONSTRAINT (COC)

Any RCF strategy in any NL must operate on continuous segments of the CH.

Thus, if a given RCF strategy works on two NP positions in the CH
it necessarily works on all intermediate positions. So, e.g. no NL
has a RCF strategy that works only on subjects and oblique case

NP (e.g. objects of prepositions in English). If it works on these it must also work on direct and indirect objects.

Notice now that the COC is a constraint which the grammars of each NL obey, yet no one NL affords sufficient data to determine the COC as we have given it. For any given NL the data are usually compatible with several different ways of ordering the six NP positions listed in the CH. In many dialects of English for example all the NP positions are relativizable, so any of the six factorial = 720 possible combinations of the six NP elements would be compatible with the data. For dialects in which objects of comparison are not relativizable (e.g. *the boy Mary is taller than) we still have 120 possible orderings compatible with the data. Even languages such as German with two RCF strategies which both cut off before the end (the prenominal strategy works only on subjects, the standard strategy works on all positions except objects of comparison) still admit of 48 possible orderings compatible with the data (viz. any ordering which presents Dir Obj, Ind Obj, Oblique, and Genitive positions as a continuous segment and which places either the Subject before or after the sequence).

Consequently, it is only the data from cross language variation which can correctly determine the most general, that is, the most universally applicable, form of the constraint on relative clause formation.

2. A performance constraint on relative clause formation

In addition to the ordering expressed in the CH, there is a sense in which the Subject end of the CH expresses the 'easiest' or most 'natural' positions to relativize. Thus all NLs possess at least one strategy that works on subjects. But this claim fails for all the other positions. This suggests the idea that even in NL where all, or most, of the NP positions on the CH can be relativized, that there may be some sense in which it is 'easier' or more 'natural' to form RCs on the Subjects (or higher) end of the CH than on the lower end.

One way to attempt to directly verify this intuition would be to elicit judgments of relative acceptability on RCs formed on the various positions. Thus if English speakers generally agreed that RCs formed on subjects were more acceptable than those formed on objects, etc., then we would have direct evidence in favor of the hypothesis that RCF is more natural on the upper end of the CH. Now indeed there is some, but insufficient, direct evidence of this sort. Thus most speakers agree that it is more acceptable to relativize on the subject on a comparative construction than on the object. Thus 'the boy who is taller than Mary' is more acceptable than 'the boy that Mary is shorter than'. Further, in some

NL such as Swedish and Dutch, colloquial speech clearly prefers subject relatives over genitive relatives. Thus while Swedish offers in fact two genitive relative pronouns, vars and vilkens, and so can directly express, e.g. 'the woman whose coat was stolen' (= kvinnan, vars kappa blev stulen) it prefers to use a semantically equivalent construction in which RCF has taken place on the subject position, e.g. kvinnan, som fick son kappa stulen (='the woman that got her coat stolen'), in which the head NP woman (= kvinnen) functions as the subject of the verb get (= fick).

In fact it was these judgments of relative acceptability which led me to think that the CH, established on the basis of cross language data, might have intralinguistic validity as well. Nonetheless, it must be admitted that the judgments of relative acceptability for all NP positions on the CH are neither reliable nor public enough to constitute the data of a serious scientific claim. This is particularly true when the NP positions considered are adjacent on the CH. Thus there is simply no reliably elicitable judgment that the acceptability of 'the farmer whose pig John stole' (a Genitive RC) is less than or equal to that of 'the farmer that John stole the pig from' (an Oblique RC). So to verify our hypothesis that RCF is more natural on the higher end of the CH than on the lower end we shall have to have recourse to indirect evidence. That is, let us assume the hypothesis and attempt to directly verify various of its consequences. Below we give three performance-based predictions which are entailed or at least naturally suggested by the hypothesis. We substantiate the predictions and consequently present confirmation (partial only of course) of the hypothesis.

3.1 First Prediction (P-1)

The frequency with which people relativize in discourse conforms to the CH, subjects being the most frequent, then direct objects, etc.

To substantiate P-1 we have collected over 2200 RCs from a variety of written materials (whose choice will be discussed shortly). In Figure 1 we present the distribution of the RC with respect to the relativized NP positions which occur in the CH. Note that we have collapsed the indirect object position with the oblique case NPs since for purposes of RCF in English it behaves in just the same way--a preposition (to) must be retained, and is either stranded, or fronted with the relative pronoun. Hence, when applied to English, the CH has only five, not six, positions. We note also here that the Genitive position includes relativization into of complements of NPs, e.g. 'the gate the hinges of which were rusty', 'the gate of which the hinges were rusty', etc.

FIGURE 1.

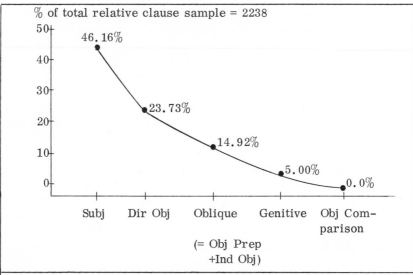

% of total relative clause sample = 2238

46.16%

23.73%

14.92%

5.00%

0.0%

Subj   Dir Obj   Oblique   Genitive   Obj Comparison

(= Obj Prep
+Ind Obj)

Positions not represented on the figure include locatives, i.e. 'the place where. . .' which represent 4.87% of the total; temporals, i.e. 'the time when . . .' which represent 3.31% of the total, and a miscellaneous category which represents 1.79% of the total. The statistical differences between the figures for adjacent NP positions on the CH are in all cases highly significant, using the standard tests discussed in Hayes (1966) and Reed (1949). In fact, no matter what pair of adjacent positions on the CH we pick, the chances that that difference in frequency would arise on a random basis is much less than .00005734%. That is, much less than one in a million.

We note furthermore that these results are in substantial agreement with those obtained by D. Block (1973) who considered a RC sample similar in size to ours for early Scots English (c. 1400).

Unfortunately these figures constitute only weak confirmation of our hypothesis, since there is an alternative (but undemonstrated) hypothesis which would explain them. Namely, that RCF in English applies randomly with respect to NP positions that are relativizable at all, and the observed distribution in Figure 1 is due to the general distribution of NPs in discourse, i.e. NPs occur most frequently as subjects, then as direct objects etc. This latter hypothesis has not been demonstrated, although it is consistent with some very small sample checks performed. Thus, while the frequency distributions in Figure 1 support our hypothesis they are insufficient to establish it. For more conclusive support, we must turn to a closer analysis of our data and somewhat finer predictions.

3.2 Second Prediction (P-2)

Authors who are reliably judged to use syntactically simple sentences will present a greater proportion of RCs near the high end of the CH than authors independently judged to use syntactically complex sentences.

Note that P-2 is certainly reasonable. For if an author generally uses complex sentence structures we would not expect him to eschew the more 'difficult' or less 'natural' end of the CH when he forms RCs. Authors which restrict themselves to simple sentence structures, however, would naturally be expected to restrict themselves more to the 'easy' or more 'natural' end of the CH.

To substantiate P-2 we have taken RCs from two sources judged to be 'simple' and compared them with two sources judged to be 'complex'. (By 'simple' and 'complex' we refer here only to internal sentence structure, of course, not, for example, to the structure of the entire discourse in which the sentences may occur.) Our first source of simple structures consisted of all the relative clauses (there were 421 RCs) found on pages 1 and 2 of a collection of issues of the Sun and the Daily Mirror. (These are among the most popular newspapers in Europe. They are in tabloid form, have lots of pictures, large headlines, short sentences, frequent paragraphs, and are obviously designed for 'snapshot' reading.) Clearly they are to be judged, pre-theoretically, as sententially simple. Any formal simplicity metric which judged them complex would simply be an inadequate metric.

Our second source of simple structures were all the RC found in George Orwell's Animal Farm (there were 344 RCs). Again, there is very general agreement that Orwell's sentences, which often present the world as seen through the eyes of the 'lower animals', are syntactically simple. A not atypical sample would be:

The very next morning the attack came. The animals were at breakfast when the look-outs came racing in with the news that Frederick and his followers had already come through the five-barred gate. Boldly enough the animals sallied forth to meet them, but this time they did not have the easy victory that they had in the Battle of the Cowshed. There were fifteen men, with half a dozen guns between them, and they opened fire as soon as they got within fifty yards. The animals could not face the terrible explosions and the stinging pellets, and in spite of the efforts of Napoleon and Boxer to rally them, they were soon driven back. A number of them were already wounded. They took refuge in the farm buildings and peeped cautiously out from chinks and knot-holes. The whole of the big pasture, including the windmill, was in the hands of the enemy. For the moment even Napoleon seemed at a loss. He paced up and down without a word, his tail rigid and twitching. Wistful glances were sent in the direction of Foxwood. If Pilkington and his men would help them, the day might yet be won. But at this moment the four pigeons, who had been sent out on the day before, returned, one of them bearing a scrap of paper from Pilkington. On it was pencilled the words: 'Serves you right' (p. 87).

Similarly, we considered two sources of complex sentence structures: First, all the RC (there were 675) in Virginia Woolf's To the Lighthouse. And second, all the relative clauses (there were 798 RCs) found in a collection of P. F. Strawson's works. [1] These authors are clearly sententially complex, although in stylistically quite different ways. Even Ph.D.'s in linguistics often have to read their sentences several times to understand them--whereas one never has this difficulty with Orwell or with the Sun/Mirror.

Figure 2 presents in summary form the distribution of RCs, with respect the CH applied to English, for the simple group, and Figure 3 for the complex group.

Clearly RCs from the complex sources are far less frequent on subjects (40.1%) than is the case for those from simple sources (57.8%). (The difference is significant well past the .00005734 level, i.e. the probability of producing such a difference by chance is much less than one in a million. In general all differences we explicitly discuss have been checked for statistical significance and are usually several degrees of magnitude more significant than is required in the literature.) On the other hand, RCs from complex sources occur significantly more frequently on Dir Objs, Obliques, and Genitives than do RCs from simple sources. (We should also note that Temporal relatives occurred with a frequency of 6.0% in the simple group, and only 1.9% in the complex group, again a very significant difference.) These figures clearly support P-2, so our hypothesis is (partially) confirmed.

Having established that RC distribution with respect to the CH can discriminate syntactically complex authors from syntactically simpler ones, we can now use the criterion to distinguish cases which are not so clear on impressionistic grounds.

FIGURE 2. 'Simple' sources: G. Orwell and Sun/Mirror

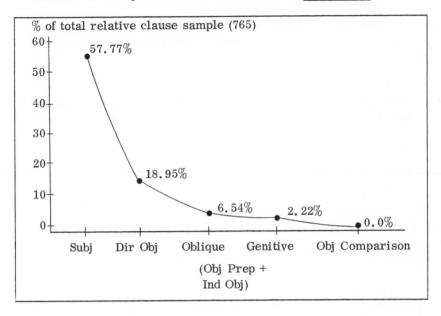

FIGURE 3. 'Complex' sources: V. Woolf and P. F. Strawson

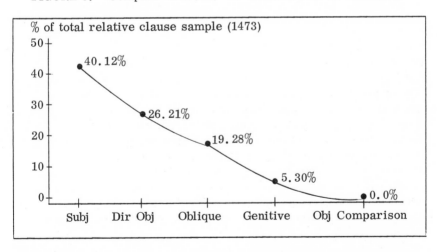

Consider first the difference between the members of the simple group: Orwell's Animal Farm on the one hand and the issues of the Sun and Mirror on the other. Impressionistically one feels that Orwell's sentences are somewhat more complex syntactically than those of the Sun and Mirror, although our judgments here carry much less conviction than they did when we compared the simple group as a whole with the complex group.

Applying our complexity criterion, however, we can see from Figure 4 that Orwell is somewhat more complex than the Sun/Mirror.

FIGURE 4.

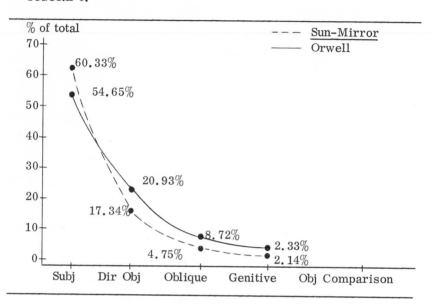

Orwell relativizes significantly less frequently on subjects than does the Sun/Mirror and relatively more in the Oblique NP position. The difference between the other positions on the CH are not significant.

Even more interesting perhaps is the comparison between the members of the more complex group--Woolf and Strawson. Impressionistically both are complex but in quite different ways. Woolf's style is clearly more flowing--it is easy to get caught up in the rhythm, or better, the momentum that her sentences impart. Strawson, on the other hand, is less overwhelming, more obviously thought out, and impressionistically, his sentences are more highly structured. Compare in this respect the beginning of V. Woolf's To the Lighthouse with the introductory paragraphs of Strawson's Individuals:

'Yes, of course, if it's fine tomorrow,' said Mrs. Ramsay. 'But you'll have to be up with the lark,' she added.

To her son these words conveyed an extraordinary joy, as if it were settled the expedition were bound to take place, and the wonder to which he had looked forward, for years and

years it seemed, was, after a night's darkness and a day's
sail, within touch. Since he belonged, even at the age of six,
to that great clan which cannot keep this feeling separate from
that, but must let future prospects, with their joys and sorrows,
cloud what is actually at hand, since to such people even in
earliest childhood any turn in the wheel of sensation has the
power to crystallize and transfix the moment upon which its
gloom or radiance rests, James Ramsay, sitting on the floor
cutting out pictures from the illustrated catalogue of the Army
and Navy Stores, endowed the picture of a refrigerator as his
mother spoke with heavenly bliss. It was fringed with joy.
The wheel-barrow, the lawn-mower, the sound of poplar
trees, leaves whitening before rain, rooks cawing, brooms
knocking, dresses rustling--all these were so coloured and
distinguished in his mind that he had already his private
code, his secret language, though he appeared the image of
stark and uncompromising severity, with his high forehead
and his fierce blue eyes, impeccably candid and pure, frown-
ing slightly at the sight of human frailty, so that his mother,
watching him guide his scissors neatly round the refrigerator,
imagined him all red and ermine on the Bench or directing a
stern and momentous enterprise in some crisis of public
affairs (V. Woolf, To the Lighthouse, p. 5).

BODIES

I. The Identification of Particulars

[1] We think of the world as containing particular things
some of which are independent of ourselves; we think of the
world's history as made up of particular episodes in which
we may or may not have a part; and we think of these particular things and events as included in the topics of our
common discourse, as things about which we can talk to
each other. These are remarks about the way we think of
the world, about our conceptual scheme. A more recog-
nizably philosophical, though no clearer, way of expressing them would be to say that our ontology comprises objective particulars. It may comprise much else besides.

Part of my aim is to exhibit some general and structural
features of the conceptual scheme in terms of which we
think about particular things. I shall speak, to begin with,
of the identification of particulars. . . . (P. F. Strawson,
Individuals, p. 15)

Figure 5 summarizes the differences in RC patterning between
Strawson and Woolf.

FIGURE 5.

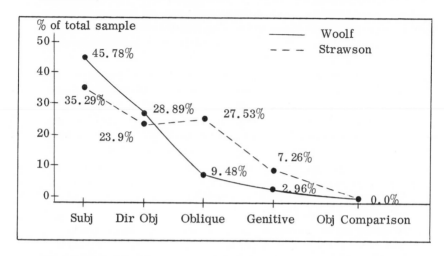

Clearly Strawson relativizes significantly less on both subjects and direct objects than does Woolf, but relatively more on oblique case NPs and genitives. Note in fact that Strawson relativizes much more frequently on objects of prepositions than he does on direct objects. Thus the complexity ordering of our four texts determined by RC distribution on the CH is: Sun/Mirror the least difficult; then Orwell, then V. Woolf, and finally P. F. Strawson, the most difficult. This ordering accords well with our pre-theoretical intuitions and so not only supports P-2 but provides a diagnostic for syntactic complexity useful in cases where our pre-theoretical judgments are less than overwhelming.

3.3 Third Prediction (P-3)

There is a tendency in 'simple' authors to move underlying direct objects into superficial subject position (e.g. by PASSIVE) under relativization.

P-3 is reasonable in that if it is really grammatically more natural to relativize subjects than objects it is natural that authors should move objects into subject position, as PASSIVE would do, in order to relativize the NP from the easiest position. We would expect this particularly in authors who are the more constrained to present their RCs high on the CH anyway.

So far we have only attempted to confirm this prediction in Orwell but there the results are very encouraging, and perhaps sufficient to establish the 'tendency' referred to in P-3. To confirm P-3 we first computed the total number of underlying direct objects present in the text as a whole (there were 1846 such). Of these, 480 occurred as derived subjects. That is, in the text as a whole, one has a 26.00% chance of presenting an underlying direct object as a superficial subject. Now, restricting ourselves to underlying direct objects that were relativized, we would predict that a greater percentage occurred as superficial subjects, i.e. that Orwell moved them into subject position 'in order' to relativize them. And this is correct. Of a total of 116 underlying direct objects that appeared as head NPs of RCs 44 were in fact superficial subjects of the subordinate verb. That is, there was a 33.93% chance of presenting an underlying direct object as a superficial subject if you were going to relativize it. (And again, given our large sample size, this difference is highly significant.)

3.4 Some additional predictions

In addition to P-1 through P-3, several other performance tests of our basic hypothesis suggest themselves. One very interesting one, not so applicable to English as certain other languages, has in fact been validated by D. Block (1973) for early Scots English. Namely, in languages which have a word order norm but which admit of variations on it with only very minor (or no) differences in meaning we would expect that word order freedom would decrease so as to approach the norm in RCs formed on the low end of the CH. That is, the more difficult the position relativized the greater the tendency to present the rest of the material in the most unmarked way, that is, the easiest way, possible.

Further the basic idea behind this hypothesis has also been validated in Givón (1973) who has shown that word order freedom in Hebrew relative clauses decreases according as the NP relativized is the less accessible (but the NP positions Givón considered were even more difficult than those represented in the CH).

A second prediction suggested by the CH is that RC comprehension is a function of the CH. Thus we predict that, on recall tests, native speakers will do less well if the basic information were presented in RCs formed low on the CH than in one formed high on the CH. We are currently testing this hypothesis in a series of tests given to school children of different ages, but we have as yet no concrete results to report.

4. Conclusion

We have shown that cross language variation in syntactic structures can serve not only as the basis of universal constraints on the grammars

See Jakobson (1941)

of languages, but can determine performance constraints within languages. This rather suggests that competence and performance are merely two ends of a scale, rather than exclusive categories.

NOTE

1. The works were the first two chapters of Individuals, Methuen, London (1959), and the articles 'Identifying reference and truth-values' in Thoeria, Vol. 30, Part 2 (1964), pp. 96–118, and 'Singular terms and predication', in Journal of Philosophy, Vol. 58, No. 15 (1961), pp. 393–412.

REFERENCES

Block, D. 1973. Relativization in early middle Scots. Paper read at the meetings of the Midwest Modern Language Association, Chicago, November 2, 1973.
Givón, Talmy. 1973. Complex NP's, word order and resumptive pronouns in Hebrew. In: Supplement to CLS IX, Chicago.
Hayes, C. W. 1966 [1970]. A study in prose styles: Edward Gibbon and Ernest Hemingway. In: Linguistics and literary style. Edited by Donald C. Freeman. New York, Holt, Rinehart and Winston.
Keenan, E. and Comrie, B. 1972. Noun phrase accessibility and universal grammar. Paper presented at the Linguistic Society of America Meetings, Winter, 1972 and at the Linguistic Association Meetings, Hull, 1973.
Reed, D. W. 1949. A statistical approach to quantitative linguistic analysis. Word V:235-47.

A 'MARKEDNESS' HIERARCHY
OF QUANTIFIED NOUN PHRASES

PATRICK F. McNAMER

McGill University

Comparatively few studies in a transformational framework have been made on selectional restrictions among quantifiers within a noun phrase. Most studies done on the quantified noun phrase have dealt mainly with its general structural format--the constituent relationships among the noun phrase(s), determiner(s), and other elements. [1] Jackendoff (1968) and others, including structural linguists, have proposed a classification of quantifiers according to position within the noun phrase. These are in a sense statements of quantifier restrictions, but are nevertheless also oriented toward a study of noun phrase constituent structure. One study that is different is that of McKeon, who recently adapted a system of cross-classificatory features previously proposed by Dougherty for a description of co-occurrence restrictions among English noun phrase quantifiers. Here, classification based on internal properties of quantifiers was much more directly involved.

Again, a number of transformational studies have attempted to fit directly quantified noun phrases (such as 'some men') and partitive noun phrases (such as 'some of the men') into an identical tree structure. McKeon, on the other hand, found more basic structure to the partitive noun phrase than to the directly quantified one. Further, there were more restrictions found between the head quantifier and the complement quantifier in partitives whose complements were introduced by the quantifiers each and every (as 'two out of every five students') than there were for partitives whose complements were introduced by a definite element. And finally, partitives with complements introduced by indefinite quantifiers (as 'three of some

men', 'many of a hundred books', etc.) were considered highly restricted and almost always anomalous (we shall refer to these latter
partitives as type 4 noun phrases in this study).

These conclusions in fact tell only half the story. Inadvertently,
the phenomena have been studied in a non-gradient framework: they
could only be valid for one particular set of idiolects at a time and
could not represent acceptability patterns for a larger portion of the
language community. McKeon himself had mentioned 'dialect' differences among permissible types of quantified noun phrases--following
general practice in transformational studies--and one interesting
difference was pointed out between his own speech and that of Barbara
Partee, where Partee, as opposed to McKeon, apparently permits
type 4 noun phrases with restrictive relative clauses. At any rate,
it appears that degree of acceptability (based on the number of
speakers who accept noun phrase X) correlates inversely with the
degree of constraint which McKeon found for the occurrence of the
different noun phrase types in the grammar. [2] In addition, data from
other languages corroborate in a general way the conclusions arrived
at by McKeon for English.

One can then postulate a syntactic condition which seems to occur
throughout language and which concerns the probability of specific
types of quantified noun phrases occurring as one unit. Perhaps we
can define its import as being that a partitive whose complement is
introduced by a quantifier other than a definite element preferably
does not occur in language; however, language-specific instances are
permitted in which such noun phrase types may occur, but they are
more 'marked' in some way: either more structured or less acceptable. From our point of view, the four-way classification of quantified noun phrase types hinted above seems to be the most relevant:
the directly quantified noun phrase, the partitive noun phrase with
definite complement (as 'some of the men',) the partitive noun phrase
with complement introduced by a distributive quantifier or a numeral
(as 'three out of every five men', 'much of each gallon', etc.) (type
3), and the partitive noun phrase with complement introduced by an
indefinite quantifier other than a numeral (as 'three of some men')
(type 4). The condition noted above then assumes in addition that the
partitive noun phrase with definite complement will be more 'marked'
in some way than a directly quantified noun phrase, and that a
partitive noun phrase of type 3 will be more acceptable than a partitive noun phrase of type 4. Hence it defines a hierarchy of markedness among four noun phrase types; that is, there is a gradient,
based on a number of factors, which can be compared across languages.

In English, the definite complement of a partitive noun phrase
appears to have no cooccurrence restrictions with quantifiers beyond

those that occur with directly quantified noun phrases (every must occur together with one, in partitives: 'every one of the books', but '*every of the books'). Both of these noun phrase types seem equally acceptable in all sets of idiolects in English. Technically speaking, approximately the same general range of cooccurrence relationships with the head quantifier appear possible with partitive noun phrase whose complements are introduced by each or every. This range occurs under very much the same restrictions. In addition, there are special restrictions, including one in which quantifiers which occur only before plural nouns (several, many, five, etc.) can occur as head quantifier only when each/every introduces a numeral plus plural noun ('five out of every hundred students'). Otherwise, each/ every introduces only singular count nouns--mass nouns are introduced with the help of measure nouns--and the occurrence of specific head quantifiers follows the restrictions that this entails. Hence it should be possible to find an idiolect which accepts a noun phrase such as 'several out of every 400 students', as opposed to '*several out of every student' or '*several out of every gallon of milk' (compare 'several of the 400 students', '*several of the student', '*several of the gallon of milk'). And we must also exclude the possibility of noun phrases such as '*each/every one out of every 400 students' as being acceptable in any idiolect. This latter restriction seems to correspond to a similar one governing definite elements, blocking noun phrases such as '*those of the books' (noun phrases such as '??ours of the books' seem marginal at best).[3]

Likewise, it is technically possible to find an idiolect where a partitive noun phrase introduced by a numeral can cooccur with the full range of quantifiers that can occur with count noun phrases: 'some of a hundred students', 'many of a hundred students', 'four out of 25 apples', 'any of 300 mice', 'every one of 25 leprechauns'. Such noun phrases, nevertheless, would have a much lower degree of acceptability among English speakers than would corresponding noun phrases with definite articles: 'some of the hundred students' 'four of the 25 apples', etc.

Finally, Barbara Partee's idiolect shows that it is possible to find instances where a partitive noun phrase whose complement is introduced by an indefinite quantifier like some or many may occur, at least when the complement noun phrase itself contains a restrictive relative clause. We can then presume that in such an idiolect, sentences of the following type have the highest probability of being accepted or at least used:

(1) Three of some people that just came in were wearing neckties.

    (2) Eighty-five out of <u>some</u> students who took the test did
        quite well on it.

    (3) A few of many people who attended the session on liquid
        properties were drunk.

On the other hand, the status of noun phrases like 'three of <u>some</u>
people', '85 out of <u>some</u> students', and 'a few of many people', without their restrictive relative clauses, in such a dialect, was not discussed by McKeon. Apparently, they would be rendered unacceptable,
or marginal at best, just as in the other dialects.

    For these last three types of quantified noun phrases--partitives
whose complements are introduced by <u>each</u> or <u>every</u>, by a numeral,
or by another indefinite quantifier, the patterns of acceptability
among speakers are clearly different from those associated with the
directly quantified noun phrase or partitive noun phrase with definite
complement. Speakers of English are far less unanimous about their
acceptability: this may be considered one possible consequence of the
condition defined at the beginning. Here, a measurement of the degree of acceptability among speakers is complicated by the variability in the type of reading that a noun phrase in these categories
may take. Interpretations for these types of noun phrases, wherever
they are acceptable at all, are no longer uniform: this is unlike the
case of the directly quantified noun phrases and the noun phrases with
definite complements. [4] Of course, this situation in readings applies
only to relationships internal to the noun phrase itself and not to
semantic influence across sentence elements.

    This phenomenon is best described through example sentences.
In the sentence:

    (4) Eighty-five out of a hundred students who took the test did
        quite well on it.

the complement noun phrase of the partitive is introduced by a <u>hundred</u>;
furthermore, it has a restrictive clause: this will be an essential
factor in some reading types. One possible reading for the noun
phrase is that of a ratio; i.e. 85/100ths of all the students who took
the test did quite well. The other possible reading is that of a
group: 85 students out of a group of 100 students who took the test
did quite well. In the example sentence:

    (5) Eighty-five out of every 100 students who took the test did
        quite well on it.

there are again two possible readings. First, there is the ratio
reading, this time rendered more explicit with the use of <u>every</u>,

where every 100 students ranges indiscriminately over a single set
of students. The second reading for this sentence would be: 85 out
of every group containing 100 students each--perhaps a hundred students in each room--who took the test, did quite well on it. Here,
unlike the first reading, there are separate sets of students involved.
The two readings are not equivalent and may have different truth
values: the statement that 85 out of every group containing 100 students each did quite well on the test implies that 85/100ths of all the
students did quite well on the test, but not vice-versa.

In contrast, the following two example sentences:

(6) Some out of a hundred students who took the test did quite
    well on it.
(7) Some out of every hundred students who took the test did
    quite well on it.

where the partitive noun phrase is introduced by some and not by a
numeral, can only take the non-ratio readings. That is, for the first
one, only a certain group of 100 students is involved; for the second
one, potentially several separate groups of 100 students each are.
Almost by definition, a ratio requires a cooccurrence of two numerals, or measure nouns, or both.

Finally, it is possible that sentences (1), (2), and (3) above may
each take an interpretation in the form of a stylistic combination of
two statements. [5] The first sentence would then say, in effect, that
some people just came in, and three of them were wearing neckties;
the second one that only some students in the school took the test,
and 85 out of these students did well on it. Similarly, the third sentence would say that many people attended the session, in addition to
stating that a few of them were drunk. This type of reading is related
to the non-ratio readings for the previous sentences, in that the complement of the partitive noun phrase semantically represents the entire
set of objects that are qualified by the lexical semantics of the complement noun phrase. That is, 'some people that just came in' refers
to the entire set of people that just came in; similarly, the total number of students who took the test was a hundred, and the noun phrase
'some students who took the test', again, represents the whole set
of students who took the test. The stressed some would contrast
this set of students with another set of students, which did not take
the test. Such a semantic relationship between quantifier and relative clause is different from the one found in the following sentence:

(8) Some students who took the test did well on it; others
    didn't do so well.

where the noun phrase in the first part of the sentence now semantically represents only a portion of the set of students who took the
test, even though it is the same noun phrase that occurs as the partitive complement in sentence (2). The question, then, is whether
such a reading, involving a portion, could be applied to the partitive
complement. There seems to be indication that it could.

These readings do not exclusively involve noun phrases with restrictive relative clauses in their complements. Partitive noun
phrases such as 85 out of a hundred students, where both quantifiers
are numerals, seem acceptable to almost all of the speakers that I
interviewed (see below). There are two readings for these, just as
there are two readings for the same noun phrases with their relative
clauses: that of the ratio, and that of one particular group of 100
students. For the latter reading, the connection with contextual presupposition is more salient; it may possibly include a 'hidden' relative clause. For example, in the sequence of sentences

(9) Some of the students in the school decided to take the test;
altogether, 85 out of a hundred students did well on it.

the phrase 'a hundred students' would be interpreted as 'the students
who took the test, which numbered 100'. The study of such a connection with contextual presupposition is a somewhat separate matter
which we will not go into here.

The classification postulated above thus implies that partitive
complements introduced by each or every and those introduced by
a numeral will have similar ranges of acceptability, both being more
acceptable than type 4 noun phrases. Further, the above discussion
implies that partitive complements for type 3 or type 4 noun phrases
with relative clauses should be more acceptable than complements
without relative clauses. The first point was fairly well borne out
in a survey carried out among native speakers, but there was a
significant difference in acceptability depending on whether the head
quantifier was a numeral or some. Sentences A, B, and C in Chart I
were much more acceptable than sentences F, G, and H. However,
sentences D and E, with some as head quantifier, are considerably
less acceptable than A, B, or C, and there is a great deal of disagreement. In both these cases, sentences with and without every
behave very much the same, although there seems to be more hesi-
tancy in accepting sentence C with every than there is in accepting
A or B, which do not have every.

The second point mentioned above was not borne out in the survey;
sentences A and B have virtually equal acceptability, although B has
a relative clause and A does not. And perhaps here we may note the

CHART I. Tentative percentage of acceptability of certain noun
phrase types among English speakers surveyed
(N = 70)

A = 85 out of a hundred students did quite well on the test.
B = 85 out of a hundred students who took the test did quite
well on it.
C = 85 out of every hundred students who took the test did
quite well on it.
D = Some out of a hundred students did quite well on the test.
E = Some out of every hundred students did quite well on the test.
F = Three of some people that just came in were wearing neckties.
G = Three of many women that John has been visiting lately
received a telephone call from his wife.
H = Four of many apples were still green.

	Acc.	Funny	Unacc.
A	98.6	–	1.4
B	97.2	–	2.8
C	80.0	8.6	11.4
D	32.8	25.7	41.5
E	28.6	22.8	48.6
F	0.0	41.4	58.6
G	27.1	32.8	40.1
H	8.5	28.5	63.0

difference between sentence F and sentence G in the chart: sentence
G is more acceptable among English speakers than F, although the
quantifiers in the partitive complements for both sentences are indefinite. The acceptability patterns of G, in fact, are similar to
those of D and E, where there is more disagreement among speakers.
And note again the steep difference in acceptability between noun
phrases with the numeral as head quantifier and those with some as
head quantifier. These findings underline the point that the hierarchy
proposed can predict only a very general trend in the acceptability of
partitive noun phrases, but since it is based only on the complement
part of the partitive, it does not directly predict differences among
partitive noun phrases which are due to particular occurrences of
first quantifiers. Several possible hypotheses for readjustment present themselves, but they require further testing to be borne out.

It also appears obvious that possible reading type does not correlate with degree of acceptability. The non-ratio interpretation in
which the partitive complement refers to a group is here coincident
with the indefinite quantifiers, including the numerals (putting aside
the definite elements for the present time). The ratio reading is here
connected exclusively with every or each and the numerals, and only

when the first quantifier is a numeral. Since these noun phrases are more acceptable, it would be easy to conclude that the ratio interpretation is preferable to the whole group interpretation within sentences that permit either reading: that is, the ratio reading should have a 'privileged' status. But this is not the case, apparently. Among the speakers interviewed, the group interpretation for these sentences strongly predominates, and only in sentence E in the set shown in Chart II are both interpretations equally probable. Again some hypotheses present themselves in regard to the difference between sentence E and the four preceding sentences--one of them perhaps involving numerical differences, and these would also require testing.[6]

CHART II. Percentage of reading probabilities among English speakers interviewed (N = 70)

A = 85 out of a hundred students did quite well on the test.
B = 85 out of a hundred students who took the test did quite
    well on it.
C = Four out of twenty-five apples were still green.
D = Four out of twenty-five apples that were brought in were
    still green.
E = Four out of five doctors recommend Jenkin's foot pads.

	Group	Ratio	Both	Unacc.
A	61.4	20.0	17.2	1.4
B	65.7	7.2	24.3	2.8
C	74.3	8.6	14.3	2.8
D	54.3	24.3	17.1	4.3
E	35.7	38.5	25.8	0.0

More generally, the results indicate that type of reading has very little bearing on the acceptability patterns pointed out so far. Note further, in Chart I, the weaker acceptability of sentence C, containing every, in comparison to the two preceding sentences, a fact that we have already noted.

Finally, we had assumed that the interpretation where the complement quantifier describes a portion of a set would not be applied as much as would an interpretation defining the entire set (see my discussion of sentences (1), (2), and (3) above). For a large number of speakers, those sentences where such a difference is relevant are unacceptable, except where the partitive complement is introduced by a numeral. The small amount of data taken from those who do accept these sentences appear not to bear out our assumption.

Up to now we have dealt only with English examples; however, the hypothesis above has been stated in the form of a universal: it claims that every language must have this general trend. We may, in this

CHART III. Number of speakers who selected entire versus portion set readings (N = 69)

A = 85 out of some students who took the test did quite well on it.			
	Entire set	Set portion	Both	Unacc.
A	11	17	5	36

light, compare the situation in English with that in French. We find that in French, just as in English, the partitive with definite complement may share the same permitted range of first quantifiers, with the directly quantified noun phrases (here I am considering noun phrases with de but no article as a directly quantified noun phrase (e.g. beaucoup de pommes, peu d'argent, etc.): the same applies to similar noun phrases in English: plenty of food, lots of toys, etc.). There is one additional restriction in some idiolects at least, where a partitive complement with the definite article is more acceptable with a restrictive relative clause or some other restrictive element than without one; that is, beaucoup des pommes qui étaient sur la table is more acceptable than simply beaucoup des pommes. Otherwise, the demonstrative ce is often used: beaucoup de ces pommes. For the other types of partitive noun phrases, it appears that the restrictions on acceptability involve significant differences between French and English, although the same general hierarchical relationships are maintained. This is brought out in a survey for French which was similar to the survey given in English, and perhaps we can make a comparison of some of these results.

CHART IV. Percentage of acceptability of certain noun phrase types among French speakers surveyed (N = 33)

A = 85 sur cent étudiants ont réussi l'examen.
B = 85 sur cent étudiants qui ont passé l'examen l'ont réussi.
C = 85 sur chaque centaine d'étudiants qui ont passé l'examen l'ont réussi.
D = Quelques-uns sur cent étudiants ont réussi l'examen.
E = Quelques-uns sur chaque centaine d'étudiants ont réussi l'examen.
F = Trois d'entre des personnes qui viennent d'entrer portaient des cravates.
G = Trois parmi plusieurs filles à qui Jean rendait récemment visite ont reçu un coup de téléphone de sa femme.
H = 85 parmi quelques étudiants qui ont passé l'examen l'ont reussi.
I = 85 sur chaque centaine d'étudiants ont réussi l'examen.

CHART IV. Continued

	Acc.	Funny	Unacc.
A	54.4	22.8	22.8
B	54.5	27.2	18.3
C	21.2	54.6	24.2
D	33.3	45.5	21.2
E	21.2	27.2	51.6
F	15.1	15.1	69.8
G	18.7	37.4	43.9
H	27.2	15.2	57.6
I	25.0	40.6	34.4

There was more disagreement in the acceptability of sentences A and B in Chart IV than there was for their English counterparts in Chart I. The use of chaque before a number in the same manner as every in the English partitive complement is much less acceptable, to such an extent that its degree of acceptability is not much higher than that of type 4 noun phrases. These differences in acceptability between the two languages can only be stated at present as being due to language-specific factors, and we will probably need to search out typical patterns in other parts of the grammar before we can account for these differences. There is also the danger that the surveys may have lost some of their sensitivity to crucial differences because of neglect of variables in other parts of the sentence or of the grammar, or an un-awareness, in either language, of the existence of equivalent locutions having different structural forms.

Looking briefly at Mandarin Chinese, we note right away that the directly quantified noun phrase is the only permitted type. Such noun phrases as '85 out of (every) 100 students' must be expressed by means of two separate noun phrases:

(10) dzài (měi)   yî-bǎi-míng tsān-jyā   kǎu-shr̀
     at   (every) one-hundred partake-in exam

    de̊   sywéshēng jr̄-jūng yǒu   bā-shŕ-wǔ-míng jî-gé-le.
    (Part.) students   among there-are eighty-five   passed.

This corresponds roughly to: 'Among (every) one hundred students who took the test, there were 85 that passed'. Separation of noun phrases occurs also in French and English, and these occurrences are related to the unified partitive noun phrase by means of movement transformations. Such a separation seems predictably more accept-able if the partitive complement is a 'heavy' noun phrase, as in the following sentences:

(11a) Out of a hundred students that took the test, 85 passed.
(11b) Out of every hundred students that took the test, 85 passed.
(11c) Sur cent étudiants qui ont passé l'examen, 85 l'ont réussi.

In French, the two components in this type of partitive noun phrase are in fact much more acceptable when separated than when combined under one NP node. This is shown in the two pairs of sentences in Chart V:

CHART V. Comparison of acceptability patterns for combined and separated components of partitive noun phrases in French

F = Trois d'entre des personnes qui viennent d'entrer portaient des cravates.			
G = Trois parmi plusieurs filles à qui Jean rendait récemment visite ont reçu un coup de téléphone de sa femme.			
FF = Parmi des personnes qui viennent d'entrer, trois portaient des cravates.			
GG = Parmi plusieurs filles à qui Jean rendait récemment visite, trois ont reçu un coup de téléphone de sa femme.			
	Acc.	Funny	Unacc.
F	15.1	15.1	69.8
G	18.7	37.4	43.9
FF	45.5	30.3	24.2
GG	78.8	21.1	0.0

Obviously, the hierarchy that we have proposed in the beginning predicts only a very general trend. Its purpose was to provide a general frame for expectations within which additional work can be done. There is still a question as to what notation will be the best means for finding generalizations from a study of these facts. Throughout the study, I have assumed the validity, in the transformational framework, of Dougherty's system of cross-classificatory features (which includes such features as [± exhaustive], [± count], [± definite], etc.), although I did not formulate the description in terms of this formal notational system. I felt that a less formal presentation would be adequate for our purposes; a more detailed study, however, will require a formal notation. It may be possible that, ultimately, specific features in Dougherty's system will need to be changed, or eliminated, or added, and quite probably such a feature system in toto is too superficial to some linguists, notably to those who have been in favor of a deeper, more abstract syntactic-semantic base. However, up to now, this has been the framework in which study of the partitive noun phrase has been developed the

furthest. In a situation where we wish to measure degree of acceptability among speakers of a language--and we are not aware of any
social parameters--the degree of probability of a restriction on a
certain cooccurrence of key features, or quantifiers, could be indicated by a percentage figure, following conventions for its application
in the quantificational approach. I have not attempted to propose an
implicational pattern in this study, and have retained the weaker hypothesis of a general gradation in degree of acceptability. A closer
examination of the possibility that the acceptability patterns correlate with cooccurrence of specific quantifier features will require a
great deal of further testing.

NOTES

I wish to thank Elyse Piquette, John Reighard, Norman Segalowitz,
Ann Roberts, and Irena Bellert for their assistance in carrying out
the surveys. Without their help, this study would not have been possible. All errors, of course, are my own.

1. The notion 'determiner' has covered a variable range of phenomena, depending on the description. It referred in fact not to a
class of words but to a particular node in the syntactic tree, whose
structural relationship with the noun phrase has varied with the
description. Other terms, such as 'pre-determiner' and 'post-
determiner' (or 'pre-article' and 'post-article') have also appeared.

2. Since the last three types of noun phrases mentioned above,
being partitives, have the same tree structure in McKeon's framework, the differences in grammaticality or degree of acceptability
must depend on the cross-classificatory features which occur in the
head and in the complement quantifiers.

3. These restrictions are discussed in McKeon (1972).

4. This last point is true in part; in English and perhaps other
languages directly quantified noun phrases often replace definite
complement noun phrases; hence one can say that directly quantified
noun phrases also vary in interpretation. For example, in the sentence 'A hundred boys took the test, and two boys failed it', 'two
boys' equals 'two of the boys (who took the test'). But this variation
seems fairly well constrained--the definite complement reading
would occur only if there was something in the preceding context
that facilitated it. This does not seem to be necessarily the case
for the other noun phrase types.

5. I wish to thank Rose-Marie Weber for her comments on these
sentences, which have led me to this observation.

6. On this point, nonlinguistic influences such as television ad-
vertising could also have a strong bearing: this was mentioned by
two or three of the speakers that I surveyed. Mention of external

influences such as this already assumes that the most natural reading for this sentence is not the ratio reading.

REFERENCES

Bickerton, Derek. 1971. Inherent variability and variable rules. Foundations of Language 7. 457-492.

Carden, Guy. 1973. Disambiguation, favored reading, and variable rules. In: New ways of analyzing variations in English. Edited by C-J. N. Bailey and R. W. Shuy. Washington, Georgetown University Press. 171-182.

Dougherty, Ray C. 1970-71. A grammar of coordinate conjoined structures I and II. Language 46. 850-898, 47. 298-339.

Jackendoff, Ray. 1968. Quantifiers in English. Foundations of Language 4. 422-442.

Lakoff, George. 1971. On generative semantics. In: Steinberg and Jakobovits. 232-296.

McCawley, James D. 1971. Where do noun phrases come from? In: Steinberg and Jakobovits. 217-231.

McKeon, Donald W. 1972. A grammar of quantified noun phrases in English. Ann Arbor, University Microfilms.

Perlmutter, David M. 1970. On the article in English. Unpublished.

Steinberg, D. D. and L. A. Jakobovits, eds. 1971. Semantics: An interdisciplinary reader in philosophy, linguistics, and psychology. New York, Cambridge University Press.

CARRYING THE NEW WAVE INTO SYNTAX: THE CASE OF BLACK ENGLISH BÍN[1]

JOHN R. RICKFORD

University of Pennsylvania

1. Introduction. Ever since the first conference on New Ways of Analyzing Variation in English was held in 1972, the abbreviated title-- NWAVE--has become something of a rallying cry ('The New Wave') to those interested in the study of linguistic variation. The enthusiasm is doubtless justified. Uneasiness with categorical frameworks has been growing for some time, and the remarks made by C.-J. N. Bailey in the introduction to the papers from NWAVE I (Bailey and Shuy 1973) would probably be endorsed by a great many (though by no means all) linguists today:

> I am happy to be rid of static homogeneous models and to be rid of the fudges represented by 'my dialect', 'performance component', 'optional', and the rest . . . (xiv)

However, as we move beyond initial revolutionary fervour, and begin a more sober stock-taking, certain weaknesses in our line of attack become increasingly clear. One salient limitation is the extent to which we have become preoccupied with morphophonemic and phonological variation to the exclusion of everything else. Syntax and semantics, for instance, have come to represent lone islands far out at sea, increasingly untouched by any waves--old or new.

The problem is particularly acute for those 'variationists' whose data consists of large samples of tape-recorded speech, covering as wide a range of stylistic contexts as possible (cf. Labov 1966, Bickerton 1972). While the advantages of this method in terms of 'accountability' etc. should be clear to most of us by now, it has a built-in

162

limitation in providing large masses of data only on those phenomena which show up with high frequency in natural speech. In most cases, these are phonological variables; hence the disproportionate number of variation studies in phonology.

It was precisely in response to this problem that Gillian Sankoff (1973) entitled her paper presented at the first NWAVE meeting 'Above and beyond phonology in variable rules'. There can be little doubt about the soundness of her primary thesis--that 'variability occurs, and can be dealt with, at levels of grammar above (or beyond) the phonological'. However, we can hardly fail to note that the pool of data examined in some of the studies she cited (for example, bai in Tok Pisin) is far smaller in the more customary studies of phonological phenomena. And that in others (Montreal que; cf. also the English copula as examined by Labov 1969) phonological features in the environment act as significant variable constraints. What of the other syntactic variables which show no or very little phonological conditioning? (We certainly know such cases exist.)

Finally, what of the other syntactic phenomena which tend to occur even less frequently than these--things about which not even the most basic linguistic facts are known, much less the kind of variation they display? Bickerton, in a recent issue of the Lectological Newsletter (March 1973) complained about the 'reams that have been written about the different things Black speakers do with their D's and Z's', but the 'next to nothing that has been written about the different ways Black speakers organize their tense systems'. But this is again because of the low frequency with which many of the most interesting Black English tense and aspect markers (e.g. Invariant Be, Remote BÍN) tend to show up in tape-recorded speech. This in turn is so not only because speakers have some awareness of the stigmatized nature of such forms, but also because the semantic conditions which they are normally introduced to express may occur rarely, if at all, in the course of a sociolinguistic interview.

Overcoming these limitations of tape-recorded data should certainly rank as one of the major challenges to riders of the 'New Wave'. But the problem has so far not received the attention it deserves. Innovations made in this area (cf. Labov 1972a) have not sparked off a chain of repeat performances (as many of Labov's innovations in sociolinguistic interview technique did in the 1960's). And issues of validity and reliability involved in such innovations still remain to be raised.

The purpose of this paper is to draw attention to some of the innovations in methodology which have already been achieved, and to demonstrate the application of two such methods to a syntactic case about which very little has been written so far--BÍN in Black English. Let us first review some of the methods available for overcoming the limitations of tape-recorded data with respect to syntactic and other low-frequency phenomena.

One possibility is the method of 'surreptitious' or 'candid' recording. As it has been demonstrated publicly and dramatically for us most recently, this method involves tape-recording what people say without their knowledge or permission. The hope of the strongest advocates of this method is that speakers, unhampered by the constraints of the typical interview situation, will produce more of those syntactic and other variables which are normally stigmatized. While this is certainly true to the extent that other aspects of the speech-situation (for example, nature of the participants) do not have a more powerful over-riding effect, it is simply the case that we cannot have our 'hidden tape-recorder' with us at all times. We will always be exposed to more speech than we shall ever have the opportunity to record. The other disadvantages of this method--poor quality of recordings, discovery and its consequences, quite apart from the ethics involved, are also well known. Together, they suggest that despite its devilish appeal, this possibility will be of limited utility.

Another method involves 'enriching the data of tape-recorded conversation' by including questions and topics which stimulate more frequent use of rare forms or environments than might occur naturally (Labov 1972b). The method works excellently in some cases. If you will pardon the use of a phonological example for effect, let me cite one case from recent studies at the University of Pennsylvania, of the tensing and raising of (æ). The problem was to elicit a natural production of the word 'sad'. One student discovered that a highly successful way of doing this was to ask interviewees if they had ever seen the movie 'Love Story'. Almost inevitably the word would crop up--repeatedly--in the ensuing discussion.

The method demands careful attention to the nature of everyday conversational interaction. But it demands more. Most of the crucial syntactic/semantic variables (like B. E. BÍN) are extremely difficult to elicit, paradoxically, unless we already know a great deal about their meaning and use.

The final two methods are more immediately feasible to the researcher. Both move beyond the use of tape-recorded data, though in very different ways. The first has been used extensively by students of variation in 'abstract syntax', for example, those interested in syntactic features which have no clear regional or social roots. In its more sophisticated form, this method involves eliciting the intuitions of other people and analyzing the results for patterns of variation, increasingly, with the help of implicational scales (Elliot, Legum, and Thompson 1969; C. J. Bailey 1970; Baltin 1973; Carden 1971; Sag 1973). The method has been extended, with important innovations, to the study of syntactic variation which is governed by

regional and social factors (Labov 1972a), and is being hailed by
others (Butters 1973) as the most promising methodology for overcoming the limitations of tape-recorded data. However, as mentioned
before, issues of validity and reliability are most acute with this
method, and as it is usually employed, no independent check on the
results is available.

The final method is one which has been used very rarely in studies
to date. It involves careful and intense participant observation.
Whether our interest is in Black English, Puerto-Rican English,
British English, or more abstract varieties, we exploit our contacts
with native speakers to record on 3-by-5 cards every possible use of
the variable in which we are interested. At the suggestion of Bill
Labov, several students at the University of Pennsylvania have been
using this method for some time now. We never cease to be amazed
at the frequency with which even the rarest variables begin to show up
once we are constantly attending to them in this way. The advances of
this method over the others are also clear. Not only are we able to
gather the most reliable data--from natural conversation--but we can
gather it anywhere, anytime, without the need of any technical equip-
ment. (Note too that permission to scribble away in the midst of on-
going conversations is more easily extended than permission to run a
tape-recorder, partly because it is less potentially damaging to participants.)

My own studies of B. E. BÍN have depended largely on a combination of the last two methods. The 'intuitive data' consists of the
responses of a sample of twenty-five Black and twenty-five White
subjects to a questionnaire designed to explore their ability to interpret, predict, and evaluate the use of BÍN. This questionnaire, entitled Q-SCOM-IV, was an extension of similar ones (Q-SCOM-I to
III) which had been developed and used by Bill Labov and other members
of a research group in which I participated two years ago (cf. Labov
1972a). In Q-SCOM-IV, several more aspects of BÍN usage were attacked, and the questions about other variables served principally as
'distractors'. The subjects were drawn from very diverse geographical backgrounds (including Pennsylvania, New York, California, North
Carolina, and Massachusetts), and were interviewed individually. [I
should like to thank here Angela Rickford and Karl Reisman for their
help with this time-consuming process.]

Participant observation was carried out in two widely separate
Black communities--one in West Philadelphia, the other in the Sea
Islands off the coast of South Carolina. Living in these communities,
I was able to draw on a wide range of conversational encounters in
which BÍN, supposedly rare, was frequently used. Although I heard
many more than I was able to note down, I was able to gather about
sixty-six sentences with stressed BÍN. Most of my sentences, it

should be noted, come from adults over the age of twenty-four--pro-
viding strong contradictory evidence to the frequently voiced claim
that the central syntactic structures of Black English are regularly
used only by young Black children or adolescents.

It is clearly impossible to present all the findings of this research
in the time available to me today. I shall consider only three central
aspects about BÍN on which there seems to be disagreement or limited
information in the published literature: (A) The significance of stress
(i. e. BÍN = bĭn ?); (B) Meaning and Use; (C) Productivity--Cooccur-
rence Relations. I shall try to maintain a balance between substantive
findings about BÍN itself and theoretical questions about the two methods
employed. In particular I shall be interested in the internal consistency of the intuitive responses, and the extent to which they are supported by data from participant observation.

2. Three issues in the study of Black English BÍN

A. The significance of stress (i. e. BÍN = bĭn ?). The been which
we are interested in is the form which has been mentioned in the literature as signalling some 'remote' past tense or perfective aspect. [2]
We shall explore the precise meaning of the form in the next section.
Here we simply want to know how significant stress is to the remote
function with which the form has typically been associated.

Previous researchers have been quite divided on this point. [3]
Stewart (1965), the first to draw attention to the form, indicated that
stress was obligatory. Fasold and Wolfram (1970) feel that stress
on been is an optional element only, its function being to 'doubly
emphasize the total completion of an action'. Fickett (1970) shares
their view on the optionality of stress, but for her its function is to
distinguish been as a Phase Auxiliary (with remote function) from
been as the auxiliary of a passive. The latter, in her analysis,
never receive stress.

Dillard (1972) suggests that there may have existed two systems
all along: one in which stressed BÍN is a remote, and unstressed
bĭn a recent perfective; and another in which been (regardless of
stress) is remote, and done a recent perfective. He adds that the
latter system 'has had most widespread influence in the U. S. ' but
that the former 'still survives in some forms of Black English'.

When we turn to the intuitive responses of Black subjects on this
point, we find similar divisions and ambiguities. (1) below indicates
the questions relevant to this is Q-SCOM-IV:

(1) 17b. Could you say 'I bĭn know it' (unstressed) and mean
the same thing as 'I BÍN know it' (stressed)? Yes___
No___

9a. He BÍN had one. 9b. He bĭn had one. Same___
Different___
15a. He BÍN sick. 15b. He bĭn sick. Same___
Different___

Question 17b for instance, was asked after subjects had responded
to the meaning of stressed BÍN, usually with tremendous agreement
on the remote function of this form. The question was whether one
could say the unstressed form bĭn and mean the same thing. Nine
said yes, ten said no. Similarly, twelve felt that 9a and 9b were the
same, and ten that they were not.

As Table 1 indicates, the number of informants who were consistent in their responses on this issue is even smaller:

TABLE 1. Consistency response of Black subjects to 17b, 9
and 15 in Q-SCOM-IV

N	Positive responses			Negative responses		
	Yes to 17b	Yes 17b Same 9	Yes 17b Same 9 Same 15	No to 17b	No 17b Diff 9	No 17b Diff 9 Diff 15
19	9	8	6	10	7	7

Positive responses are those which suggest that BÍN and bĭn are
equivalent. Negative responses, that they are different. While there
are only six informants who consistently see the two forms as equivalent, and seven who consistently see them as different, note again
what an even split this is. This is the pattern that is repeated regularly, no matter how the question of BÍN = bĭn is put, nor how the
answers are analyzed. This might be taken to suggest that Dillard
(1972) is right--that there are two systems for signalling 'remote'
tense. In one the stress on been is significant, in the other it is not.

As variationists, there should be nothing uncomfortable about this
conclusion. But before we accept it, let us turn to the data gathered
in participant observation. From a total of sixty-six BÍN sentences,
and over two hundred with unstressed bĭn, the data is quite clear and
conclusive on this point. Only stressed BÍN can signal remote function by itself, as is clear from the contexts in which it is used.

Unstressed bin occurs frequently with temporal adverbs or
'specifiers', as in

(2) I bĭn playing cards since I was four. (BF 38, Pa)[4]

Since this is often the case, it is possible to see how one might
arrive at the mistaken impression that unstressed bĭn signals remote

aspect. However, it is the time adverbial that signals the function in these cases, not the unstressed bĭn form. Not only are such time-adverbials unnecessary with stressed BÍN, they are restricted from co-occurring with it. This syntactic consequence of the semantic difference between the two forms is illustrated most strikingly when the two follow close upon each other in the discourse:

(3) I BÍN know you, you know. I bĭn knowing you for years.
    BM 59, Pa)

The only case in which time adverbials appear to co-occur with BÍN is in utterances like (4):

(4) He BÍN home--since last week. (BM 41, Pa)

However the time adverbial here does not, as in (2) or (3) occur as part of a single 'sentence intonation pattern'. It is separated from the main clause both by pause and by falling intonation on home. And in fact an analysis of (4) as derived from (4') seems quite sound:

(4') He BÍN home. He bĭn home since last week.

There is other evidence that BÍN and bĭn are different. Note the following sentence:

(5) He bĭn doing it ever since we was teenagers, and he still doing it. (BM 41, Pa)

The conjoined qualification 'and he still doing it' would be redundant if BÍN+V-ing were used. As we shall see in a moment, the meaning 'Remote Phase Continuative' would be implicit in the form itself.
    Although most of the examples with unstressed bĭn are not preceded by forms of have, there are a few which are, and seem nevertheless to carry the same semantic force. For instance:

(6) Cause I've bĭn through it. I've bĭn through them changes.
    (BM 26, Pa)

On the basis of this, it may be possible to describe most instances of B. E. bĭn for Philadelphia, at least, as 'Present Perfects'. This is not the case with stressed BÍN.
    There are also several cases of unstressed bĭn with done as first auxiliary, as in:

(7) Get to work, start talking to them girls, they done bĭn locked up fifteen times! (BF 38, Pa)

There is a rare occurrence of BÍN + done, as in the Sea-Island sentence:

(8) Boy, if we had shrimp, we'd a BÍN done got us some fish! (BM 11, SI)

but none whatsoever of done + BÍN.

In the Sea-Island data, stressed BÍN and unstressed bĭn must also be separated on syntactic and semantic grounds. One difference between the two forms, here as in Philadelphia, is the possibility of treating many instances of bĭn as 'Present Perfects'. But there are other differences here. Unstressed bĭn is sometimes used as a straight equivalent of was, indicating simple past tense. Note the close alternation between the two forms in (9):

(9) I don't know if that snake bĭn coil, or either was stretch out or what. (BM 52, SI)

Used before a verb-stem, unstressed bĭn has the additional ambiguity of signalling either 'Past' or 'past before the Past':

(10) But the real medicine what I bĭn want fuh get fuh Joo-Joo . . . (BF 78, SI)
'But the real medicine which I had wanted to get for Joo-Joo . . .'

Finally, bĭn but not BÍN occurs before continuative a:

(11) How bout that thing wuh B bĭn a tell you? (BM 67, SI)
'How about that thing which B was telling you?'

These uses of unstressed bĭn are of course well known in other creole areas (cf. for Jamaican Creole, B. Bailey 1966; for Sierra Leone Krio, Jones 1968; for Guyana Creole, Bickerton 1974). The point here is not to pursue the use of bĭn in any detail, but simply to indicate the ways in which it differs from BÍN in semantic function and syntactic co-occurrence restrictions.

Enough has been said so far to demonstrate the point with which I started out, that on the basis of the participant observation data, BÍN and bĭn must be distinguished. In the light of this, what are we to make of the intuitive judgments of Black respondents, who, as indicated above, were evenly divided on this issue? It may be that those

who claimed the forms were equivalent were speakers of some 'other'
dialect which has simply not been tapped in my own participant observation. This is possible, but I think, unlikely. First of all, the respondents were, as we shall see, in unanimous agreement on the
meaning and interpretation of stressed BÍN. Secondly, I know that
at least one of the respondents who suggested that the two forms were
equivalent, consistently distinguishes them in his everyday speech.
I am more inclined to think that what we are dealing with here is a
weakness of the 'intuitive method' itself.

Let me mention two possible sources of error which have already
come to light. One is the real difficulty which some subjects had in
hearing 'unstressed' forms of bĭn. They would repeat question 9b, for
instance, with lighter stress on bin than the stress on BÍN in 9a, but
it would still be primary in that sentence.

This difficulty may have been the result of a second factor. For
some informants, unstressed bĭn + V-ed (non-passive) is not a real
possibility at all. These informants accept and say 'I BÍN had that'
but not 'I bĭn had that'. Faced with the latter, they cannot see it as
contrastive, may not even hear the difference in this environment.
Note that when BÍN and bĭn are contrasted in another environment in
which both are possible for all informants, as in question 15: He
BÍN sick vs. He bĭn sick, five of the twelve informants who had seen
them as equivalent in 9 now saw them as different. It is clear that
in any repeated version of this questionnaire serious attempts to
overcome these difficulties will have to be made. What is demonstrated here, in this very first issue about BÍN, is the value of data
from participant observation in challenging and qualifying the data
from intuitive responses.

    B. BÍN--meaning and use. Previous researchers have applied
a variety of labels to the Black English form BÍN (I ignore hence-
forth the issue of stress): 'Completive Perfect' (Stewart op. cit.)
'Remote Past' (Fasold and Wolfram 1970), 'Remote Perfective'
(Dillard 1972) 'Perfect Phase' (Fickett 1970). What they are all
trying to express via these different labels is essentially the same.
That BÍN places the action in the distant past (relative to the present
axis) and/or that it expresses 'total completion of the event'. One
Standard English paraphrase that has been used frequently to register
this fact is the time adverbial 'a long time ago'. This is perfectly
appropriate for some of the BÍN sentences which I collected in Philadelphia and the Sea Islands, for instance (12):

    (12) She ain't tell me that today, you know. She BÍN tell me
         that. (BF 32, SI)
         'She told me that a long time ago'

However, this gloss, and the semantic notion of a totally completed action in the distant past, is appropriate only for a subset of the Participant-observation data--those in which BÍN is followed by non-stative verbs. With stative verbs, or with either kind in the progressive, the function of BÍN is different. Instead of expressing completion of the associated process (a cover term for action or state) it asserts only that it began in the distant past and is still very much in force at the moment of speaking. In both of these cases, a better S. E. paraphrase would be 'for a long time', e.g.:

(13) I BÍN had this. (BM 6, Pa)
   'I've had this for a long time'
(14) I BÍN treating them like that. (BF 25, Pa)
   'I've been treating them like that for a long time'

The similarities and differences between BÍN as used with non-statives on the one hand, and statives and progressives on the other, is more graphically illustrated in (15)

(15)

	Remote Anterior	Anterior	Point of Orientation
Statives	X-----------------|-----------------|------		
Non-statives	XY		
Progressives	X-----------------|----------|------		

In (15), X indicates the initiation of the 'process' and Y the end-point.

If we wish to formulate a conjunctive definition for BÍN we would have to say that it places the initiation of a process at some point in the distant past. 'Remote Phase' is perhaps the most appropriate label for this function. [5] It could then be extended (Remote Phase Continuative, Remote Phase Completive) to describe the particular effect of using the form with statives and progressives as against non-statives. It should be mentioned here that almost all the examples given by previous researchers involve non-stative verbs. This may be one element in their failure to perceive the more comprehensive nature of BÍN. This failure in turn is reflected in the labels they chose for the form--all of which suggest a Remote Phase Completive function only. Let us now turn to the intuitive responses on the meaning and use of BÍN to discover the extent to which they support or qualify the above analysis. In (16), the main questions in Q-SCOM-IV relevant to this issue are presented. Note that they go beyond simply asking what the form means, and try to get subjects to look through the grammar into the real world (cf. Labov 1972a).

(16) Q-SCOM-IV questions on the meaning of BÍN:

1. Someone asked, 'Is she married?' and someone else
    answered, 'She BÍN married'. Do you get the idea
    that she is married now? Yes___ No___
3. Bill was about to be introduced to this guy at a party,
    but when he saw him, he said, 'Hey, I BÍN know his
    name!' Which of these three things do you think he's
    most likely to say next:
    a. Give me a minute and I might remember it.
    b. He's John Jones. I saw his picture in the papers
        yesterday.
    c. He's John Jones. I've been hearing about him for
        years.
    So, what do you think Bill meant when he said, 'I
    BÍN know his name?' Choose the one that is closest
    to what you think:
    d. Used to know.
    e. Already knew.
    f. Know, but can't quite remember.
    g. Know right now.
    h. Have known for a long time, and still do.
    i. Other_____.
16. Frank asked his friend if he had paid off the bill on
    his new stereo, and got the answer, 'I BÍN paid for
    it'. Does he mean:
    a. I've already paid for it.
    b. I was paying for a long time, but I'm finished now.
    c. I paid for it long ago.
    d. I've been paying for it for a long time, and
        haven't finished yet.
    e. Other_____.

The responses appropriate to a 'Remote Phase' interpretation of
BÍN were: Yes to 1, (c) and (h) to 3, (c) to 16. If we multiply the
number of responses by the number of individuals in each group, we
derive a total of one hundred possible responses. From the start,
the difference between Black and White respondents on this issue is
clear. For the Blacks, 87 percent of the responses were appropriate to a 'Remote Phase' interpretation. Only 37 percent of the White
subjects' responses were.

The overwhelming agreement among Black respondents and their
difference from White subjects on this issue is demonstrated even
more clearly in Table 2, which displays the number of consistent
Remote Phase interpretations:

TABLE 2. Consistent 'Remote Phase' interpretations to Q's
1, 16, 3

Group	N	Yes to 1	Yes to 1 (c) to 16	Yes to 1 (c) to 16 (c) to 3	Yes to 1 (c) to 16 (c) to 3 (h) to 3
Blacks	25	23	21	19	15
Whites	25	8	4	1	1

Note that while fifteen of the Black respondents end up giving completely consistent 'Remote Phase' interpretations, only one of the White respondents manages to do so. As it turns out, he is a native of Greensboro, North Carolina, who claims to have extensive contact with Blacks throughout his life.

The responses can be just as dramatically reviewed the other way around. In Table 3, the consistent Non-'Remote Phase' interpretations of Blacks and Whites are tabulated:

TABLE 3. Consistent Non-'Remote Phase' interpretations to
Q's 1, 16, 3

Group	N	No to 1	No to 1 ~ (c) to 16	No to 1 ~ (c) to 16 ~ (c) to 3	No to 1 ~ (c) to 16 ~ (c) to 3 ~ (h) to 3
Blacks	25	2	1	0	0
Whites	25	17	14	12	10

Note that there are only two Black respondents who give Non-'Remote-Phase' interpretations to 1 to begin with, and by the time non-remote interpretations to 1, 16, and 3 are combined, none of the Black respondents are involved. By contrast, seventeen of the White respondents gave non-remote interpretations to 1, and ten maintained the same interpretation throughout.

Considering that a certain amount of chance error may always be present in investigations of this type, the tremendous regularity that is revealed here is highly significant. Both the 'participant observation' and the 'intuitive' data converge strongly to endorse a 'Remote Phase' interpretation for Black English BÍN. In addition, both data sources suggest that Black and White speakers are sharply divided in their abilities to use and interpret the form. The only other feature which has ever been shown to differentiate the two groups so sharply and reliably is their ability to understand the African-derived forms

'Cut-eye' and 'Suck-Teeth' and enact the non-verbal behavior to which these refer (cf. Rickford and Rickford 1974).

Finally, we may consider the overt responses of Black and White subjects to questions designed to explore their familiarity with and use of BÍN. The results are tabulated in Table 4.

TABLE 4. Positive responses to familiarity and use questions

Group	Have you ever heard BÍN?	Do you say BÍN yourself?
Blacks	24/25 = 96%	17/25 = 68%
Whites	16/24 = 67%	3/22 = 13%

Insofar as these results indicate what we would have suspected from participant-observation anyway, that more Blacks have heard and use BÍN than Whites, they seem generally valid. But the details are questionable. Sixteen Whites claim to have heard BÍN, and three to use it themselves. But in view of their responses on the 'meaning' questions reported on above, these claims are at least suspect. Interestingly enough, of the three Whites who claimed to 'say BÍN' themselves, two gave consistent Non-'Remote-Phase' interpretations to all four meaning-questions, and the other one gave a similar interpretation to two out of four. It is probable that these particular subjects were trying to claim familiarity with what they perceived as a 'Black' idiom because it was in some sense fashionable to do so.

The reverse process undoubtedly operated in the case of some Black subjects. Some of those who claimed not to say the form themselves modified it in subsequent discussion to 'at least not anymore'. For them, BÍN as a non-standard feature had a stigma which they would just as soon avoid.[6] In any case, the almost unanimous claim of Black subjects that they had at least heard the form is more credible, in the light of the high percentage of 'Remote Phase' interpretations on the meaning questions.

I might only add that BÍN is understood by a range of Black subjects considerably wider than is normally associated with the Black English vernacular. I once informally asked a few of the 'meaning' questions at a dinner party. The lone Black informant in this group, a Philadelphia judge, was rather surprised to discover that he was immediately distinguished from the other 'subjects' by his ability to give the 'correct' Remote-Phase interpretations. From his normal level of speech, one would hardly have classed him as a speaker of 'Black English'. But his ability to interpret BÍN in the same way that other B. E. speakers do, indicates the deep-seated sensitivity and exposure to this form that exists among Black Americans, of all levels, and suggests a possible creole history. It also raises the crucial issue of whether linguistic grammars should be written on the basis of 'productive' or 'receptive' competence. To explore this issue at any further length is clearly beyond the scope of this paper.

C. The productivity of BÍN--co-occurrence relations. The final issue which I shall take up is the productivity of BÍN in the grammar of Black English. The only environment in which earlier investigators found BÍN to occur was before V+ed. Dillard (1972) also found it before V-ing. But the picture that emerges from the participant-observation data is that BÍN is far more productive in Black English than this. In addition to V+ed and V-ing, it can be followed by:

(a) Locatives:
    (17) Oh, it BÍN in this house. (BM 6, Pa)

(b) Adverbs:
    (18) Them crab BÍN off. (BM 46, SI)

(c) Verb-Stem alone
    (19) She BÍN quit school. (BM 15, SI)

(d) Passive Participles (contrary to Fickett 1970's claim), both with and without got:
    (20) My hair BÍN cut. (BM 29, SI)
    (21) He shoulda BÍN got shot. (BM 25, Pa)

(e) Modal or Done + Verb-(ed):
    (22) I BÍN could walk on them stilts. (BF 16, SI)
    (23) Boy, if we had shrimp, we'd a BÍN done got us some fish. (BM 11, SI)

Finally, as some of the examples here have already indicated, BÍN is frequently preceded by the modals coulda, shoulda, and woulda.

In order to discover the reliability of co-occurrence patterns which showed up in the participant-observation data and to discover the status of patterns which had not been attested at all, we included a series of sentences (a-n) in Q-SCOM-IV, and asked subjects to indicate whether they found them acceptable ('Given that you could say "I BÍN know that", could you also say . . . ?'). The sentences themselves are reprinted in Table 6 which displays the results in the form of an implicational array. First, however, we want to consider the extent to which Black and White groups differed in their acceptability ratings in general. This data is tabulated in Table 5.

TABLE 5. Positive acceptability ratings for sentences in Q. 18,
Q-SCOM-IV

Group	N	a	b	c	d	e	f	g	h	i	j	k	l	m	n
Blacks	25	23	23	18	18	19	8	15	15	15	18	19	23	22	5
Whites	23	17	14	17	18	13	8	12	17	10	15	14	11	14	7

There are one or two striking differences in the acceptability ratings
given to particular sentences by members of the two groups: twenty-
three Blacks but only eleven Whites endorsed (18l): 'They BÍN ended
that war'; twenty-two Blacks but only fourteen Whites endorsed (18m):
'I BÍN knowing that guy'. But these are sentences which were already
well-documented from the participant observation data. On the acceptability ratings of lesser attested or unattested sentences, the difference
between the two groups are virtually identical (cf. ratings for (18d) and
(18f). This is surprising, in view of the overwhelming difference between the two groups which was registered in their interpretations of
the meaning of BÍN. This equivalence in the ratings of the two groups
is the first piece of evidence to suggest that there is more random
variation here; that somehow, in this section of the questionnaire, we
have failed to elicit the richer knowledge of the syntactic relations of
BÍN which Black speakers must certainly possess in order to understand and use it as consistently as we know they do. Many different
interpretations for our failure here suggest themselves. Part of the
difficulty may lie in the technique of asking subjects to rate a string
of sentences all at once. But Labov's (1971) remarks on idiosyncratic
judgments made by informants to extremely rare alternants undoubtedly
also apply here. Labov suggested that these might not be part of
langue, but rather some kind of intuitive parole, and 'if so, we need
techniques that will enable us to stop short of (such) intuitive judgments' (1971:447-448). Finally, it may be that both groups predict
the extension of BÍN to other points in the grammar on the basis of
their knowledge of the syntactic possibilities with Standard English
unstressed beĕn. If this is so, we have again failed to get at the true
set of possible co-occurrence patterns with Black English BÍN, for as
indicated in section A above, these can be quite different from bĭn.

I have not yet identified the real source of the problem here, nor
have I attempted as yet any workable solutions. However, the data
remains useful--if only for demonstrating the kinds of difficulties
which we might encounter in asking for acceptability ratings for sentences. There are more. Disregarding the questions Table 5 has
already led us to raise concerning the reliability of the data we are
getting here, let us go on to squeeze it, as is usually done, for all
that it is worth.

Table 6 represents the results of the acceptability ratings of Black subjects in the form of an implicational array. As usual, what this 'implicational scale' implies is: (a) sentences to the left are more generally acceptable than sentences to the right; (b) if a subject finds a certain sentence acceptable, he will also find all sentences to the left of this (in the implicational array) acceptable.

In general, the hierarchical ranking of these sentences in terms of acceptability can be supported somewhat by the participant observation data. As already indicated, the two sentences most acceptable (furthest to the left) are well represented in the data from actual speech. And the three least acceptable (or furthest to the right): (h) He done BÍN locked up, (f) He BÍN bin gone, and (n) I have BÍN had that, have never been attested. The two next least acceptable sentences, including BÍN-could and BÍN-done have been attested only rarely, and only in the Sea-Islands. Since none of the respondents were from this area, their low acceptability rating is understandable. However, there are a few striking surprises. For instance, 'He BÍN got messed up', a pattern represented in the Philadelphia data, is ranked much further down the line than we would expect. And the BÍN-NP pattern represented in (a) He BÍN the leader, is ranked as third most acceptable, but has never been attested. Thus the ranking of the sentences cannot be simply taken at face-value either.

To continue the discussion at this level would be to miss the whole point of the methodology of 'implicational scaling' as it is usually applied to linguistic behavior or intuitions (cf. Bailey 1970, Bickerton 1973). Implicational scales are less valuable for the ranking of particular sentences (we could achieve more or less the same results just by noting percentages of positive responses) than for isolating the 'lects' (and their membership) which they may be taken to define. If we follow the solid line as it cuts upward and to the right across the table, separating mainly 'positive' ratings from mainly 'negative' ones, we find that no less than eleven different 'lects' are found to exist among these twenty-five different subjects. (For instance, B15 and B5 share lect 1, the most 'liberal' lect; and B1 is the only representative of lect 11, the most 'conservative' one). This by itself seems highly questionable. If we could find so many 'lects' among only twenty-five speakers, what would happen if we increase both the number of sentences, and the pool of subjects, to any significant extent? Would we truly be prepared to accept the proliferating number of 'lects' as having any solid basis in reality?

Furthermore, there is absolutely no evidence in the participant-observation data for these eleven different lects. Obviously, the method here is telling us far more than we can reasonably assume to be true. Its results are not supported by any of the independent evidence presently available. All this is the more striking because of the

TABLE 6. Implicational array for Black subjects' acceptability ratings to BÍN sentences in question 18, Q-SCOM-IV (Deviations circled, Scalability = 88.9%)

Subjects	Ved: They BÍN ended that war. (l)	Ving: I BÍN knowing him. (b)	NP: He BÍN the leader. (a)	've had: I've BÍN had that car. (m)	Pass.: The chicken BÍN ate. (d)	knew: I BÍN knew your name. (k)	got Pass.: He BÍN got messed up. (e)	have: I BÍN have that. (j)	Adj.: She BÍN nice. (c)	Modal: I BÍN could do that. (i)	done: He BÍN done gone. (g)	done: He done BÍN locked up. (h)	bin: He bin bin gone. (f)	have had: I have BÍN had that. (n)
B 15	+	+	+	+	+	+	+	+	+	+	⊕	+	+	+
B 5	+	+	+	+	+	+	+	+	⊕	+	+	+	+	+
B 19	⊕	+	+	+	+	+	+	+	+	+	+	+	+	−
B 8	+	+	+	+	⊕	+	+	+	+	+	+	+	+	−
B 21	+	+	+	+	+	+	+	+	+	⊕	+	+	−	−
B 12	+	+	+	+	⊕	+	+	+	+	+	+	+	−	−
B 3	+	+	+	+	⊕	⊕	+	+	+	⊕	+	+	−	−
B 24	+	+	+	⊕	+	+	+	+	+	+	+	+	−	−
B 4	+	⊕	+	+	+	⊕	+	+	+	+	+	+	−	−
B 22	+	+	+	⊕	+	+	+	+	+	+	+	+	−	−
B 25	+	+	+	+	+	+	+	+	+	+	+	+	−	−
B 6	⊕	+	+	+	+	+	⊕	+	+	+	+	+	−	−
B 11	+	+	+	+	+	+	+	+	+	+	+	+	−	−
B 16	+	+	+	+	+	+	−	+	+	+	+	+	−	−
B 23	+	+	+	+	+	+	−	−	+	+	−	+	⊕	⊕
B 13	+	+	+	+	+	+	⊕	−	−	−	⊕	⊕	−	−
B 14	+	+	+	+	+	+	−	−	−	−	⊕	⊕	−	−
B 7	+	+	⊕	+	+	+	−	−	−	−	⊕	−	−	−
B 17	+	+	+	+	+	+	−	−	⊕	−	⊕	−	−	−
B 18	+	+	+	+	+	+	−	⊕	⊕	−	−	−	−	−
B 2	+	+	+	+	+	+	−	−	−	−	⊕	−	⊕	⊕
B 20	+	+	+	+	+	+	−	−	−	−	−	⊕	−	−
B 9	+	+	+	+	−	−	−	−	−	−	−	⊕	−	−
B 10	+	+	−	−	⊕	⊕	−	⊕	−	−	⊕	−	−	−
B 1	+	−	⊕	⊕	−	−	−	⊕	−	−	−	−	⊕	−

high scalability (88.9%) which this table manages to achieve.[7] Scalability figures like these are often included in the literature, supposedly to represent the 'statistical reliability' of the implicational array. But the evidence suggests that in this case, and perhaps others, such figures may mean very little. Far more work remains to be done in developing reliable statistical and linguistic measures of the reliability and validity of implicational arrays.[8]

3. Conclusion

The weaknesses in the intuitive data revealed at various points in the preceding discussion of BÍN merit serious attention. For it is precisely the same method, eliciting judgments of the equivalence or acceptability of various sentences, and arranging the results in implicational arrays, which, as mentioned before, is most frequently used in the study of abstract syntactic 'squishes', and is winning devotees among those interested in social and regional variation. The results revealed in this paper, along with other limitations previously noted (Labov, Hindle, and Baltin [to appear]) should give us pause. They should also force us to consult, perhaps for the first time, a handful of research which has already explored in some detail various issues involved in the elicitation of linguistic judgments (Bolinger 1968, Gleitman 1967, Quirk and Svartvik 1966). I discovered these too late to affect the course of my own elicitations. But most work involving the study of linguistic intuitions seems equally uninformed by the insights and suggestions represented in this tiny literature.

We might indicate in closing one way in which the work on BÍN discussed in this paper seems to relate to some of this work on 'intuitive judgment methodology'. Bolinger (1968:39) had suggested:

> Perhaps we are not asking the right question when we inquire whether a given sentence or sentence-type is grammatical-- we should ask instead whether it has a meaning, (and) determine what the meaning is . . .

The highly successful results of our 'intuitive data' on the meaning of BÍN, contrasted with the far more ambiguous and questionable results on the acceptability of BÍN sentences, suggests that Bolinger may well be right on this point. (Cf. also the successful investigations of the meaning of 'Cut-Eye' and 'Suck-Teeth'--Rickford and Rickford 1974). But this again is exactly the opposite of what is being done in the growing number of variation studies employing 'intuitive' data.

It is clear that we shall have to be far more critical about the use of elicited intuitive data than we are presently. Intuitions can be

invaluable resources. But, contrary to past and present expectations,
they are not necessarily or universally so. What questions we can
ask, what answers we can accept, and what we can do with such answers, are things that remain very much to be worked out, both in
general, and for specific cases. There is much work to be done
here, and much work to be done also in developing other methods,
like participant observation, [9] which can serve as independent 'checks
and balances'.

The prospects for overcoming the limitations of tape-recorded data
and carrying the 'New Wave' into syntax, seem promising but not
easy. However, there is no reason to limit our goals and methods
to those that require the least effort and/or imagination. This is no
way to run a revolution.

NOTES

1. This paper is full of references to the work and influence of
William Labov. It is not inordinately or accidentally so, however,
for he has been in the forefront of innovations in (socio-) linguistic
methodology for the past ten years. I welcome this opportunity to
thank him for provoking me to a critical awareness of the importance
of 'methodology' and for stimulating my own work both by example
and suggestion.

2. As used in this paper, been is an abstract form in which stress
is not distinguished. It is introduced primarily to facilitate discussion of the work of previous researchers. BÍN and bĭn are more con-
crete--the former referring to the stressed form, the latter to the
unstressed.

3. The work of Loflin (1969) is omitted in the body of this paper.
This might be surprising to some, since Loflin does discuss BÍN, and
his paper is often cited as a high point in the formal analysis of Black
English. But we must not be 'snowed' by apparent applications of the
transformational-generative framework to the field of 'sociolinguistic
variation'. Loflin 'accounts' for BÍN by 'postulating a formative E
of emphatic stress which could be given in the rule rewriting VP and
which could be converted into appropriate realizations, e. g. E+V+ed
⇒ BÍN+V+ed'. In recognizing the obligatory nature of stress, Loflin
is justified. But his rule for generating the form is totally ad hoc and
unmotivated, most seriously because the meaning of the form is not
discussed at any point. Loflin's methodology, drawing on the intuitive reactions of an isolated fourteen-year-old informant, has also
received widespread criticism.

4. The notation in parentheses following each sentence records in
this order the following information: race, sex, age, and geographical community of the speaker.

5. We cannot explore here in any depth the fascinating issue of how 'remote' the initiation of a process must be to justify the use of BÍN. One thing is certain--no absolute distance in objective time from the point of orientation can be set. What BÍN expresses is the speaker's subjective feelings about the event and the 'time' involved. Thus an old woman stepping out of a dentist's office she had entered only a few minutes before said, 'He finish so quick. I ask him was he finished, and he say "I BÍN finished"'.

There are, however, 'consensus definitions' of how 'remote' the initiation of a process must be, relative to certain cases. And there is a rich arena for research in the use of BÍN contrary to such 'consensus' definitions for dramatization and self-aggrandizement, or 'styling'. Thus a young woman who was complimented on the fine dress she had bought only the day before replied nonchantly, 'Oh, I BÍN had this!' This 'styling' use of BÍN is open to challenge, however.

These considerations are not totally irrelevant to the methodological issues with which we are concerned in this paper. For instance, Gary M. of New York hesitated before giving the 'Remote Phase' interpretation to question 3 in Q-SCOM-4 (see (15) below), because, in his words 'I don't know if he bin know that guy. A lot of dudes go around running off at the mouth bout how they BÍN know this and they BÍN know that. Ain't nothing but a bunch of jive!'

6. This section may be taken to illustrate the general principle that questioning people on their own use of linguistic forms or varieties which have high social effect (either positive or negative) is likely to produce unreliable results unless checked against other evidence.

7. The scalability figure is arrived at by the formula:

$$100 - (\frac{\text{No. of deviations}}{\text{No. of cells}} \cdot \frac{100}{1})$$

In this case: $100 - (39/350 \cdot 100)$.

8. The whole question of what is to be retained, what modified in borrowing techniques like 'sociometric scaling' from social-survey methodology is quite problematic. For instance, 'factors' which are marked by a high number of 'deviations' are often omitted in psychological and sociological work. But so far no one has suggested in linguistic circles that sentences like 18g should be thrown out of consideration altogether. (I am thankful to Wolfgang Wölck for raising this issue.) The closest anyone has come to this is Labov (1971), see page 176 above.

9. At the risk of being accused of descending to the trivial or ephemeral, let me suggest here one or two methods for extending

the method of participant-observation to include information on the frequency of pre-coded variables which occur more often than BÍN. The art is to develop idiosyncracies like doodling or breaking matches in half. With each occurrence of a variant (for example que vs. Ø) one makes the appropriate 'doodle' on a handy napkin or whatever, or puts the broken half of a matchstick in the appropriate pile. So long as one remembers to collect the napkins, or put the matchstick pieces into different pockets, these 'extensions' can prove extremely informative and reliable. Needless to say, however, they put a tremendous strain on the 'participant-observer' of natural conversation, and require some practice.

REFERENCES

Bailey, B. L. 1966. Jamaican Creole syntax. London, Cambridge University Press.
Bailey, C.-J. N. 1970. Using data variation to confirm, rather than undermine, the existence of abstract syntactic structures. Working Papers in Linguistics 2.8:77-86. Honolulu, University of Hawaii.
_____ and R. W. Shuy, eds. 1973. New ways of analyzing variation in English. Washington, D.C., Georgetown University Press.
Baltin, Mark. 1973. A reanalysis of quantifier-negative dialects. Mimeo. University of Pennsylvania.
Bickerton, Derek. 1972. The structure of polylectal grammars. In: GURT 1972. 17-42.
_____. 1973. On the nature of a creole continuum. Lg. 49:640-669.
_____. 1974. Bin in the Atlantic Creoles. In: Journal of African Languages, Special Issue devoted to the English Pidgins and Creoles. Edited by I. Hancock.
Bolinger, D. 1968. Judgments of grammaticality. Lingua 21:34-40.
Butters, R. 1973. Acceptability judgments for double modals in Southern English. In: Bailey and Shuy (1973). 276-286.
Carden, G. 1971. A note on conflicting idiolects. Linguistic Inquiry 1.3.
Dillard, J. L. 1972. Black English--Its history and usage in the United States. New York, Random House.
Elliot D., S. Legum, and S. Thompson. 1969. Syntactic variation as linguistic data. In: Papers from the Fifth Regional Meeting, Chicago Linguistic Society. Edited by Binnick, et al. Chicago, University of Chicago. 52-59.
Fasold, R. W. and W. Wolfram. 1970. Some linguistic features of Negro dialect. In: Teaching Standard English in the inner city. Edited by R. W. Fasold and R. W. Shuy. Washington, D.C., Center for Applied Linguistics. 41-86.

Fickett, Joan G. 1970. Aspects of morphemics, syntax, and semology of an inner-city dialect. West Rush, New York, Meadowbrook Publications.

Gleitman, Lila R. 1967. An experiment concerning the use and perception of compound nominals by English speakers. Unpublished Ph.D. dissertation, University of Pennsylvania.

Jones, E. D. 1968. Some tense, mode, and aspect markers in Krio. African Language Review 7:86-89.

Labov, William. 1966. The social stratification of English in New York City. Washington, D.C., Center for Applied Linguistics.

_____. 1969. Contraction, deletion, and inherent variability of the English copula. Lg. 45.4:715-762.

_____. 1970. The study of language in its social context. Studium Generale 23:30-87.

_____. 1971. Linguistic methodology. In: A survey of linguistic science. Edited by W. O. Dingwall. College Park, University of Maryland. 412-497.

_____. 1972a. Where do grammars stop? In: GURT 1972. 43-88.

_____. 1972b. Some principles of linguistic methodology. Language and Society 1:97-120.

_____, D. Hindle, and M. Baltin. [To appear] For an end to the uncontrolled use of intuition in linguistic analysis.

Loflin, M. 1969. On the structure of the verb in a dialect of American Negro English. Linguistics 14-28.

Quirk, R. and J. Svartvik. 1966. Investigating linguistic acceptability. The Hague, Mouton and Co.

Rickford, John and Angela Rickford. 1974. Cut-eye and suck-teeth. In: Journal of African Languages. Special issue devoted to the English pidgins and creoles. Edited by I. Hancock.

Sag, Ivan. 1973. On the state of progress on progressives and statives. In: Bailey and Shuy (1973). 83-95.

Sankoff, Gillian. 1973. Above and beyond phonology in variable rules. In: Bailey and Shuy (1973). 44-61.

Stewart, William A. 1965. Urban Negro speech: Sociolinguistic factors affecting English teaching. In: Social dialects and language learning. Edited by Roger W. Shuy. Champaign, Illinois, The National Council of Teachers of English. 10-18.

POLYSEMY OR MONOSEMY:
DISCRETE MEANINGS OR CONTINUUM?

CHARLES E. RUHL

Recent developments in Transformational Grammar have led to a linguistic methodology which is not exclusively committed to the use of discrete, all-or-none processes and categories. The result of such a methodological change will prove to be more revolutionary than the advent of TG itself. The following heuristic principles suggest the magnitude of that change:

(A) Locating a distinction is not enough; it may be the product of a distorted selection from an underlying continuum.
(B) To uphold a discrete distinction, the lack of a continuum must be demonstrated.
(C) Even if a discrete distinction seems to hold, its legitimacy may rest on another, illegitimate distinction in the grammar, or in the defined limits of the grammar.
(D) An apparent distinction may be legitimate in some areas of the grammar, but illegitimate when extended over the whole grammar.

In the perspective of these principles, discrete processes are a special case; the initial assumption in all analysis is that variable conditions obtain. As Principle C asserts, not even the basic idealization of a grammatical approach--the idealization of TG has discrete breaks between sentence and discourse, and between linguistic and nonlinguistic factors--is immune from re-evaluation. Nor are distinctions supported only by tradition: those between concrete and abstract, literal and metaphoric, and hyperbolic and non-hyperbolic. In addition, certain seemingly clear distinctions, such as those between action and inaction, and purposeful and non-purposeful conditions, become as problematic in linguistic analysis as they are in real life, once we include data which discrete analysis either ignores or misinterprets. As Principle D asserts, such distinctions may be sharp and clear in some areas of the grammar, but fuzzy or irrelevant in others; an analysis which posits them as breaks cutting through the whole grammar thereby imposes distorting requirements, and inevitably produces spurious complexity.

One of the undesirable consequences of a methodology oriented exclusively to discrete distinctions has been the creation of excessive polysemy in the lexicon. It would seem to be a self-evident goal in any linguistic theory to find unified semantic senses for phonological forms, foregoing this goal in particular cases only in the face of compelling evidence to the contrary. Such a goal acts as a natural constraint of a theory, guarding against the use of inappropriate criteria. But since homonymy and polysemy do unmistakably occur in some instances, the tendency has been to assume that they exist in any instance where an analysis requires it; the unity of the form is sacrificed heedlessly, with automatic acceptance given to the criteria which forced the division. Consider the question of how extensive the distinction of concrete and abstract should be in a grammar of English. Since a large number of words--such as the verbs run, go, take, hit, break--range over both, the correct analysis is that they are neutral to such a distinction, and that the distinction thus has a limited domain. To assume the contrary is to make by fiat an unsupported claim about cognitive organization--a claim directly disproved by the neutrality these words exhibit.

As another example, consider the pronouns. Pronouns can be anaphoric to nominals in the same sentence, in the accompanying discourse, or to something nonlinguistic. Because of the TG idealization, these three possibilities have been treated as distinct, and can not presently be defined in some versions of TG with one general statement. But since pronouns have this range, the correct generalization is that the distinctions between sentence, discourse, and nonlinguistic factors are illegitimate when applied to the pronouns. Such a conclusion is the only one which accords with the theoretical requirements of simplicity and generality. Of course, the syntactic and semantic environment of a pronoun may vary under these three conditions, but the conclusion to be drawn is that the variation occurs in the environment and not in the pronoun.

Problems stemming from inhibiting idealizations suggest the following additional principles:

(E) In attempting to simplify one's task by limiting the domain of study, one may eliminate the full range of data which would reveal the simplifying principles.

(F) Improper simplification can lead to the burdening of certain elements, such as words, with syntactic or semantic information which should be ascribed to more general processes.

(G) Improper simplification may so obscure the structural principles of the language that structural principles from other highly valued cultural creations, such as the current models of logic, may be resorted to so as to create some order.

An illustration of Principles E and F involves a problem addressed by the UCLA Syntax Project (Stockwell, et al. 1973:728). The Project notes that for three nouns representing three biologically bisexual species--the nouns 'neighbor', 'horse', and 'fruitfly'--the permitted pronouns vary (my sentences):

he

(1) My neighbor is fascinating, but she is also unreliable.

*it

he

(2) That horse is beautiful, but she is completely unmanageable.

it

*he

(3) This fruitfly appears to be dead, but *she may simply be resting.   it

The Project devises three different feature notations for these three nouns; in addition, the differing interrelationships of the pronouns suggest multiple feature designations on them. But the simplifying generalization lies not in the isolated properties of the nouns and pronouns, but in the semantic hierarchy (Lakoff 1972) which all speakers use:

(H) The higher in the order of animals, the more necessary it is to make sexual distinctions.

(Principle H assumes another principle defining the order of animals.) Except for babies, it is always necessary to make distinctions with humans, but optional with horses, and unnecessary, and usually impossible, with fruitflies. Once Principle H is included in the grammar, the feature designations on the nouns can be eliminated. This accords with McCawley's (1968) judgment that 'neighbor' is not ambiguous, in spite of the pronoun variation, a judgment which applies equally to 'horse'.

Principle G can be illustrated by the enigmatic behavior of the conjunction and. Unlike logical conjunction, and appears between elements of less than propositional (in analogy, 'sentential') rank, and in asymmetric constructions. With logical conjunction as an apparent implicit norm, there have been several attempts to convert non-sentential conjoinings into sentential ones, in spite of the deep structural complications required for a sentence such as:

(4) John, Bob, and Sam are an unlikely combination.

Asymmetric constructions with sentential conjuncts, such as

(5) John shot Bob and rode off down the trail.

can be handled by several strategies, such as McCawley's (1971) positing of a tense sequence in the verbs. But for sentences such as

(6) She's gone and ruined her dress.
(7) I've got to try and find that screw.
(8) One more can of beer and I'm leaving.

the temptation is great, as Schmerling (to appear) notes, to conclude that there are several different and's in the language, serving as low level variants of conditional or infinitival constructions. Yet, there seems to be no reason why the syntactic puzzles should be solved by a proliferation of and's, except through an illegitimate comparison of 'and' with logical conjunction. In fact, the infatuation with logical conjunction--and, in general, the shortsighted assumption that natural language should accord with the requirements of some artificial language--actually blocks research into communicational requirements and possibilities which account for the 'illogical' syntax of (6)-(8).

But the most striking illustration of Principles E, F, and G can be seen in Postal's (1970) argument that the verb remind is polysemic. In a brilliant and detailed analysis, Postal inadvertently demonstrates the folly of an exclusive reliance on the most favored methodological tool of General Semantics: the analysis by synonymy. The extreme significance given to considerations of synonymy in GS analyses is baffling. Synonymous relationships are defined by paraphrasing (even when this is disguised as features or predicates); but as is well known, paraphrasing is characteristically inexact, the two related forms differing in range, connotation, and degree of specification. Yet, in the interest of capturing generalizations involving synonymy, complex deep structures and elaborate rule schema are devised, discrepancies are ignored by appeals to greater abstractions or more powerful rules, and the phonological identity of a form over a closely related range of meanings, one of the most obvious and certain bits of data a linguist can ever have, is almost contemptuously rejected. Such is the fate of remind. Again, the influential image of artificial languages, where complex terms can be precisely and exhaustively defined by more primitive terms, [1] appears to be irresistible in a heuristic context where communicational factors have been ignored. Postal claims that remind has at least two meanings, 'cause to remember' and 'strike as similar', illustrated respectively in (9) and (10):

(9) Harry reminded Betty to visit her sick uncle.
(10) Harry reminds me of Fred Astaire.

But the paraphrase 'strike as similar' is both too weak and too strong, as Bolinger (1971) points out: remind presupposes 'previous knowledge' while strike does not, and remind presupposes only a 'connection', not a similarity. Bolinger contrasts the appropriateness of (11)-(12), the setting 'that of a person meeting two sisters, Jane and Mary, for the first time. The one presenting them asks:

(11) *Doesn't Jane remind you of Mary?
(12) Doesn't Jane strike you as similar to Mary?' (1971:525)

Remind is inappropriate because there is no previous knowledge. Also, a sentence such as (13) shows that only a link, not a resemblance, is required:

(13) Your story reminds me of the time I went hunting in Maine.

Bolinger claims that the notion of similarity or resemblance, when it is possible as in (10), is not 'referential' but 'inferential' (1971:522); that is, as he restates it later (528), it does not involve the 'definition' of remind, but the 'circumstances' of the context in which remind occurs. What is involved here is 'the integrity of remind as a lexical item' (528);[2] if a common core of meaning can be found for 'remind' in all its occurrences, then we should first investigate the possibility that any variation of meaning is contributed by other elements or factors. It is at this point where the principles thus far enumerated become so crucial; their implications can be summarized in Principle I:

(I) The total 'meaning' of a sentence is a product of more than its lexical items and its syntax.

Principle I explicitly denies the TG idealization: semantic information can not be apportioned compositionally to the lexical items, because the inevitable result will be 'semantic overloading' (Bolinger's term; recall Principle F). In Ruhl (1973a) I discussed evidence which shows that linguistic expressions are characteristically 'underdetermined'; that is, conveying more information than the lexical items and syntax contribute. Sometimes the additional information is highly specific, as in

(14) I tried the new pool.

where it is suggested that I went swimming in the pool. But as (15) shows, the 'trying' varies according to context:

(15) I looked for my kids everywhere. Finally, I tried the pool.

Although in isolation, (14) is biased toward a particular specific reading involving swimming, a natural inference, since swimming relates strongly in human experience to (swimming) pools, the lexical items merely permit the inference. Similarly, in

(16) We decided on the boat.

specific circumstances, both in the discourse and in the setting, may bias the meaning toward

<pre>
                     buying
(17) We decided on selling the boat.
                     painting
</pre>

or other possibilities. Another intriguing inferential property of (16) is that it suggests a positive decision, which need not be the case:

(18) A: We decided on the boat.
    B: And what did you decide?
    A: We're not going to sell it.

Bolinger notes also that 'I'm starved' can carry the additional meaning of 'Serve me dinner'. A parallel case, he claims, accounts for a shift in the meaning of the verb want. Although it originally meant only 'lack', the natural inference of desire eventually shifted its meaning, so that the verb typically now means in itself 'desire' (note contrast of 'I want food' and 'I want for food'). A sign that the shift has become definitional is the fact that now 'lack' is inferential;

we can now 'want' something which we have already (L. Anderson 1973). Not incidentally, the shift of meaning from inferential to referential is difficult to handle for a theory of language change based on the TG idealization.

Although linguists may ignore Principle I, teachers of rhetoric ignore it at their peril. While the major problem in teaching writing is that students write too generally and disjointedly, leaving too much detail and structure for the reader to supply, they also are frequently guilty of the opposite offense, that of supplying material the reader can infer, or laboriously using 'for example', 'but', and the like when the structure is transparent. Actually, both problems can exist in the same composition; an essay bristling with signposts at lower levels can be structurally mysterious as a whole. Even short stretches of prose can err in both directions, as (19) shows:

(19) My father was a difficult man. When my family moved to the West Coast, into the Pacific Time Zone, I was only six, and being a child my memory wasn't so good. When we moved, we took everything we had. For example, even my old crib was put in the trunk when we moved.

What a student must be led to see, and to exemplify, are two principles which at first glance appear to be contradictory (Ruhl 1973a):

(J) People need familiarity and unity, the 'expected' and the 'explainable', and this need requires that any human activity have continuity, repetition, and structure.

(K) People need variety and freedom, the 'unexpected' and 'challenging', which requires that new information be prominent, and predictable elements be minimal or implicit.

The effect of these principles is that the signs and cues of structure in any human activity are rarely obvious; and language is no exception. Pronouns, and other forms of anaphora, derive their explanation from these two principles; and it is significant that artificial languages, which do not require anaphoric elements, are created independently of the contingencies of communication. It is also significant that GS, viewing anaphora from the perspective of coreferentiality (which is another aspect of the synonymy criterion), must labor under complex deep structures and still more complex systems of rules, and that TG in general grossly underestimates the extent of implicit information in linguistic expression. A good example is

(20) I answered the door

in which the semantics seems so strange that the UCLA Project (p.
721) had to conclude that 'answer' was a different verb from the
'answer' of

(21) Nobody answered the question.

(In addition, the 'answer' of 'he answered the letter' "raises other
questions".) The requirement that all semantic information be
distributed among the lexical items in fact precludes any other
choice; Green (1969:81), from the same perspective, concludes that
on the basis of:

(22) Harry refused Bill's request.
(23) Harry refused Bill's offer.

there are two refuse's (at least) in the language, one parallel to
'refuse to grant', the other to 'refuse to accept'. She proposes that
'unpleasant implications follow from the claim that there is . . .
only one lexical entry for the lexical item refuse (81); but there
should be equally unpleasant implications about a proliferation of
refuse's. The problem is created by the needless requirement to
account for 'grant' and 'accept' in the lexical portions of (22)-(23).
Rather, these senses are supplied by inference, because the communication situation includes a hearer who can infer the full meaning
from the experiential properties of requests and offers.[3] In still
another typical example, the UCLA Project (p. 729) opts for two
different 'remember's in

(24) He remembered telling her.
(25) He remembered to tell her.

because the first is factive and the second is not. With such disre-
gard for lexical integrity in these cases, it is no wonder that Postal,
in a more subtle case, quite naturally divided remind.
    The TG idealization thus leads inexorably to methods and assump-
tions of discrete analysis, which in turn create unnecessary polysemy; since the idealization is itself an illegitimate discrete distinction, it creates others in its wake. But it is not questioned on
these grounds because it draws powerful support from the very cultural influences which it denies; by eliminating the cultural ground
of language, TG follows Structuralism in adopting the mechanistic,
reductionist perspective which has been culturally dominant for
several centuries, but which has already been abandoned for field

or ecological perspectives in other sciences. Two epistemological views are involved, which sharply conflict in their implications for linguistic research. Mechanistic research is a bit-by-bit, compositional methodology, of building from nothing, combining a primitive set of discrete elements into larger constructions, which are the sum of their parts; this is the method of artificial language. Ecological research, on the other hand, starts from a given whole, and delineates out, the elements and structure of the delineation both selective and suggestive of the initial whole. The differences between the two views are so basic and global that a methodology based on one, but analyzing a reality closer to the other, will produce wide-reaching distortions. The two views can be particularized by Structuralism on one side, with its laborious accumulation of phonemes and morphemes, and by Rhetoric on the other, with its seemingly foreign preoccupation with central ideas, unity, coherence, tone, levels of usage, and strategies of organization.

Transformationalists are aware of what an explosive change can take place in a field which shifts from a piecemeal to a holistic framework: with the assumption that a sentence was more fundamental than its parts, the linguist's preoccupation changed from isolated elements and constructions to the complex and heterogeneous unity of the whole grammar. The transformational revolution was a striking demonstration of Principle E, and the enlarged domain of permitted data enabled transformationalists to discover and systematize regularities which had not even been suspected before. But it was an incomplete revolution: with its avoidance of discourse, situational factors, and dialectical variation, TG as conceived in Aspects reverted to piecemeal analysis again; a self-sufficient competence grammar was to be an independent prerequisite for some more complex performance grammar, and in a startling echo of Structuralist dogma there was to be no mixing of levels.

What is needed, then, is an adoption of the initial Transformational proposal to a wider domain of evidence. This entails allowing 'knowledge of the world' to intrude upon 'knowledge of the language', and any objection to such a course on the basis that a formal system is thus rendered impossible or difficult is merely an uninteresting indication that the objector prefers systematizing to actually comprehending the language. But there are methods that even 'closet' linguists can use to advantage, even without exhaustive research on the particular real world factors that need to be considered. One method is illustrated in the now largely ignored generative component of a TG grammar, that of 'specification', rewriting general structures as more specific ones. This method contrasts with that of synonymy, which came to be the method of the transformational component, and which in CS has largely pre-empted any interest in general-specific relationships. Consider, in this regard, the verb 'take', which in the dictionaries is a highly polysemic word, and would be considered as such by discrete analysis. In an earlier paper (Ruhl 1973b), I argued for a monosemic status for take, and by the use of the method of specification, shown below, factored out specific accretions of meaning on take which it seems to have in isolated sentences. I began with sentence (26), in which take can be glossed variously as equivalent to 'seize', 'steal', 'accept', 'win', 'choose', and 'buy'. I compared this sentence with other sentences in which modifying material has been appended, to show that some specifics are not part of take, but are merely inferential attempts to make a highly general sentence more specific. Once the specifics are factored out, it is surprising what a minimal amount of information take actually conveys:

(26) John took the book from Bob.
(27) John gratefully took the book from Bob.
(28) John illegally took the book from Bob.
(29) John arrogantly took the book from Bob.
(30) John accidentally took the book from Bob.
(31) John took the book from an unsuspecting Bob.
(32) John took the book from a helpless and angry Bob.
(33) John took the book from an insistent Bob.
(34) John took the offered book from Bob.
(35) John took the book from Bob in exchange for the tapes.
(36) John took the book from Bob with a beautiful play on the second round.
(37) John$_i$ took the book from Bob$_j$ without his$_k$ knowledge. (i=k, j=k)
(38) John$_i$ took the book from Bob$_j$ against his$_k$ will. (i=k, j=k)
(39) John begrudgingly took the book from an equally begrudging Bob.

Each modification biases the meaning of the original sentence in a particular direction, attributing varying degrees of, to name some 'feature' factors, activity, willingness, awareness, purposefulness, knowledge, and attitude to John and Bob. But the original sentence is neutral to all these variations. Nor are these variations merely a small set of distinct options--the crucial assumption behind all feature analysis--but an infinitely variable continuum, as any detailed list of modifications can readily show. Specific modifications or specific glosses such as 'steal' pinpoint various portions of the continuum, and any division of its sense only introduces distortion. There is nothing unique about this situation; the same thing applies to 'man' in (40), which can also be shown to be infinitely variable:

(40) I see a man outside.
    (41) I see a man <u>in a blue suit</u> outside.
    (42) I see a man <u>who looks familiar</u> outside.

Seen with holistic eyes, what is remarkable about sentences (26)-(42), or, for that matter, any sentence, is how ill-defined many details are, and yet how easily a listener or reader supplies more precise definitions, automatically, as they are needed. Sentences (26)-(39) leave undefined whether John was personally present with Bob when the transfer of the book occurred, or whether an agent intervened; yet, readers more than likely assumed he was in fact present. In (27), we do not know who John was grateful to, or why; yet, by default we assume that he is grateful to Bob, and for the book. (Someone could be holding a gun on Bob, and John, grateful for the help, seizes the book.) We do not know in (29) whether the arrogance was highhanded or merely a brave front in the face of a disagreeable act. Who offers the book in (34)? Every sentence can be quibbled with, but usually only by a pedant or a linguist doing analysis. What is impressive about such quibbling, however, is the realization that much of what we assume is 'in' the sentence really isn't. But this is a natural effect of a language with an ever-present cultural ground.

Some specifications may come from the manner of a speaker. Consider the following two sentences, uttered by my daughter Jennifer, age 10. On the occasion of the first, she came running into the house, flushed and angry, shouting in a belligerent, demanding tone. On the occasion of the second, she was shy, even bashful, and quiet almost to the point of being inaudible:

(43) Josh took my bike.
(44) The teacher took my poem.

If I were to quote what she said later to someone else, I might introduce paraphrases such as:

(45) Josh stole my bike.
(46) The teacher chose my poem.

Where would I get those specific glosses? Partly from <u>take</u> and the other lexical items, partly from my wordly knowledge, but most crucially I think from Jennifer's manner. Her angry tone in (43) prevents me from assuming, for example, that she had forced her bike on a desperately protesting Josh. Also, her quiet pride in (44) prevents me from assuming that her teacher snatched the poem out of her hand. A discrete analysis of <u>take</u> would interpret the role of the situation as merely resolving a choice of discrete possibilities;

if, as I claim, the possibilities are infinite, then the manner can be excluded only from a linguistic description that provides take with a general meaning. But if the sentence is burdened with accounting for the full meaning it conveys, then such an option is precluded: discrete analysis stumbles onto a contradiction, one which can only be evaded by ignoring the infinite range of data--which is, in fact, what happens in discrete analyses. Hopefully, it will be possible to draw a line between linguistic and non-linguistic contributions to meaning; but that line can not be drawn as it is presently drawn.

Any judgment concerning the locus of meaning is a highly vulnerable one, especially so when one's assumptions force a compositional analysis. However, there is one transformational test (or, rather, a set of such tests) which is intended to guard against improper judgments by showing clearly when two senses of a form are distinct from each other. This is the Reduction Test, the premise of which is that forms with identical meaning should be able to delete when they recur in comparative or conjoined structures. According to this test (McCawley 1968), there is one heavy in (47)-(49) and one take in (53)-(55), but, because reductions are not permitted, there are two sad's in (50)-(52) and two take's in (56)-(58):

(47) John is heavy.
(48) This box is heavy.
(49) John is as heavy as this box.
(50) John is sad.
(51) This book is sad.
(52) *John is as sad as this book.
(53) I took a pear.
(54) John took an apple.
(55) I took a pear and John an apple.
(56) Joe took the jewels.
(57) Bill took a lot of punishment.
(58) *Joe took the jewels and Bill a lot of punishment.

Unquestionably, there is a difference of meaning in (50)-(51) and (56)-(57), and the improper reductions indicate this. It can even be claimed that the differences are distinct, and not slight shadings of meaning: McCawley glosses the two sad's as 'experiencing sadness' and 'evoking sadness', and these glosses are assuredly distinct, as the lexical difference of 'experience' and 'evoke' indicates. Similarly, the active sense of taking jewels differs from the passive sense of taking punishment. But while the sentences convey a different impression, especially when compared in isolation to each other, is it because certain words are polysemic? Or, is it rather that different inferential factors prevent the reductions?[4]

The whole issue of what constitutes 'the same word' is needlessly complicated in TG because different conclusions are reached with similar processes in different parts of the grammar. Note the following patterns with a noun instead of a verb at issue:

(59)   The man$_i$ is happy.
(60)   The man$_i$ is rich.
(61)   The man is happy and rich.
(62)   The man$_i$ is happy.
(63)   The man$_j$ is rich.
(64)   *The man is happy and rich.

A reduction can only occur when the man has the same 'reference'. Note that the difference here is not put in the noun; no one claims that (62)-(64) shows that there are at least two man's in the language. In other words, with nouns transformationalists recognize the possibility of distinct differences without creating polysemy. Of course, a number of built-in assumptions concerning the difference of nouns and verbs prevents us from dealing with a similar phenomenon in both in a similar way. Since those assumptions lead to excessive polysemy in verbs, they should be re-examined.

An analysis which respects lexical integrity would be more concerned, before making judgments of synonymy, with determining the full range of a word. Thus, before making an equation (perhaps on a more 'abstract' level) of kill to 'cause to die' and 'cause to be not alive', we should note such sentences as:

(65)   I was just killing time.
(66)   My feet are killing me.
(67)   Bob just kills me when he makes that crocodile mating call.

Our immediate reaction is to argue that these kill's are metaphoric or hyperbolic. [5] But, again, since kill does not respect a boundary such as literal-metaphoric, what justification do we have for making this such a fundamental distinction? The only justification comes from philosophical axioms which, no matter how culturally entrenched they are, kill happens not to adhere to. Of course, speakers can tell the difference (some or most of the time) between literal and metaphoric uses of a word, just as they can tell the difference between man applied to one person or to another. But even the line between literal and metaphoric is not a distinct one; what is literal to one person may not be so to another. Di Pietro (to appear) reminds us of how we use, and need to use, metaphors in linguistic analysis, and how quickly we come to think of them as literal:

In transformational generative grammar . . . many of the
terms derive from plant imagery. 'Trees' are produced,
with 'branches' that can be 'pruned' or attached, as if grafted,
to other trees. There are 'kernal' sentences, as well. Just
as birds nest in real trees, so do constructions in grammar
trees. Other metaphors come from mathematical logic, such
as 'transformation' and 'recursion'. Still others derive from
the engineering sciences: 'power of generation', 'simplicity'
of design, and so on.

In the process of rejecting earlier theories of grammar,
the metaphors of those theories were devalued. No one in
transformational grammar draws 'box diagrams' as did the
structuralists. Whereas 'trees' are supposed to reflect a
reality of language design, boxes do not. The advocates of
each school defend their metaphors vigorously. Lakoff (1970),
when attempting to reconcile the notion of transformational
rule with the observations of researchers in language related
fields, avers that '. . . there is a very good reason to believe
that transformations do exist' (Lakoff 1970:637) and proceeds
to make such rules more inclusive or global. He apparently
believes that when the metaphorically derived rules of a grammar are made to be more general, their literal senses will
no longer be questioned. Regardless of how sophisticated we
make our grammars, we shall do nothing more than postpone
the day when an empirical foundation must be found for them.

Logics, artificial languages, grammars, philosophies, and philosophical distinctions such as those between literal and metaphoric are
all metaphoric--all witness to man's creative spirit, his attempt to
find some order in some life. Natural language is also a witness of
that creative spirit, but its tides run at a much greater depth. Compared to it, our grammars represent gross political maneuvers, im-
patient and imperious attempts to impose order at any cost, to keep
the rabble in line. And minor political maneuvers are usually linked
to major: the excessive mechanization and literalization of modern
culture is reflected in linguistic approaches which ignore or postpone
'performance' and metaphor. All incorrect orders bring disorder;
excessive polysemy is transformational disorder. Typically, disorder comes at levels which are politically devalued, usually because
they remain disorderly. In TG, where a specific language has the
air of an imperfect (and often cantankerous) tool for expressing a
deeper, truer universal language, the 'low level' reality of mere
lexical items is naturally going to be messy.

The process of politicization is especially crucial to linguists, all
of whom have successfully passed through one of the most political

organizations of our society: the schools. As linguists search their 'intuitions', they are coping with at least three different modes of organization: the first, language as they learned it as children, speech linked naturally with environment; the second, language as prescribed in schools, language as writing, where environment is stylized and diminished; and the third, language as seen by a linguist, subject of investigation, subject to theoretical structuring and preconceptions. All three may co-exist in wild disagreement with each other; each is developmental, not synchronic or homogeneous. A caution for linguistic research is that linguists searching their intuitions probably find the organization of modes two and three. As academics, who (perhaps too) easily and typically separate language from situation, the separation extends to affective qualities of language as well, they are unlikely to be able to get back to mode one, where no such distinction existed. Yet, it is the first mode which is the most complete, probably the best organized, and the one in which elemental words such as take can best be comprehended. Such observations are sobering for linguists who trust too much to intuitions, or who think there is a neatly organized, homogeneous grammar lurking somewhere inside us.

The importance of the linguist's potentially distorting academic personality in his research can be generalized to his whole role as a scientist. The lesson learned painfully--because the mechanistic framework denied it--in other sciences is that the scientist is both affected by and affecting what he is doing. Although I have always been a compulsive writer of poems, stories, and parables, and can be a notorious punner, in the five years when I was enthralled by 'ideal speaker-hearers' all of my natural linguistic exuberance diminished; I doubt that this was mere coincidence, and other linguists I'm sure have similar experiences. And as Labov (1972) found when doing field work, the crucial factor is the investigator's wide and specific knowledge of life and his ability to establish a sense of trust with his informant:

. . . one must turn back to the basic sociolinguistic conundrum: 'Why does anyone say anything?' There are three content themes which have the greatest force for evoking speech from the broadest range of speakers: (1) death, and the danger of death, including any form of physical violence (fights, accidents, sickness, operations); (2) sex and all the machinery for interaction between the sexes (proposals, dating, household negotiations); (3) moral indignation (e. g. 'Did you ever get whupped for something you didn't do?') Beyond such general considerations, there are a vast array of local issues, humor and gossip which the field worker must seize as a

by-product of participant-observation. Questions in specific
local areas are constructed by a feedback technique which
progressively assumes more as the field worker knows more.
An initial question 'Do you play the numbers?' would thus give
way to 'Did you ever hit big?' In talking to deer hunters, an
initial question such as 'Where do you aim?' would give way
to 'Is it worth trying a rump shot?' As the outsider gradually
becomes an insider, the quality of the speech obtained and the
speaker's involvement in it rises steadily. A field worker who
stays outside his subject, and deals with it as a mere excuse
for eliciting language, will get very little for his pains. Almost any question can be answered with no more information
than was contained in it. When the speaker does give more,
it is a gift, drawn from some general fund of good will that
is held in trust by himself and the field worker. A deep knowledge implies a deep interest, and in payment for that interest
the speaker may give more than anyone has a right to expect.
Thus the field worker who can tap the full linguistic competence of his subjects must acquire a detailed understanding
of what he is talking about, as well as broad knowledge of the
general forms of human behavior. (Labov 1972:115)

What we need is the understanding of the anthropologist, the
psychiatrist, the writer, the critic, as well as the logician and the
systems analyst. In short, linguists are humanists as well as scien-
tists; linguists should be the first to know that the discrete distinction
of scientist and humanist is also illegitimate.

All of this may seem overly portentous when the subject of the
paper has been polysemy. But the conditions creating polysemy run
this deep. If you doubt it, I suggest an exercise: you 'know', of
course, that 'kick the bucket' is an idiom, and means something like
'die'. You've never given much thought to it, but it's pretty obvious,
isn't it? Or is it? Why not look around a bit? Perhaps you might
find a phrase like 'kick the habit'. And other things too. And, regardless of what you might find, then ask yourself: if even this
idiom may not be as idiomatic as you thought, what about all the
other obvious idioms you keep confidently in store? You might go
next to 'take place', which is a rather easy one.

NOTES

1. At the dawn of transformational semantics (Katz and Fodor
1963), Bolinger (1965) issued a warning that was not heeded: 'I am
inclined to think that K-F's example of bachelor is a special kind of
word where we 'find' the markers we have already put in. An uncle,

similarly, is one who bears a socially defined relationship to parent
who in turn bears it to an offspring--the markers are there because
we put them there. It is something different to find markers in anything that has a life history independent of our naming-operations.
A bachelor is a bachelor because he is unmarried, and marriage is
an arbitrarily defined social ceremony; we impose the conditions.
A bird or a fish is something that we take as we find it, and the
markers are adjusted like a suit of clothes, often badly. The fit is
crude, metaphorical, subject to revision, and above all subject to
change as the entity itself grows or decays through time. This distinction is fundamental. A CONSTRUCTIVE definition applies to a
social construct, with markers defined a priori. A SUBSTANTIVE
definition applies to the hard objects of the natural world' (Jakobovits
and Miron 1967:443). As far as I know, no transformational semanti-
cist had anything to say about birds until Lakoff (1972) illustrated the
semantic hierarchy of birds: a non-discrete phenomenon. (Lakoff's
work on 'fuzzy logic' is one of the seminal works on non-discrete
analysis.)

  2. A number of reactions to Postal argued the same point: Bowers
(1970), Wolf (1970), Kirsner (1972). Commenting on the possibility
that 'remind' may be split along active versus stative lines, Kirsner
notes (1972:497): 'Just as it could be claimed that the genitive structure A's B--e.g. John's book--does not itself specify exactly how A
is related to B, so could it be claimed that A reminds C of B does not
really specify exactly how it is possible for A to remind C of B. A
spliting of the two senses of remind into two separate verbs remind
might then be a form of overanalysis.' As my subsequent discussion
shows, I think Kirsner is right; 'overanalysis' is related to Principle
I, which follows directly in the text. Not only is Kirsner right about
the genitive structure, but the same analysis of noun compounds
(Ruhl 1973a) would clear up the supposed semantic difficulties there.
Kirsner also shows that 'cause to remember' is not an accurate gloss
either (1972:498):

  (i) The current which the neurosurgeon fed to the micro-
       electrode implanted in Gertrude's cerebrum made her
       remember events which had occurred over fifty years
       ago.
  (ii) ?The current which the neurosurgeon fed to the micro-
       electrode implanted in Gertrude's cerebrum reminded her
       of events which had occurred over fifty years ago.

Cruse (1972) also shows how 'teach' can be analyzed as several
verbs, but rejects the proposal.

3. Green discusses in more detail the verb ask, which also requires a highly polysemic approach. Like Postal, her work is significant and valuable because it details exactly what present semantic
proposals entail; not having recourse to an inferential solution, she
is nevertheless less than happy with the polysemic conclusion.

4. Perhaps significantly, reductions are permitted with Green's
two refuse's (see my sentences (22)-(23):

(iii) I refused Bill's offer and Bob's request.

The notion of 'inference' is not an empty one. I discuss inferential
principles in Ruhl (1973a).

5. 'Kill', 'die', and 'alive' have overlapping uses--which is only
natural, since they refer to some common phenomena--but their full
ranges are also varied; none of the three can be accounted for exclusively by reference to another.

REFERENCES

Anderson, Lloyd. 1975. Using three traditions: The classical study
of grammatical-category-space, the gradient (or 'squishy') data of
meaning-shifts, and lexical decomposition in generative semantics.
In: Shuy and Fasold (1975) [this volume, pp. 241-268].
Bolinger, Dwight. 1965. The atomization of meaning. Lg. 41.4:
555-573.
_____. 1971. Semantic overloading: A restudy of the verb remind.
Lg. 47.31:522-547.
Bowers, John. 1970. A note on 'remind'. Linguistic Inquiry
1.4:558-560.
Cruse, D. A. 1972. A note on English causitives. Linguistic
Inquiry 3.4:522-527.
Di Pietro, Robert J. To appear. The role of metaphor in linguistics.
Green, Georgia M. 1969. On the notion 'Related Lexical Entry'.
Papers from the Fifth Regional Meeting, Chicago Linguistic
Society. 76-88.
Jakobovits, Leon A. and Murray S. Miron, eds. 1967. Readings
in the psychology of language. Englewood Cliffs, N.J., Prentice-
Hall.
Katz, Jerrold J. and Jerry A. Fodor. 1963. The structure of a
semantic theory. Lg. 39.2:170-210.
Kirsner, Robert S. 1972. About 'about' and the unity of 'remind'.
Linguistic Inquiry 3.489-500.
Labov, William. 1972. Some principles of linguistic methodology.
Language in Society 1.1:97-154.

Lakoff, George. 1970. Global rules. Lg. 46.3:627-634.

_____. 1972. Hedges: A study in meaning criteria and the logic of fuzzy concepts. Papers from the Eighth Regional Meeting, Chicago Linguistic Society. 183-228.

McCawley, James D. 1968. The role of semantics in a grammar. In: Universals in linguistic theory. Edited by Emmon Bach and Robert T. Harms. New York, Holt, Rinehart and Winston, Inc. 125-170.

_____. 1971. Tense and time reference in English. In: Studies in linguistic semantics. Edited by Charles J. Fillmore and D. Terence Langendoen. New York, Holt, Rinehart and Winston, Inc. 97-114.

Postal, Paul. 1970. On the surface verb remind. Linguistic Inquiry 1.1:37-120.

Ruhl, Charles E. 1973a. Semantic anaphora. Ninth meeting, Southeastern Conference on Linguistics, University of Virginia.

_____. 1973b. The verb 'take'. Summer Meeting, Linguistic Society of America, University of Michigan.

Schmerling, Susan F. To appear. Asymmetric conjunction and rules of conversation. In: Syntax and Semantics III. Edited by P. Cole and J. L. Morgan. New York, Seminar Press.

Stockwell, Robert P., Paul Schachter, and Barbara Hall Partee. 1973. The major syntactic structures of English. New York, Holt, Rinehart and Winston.

UCLA Syntax Project. See: Stockwell et al.

Wolf, Meyer. 1970. A note on the surface verb 'remind'. Linguistic Inquiry 1.4:561.

DISCORD

CLARE M. SILVA AND ARNOLD M. ZWICKY

Ohio State University

1. Introduction. The existence of various 'styles', 'levels', or 'tones' of spoken and written language has long been recognized, and there is now a considerable literature--much of it prescriptive-- dealing with particular examples and their classification. [1] Our concern here is with the distinction between 'formal' language and 'casual' language, [2] as reflected in the lexicon, in phonology, and in syntax. In all of the following pairs, the (a) examples are more formal than the (b) examples:

(1a) She was quite tall.
(1b) She was pretty tall.
(2a) I am unhappy with these avocados.
(2b) I'm unhappy with these avocados.
(3a) He won't eat fava beans.
(3b) Fava beans he won't eat.

The sentences in (1) are distinguished by the choice of lexical item, the adverb quite as opposed to pretty; the sentences in (2), by the nonapplication versus application of a phonological contraction rule, auxiliary reduction; and the sentences in (3), by the nonapplication or application of the syntactic rule of topicalization (or Y-movement). Compare DeCamp (1971:352-353):

> If I shift into a formal, oratorical style, several rule-predict-
> able things happen to my grammar: the contraction transfor-
> mation is blocked, so that I say is not and he has instead of
> isn't and he's; the ordering of the rules for case marking and

for relative attraction is reversed, so that whom appears in
my surface structures; conversely an otherwise dormant rule
of disjunctive pronominalization makes me sprout it is he and
it is I; several phonological rules of assimilation and vowel
reduction are blocked.

Although there are complex interrelationships, we propose to discuss formality separate from other categorizations of language--for
instance, categorization by geographical origin of the speaker, social
class of the participants, their sex, their ages, their personal involvement in the discourse, politeness, occurrence of grammatical
shibboleths or simple errors, poetic texture, or 'specific' context of
discourse. This idealization permits us to treat a wide variety of
cases within a single framework. The idealization also reflects the
fact that speakers seem to be able (within limits) to make judgments
about which of two examples is the more formal, about whether a
single example sentence is formal or casual, and even about whether
an example is extremely, fairly, or only a bit formal (or casual).
Now it may turn out that this ability is not at all simple--in section
3. 2 below, in fact, we consider some possible difficulties--but it
seems sensible to examine less complex treatments of linguistic behavior before taking on elaborate models.
    Again, compare DeCamp's statement:

Of course the sociological correlates of the linguistic variation are multidimensional: age, education, income bracket,
occupation, etc. But the linguistic variation itself is linear
if described in linguistic terms rather than in terms of those
sociological correlates (1971:354).

In general, we must stress that our work is in several ways quite
exploratory.
    We have restricted our discussion largely to our own judgments
about levels of formality and about stylistic anomaly in American
English. The restriction to two informants (occasionally supple-
mented by others) is a matter of convenience only; we would hope to
see careful studies of informant reactions on a large scale. Our
reference to informant judgments rather than to properties of masses
of elicited or collected data is intentional, however. Although we
recognize the significance of the work of Labov and those influenced
by him, we do not wish to dismiss informant judgments as sources
of insight into linguistic systems.
    In the next section we consider a simple account of stylistic level
and observe that this account is insufficiently delicate to categorize
our judgments. Sentences exhibiting stylistically discordant elements

are then used to get at fine distinctions in level. A more complex 'gradation model' is outlined in section 3.1, where a catalogue of elements is also provided, and the ways in which this model could fail to be adequate are canvassed in section 3.2. In section 3.3 we consider several cases that might illustrate one type of failure, the grammatization of instances of discord into conditions on rules.

2. A simple account

A straightforward categorization of lexical entries and rules with respect to stylistic levels would be: formal, neutral (usable in all styles), casual. Using these categories, (1a) is formal, (1b) casual; (2a) formal, (2b) neutral; (3a) neutral, (3b) casual. Other examples of lexical items and rules that distinguish among the three styles are considered below.

2.1. Some examples. A (peremptory) request with if you please is formal, while the corresponding request with please is neutral:

(4a) Give me that negative, if you please.
(4b) Give me that negative, please.

Interested in is neutral, but go for is casual:

(5a) He's not interested in yoga.
(5b) He doesn't go for yoga.

The preposing of negative adverbials (together with subject–verb inversion) is formal, while sentences without preposing are neutral:

(6a) Nowhere does he state the nature of the process.
(6b) He doesn't state the nature of the process anywhere.

A question tag with opposite polarity from its main clause (a 'flip tag') is neutral, but a tag with matching polarity (an 'alpha tag') is casual:

(7a) She's the chairman, isn't she?
(7b) She's the chairman, is she?

A sentential subject is formal, but extraposition gives a neutral sentence:

(8a) That he paid only $1800 in taxes was no surprise.

(8b) It was no surprise that he paid only $1800 in taxes.

The deletion of certain sentence-initial elements transforms a
neutral utterance into a casual one. [3]

(9a) Are they going with us?
(9b) They going with us?

The phonological process of initial glide deletion in unstressed
words is suppressed in the formal (10a), but applies in the neutral
(10b). Flap deletion and desyllabication give the casual (10c).

(10) It would be easier to say.
(10a) [It wvd bi izir̩ tu se]
(10b) [Irəd bi izir̩ tə se]
(10c) [Id bi· zir̩ tə se]

2. 2. Evidence that the simple analysis is inadequate. The three-
way distinction, although initially attractive because of its simplicity,
is insufficient for a comprehensive analysis of stylistic levels; and,
in fact, most writers on the subject have seen more than two marked
levels. [4] Intuitively, certain items or rules have a much more extreme effect than others; uncontracted let us in

(11) Let us go now.

is much more formal than uncontracted I am in (2a). Preposing the
adverbial phrase of (12a) gives a more formal sentence, (12b), than
preposing the appositive, as in (12c):

(12a) John went back to work, somewhat ill and utterly
       depressed.
(12b) Back to work John went, somewhat ill and utterly
       depressed.
(12c) Somewhat ill and utterly depressed, John went back
       to work.

So plus a clause is felt by some speakers to be more casual than the
same clause with an alpha tag, even though the two constructions have
similar meanings and uses:

(13a) So you're a man-hater now.
(13b) You're a man hater now, are you?

In addition to judging relative levels directly, we can get at fine distinctions in stylistic level by considering cases of discord, conflict in level between elements. In what follows, we consider only discord between elements from different components of grammar; here the effects are quite striking (sometimes definitely funny), although discord within a component deserves study too. We present below a sampling of cases in which formal and casual lexical entries, syntactic rules, and phonological processes are variously juxtaposed. To indicate degrees of deviance, we have used the question mark quantitatively--that is, the more deviant the sentence is thought to be, the greater the number of question marks assigned to it (up to three). The asterisk is used to mark sentences we judge to be so far beyond the pale they are ungrammatical (though we return to these examples in later sections).

Formal lexicon, casual syntactic processes. Casual topicalization of NP conflicts with the formal lexical items in

(14)   ?Men who eschew controversy we are not in need of.

Discord results when the formal impersonal <u>one</u> appears in casual pseudo-imperative conditionals or in a sentence with a casual tag:

(15)   *Wash oneself every day, and one's skin gets dry.
(16)   *One should eat violet leaves, should one?

Formal lexicon, casual phonology. Discord (in different degrees) arises in the association of formal lexical entries with the casual phonological processes that give <u>gonna</u>, <u>wanna</u>, and <u>lemme</u>:

(17)   I submit that what they are $\left\{ \begin{array}{l} \text{going to} \\ \text{? ?gonna} \end{array} \right.$ do might well dis-
       credit the program in its entirety.
(18)   I $\left\{ \begin{array}{l} \text{want to} \\ \text{?wanna} \end{array} \right.$ make one thing perfectly clear.
(19) $\left\{ \begin{array}{l} \text{Let me} \\ \text{? ? ?Lemme} \end{array} \right.$ assure you of my dedication to this office.

Formal syntax, casual lexicon. Adverbial preposing conflicts with the casual entries <u>go for</u> and <u>you knów</u>:

(20)   ? ?Never did he go for rock or cool jazz, you knów.

The casual impersonal pronoun <u>they</u> and the predicate <u>great</u> are discordant with a sentential subject. Compare casual (21a) and formal (21b) with the juxtaposition of styles in (21c).

(21a) It's great they finally caught up with those hoods.
(21b) That the miscreants were finally apprehended is splendid.
(21c) ??That they finally caught up with those hoods is great.

Formal syntax, casual phonology. Casual processes of flap
deletion, auxiliary reduction, and desyllabication (illustrated in (22a))
are at variance with the formal sentential subject of (22b).

(22a) [hi dIn se Id bin izɨ wr̥d tǝ se]
       He didn't say it would be an easy word to say.
(22b) ??[ðæɾId bin izi wrd tǝ se dIn mærr]
       That it would be an easy word to say didn't matter.

Formal phonology, casual lexicon. Suppressing contraction
renders (23) discordant.

(23) ???Let us cut out now, baby.

The sentential idioms of (24) lose their idiomatic understanding when
casual phonological processes are suppressed, as in (25).

(24a) What's up?
(24b) You're telling mé!
(24c) So's your old man!
(25a) What is up?
(25b) You are telling mé!
(25c) So is your old man!

Formal phonology, casual syntax. The casual tag of (26) conflicts
with the formal suppression of contraction.

(26) ?She is the chairman, is she?

The casual deletion in (27) conflicts with suppression of contraction.

(27) *Have not seen George around for a long time.

3.1. A more complex linear model

Given that a three-way division is not adequate, the next possibility to explore is that there are merely more degrees of casualness
and more degrees of formality, as various writers have suggested.
A gradation model of this type might provide two scales deviating
from the neutral, or zero, position--say, from +1 to +10 for formal
elements and from -1 to -10 for casual elements (the choice of the

number 10 here is without significance). Each linguistic element (lexical entry or rule) would be assigned a value between -10 and +10, and the degree of stylistic deviance of a sentence could be calculated as the difference between the values of the most extreme elements in it. [5] Thus, a sentence having a very formal element in it, one assigned the value +9, and also a fairly casual element, one with the value -5, would receive the deviance index 14, and would be predicted to be more anomalous than a sentence with the same formal element in combination with an only slightly casual (-2) element (index 11), or a sentence with the same casual element in combination with a moderately formal (+4) element (index 9).

Our gradation model is quite similar to (but distinct from) DeCamp's 1971 model. DeCamp proposes to order linguistically variable elements on a linear scale, each point on the scale separating occurrence of the element from its nonoccurrence. DeCamp does not incorporate neutral elements into his model, nor does he provide a mechanism for distinguishing larger or smaller distances between two elements (except insofar as there are intervening elements on the scale; but nothing guarantees that such intervening elements will happen to occur). On the other hand, DeCamp (1971:354) assumes that his scales are indefinitely divisible ('by calling it a continuum I mean that given two samples of Jamaican speech which differ substantially from one another, it is usually possible to find a third intermediate level in an additional sample'), whereas the number of levels in our model is bounded by speakers' abilities in discriminating styles. This last difference between the two models points to the major distinction between DeCamp's treatment and ours; he is primarily interested in systematizing variation across speakers, while our purpose is to systematize variation across contexts for a single speaker. These are related types of variation, but not necessarily the same.

In a more recent paper, DeCamp (1973) has investigated a model quite similar in spirit to ours, though his interest focuses on the correlation between the extent to which grammatical features are related and the extent to which they are implicationally dependent on each other. He does, however, see features varying in stylistic import on a number of scales.

Within our present framework, the linguist's problem is to determine which rules and lexical entries are stylistically marked and then to assign them values in a way that predicts both the correct ordering of elements and the correct relative ordering of discords. A first attempt at a sample of this catalogue is given in the next section.

3.1.1. Phonological rules.[6]

+10: uncontracted <u>let us</u>

+9: suppression of t → ʔ ʔ __##, as in <u>right</u>, <u>got</u>, <u>eat</u>, especially before word-initial consonants or in pausa; suppression of a rule that deletes morpheme-final t and d after certain continuant consonants, as in <u>and</u>, <u>soft</u>, <u>must</u>, especially before other consonants.

+7: suppression of n → ∅ / V__C, as in <u>can't</u>, <u>hand</u>; suppression of a rule syncopating vowels, roughly

$$\begin{bmatrix} V \\ -\text{stress} \end{bmatrix} \rightarrow \emptyset \ / \ C\underline{\quad}R \begin{bmatrix} V \\ -\text{stress} \end{bmatrix}$$

as in <u>hindering</u>, <u>pedaling</u>, <u>happening</u>.

+4: failure to delete initial glides h and w in unstressed words, as in <u>his</u>, <u>would</u>; suppression of auxiliary reduction; failure to reduce Vn to n in <u>in</u>, <u>on</u>, <u>an</u>, <u>and</u>

0: obligatory morphophonemic rules.

-1: rules yielding <u>wanna</u> from <u>want to</u>.

-3: rules yielding <u>gonna</u> from <u>going to</u>.

-5: vowel centralization (Shockey (1973) observes a significant degree of centralization in the conversational style of her subjects); flap deletion, as in <u>magnetic</u> and <u>about it</u>.

-7: desyllabication (after flap deletion), as in <u>being</u> [biŋ], <u>be an</u> [bin], <u>it'd</u> [Id]; rules yielding <u>lemme</u> from <u>let me</u>.

Note that formality in phonology largely derives from suppressing rules rather than from applying them.[7] Also note that it is very hard to find an optional phonological rule without any stylistic import whatsoever. In these respects, phonology is different from syntax, and it would be very interesting to try to explain why.

3.1.2. Syntactic rules. [8]

+10: counterfactual inversion, as in 'Were John here, we could discuss your problem'.

+8: subject-verb inversion after preposed negative elements, as in 'Nowhere does he state the nature of the process'.

+7: pied piping in questions and relatives, as in 'At whom are you smiling?' and 'The person to whom he spoke was a former dean'; preposing of adverbial phrases as in 'To her closest friends we related what was happening' and 'On your answer our future lives depend'; preposing of appositive clauses, as in 'Feeling that he might be in danger, I ordered him to return' and 'The largest single campus university in the U.S., Ohio State offers 250 programs of study'.

+5: failure to extrapose sentential subjects, as in 'That the test case was disappointing surprised no one' and 'For the test case to be disappointing surprised no one'.

+3: use of existential there with verbs other than be, as in 'There are said to be several candidates for the job', 'There remained several matters to attend to'.

0: passivization; flip tags, as in 'This dog is handsome, isn't it?' and 'This dog won't bite, will it?'; VP deletion, as in 'These machines can handle that job, but the new ones can't'.

-2: extraposition from NP, as in 'A man came in who was wearing a headphones stereo'; topicalization of NP, as in 'This paper I'm going to regret ever having begun'. (Huddleston 1971:315 finds that the focusing achieved by topicalization of NP 'is effected just about exclusively' by passivization in scientific English.)

-4: alpha tags, as in 'You're going to town, are you?'; pseudo-imperative conditionals, like 'Add acid and the solution will turn blue'; retention of pronouns in 'Don't you talk to me that way!' and 'I got me a wife'; left dislocation, as in 'That guy, he's a bum'; right

dislocation, as in 'He's a bum, that guy'; emotive negative tags, as in 'Not this bottle, you won't!' fractured
whimperatives (Sadock 1970), as in 'Close the door,
will/won't you?'

-5: topicalization of VP, as in 'Call a cab I never could';
emotive extraposition of NP, as in 'It's great the way
he's handling the ball' (Elliott 1971); possessive deletion, as in 'John getting home late was no surprise'.

-9: various deletions of sentence-initial elements, illus-
trated by 'Think I'd better get this in the mail today',
'See where he went?', 'Can't be many people here',
'Ask me, I'd say he went that way'.

A question that deserves more study is: can we predict which 'optional'
syntactic rules will have stylistic import, and if so, can we predict
whether a particular rule will give casual or formal results? A few
general observations are possible. For instance, sentences that are
heavy on the left tend to be associated with formal style. Also notice
these suggestive remarks by Fraser (1973:6):

Contrary to the rules in B ['rules to adjust grammatical detail',
like number agreement], which for some dialects are seldom
optional, the rules in C ['rules to reduce redundancy'] are, I
believe, always optional though the frequency of application
and thus the degree of obligation will depend on the speech context. We can hypothesize that the optionality for such rules
will increase as the style of discourse becomes less formal.

The rules in Fraser's classes E ('rules to topicalize') and F ('rules
to increase variety') sometimes have stylistic import and sometimes
do not. [9]

3.1.3. Lexical items [10]

+9: hereby

+8: performative formulas like I submit, let me say, I
should point out, I conclude, etc.

+7: impersonal one (rather than you); eschew

+2: subsequently, in this respect/regard, in conjunction
with, in the event

0: <u>then</u>, <u>and</u>, <u>after</u>, <u>chair</u>, . . .

-3: intensifying <u>pretty</u>, <u>really</u>, <u>awful</u>; <u>you know</u> and similar filler items; impersonal <u>they</u>

-5: many slang expressions, for instance exclamatory <u>boy</u>!, <u>great</u> [good], <u>beat it</u> [leave], <u>step on it</u> [hurry up], <u>bust</u> [arrest], <u>go for</u> [be interested in]

-8: many obscene expressions

We return now to the discordant example sentences of section 2.2 to see what deviance indices would be assigned to them by the scheme just outlined. Table 1 includes all question-marked (but not asterisked) examples:

TABLE 1.

Example number	Deviance index	Question marks
(14)	9	?
(17)	11	??
(18)	9	?
(19)	15	???
(20)	11	??
(21c)	10	??
(22b)	12	??
(23)	15	???
(26)	8	?

Our assignment of values to the elements in these sentences is consistent with our original judgments of the relative deviance of the sentences; an index of 8 or 9 corresponds to one question mark, 10 to 12 corresponds to two, and by 15 we have reached three question marks. We discuss the asterisked examples in section 3.3.

3.2. Potential difficulties

The model of stylistic level outlined above could be inadequate in a number of ways. In fact, several of these difficulties are implicit in the previous discussion. But let us take up the problems one by one.

Variation in values by environment. It might be impossible to assign invariant values to an element because the degree of formality of the element is different in different linguistic environments. In particular, it might be impossible to assign an invariant value to a rule because application of the rule to different lexical items or structures yields results not on the same stylistic level. We have already seen a few cases of this difficulty. For instance, as noted in the previous section, existential there with verbs other than be is somewhat formal. But there with predicative be is neutral; there is nothing marked about sentences like

(28) There is a car in the driveway.

Consequently, unless it can be argued that there are two or more there-insertion rules, we have here an example of a rule that gives different values in different environments.

Similarly, pied piping is not a rule, but a mode of application of rules. Yet the result of moving wh-words in questions and relatives has different values, depending upon whether or not these rules pied pipe.

We have also pointed out that topicalization of NP is less casual than topicalization of VP. For some speakers, moreover, topicalization in negative sentences is less casual than topicalization in positive sentences, so that (29) is less casual than (30):

(29) Beans I never eat.
(30) Beans I eat often.

Other cases are easy to find. Preposing of adverbials has quite different effects depending upon what sort of adverbial is fronted. Contrast the formal sentences in 3.1.2, which have preposed negative elements and the phrases to her closest friends and on your answer, with sentences with preposed time adverbials, which are stylistically neutral:

(31) Yesterday we went to Philadelphia.
(32) At the beginning of the week they should receive the letter.

The effect of preposed negative elements isn't constant, as a matter of fact, since the not only construction is not particularly marked:

(33) Not only do I read Spanish, (but) I also play polo.

For syntax, it seems to be that stylistically marked elements typically vary in their effect according to environment. Phonological rules and lexical items don't seem to exhibit variation to this degree. We have, however, illustrated a few cases of variation within phonological rules. Presumably, the rules yielding lemme, gonna, and wanna are drawn from the same set, yet the three results are not on a par stylistically. And perhaps the contraction in let's can be argued to be part of a more general contraction process, in which case this general process would have different stylistic values in different environments. Moreover, extension of phonological processes has been widely noted by students of casual speech. Nevertheless, the syntactic cases are much more striking than the phonological ones, and there is no obvious syntactic parallel to the paths along which phonological processes extend with increasing casualness of speech.

Complexity of the deviance function. The deviance function might be more complex than F-C, where F is the extreme formality value and C the extreme casualness value. The correct function might involve coefficients, or assign different weights to different components of grammar, or even be nonlinear. We see no indication that this is so, except in the cases discussed in section 3.3.

Range and distribution of values. The presentation of the model above claims that the most formal possible element is as marked as the most casual possible element, and provides equally spaced degrees between a neutral point and these extremes. It is not required that each component of the grammar of a language, or even each language, exhibit elements at the extremes. Moreover, it is not required that the value within some component, or the total set of values for a language, distribute themselves evenly over the range from +10 to -10. Values might cluster at (say) +10, +8, +2.5, 0, -5, and -7. Restricted ranges and skewed distributions are consistent with the model as presented. But they would indicate--especially if they recurred in many languages--that the model was insufficiently restricted. We have not surveyed a large enough body of phenomena to tell whether this problem arises.

At the moment, then, it appears that the major difficulty with the gradation model is the variability of elements according to environment. This is a very serious difficulty, and it is not easy to see how to accommodate the sorts of facts exemplified above. A brute force solution would be to mark subrules of rules for their stylistic level, and to mark, in the same way, lexical items to which rules apply-- that is, to treat formality as squishy (Ross 1972) in several dimensions 'below the level of the rule'.

David Dowty has pointed out to us that our observations can be taken as leading to quite a different conclusion: since the stylistic level of transformational operations seems to be psychologically real, facts about discord can be interpreted as evidence that similar operations with different stylistic levels constitute different rules. That is, we might simply conclude that there are two or more distinct there-insertion rules, several adverbial preposing rules, several topicalization rules, distinct rules of wh-movement according to

whether or not pied piping takes place, and so on. In some cases--
there-insertion, for instance--this conclusion would not be surprising, but in others--as in the pied piping examples--it would be dis-
tasteful, since we would have to break up a number of rules in a
parallel way.

3.3. Grammatized discord

The examples in (24) and (25) of section 2.2 illustrate a specialized
form of deviation from the simple gradation model; the combination
of a casual lexical item (in each case a sentential idiom) with formal
phonology (failure to contract auxiliaries) is simply impossible.
Apparently, the English sentential idioms What's up, You're telling
mé, and So's your old man must either be marked as obligatorily
undergoing deletion of the vowels in is and are, or lack these vowels
in their phonological underlying representations. Note that degree
of discord by itself is not sufficient to explain our judgments; on the
assumption that the sentential idioms are simply slang, or just a bit
more casual than the slang expressions listed in section 3.1.3, the
deviance index for (25) is only 9 to 11.

In (27) above, we saw a similar example, this time involving a
syntactic deletion rule in combination with the suppression of contraction. Apparently, contraction is obligatory in certain reduced sentences. Again, the deviance index for (27) is 13, which is less than
the index for (19) and (23).

Sentence (15) (similarly (16)) illustrates an interaction between a
syntactic rule and the formality of the lexical item one. The syntactic rule in question is one that forms imperative-looking sentences
from conditional remote structures. The source of (15) would be the
grammatical

(34) If one washes oneself every day, one's skin gets dry.

parallel to the derivation of

(35) Wash yourself every day, and your skin gets dry.

from

(36) If you wash yourself every day, your skin gets dry.

(understood with the impersonal you). Apparently, this rule of
pseudo-imperative conditional formation must require the subject
you in the antecedent of the conditional; antecedents with one in
them cannot undergo the rule, even though there is no semantic

anomaly. Although the deviance index for (15) is only 11, we suggest that the explanation for the restriction on the rule is the stylistic discord between the rule and the lexical item <u>one</u>. Like some of the perceptual constraints studied by Grosu (1972), the condition has become grammatized, made absolute rather than graded. Grosu notes that different languages grammatize different constraints--English, for instance, has grammatized a constraint against complex prenominal modifiers, while German has not. Similarly, we would not be surprised to find other languages in which the translations of (15) and (16) were merely somewhat odd.

We conclude that the most attractive accounts of stylistic level are inadequate in several ways. Apparently, what is called for is a descriptive device of at least the complexity of subrule hierarchies (or the partition of standard rules into many rules each), plus the postulation of conditions on rules which are motivated by stylistic discord but are categorical.

NOTES

This work was supported in part by the John Simon Guggenheim Memorial Foundation. Our thanks to Bruce Johnson, William Labov, and J. R. Ross for their comments.

1. Traditional discussion of usage--the surveys by Fowler, Gowers, Partridge, and the Evanses, for instance--tend to concentrate on lexical choices, and their judgments of stylistic levels are not clearly distinguished from judgments about grammaticality, clarity, beauty, regional or archaistic character, and other matters. Technical linguistic discussions have concentrated on phonology (as in Dressler (1972) and Zwicky (1972b)) or on correlations between linguistic and sociolinguistic variables.

2. To classify styles we use the terms 'formal' and 'casual' where Labov (1966) uses 'careful' and 'casual', respectively (he reserves 'formal' and 'informal' to characterize contexts, noting that styles and contexts are correlated but not coextensive).

3. See Schmerling (1973) for a discussion of subjectless sentences. Schmerling (1973:582-583) notes that 'some elusive element of spontaneity and impulsiveness' is involved in uttering sentences like <u>Guess I should be going</u>. Thrasher (1973) treats all sorts of sentence-initial deletions, but without a discussion of their stylistic effects.

4. Thus, Labov's studies see five or more stylistic levels, ranging from casual speech to the reading of minimal pairs, and many scholars of French have posited several levels--for instance, Fouché (1959), treating liaison, distinguishes two styles (labeled

conversation sérieuse et soignée and style soutenu) more elevated than a basic style (conversation courante).

5. This proposal has something of the flavor of Ross' (1964) treatment of degrees of grammaticality for superlative constructions. In addition to rules which have no effect on grammaticality, there are rules whose application is said to raise or lower grammaticality by a specified number of degrees.

6. These examples are drawn from various sources, in particular Zwicky (1972a).

7. Lawrence Schourup has pointed out to us that contracted mightn't and shan't are more formal than uncontracted might not and shall not.

8. The examples are taken from various sources, in particular Ross (1967).

9. It is unfortunate that in transformational grammar those rules which have come to be called 'stylistic', in that they yield 'stylistic variants' (following Chomsky's usage in a number of places), are quite often those without apparent stylistic import, like particle movement and dative movement.

10. Wells (1960) observes a general preference for nominal forms in formal style, where verbal expressions would be used at a non-formal level. He contrasts at the time of our arrival with when we arrive/arrived, in the event of his doing that with if he does that.

REFERENCES

DeCamp, David. 1971. Toward a generative analysis of a post-creole continuum. In: Pidginization and creolization of languages. Edited by D. Hymes. Cambridge University Press. 349-370.
_____. 1973. What do implicational scales imply? In: New ways of analyzing variation in English. Edited by C.-J. N. Bailey and R. W. Shuy. Washington, D. C., Georgetown University Press. 141-148.
Dressler, Wolfgang. 1972. Allegroregeln rechtfertigen Lentoregeln: secondäre Phoneme des Bretonischen. Innsbrücker Beiträge zur Sprachwissenschaft, Band 9.
Elliott, Dale. 1971. The grammar of emotive and exclamatory sentences in English. Ohio State University Working Papers in Linguistics 8. viii-110.
Fouché, Pierre. 1959. Traité de prononciation française. (2nd ed.) Paris, Klincksieck.
Fraser, Bruce. 1973. Optional rules in grammar. In: GURT 1973. 1-15.
Grosu, Alexander. 1972. The strategic content of island constraints. Ohio State University Working Papers in Linguistics 13.

Huddleston, Rodney D. 1971. The sentence in written English. Cambridge, Cambridge University Press.

Labov, William. 1966. The social stratification of English in New York City. Washington, D. C., Center for Applied Linguistics.

Ross, J. R. 1964. A partial grammar of English superlatives. Unpublished Master's thesis, University of Pennsylvania.

_____. 1967. Constraints on variables in syntax. Unpublished Ph. D. dissertation, Massachusetts Institute of Technology.

_____. 1972. The category squish: Endstation Hauptwort. CLS 8.316-328.

Sadock, Jerrold M. 1970. Whimperatives. In: Studies presented to R. B. Lees by his students. Edited by Sadock and Vanek Edmonton, Linguistic Research, Inc. 223-228.

Schmerling, Susan. 1973. Subjectless sentences and the notion of surface structure. CLS 9.577-586.

Shockey, Linda. 1973. Some phonetic and phonological properties of connected speech. Unpublished Ph. D. dissertation, Ohio State University.

Thrasher, Randy. 1973. A conspiracy on the far left. University of Michigan Working Papers in Linguistics 1:2.169-179.

Wells, Rulon. 1960. Nominal and verbal styles. In: Style in language. Edited by T. A. Sebeok. Cambridge, The MIT Press and New York, John Wiley and Sons.

Zwicky, Arnold. 1972a. Note on a phonological hierarchy in English. In: Linguistic change and generative theory. Edited by R. Stockwell and R. Macaulay. Bloomington, Indiana University Press. 275-301.

_____. 1972b. On casual speech. CLS 8.607-615.

FIGURATIVE LANGUAGE
AND THE TWO-CODE HYPOTHESIS

MARTIN STEINMANN, JR.

University of Minnesota, Minneapolis

What is the difference between speaking literally and speaking figuratively? My thesis is that this is a puzzle that the one-code hypothesis about a speaker's competence in a language does not permit linguists to solve but that the two-code hypothesis may. Before stating these two hypotheses and supporting this thesis, however, I must anticipate a possible confusion and make explicit an assumption.

Literal/Figurative vs. Serious/Nonserious. The distinction between speaking literally and speaking figuratively and the distinction between speaking seriously and speaking nonseriously, though often confused (for example, by Mack 1973b:75), are not the same; they cut across one another (cf. Austin 1962:121, Searle 1969:57). To speak figuratively is to utter tropes: not only metaphor but metonymy, synecdoche, oxymoron, rhetorical questions, polite requests, and so on. To speak nonseriously is to do such things as writing fiction, speaking lines in a play, telling jokes, conducting pattern practice, and testing public-address systems by uttering sentences. Not all figurative language is nonserious, and not all nonserious language is figurative. Figurative language often occurs in textbooks, cookbooks, news stories, television commercials, and traffic signs, for example. On the other hand, many ballads contain no figurative language at all; and much fiction--Hemingway's, for instance--uses it very sparingly.

Assumption. I assume that figurative language is a definable concept--that is, that speakers draw an intuitive line between speaking literally and speaking figuratively and therefore that there is a theoretical line for linguists to draw. This assumption may, of course, be false; the line may be only verbal, or it may be drawn differently by different speakers (cf. Di Pietro 1973). It may be that there is no set of properties shared by all instances of language we call 'figurative' but only a set of properties at least one of which is possessed by each instance, in Wittgenstein's famous expression (1953:32), only Familienähnlichkeiten. Obviously the only way to show that this assumption is not false is to successfully draw a theoretical line (cf. Donagan 1962:104).

One-Code Hypothesis vs. Two-Code. Until recently, virtually all linguists (e.g., Chomsky 1965) accepted the one-code hypothesis: that a speaker's competence in a language consists solely of his tacit knowledge of one set of rules, namely, the grammatical (that is, syntactic, semantic, and phonological) rules of the language, rules for sentences. This hypothesis does not, of course, hold that a speaker's knowledge of these rules uniquely determines his performance, only that, whatever the other determining factors may be (intelligence, for example, or memory capacity or degree of fatigue), they are not linguistic rules.

To this set of rules, the two-code hypothesis, not novel but now gaining more acceptance (cf. Lakoff 1972), adds another--namely, speech-act rules, rules for using sentences in the performance of speech acts (Austin 1962, Searle 1969).

On this hypothesis, the grammatical rules of a language constitute each of an infinite set of abstract entities, sentences, by generating three associated structures: at least one semantic structure, at least one syntactic, and at least one phonological. The semantic structure of a ('typical') sentence is a set of potentials (cf. Steinmann 1973):

(1) An illocutionary-act potential (IAPo)--a potential for use in the performance of a certain illocutionary act; making a statement (SPo), for example, or asking a question (QPo)

(2) A propositional-act potential (PropAPo)--a potential for use in the performance of a certain propositional act; that is, both (a) and (b):
   (a) A referring potential (RefPo)--a potential for use in the performance of an act of reference
   (b) A predicating potential (PredPo)--a potential for use in the performance of an act of predication

Consider the following sentences:

(S-1) The table is red.
(S-2) Is the table red?

(S-3) The table is not red.

(S-1) and (S-2) have different IAPos: (S-1) has SPo; (S-2), QPo.
But they have the same PredAPo: the same RefPo (for referring to
the same referent, an already-identified table) and the same PredPo
(for predicating the same property, redness, of it). In other words,
(S-1) has a potential for use in stating that, and (S-2) a potential for
use in asking whether, a table is red. (S-3) has the same IAPo as
(S-1). But it has a different PropAPo: the same RefPo but a different PredPo (for predicating a different property, not-redness, of the
referent).

Just as the grammatical rules of a language constitute one kind of
abstract entity (sentences) speech-act rules constitute another kind
(statements, questions, etc.). In effect, they specify the conditions
under which utterance of a sentence may realize the IAPo and the
PropAPo of the sentence (and, I shall suggest, the conditions under
which the utterance of it may realize the potentials of a different
sentence). For an utterance of (S-1) to realize the potentials of (S-1),
for instance, the speaker must, among other things, perform a certain act of reference (use the referring phrase the table to refer to
some already-identified table) and a certain act of predication (use
the predicating phrase is red to predicate redness of that table),
believe that table to be red (the sincerity condition), believe the
person-spoken-to not to know that it is (a preparatory condition),
and count utterance of (S-1) as a commitment that it is (the essential
condition). And, for utterance of (S-2) to realize the potentials of
(S-2), the speaker must perform the same acts of reference and
predication, want to know whether the table is red (the sincerity
condition), believe the person-spoken-to to know whether it is (a
preparatory condition), and count utterance of (S-2) as an attempt to
find out whether it is (the essential condition).

Figurative Language and One-Code Hypothesis. On the one-code
hypothesis, figurative language must, it seems, be explained either
as anomalous or in terms of deep and surface structures; and neither
explanation will do.

Explanation of figurative language as anomalous is very tempting.
Much of it--almost all metaphor, for instance, and by definition all
oxymoron--is semantically anomalous (violates selectional restrictions); and all of it is both intended and interpreted to mean something that the code, the grammatical rules, do not permit it to mean.
But not all figurative language is semantically anomalous:

(S-4) My father is a dictator.

Uttered as a statement by someone whose father is not a Hitler,

(S-4) is certainly figurative (metaphorical); and, taken as a literal statement, it is certainly false. But, since no semantic features of father are incompatible with any of dictator, the sentence is not semantically anomalous; and the statement, though false, is only contingently, not necessarily, so.

What is more, though speaking figuratively is even more creative than speaking literally, for not only the sentence uttered but the meanings of some of its words are novel, it shows every sign of being rule governed. All speakers do it at least as often as they speak literally and with no sense of doing something bizarre, children do it as soon as they learn to speak at all, figurative language occurs in discourse of every kind, speakers interpret it as easily as they do literal language, and it is the chief source of semantic change in the literal.

On the one-code hypothesis, one way to explain figurative language in terms of deep and surface structures is, for one surface structure, to postulate two deep structures, one corresponding to the literal meaning of the sentence and the other to the figurative. Thus explained, (S-4), for example, is ambiguous. Underlying the surface-structure dictator are two different deep-structure items: something like autocratic-chief-of-state (the literal) and autocratic-person (the figurative). Sadock (1971) explains rhetorical questions (or 'queclaratives') in much this way. Taken figuratively--that is, as a rhetorical question--(S-5), for instance, has a deep structure that conjoins a sentence something like I-ask-Is syntax easy? with one something like I-declare-Syntax is not easy:

(S-5) Is syntax easy?

Taken literally, however, (S-5) has a deep structure consisting of only the first sentence. (Cf. Mack 1973a, Kiparsky 1970, and Dahl 1972:707-708.)

The other way to explain figurative language in terms of deep and surface structures is, for two surface structures, to postulate one deep structure. Thus Ross (1973) explains (S-6) taken figuratively-- that is, as metonymy--as having the same deep structure as (S-7) (and as being synonymous with it):

(S-6) I am parked on Elm Street.
(S-7) My car is parked on Elm Street.

Underlying the surface subject of both (S-6) and (S-7) is a deep-structure subject something like I-have-a-car, but in (S-6) an optional transformation deletes car.

But neither way will do to explain figurative language in general.
For one thing, it is unlikely that all instances of figurative language
can be explained in either way. For another thing, even if they can,
neither way can draw a theoretical line between figurative language
and literal. Neither can distinguish, for instance, the ambiguity of
(S-4), which ex hypothesi has one figurative and one literal reading,
from the ambiguity of (S-8), which has two literal:

(S-8) My father is gay.

Nor can either distinguish the synonymity of (S-6) (figurative) and
(S-7) (literal) from the synonymity of (S-7) and (S-9) (both literal):

(S-9) On Elm Street is parked my car.

Figurative Language and Two-Code Hypothesis. The two-code
hypothesis may permit a solution to the puzzle of how figurative language differs from literal. For, by postulating a second code, speech-
act rules, it permits a distinction between (a) declarative, interroga-
tive, imperative, etc. sentences (abstract entities with semantic
structures constituted by the grammatical rules) and (b) statements,
questions, requests, etc. (abstract entities constituted by speech-act
rules). Thus, it permits a distinction between (a) intended meaning
(IM), the meaning the speaker intends his utterance of a sentence in
the performance of a speech act to have; (b) sentence meaning (SM),
the meaning that, by the grammatical rules, the sentence uttered has;
and (c) utterance meaning (UM), the meaning that, by speech-act
rules, his utterance of the sentence in the performance of a speech
act has.

Speaking figuratively consists, I suggest, of saying (UM) what you
mean (IM) by not meaning what you say (SM); speaking literally, of
saying (UM) what you mean (IM) by meaning what you say (SM). Thus,
in figurative language, IM $\neq$ SM but IM = UM and therefore SM $\neq$ UM;
in literal language, IM = SM, IM = UM, and therefore SM = UM. In
other words, in figurative language, some or all of the potentials
that constitute the semantic structure of a sentence are not realized
in the performance of a speech act (SM $\neq$ UM); in literal language,
all are realized (SM = UM).

Again consider (S-4), (S-5), and (S-6) taken figuratively (as
metaphor, rhetorical question, and metonymy, respectively):

(S-4) My father is a dictator.
(S-5) Is syntax easy?
(S-6) I am parked on Elm Street.

In the figurative utterance of (S-4), the IAPo (SPo) is realized, but the PropAPo is not. The RefPo of the referring phrase my father is realized but not the PredPo of the predicating phrase is a dictator. Instead the PredPo of the predicating phrase is an autocratic person is realized. In the figurative utterance of (S-5), neither the IAPo (QPo) nor the PropAPo is realized. Instead the IAPo (SPo) and the PropAPo of (S-10) are realized:

(S-10) Syntax is not easy.

Though (S-5) and (S-10) have the same RefPo (because they contain the same referring phrase, syntax), they have different PredPos (because they contain different predicating phrases, is . . . easy and is not easy). Finally, in the figurative utterance of (S-6), the IAPo (SPo) is realized, but the PropAPo is not. The PredPo of the predicating phrase be [am/is] parked on Elm Street is realized but not the RefPo of the referring phrase I. Instead the RefPo of the referring phrase my car (as in (S-7)) is realized.

On the two-code hypothesis, then, it is not sentences that are figurative or literal; it is utterances of sentences in the performance of speech acts. One utterance of a given sentence can be figurative, another literal. And whether an utterance is figurative or literal depends upon the conditions of utterance. If the two-code hypothesis is to solve the puzzle of how figurative language differs from literal, then speech-act rules must specify not only the conditions of literal utterance (that is, the conditions under which utterance of a sentence may realize the IAPo and the PropAPo of the sentence) but also the conditions of figurative utterance (the conditions under which utterance of it may realize the IAPo and/or the PropAPo of a different sentence). Austin (1962) and Searle (1969), for example, have formulated many of the literal speech-act rules; and Gordon and Lakoff (1971) and Grice (1968) have begun to formulate the figurative ones (as 'conversational postulates').

There are, of course, problems. As Gordon and Lakoff (1971), Heringer (1972), and Sadock (1971) suggest, there seem to be cases in which the grammatical rules (and therefore semantic and syntactic structure) as well as speech-act rules play a role in figurative language. Even if these cases are indeed counterinstances, perhaps they need not be fatal to the hypothesis here suggested. Like any other hypothesis or theory, it must sweep some recalcitrant cases under the rug, at least until (if ever) it undergoes a modification that can account for them (cf. Kuhn 1970).

Another problem is the semantic anomaly of many sentences used in speaking figuratively:

(S-11) My father is an amoeba.

Some semantic features of <u>father</u> (+human, for example) are incompatible with some of <u>amoeba</u> (~human). Consequently, uttered literally as a statement, (S-11) is a contradiction--something is both human (because a father) and not-human (because an amoeba)--and hence necessarily false. What is the function of this semantic anomaly? Is it to signal the person-spoken-to that an utterance of the sentence is almost certainly to be taken figuratively?

A consequent problem is that, when SM is (so to speak) semantically anomalous, UM and presumably IM are indeterminate. If (S-11) is taken figuratively, then the PredPo of the predicating phrase <u>is an amoeba</u> is not realized, but neither is the PredPo of any other particular predicating phrase. The person-spoken-to finds himself confronted with an indefinitely great range of PredPos from which he is free, with some guidance from the verbal and the situational contexts, to choose one (or more?) to realize: the PredPos of, for instance, the referring phrases <u>is very small</u>, <u>is peculiarly shaped</u>, <u>is given to creeping</u>, and <u>is naked</u>.

Still another problem is to distinguish figurative language from elliptical literal language--saying what you mean by meaning more than what you say (or by saying less than what you mean)--and from anomalous language--not semantically anomalous sentences (violations of grammatical rules), ill-formed sentences, but ill-formed speech acts (utterances of sentences containing malapropisms, dangling modifiers, or misplaced modifiers, for example). Perhaps the following scheme makes a start in dealing with this problem:

$$\text{Speech}$$

		Rule governed	Anomalous
			IM $\neq$ SM
	Literal	Figurative	IM $\neq$ UM**
		IM $\neq$ SM	SM $\neq$ UM
Full	Elliptical	IM = UM	
IM = SM	IM $\neq$ SM*	SM $\neq$ UM	
IM = UM	IM = UM		
SM = UM	SM $\neq$ UM		

*But SM = part of IM and UM.

**The person-spoken-to may, of course, correctly infer IM, but by reference to extralinguistic generalizations, not to linguistic rules, grammatical or speech-act.

REFERENCES

Austin, J. L. 1962. How to do things with words. Edited by J. O. Urmson. Oxford, Clarendon Press.

Chomsky, N. 1965. Aspects of the theory of syntax. Cambridge, The MIT Press.

Dahl, O. 1972. Review of: The Nordic languages and modern linguistics . . . Edited by H. Benediktsson. Lg. 48.705-714.

Di Pietro, R. J. 1973. The role of metaphor in linguistics. To appear in: The Hill memorial volume. Edited by Edgar C. Polome. Austin, University of Texas Press.

Donagan, A. 1962. The later philosophy of R. G. Collingwood. Oxford, Clarendon Press.

Gordon, D. and G. Lakoff. 1971. Conversational postulates. Papers from the Seventh Regional Meeting, Chicago Linguistic Society. 63-84.

Grice, H. P. 1968. The logic of conversation. MS.

Heringer, J. T. 1972. Some grammatical correlates of felicity conditions and presuppositions. Working Papers in Linguistics. Ohio State University. 11.iv-110.

Kiparsky, P. 1970. Semantic rules in grammar. The Nordic languages and modern linguistics . . . Edited by H. Benediktsson. Reykjavík, Vísindafélage Íslendinga. 262-285.

Kuhn, T. S. 1970. The structure of scientific resolutions. (2nd ed.) Chicago, University of Chicago Press.

Lakoff, R. 1972. Language in context. Lg. 48.907-927.

Mack, D. 1973a. Metaphorical ambiguities. In: Nilsen 1973: 58-63.

_____. 1973b. Metaphoring as one kind of speech act. In: Nilsen 1973:75-87.

Nilsen, D. L. F., ed. 1973. Meaning: A common ground of linguistics and literature.

Ross, J. R. 1973. Inaudibili. Paper presented at the Second Annual Colloquium on New Ways of Analyzing Variation, Georgetown University.

Sadock, J. M. 1971. Queclaratives. Papers from the Seventh Regional Meeting, Chicago Linguistic Society. 223-231.

Searle, J. R. 1969. Speech acts. Cambridge, Cambridge University Press.

Steinmann, M. 1973. On McCawley on propositions and noun phrases. In: Toward tomorrow's linguistics. Edited by R. W. Shuy and C.-J. N. Bailey. Washington, D.C., Georgetown University Press. 65-71.

Wittgenstein, L. 1953. Philosophical investigations. Translated by G. E. M. Anscombe. Oxford, Basil Blackwell.

WHERE DO CONDITIONAL EXPRESSIONS QUALIFY?: FUNCTIONAL VARIABILITY BETWEEN LOGICAL AND ORDINARY LANGUAGE CONDITIONALS

MASA-AKI YAMANASHI

University of Michigan

Introduction. In the field of linguistic variability, the study of phonetic phenomena has provided the first testing ground for research. This is not an accident, for the behavior of surface linguistic forms most clearly enabled us to construct data sets explicit enough for the analysis along many dimensions of variation and thus became a reasonable target of quantitative studies of language behavior (Cedergren 1973:13).

Semantic phenomena, on the other hand, have received relatively less attention so far. The reason for this is certainly not a lack of interest, since the study of meaning is one of the most crucial parts of linguistic research. As Labov (1973) has pointed out, it is rather due to the difficulty of the problem and its inaccessibility to currently popular methods of research.

The purpose of the present paper is to investigate the functional variability between logical conditionals and a variety of ordinary conditional expressions in natural language. The discussion in what follows is necessarily semantic and pragmatic in nature. Observations to be made below are mainly descriptive. This does not mean, however, that the underlying purpose of the present paper is to end at that level. The eventual goal is to establish the detailed specification of the functional variability of ordinary conditional expressions in natural language in connection with the truth-functionality of logical conditionals.

In the first three sections, we will investigate the interaction between the truth-functionality of logical conditionals and three different types of ordinary conditionals: (i) Indicative conditionals, (ii) Rhetorical conditionals, and (iii) Counterfactual conditionals and try to characterize their functional variability in terms of the manner of relevance between the antecedent and consequent, the existence of presuppositions in the antecedent and/or consequent, and the pragmatic nature of invited inference. In the fourth section, the non-truthfunctional nature of concessive conditionals is discussed in connection with the behavior of ordinary indicative conditionals. In the final section, we will observe a number of non-truthfunctional conditionals, which have something to do with suspension of some element in the consequent statement in terms of conversational implicature, logical or pragmatic presupposition, and a set of felicity conditions in the speech act.

1. Truth-functionality and ordinary indicative conditionals

In ordinary discourse, if one statement is a reasonable ground for another and the speaker is not certain whether the first statement is true or not, he is justified in saying something of the form, If p, then q. Thus, consider the following sentences in (1).

(1a) If it rains tomorrow, the game will be cancelled.
(1b) If you study hard, you will pass the exam.
(1c) If Bill beats his wife, he will get divorced.

When one utters (1a) for example, he does not thereby affirm that the game will be cancelled. He will not necessarily have to admit that he was mistaken if it turns out that it didn't rain and at the same time the game was not cancelled. [1] On the other hand, he should acknowledge his mistake or at least he should admit that he was misleading in his use of the conditional form, If p, then q, if it turns out that it rained and the game was still not cancelled. In other words, the statement made in (1a) can be said to commit the speaker only to the extent of ruling out the joint fulfillment of the antecedent statement and the denial of its consequent statement. The same can be basically said about those conditionals in (1b) and (1c). Characterized in this way, the conditionals in (1) are not incompatible with the truth-functional statement of the form, $p \supset q$ in that it is to be specified as false just in case the antecedent is true and the consequent is false. This, however, does not mean that ordinary conditional expressions of the form, If p, then q, can be identified with their truth-functional counterparts, $p \supset q$.

For one thing, such ordinary conditionals as in (1) should be based on the speech act situation where the normal fulfillment of the antecedent may provide some confirmation for the assertion that the existence of the states of affairs like those described by the antecedent is a good ground for expecting the states of affairs like those described by the consequent. In other words, the utterance of those in (1) should be based on some manner of relevance between the antecedent and consequent--some causal or contingent connection between them.

The truth-functional version, $p \supset q$, on the other hand, is unnatural in terms of ordinary language in that it leads us to construe the whole conditional statement as true no matter how irrelevant its antecedent statement may be to its consequent statement, so long as it is not the case that the antecedent is true and the consequent is false (i.e. the falsity of the antecedent or the truth of the consequent is equally the sufficient condition for the truth of the whole conditional statement).

Thus, let us examine the conditionals in (2).

(2a)   ?If New York is in the United States, sugar is sweet.
(2b)   ?If New York is in Japan, sugar is sweet.
(2c)   ?If New York is in Japan, sugar is salty.

In truth-functional terms, these conditionals ought to be regarded as true in that at least either the antecedent is false or the consequent is true, although in ordinary discourse of natural language they cannot be meaningful unless the user of those conditionals presumes a certain peculiar context which entails some manner of relevance between the antecedent and consequent.

Thus, we cannot merely take ordinary conditionals of type (1) to be identical with truth-functional conditionals. This is not to say, however, that there is no overlapping in function between ordinary conditionals and truth-functional conditionals. There are some cases where the truth-functional specification seems to mesh with the account for some special use of conditionals in ordinary language.

2. Rhetorical conditionals

Consider the examples in (3).

(3a)   If John is an eligible bachelor, I'll eat my hat.
(3b)   If Harry is a genius, I'm a monkey's uncle. [2]
(3c)   If Nixon is not guilty, I'm a Dutchman.

When one uses conditionals of type (3), ironically he somehow assumes the consequent to be false. Thus, the following expressions are infelicitous.

(4a) *If John is an eligible bachelor, I'll eat my hat, which
      I'll do at any rate.
(4b) *If Harry is a genius, I'm a monkey's uncle, which I
      am anyway.
(4c) *If Nixon is not guilty, I'm a Dutchman, as I am anyway.

The force of such utterances as in (3) is to lead the addressee to
understand that, since the consequent cannot be taken to be true,
the conditional statement as a whole can be true only if the antecedent
is taken to be false.[3] Virtually, this is an indirect way of asserting
the statement in the antecedent clause to be false.[4]

One might suppose, however, that even the antecedent of the
conditionals in (3) can be assumed to be false. In fact, in most contexts the conditionals in (3) strongly suggest that the antecedent is
also false. This, however, is not taken to be a logical result. In
the actual world, John might be an eligible bachelor (e.g. (3a)) or
Harry might be a genius (e.g. (3b)). But so far as the speaker's
world is concerned, all he does is to assert indirectly the antecedent to be false in virtue of the obvious absurdity of the consequent
statement.

3. Counterfactual conditionals

Now, compare the rhetorical conditionals of type (3) with so-
called counterfactual conditionals in (5).

(5a) If Pat had been wise, she would have divorced Dick.
(5b) If dodos were still alive, I would hunt them.
(5c) If Mary were not idle, she would be a good secretary.
(5d) If John had kept beating his wife, he would have been
      divorced.

As Karttunen (1971) has pointed out, although counterfactual conditionals presuppose the negation of the antecedent, they only suggest,
in the absence of disclaimer, that the consequent should be false.
Thus, take (5a) for example. The speaker cannot modify the sentence in (5a) and utter, without contradiction, such sentences as in
(6).

(6a) *If Pat had been wise, as she is anyway, she would have
      divorced Dick.
(6b) *If Pat had been wise, she would have divorced Dick,
      but she is wise.
(6c) *If Pat had been wise, she would have divorced Dick,
      and it is odd that she is wise.

Thus, the sentence in (5a) (or for that matter any counter-factual conditionals of type (5)) can be basically specified in terms of two components (i.e. (a) Presupposition component and (b) Assertion component) as in (7).

(7a) Presupposition: Pat is not wise.
(7b) Assertion: If Pat was wise, she divorced Dick.[5]

If the above observations are correct, then we can see an interesting contrast between counterfactual conditionals of type (5) and rhetorical conditionals of type (3): the former can be characterized as assuming their antecedent to be false, whereas the latter assume their consequent to be false. Schematically, the variety of ordinary conditionals observed so far can be specified as in (8).

(8)

types ⊃	p	q
(8a) Indicatives	$\emptyset$	$\emptyset$
(8b) Counterfactuals	>>(~p)	$\emptyset$
(8c) Rhetoricals	$\emptyset$	>>(~q)
(8d) ----------	>>(~p)	>>(~q)

(where p and q are the antecedent and consequent, respectively. >>(x) indicates that x is assumed to be the case. $\emptyset$ indicates that such an assumption is absent.)

As shown in the rows, (8b) and (8c), the difference in function between counterfactual and rhetorical conditionals is whether the antecedent, p, or the consequent, q, is assumed to be false. But this is by no means to say that they are equivalent otherwise. There is a crucial difference between these two types of conditionals in terms of the existence or absence of the manner of relevance between p and q. In case of rhetorical conditionals like (3), there is no direct mode of relevance between p and q. Thus, in (3a) for example, there is no direct connection between the antecedent statement, 'Nixon is not guilty' and the consequent statement, 'I'm a Dutchman'. The same is true of (3b) and (3c).[6]

Counterfactual conditionals of type (5), on the other hand, involve some aspects of manner of relevance between p and q. Given the distinction between the 'presupposition' and 'assertion' components for counterfactuals as specified in (7), the 'assertion' component (e.g. 'If Pat was wise, she divorced Dick') entails some mode of relevance between the antecedent and consequent. Thus, the counterfactual expression, 'If Pat had been wise, she would have divorced

Dick', should be based on such contexts as the one in which Pat has been married to her husband, Dick, who involved himself in some utterly lousy business. In this respect, counterfactual conditionals share the same function as ordinary indicative conditionals as in (1). The difference between these two types of conditionals consists in the existence or absence of the presupposition of the falsity of the antecedent.

Now, the combination of the antecedent and consequent in terms of the row given in (8d) is an interesting possibility. So far as I can see, there is no case in ordinary English, in which conditionals fit into (8d). We observed that counterfactual conditionals assume the falsity of the antecedent, but they only suggest (not logically imply) that the consequent should be false. Geis and Zwicky (1971:562) point out that in a wide variety of circumstances, a sentence such as 'If you mow the lawn, I'll give you five dollars', can be interpreted by a majority of speakers as if it implied its corresponding inverse form (i. e. 'If you do not mow the lawn, I will not give you five dollars'). In many cases, a statement of the form, $x \supset y$ invites an inference of the form, $\sim x \supset \sim y$. In other words, there is a tendency in natural language to perfect conditionals to biconditionals.

Given this tendency, it is natural to expect that such conditional expressions as counterfactuals in (5) should be interpreted in terms of the row given in (8d). But this result must be based on pragmatic grounds, not on purely logical grounds. [7]

So far, we have observed three different kinds of ordinary conditional expressions: indicative conditionals, rhetorical conditionals, and counterfactual conditionals. From the above observations, it is clear that they cannot simply be used truth-functionally. In case of indicative conditionals, there must be some kind of connection between the antecedent and consequent which constitutes a necesary condition for the truth of the whole conditional statement: i. e. there should be some mode of relevance between the antecedent and consequent which is part of the meaning of the indicative conditionals but not the meaning of the truth-functional conditionals. Counterfactual conditionals presume the same kind of mode of relevance between the antecedent and consequent, but differ from indicative conditionals in that they assume the antecedent to be false. In case of rhetorical conditionals, on the other hand, there is no direct connection between the antecedent and consequent. Thus, in this respect, they are more like truth-functional conditionals. But the former are distinct from the latter in that the consequent of the former is presumed to be false.

However, these characteristics of ordinary conditionals do not lead us directly to the conclusion that their use has nothing to do with the truth-functional use of logical conditionals. Take rhetorical conditionals, for example: their basic function is to exploit the inference such that given the conditional statement of the form, If p, then q (e. g. 'If Nixon is not guilty, I'm a Dutchman') plus the obvious falsity of q (e. g. 'I'm a Dutchman'), then it is truth-functionally valid to infer the falsity of p (i. e. 'Nixon is actually guilty'). In case of counterfactual conditionals, based on the pre-supposed falsity of the antecedent, the consequent is naturally invited as false. Although strictly speaking this process is not logical, there is a reasonable ground upon which this result holds: i. e. given If p, then q in counterfactual form, from the conjunction of the pre-supposed falsity of the antecedent (~p) with the invited inference (If ~p, then ~q), it follows that ~q is the case. Although the second premise here is merely invited, clearly the truth-functional process participates in the above inference.

Thus, the types of ordinary conditionals observed above cannot simply be treated as independent of truth-functional conditionals. The communicative function of the former can be interpreted in an indirect way in terms of the latter.

4. Concessive conditionals

Now, consider the conditional expressions of the following sort.

(9a) If they are poor, they are happy.
(9b) He is a good poet, if not a good novelist.
(9c) John is strong, if not young.
(9d) Harry is honest if poor.

Although the conditionals in (9) apparently have the same syntactic form as ordinary indicative conditionals, they differ in that the former have the assumption that the antecedent is to be granted as true and the latter do not. Thus, those in (9) can be paraphrased into those in (10).

(10a) If they are poor, they are happy anyway.
(10b) He is still a good poet, if not a good novelist.
(10c) John is still strong, if not young.
(10d) Harry is honest at any rate, if poor.

Or (9) can be paraphrased as in (11) with even immediately preceding if.

(11a) Even if they are poor, they are happy.
(11b) He is a good poet, even if not a good novelist.
(11c) John is strong, even if not young.

(11d) Harry is honest, even if poor.

The conditional expressions which show the above characteristics are different from ordinary indicative conditionals in that the antecedent cannot be taken to contribute to the direct determination of the truth condition for the consequent. Rather, the antecedent here is to provide a reasonable ground for expecting one of the remaining possibilities such that the consequent will still be the case. There is an interesting kind of manner of relevance between the antecedent and consequent. But the relevance here is some sort of unexpected contrast between the states of affairs expressed by the antecedent and consequent, but not the kind of relevance which connects one state of affairs that entails another, as is the case with ordinary indicative conditionals.

5. Conditionals having to do with suspension

The behavior of the following types of conditionals is also unique in that their antecedent cannot be understood to simply modify the consequent statement as such. Rather, the antecedent here can be taken to participate in the suspension of some element which can be inferred, logically or pragmatically, by the statement made in the consequent in virtue of such relations as conversational implicature and logical or pragamatic presupposition.

5.1. Implicature-suspending conditionals. First, consider the following conditionals in (12), which Horn (1972) pointed out.

(12a) Mary is pretty, if not beautiful.
(12b) I visited that spot sometimes, if not often.
(12c) It is warm, if not hot.
(12d) Sixty percent, if not more, of the electorate will be fooled.
(12e) You can find such a person somewhere, if not everywhere.

Here, the antecedent cannot literally be taken to constitute a sufficient condition, as is the case with indicative conditionals. As Horn observed, the function of those if-clauses in (12) is to suspend the quantitative implicature which is conversationally conveyed by those scaler predicates in the consequent statement (e.g. pretty, warm, some). The use of the predicate, pretty in (12a) for example, conversationally implicates a stronger predicate like beautiful on the same scale and the force of the given if-clause is to suspend this conversational implicature. The conditionals in (12) are apparently similar to those in (9). It should be noted, however, that the predicates used in the antecedent and consequent in (12) are based on the same scale, whereas those in (9) are not.

5.2. Presupposition-suspending conditionals. Another type of conditionals which cannot simply be identified with ordinary indicative (or truth-functional) conditionals are the following.

(13a) Martha stopped nagging at her husband, if (indeed) she ever did.
(13b) Steve doesn't cry anymore, if (indeed) he ever did.
(13c) John doesn't realize what, if anything, is going on.
(13d) Few men quit beating their wives, if any at all ever did.
(13e) Only Fred left the party, if (indeed) he did.

The relation which connects the antecedent and consequent statements in (13) is different from the implicature involved in the conditionals of type (12). The relation here is rather that the statement made in the consequent presupposes the propositional content of the antecedent. The fundamental function of the antecedent here is to suspend the necessary condition of the consequent statement, which would otherwise be presupposed. Thus, in case of (13a), the consequent statement (i.e. 'Martha stopped nagging at her husband') presupposes that she used to nag at her husband and this presupposition is somehow suspended or cancelled by the if–clause (i.e. 'if (indeed) she ever did'). The same relationship holds of (13b)-(13e).

5.3. Performative conditionals. Finally, let us consider the following expressions. [8]

(14a) If I may ask, how old is your wife?
(14b) Do it again, if you can!
(14c) There are some candies on the table, if you would like some.

According to Austin (1962), for every illocutionary act, there is a reasonably limited set of conditions on intensions, beliefs, and other internal and external circumstances of the speech act, which he calls 'Felicity conditions'. Thus, take (14a) for example. As was pointed out in Heringer (1972), in settings where the speaker is being deferential or polite to the addressee, the performer of an illocutionary act is to believe, among other things, that he has the permission of the addressee to perform the volitional act involved in the carrying out of that illocutionary act, that is, the addressee will allow the speaker to carry out that act. The utterance of type (14a) involves the felicity condition of this kind as part of the context of the speech act.

Similar cases are as follows.

(15a) If you don't mind (my saying so), your husband is too old.
(15b) If you'll allow me to say so, you are trying to do something impossible.
(15c) If you'll pardon me, I forgot to take out the garbage.
(15d) If it's alright with you, can you come and pick me up at one o'clock?

In fact, if one utters the sentence like, 'How old is your wife?', which consists of the consequent of (14a) alone, the utterer of the sentence is taken to presume that he has the right of performing a volitional act of questioning. The virtue of the if-clause in (14a) or (15), then, is to somehow suspend the presumption of the above sort and thereby indicates indirectly that the performer of the given act is deferential or polite to the addressee.

By the same token, in case of such imperative utterances as (14b), the speaker is to assume a set of felicity conditions such that the addressee is able to do the required act, A, that it is not obvious to the speaker that the addressee will do the act, A, that the speaker is in a position of authority over the addressee and so on. And the function of the if-clause in (14b) is to suspend the presumption of one of the above felicity conditions. Namely, he suspends the presumption of the addressee's ability to do the act, A, and by so doing leads himself to a more secure ground in the speech act situation.

In case of such apparently declarative utterances as in (14c), there is a set of underlying illocutionary forces such as that there is some reason for the speaker to believe that the addressee will benefit from his indication of the fact that p (i.e. there are some candies on the table), that the addressee will be interested in the existence of the candies, that the addressee still does not realize the above fact, and so forth. Here, again, the use of the if-clause can be viewed as contributing to the suspension of one of the above presumptions: i.e. the addressee's interest in profitting from the indication of p.

From the above considerations, it is clear that the antecedent in conditionals of type (14) cannot be interpreted as providing a sufficient condition for the consequent to be true, as is the case with ordinary indicative conditionals. Rather, they are to modify one of the felicity conditions entailed by the performance of the speech act in the consequent.

6. Residual problems

In this paper, we observed a variety of conditional expressions in ordinary English, all of which are manifested syntactically in the form of If p, then q. From the above observations, it turned out that their underlying function varies depending on the nature of manner of relevance between the antecedent and consequent, the existence or absence of presupposition, invited inference, conversational implicature, and various kinds of pragmatic conditions entailed by the speech act context.

The discussions made above are descriptive and far from exhaustive. But they are sufficient enough to lead us to ask, among others, the following questions: (1) How can we capture these various functions underlying ordinary conditional expressions in grammar? At what level of the grammar are they located?; (2) If they diverge from one another, what is the motivating ground for their manifestation in the same syntactic frame, If p, then q?; (3) Is there any discrete point which demarcates logical (or purely truth-functional) nature from pragmatic nature of conditionals? Can we say, for example, that indicative conditionals are specifiable in terms of truth conditions and performative conditionals, on the other hand, in terms of felicity conditions?; (4) Do invited inference phenomena exist cross-dialectally or do they vary depending on individual judgments?; (5) Is the presupposition of falsity in the antecedent (counterfactual conditionals) the same in nature as the presupposition of falsity in the consequent (rhetorical conditionals)?

All of these questions remain. It is hoped that the further research of functional variability in ordinary conditionals will result in clarifying the nature and the implications of such problems as raised above.

NOTES

I would like to thank Alton Becker, Larry Johnson, John Lawler, and Rich Rhodes for their valuable comments and discussions.

Needless to say, I am responsible for any errors which might have been made.

1. It should be noted, however, that from the fact that it didn't rain, one might invite the inference that the game was not cancelled. But this is not a purely logical result.

Phenomena of invited inference of this type will be discussed in section 3 in more detail.

2. This example is from Karttunen (1972:17).

3. The following idiomatic conditions seem to share the same kind of process as those conditionals in

(3i) I'll be damned if I'll marry her again.
(3ii) I'll be hanged if I'll give them another chance.
(3iii) I'll be a son-of-a-bitch if I'll do it again.

But they are more restricted than those in (3) in that so far as they are used idiomatically, the subject of the consequent must be the

first person, singular (i.e. I). Thus, the following expressions are
not acceptable in the above intended sense.

(i) * $\left\{\begin{array}{l}\text{you}\\\text{he}\\\text{she}\\\text{they}\\\text{etc.}\end{array}\right\}$ 'll be damned if I'll marry her again.

4. In truth-functional terms, this process can be characterized
by <u>Modus Tollens</u> (i.e. p ⊃ q and ~q, therefore ~p).

5. Although it might be supposed that in counter-factuals not only
the antecedent but also the consequent should be presupposed to be
false, this does not necessarily follow. Karttunen (1971:566) gave
some counterexamples against the reading suggested above that without contradiction one may utter such sentences as the following.

(i) If Harry had known that Sheila survived, he would have
gone home, which he did anyway.
(ii) If Harry had known that Sheila survived, he would still
have gone home.

6. Actually, this lack of direct mode of relevance between p and
q is one of the fundamental functions which leads the addressee to the
understanding of the rhetorical force of conditionals of type (3).

7. Also, in case of rhetorical conditionals of type (3), there is a
tendency to regard not only the consequent but also the antecedent as
assumed to be false. In fact, given the rhetorical conditionals of the
form, If p, then q plus the assumption ~q, it is valid to infer that ~p
is the case. Admittedly, this inference cannot be ascribed to an invited inference in the sense of Geis and Zwicky (1971). But still (8d)
cannot be said to be the direct underlying form of the rhetorical conditionals, for the use of rhetorical conditionals of type (3) consists in
not assuming the falsity of the antecedent but indirectly asserting its
falsity.

8. For the detailed observations of conditionals of this type, see
Heringer (1972) and Yamanashi (1973).

REFERENCES

Austin, J. L. 1962. How to do things with words. Oxford, Oxford
University Press.
Bailey, C.-J. N. and Roger W. Shuy, eds. 1973. New ways of
analyzing variation in English. Washington, D.C., Georgetown
University Press.

Cedergren, H. J. 1973. On the nature of variable constraints. In: Bailey and Shuy (1973). 13-22.

Geis, M. L. and A. M. Zwicky. 1971. On invited inference. Linguistic Inquiry 2:4.561-566.

Grice, H. P. 1968. Logic and conversation. Manuscript. Department of Philosophy, University of California, Berkeley.

Heringer, J. T. 1972. Some grammatical correlates of felicity conditions and presuppositions. Working Papers in Linguistics. Department of Linguistics, Ohio State University.

Horn, L. R. 1972. On the semantic properties of logical operators in English. Unpublished Ph.D. dissertation, University of California, Los Angeles.

Karttunen, L. 1971. Counterfactual conditionals. Linguistic Inquiry 2:4.566-569.

_____. 1972. Possible and must. In: Syntax and semantics. Vol. 2. Edited by John Kimball. New York, Seminar Press. 1-20.

Labov, W. 1973. The boundaries of words and their meanings. In: Bailey and Shuy (1973). 340-373.

Lakoff, G. 1970. Linguistics and natural logic. Studies in generative semantics. 1. Phonetic Laboratory, University of Michigan.

Yamanashi, M. 1973. Performative conditionals and scope of qualification. Paper presented at the annual meeting of the Michigan Linguistic Society, Kalamazoo, Michigan.

UNITING THREE TRADITIONS: THE CLASSICAL STUDY OF GRAMMATICAL-CATEGORY-SPACE, AND LEXICAL DECOMPOSITION IN GENERATIVE SEMANTICS

LLOYD ANDERSON

Introduction. Boundaries between the meanings of words are becoming a prominent area of study in linguistics. One can in general understand the meanings of words only by understanding the competition between them at their boundaries. Grammatical categories similarly compete with each other as expressions for meaning-structures at their boundaries. Thus there need be no artificial division between the lexical and grammatical planes (studies of verb-classes distinguishable both by ranges of meaning of the verbs and by grammatical sentence-types in which they may be used have repeatedly shown such a division to be harmful to our understanding of language).

Such category-boundaries can be handled with techniques from several traditions in linguistics, from European structuralism to modern gradient phenomena and variable rules, and the trees used by generative semanticists to represent components of meaning. In reviewing these, we find that many of our 'new' ideas have strong traditional roots.

The two major sets of examples used as illustration are (1) classical problems of meaning-space and change, the history of <u>silly</u> in English together with the space of color terms as recently developed by Berlin and Kay (1969) and the contrast of Spanish <u>hacer</u> with English <u>make, do, act,</u> etc.; and (2) varieties of 'to be' and of a grammatical category loosely called the 'passive', a detailed treatment of a small area in the general meaning-space/grammatical-space of <u>be, get, have,</u> and their relatives.

1. Graduality in meaning-change

The gradient meaning-development through time of the word spelled gisælig, iseli, seely, silly can be presented in a chart of + and 0 entries as in (1b), information traditionally displayed with time-lines from earliest to latest dates of attestation of particular meanings (1a). Focusing on the horizontal dimension instead, we get chart (1c), which can also be visualized as the mounds of earth a word-carrying mole raises as he travels through the ground of meaning.

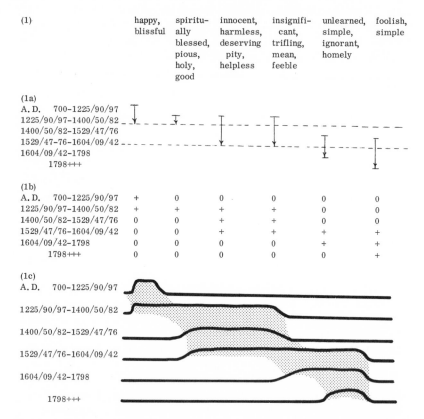

(1)

| | happy, blissful | spiritu- ally blessed, pious, holy, good | innocent, harmless, deserving pity, helpless | insignifi- cant, trifling, mean, feeble | unlearned, simple, ignorant, homely | foolish, simple |

(1b)

A.D.						
700–1225/90/97	+	0	0	0	0	0
1225/90/97–1400/50/82	+	+	+	+	0	0
1400/50/82–1529/47/76	0	0	+	+	0	0
1529/47/76–1604/09/42	0	0	+	+	+	+
1604/09/42–1798	0	0	0	0	+	+
1798+++	0	0	0	0	0	+

Chart (1) is adapted from information in Menner (1945) by collapsing some of the most closely related meanings with minor variations in dates of attestation to obtain a smaller number of categories. Charts of type (1a) may be seen for example in appendices to Closs Traugott (1972:198–200).

In the traditional approach represented by Menner, there were beginnings toward other explanatory concepts. Thus the range of meanings expressed by a single form is not to get so wide that crucial ambiguities occur unresolved by context:

(2) It is obvious that in Standard English 'pious-good' over-lapped 'innocent-harmless' and 'innocent-harmless' over-lapped 'foolish-simple', but 'pious-good' and 'foolish-simple' do not overlap historically. (Menner 1945:65)
    . . . though two or three senses may coexist for a long time the development out of the last of still another sense further removed from the first tends to coincide with the elimination of the first. (Menner 1945:64)

And methodological principles were suggested for dealing with inter-view data so as to demonstrate interference between two senses which tend not to be expressed by the same word. In the Linguistic Atlas of New England, clever may be cited by interviewees for the meanings 'good natured' or 'handy (at ploughing)'. But the relative proportions citing the word for both meanings is lower if restricted to citations when the interviewer did not suggest the word (Menner 1945:73).

The example silly in (1) shows the shift of a single category (in this example, a word) through meaning-space. The + entries in (1b) are surrounded on both sides by 0 entries in a fashion matching the middle of squish-type (3a) rather than (1a) of Anderson (1974a). A more general treatment must involve the borders between categories:

2. Border areas between neighboring categories

Meaning-spaces have traditionally been made explicit for plant and animal taxonomies, for kin-terms, and for color-terms. Some important concepts are suggested through comparison of languages with different numbers of terms distributed over the same (univer-sal?) color-space, as diagrammed in (3) (adapted from Berlin and Kay 1969:19-20). For each term there is a core area of preferred use and a periphery where it is less freely used. When an addi-tional term is added to the system, it may occupy a position formerly peripheral to another term, as when 'blue' in stage V occupies an area which in stage IV was the periphery of 'green'. This type of pattern may be anchored in external reality, physiological or other. (Berlin has informed me that there is an alternative stage IV* in which the core of the 'grue' area is 'blue' instead of 'green', the green area being the periphery of the 'blue' category. See section 3 below for further discussion of core and periphery.)

The schematic chart for stage VI suggests a different situation, in which the addition of a category 'brown' causes the neighboring category 'green' to shift its core area of use (in this example

(3)

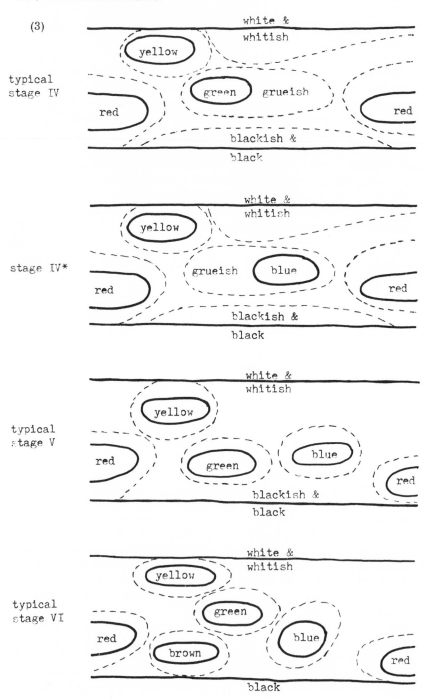

typical
stage IV

stage IV*

typical
stage V

typical
stage VI

towards lighter shades) rather than simply to withdraw its periphery. (This must be taken with a grain of salt, since the stage VI chart is based on others' reports rather than direct experimental evidence. Berlin reports stage VI may turn out to be not strictly implicationally ordered, but rather a subvariety of stage VII.) This seeming equilibrium-system avoiding collision of categories is much like so-called 'push-chains' and 'drag-chains', co-variation in phonetic space.

The diagrams in (3) also have what might be called 'lexical gaps' between category-peripheries, where no basic color term is comfortably used. There are at least two accounts for this: (a) that there is no need for terms for unusual colors (or that for physiological reasons certain colors are not as easily categorized); or (b) that complex terms such as 'sky blue' are used when needed as substitutes for simple terms. These two phrasings may in fact be a single explanation.

A clear example of this is discussed by Lehrer (1970), as given in (4):

(4) general: horse   mouse
     'female':   ⎧female horse   female mouse
                  ⎩mare   --

One could say that there is no 'need' for an 'unmotivated' (indivisible) term for 'female mouse', but this sounds like merely naming the problem. Or one could say that such an 'unmotivated' term would not survive the learning process (because of infrequent usage?), while the compound term female mouse is productively regenerable by any speaker of the language.

3. Core and periphery

Even when it is recognized that a given word or grammatical category has central meanings and peripheral meanings, this may be treated as either a discrete or a gradient structure. The central and peripheral meanings may be distinguished discretely by the context in which they occur (5), or in a gradient by the strength with which they are invited as inferences from the form (6). The version (5) of the shift looks very much like rule-inversion in phonology (Vennemann 1972, Kuryłowicz 1948).

(5) Meanings of <u>I want food</u>

	special contexts X	all contexts except Y	all contexts	all contexts except X	special contexts Y	
older English			[lack]		[desire]	A
possible			[lack]	[desire]		B
historical		[lack]			[desire]	C
intermediates		[lack]		[desire]		D
	[lack]			[desire]		E
		[lack]	[desire]			F
modern English	[lack]		[desire]			G

(6)

	strongly invited inference	weakly invited inference
older English	'lack food'	'desire food'
modern English	'desire food'	'lack food'

The above example has been cited by Bolinger, taking it as analogous to the modern 'I'm starved' from which one can usually infer 'I desire food'.

The most general model would allow both context-sensitivity (5) and quantitative strength (6), in complex combinations for which computers will probably be needed to model the dynamics. (Labov (1973: 355-356) points out that dictionary definitions incorporate quantitative strength.) I might hazard the guess that all meanings are invited inferences, core meanings invited more strongly or in a wider range of contexts. Presuppositions for example might be more weakly invited (or invited only on a semiconscious level), but invited by both positive and negative versions of a sentence ('I have/haven't stopped beating my wife').

I do not have direct information on the historical intermediates of (5), so I have allowed for different possibilities (7):

(7)

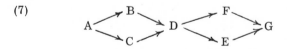

The non-viability of any discrete distinction between distinctive/ criterial and redundant/peripheral meanings has been argued by Labov (1973:esp. 342-347) and by Haas (1973). Some examples and evidence from Haas (290):

(8) Evidence that the 'focal' or 'criterial' meaning of <u>show</u>
is 'cause to see':
(a) Showing you the picture, I caused you to see it.
(tautologous, pointless)
(b) John was asleep when I showed him the picture.
(absurd, contradictory)
Counterevidence in special situations:
(c) Not realizing that Bill was blind, I
{OK showed him } some pictures.
{*caused him to see}

(9) Haas's Conclusions:
Enough meaning is left to 'show', even though a central
semantic feature of it, <u>see</u> + causative, is eliminated by
context. [in (8c)]
It happens again and again that the conversion of
semantic tendencies into rules forces us to misrepresent
the normal semantic spread of an expression as a multiple
ambiguity [the rule of causative decomposition/incorpor-
ation in generative semantics; <u>show</u> would be ambiguous,
one meaning for (8a) and (8b), another for (8c)].
There is no paraphrase relation between 'deep-structure
input' and the surface output of the [lexicalization] transformations.

Contrasts between methods of lexical (or grammatical) decomposition in generative semantics, and traditional methods of semantic (or
grammatical) space will be discussed in sections 5 and 6.

4. Meaning-space and grammatical space: Contrastive diagrams

The universal pattern of meaning-relations and of meaning-shifts
can be diagrammed so as to provide an overview. For traditional
grammatical categories this is discussed in section 7.
Form-meaning connections are traditionally the fundamental data
of linguistics. The contrast between two varieties of language can be
indicated by two superimposed partitions of meaning-space, as given
in (10) for a lexical contrast between a child's use (dashed enclosures)
and adult's use of English <u>ask</u> and <u>tell</u>.
For Smith's son Amahl (1973:254), <u>tell</u> 'was used consistently
with the meaning of 'ask'. For A, [āsk] usually meant "ask for".'
A longer study at later ages is Chomsky (1969).

(10)

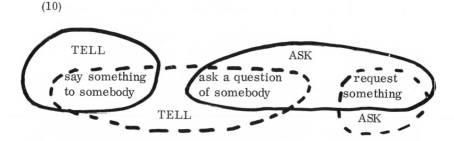

A more extended lexical contrast is given in (11) for the English words make, do, act, etc., as their range of use overlaps the range of Spanish hacer. The codes h7, m7, etc. refer to lists of meanings which Hagerty and Bowen (1973) differentiate. I have attempted to arrange the most closely related meanings next to each other But I have no direct evidence on how native speakers of the two languages classify these relations of meaning psychologically. That would be of considerable relevance for teaching strategies; at least such diagrams of lexical overlap allow us to pose the problem.

Numerals in brackets (the 15 of [h7 = m7 15] under causal hacer) are from the textual count reported by Hagerty and Bowen (1973:24); percentages of types of use indicated for do and make are from Michael West General Service List of English Words, as reported by Hagerty and Bowen (18-20). Further values for make: m6/7 (nouns) 36 percent, m8 (adjectives) 22 percent, m9 (verb-particles) 2. 2 percent.

The same approach can be used for distinctions among more grammatical forms (12), where solid enclosures represent Spanish categories, dashed enclosures represent English categories. Some interesting details on English parallels are in Bolinger (1973), especially as concerns the types 'he's all in a dither' but not 'all insane', and 'Mary thinks him sane' but not 'Mary thinks him in control of himself' for the accidental/essential contrast (in reverse order for the second pair).

Visually, the range of meanings expressed by ser is divided in two by the range of estar. Estar could be a historically later intrusion. But it does not necessarily follow from such a diagram, because the limitation to two-dimensional paper has no necessary relation to a multi-dimensional meaning-space, and may prevent linking visually two uses of a category which are psychologically related. I suspect this particular lexical/grammatical split is psychologically real because the arrangement of meanings in (12) matches closely the arrangement which traditional knowledge suggests for grammatical categories involving be; see section 7, especially (20).

(11) The Meaning-space of <u>hacer</u>, <u>make</u>, <u>do</u>, etc.

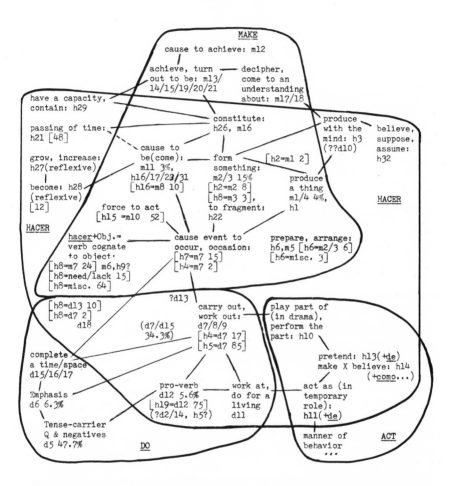

Here there are almost certainly implications for language teaching. The semantically central contrasts are perhaps two: first, between essential (<u>ser</u>) and accidental/temporary (<u>estar</u>) senses of 'being'; second, between intransitivizing <u>se</u> and impersonal occurrence (<u>ser</u>).

5. One meaning or two: Generative semantics and traditional meaning-space

The range of meanings of <u>hacer</u> given in (11) is wide. For a subset, we would have generative-semantic trees more or less as in (13), leaving out the subject NP_x. Although variety (b) may be a more-specific (c), (e) may be a more-specific (d), and (g) may be

(12) The grammatical meaning-space of be, ser, estar, etc.

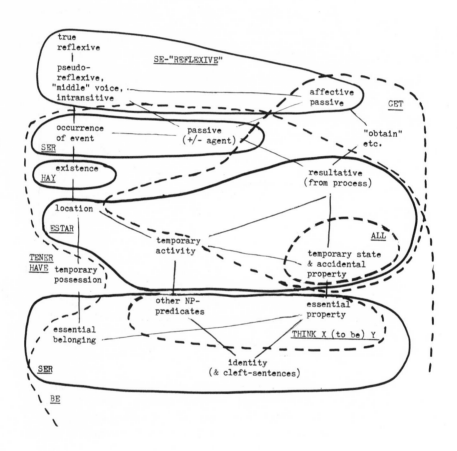

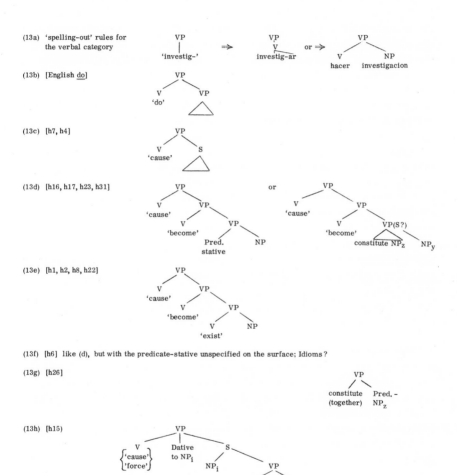

(13a) 'spelling-out' rules for the verbal category

(13b) [English do]

(13c) [h7, h4]

(13d) [h16, h17, h23, h31]

(13e) [h1, h2, h8, h22]

(13f) [h6] like (d), but with the predicate-stative unspecified on the surface; Idioms?

(13g) [h26]

(13h) [h15]

related to (d), there is apparently no sub-tree common to all uses of hacer.

The current solution for generative semanticists is to talk of a surface target-structure (the verb hacer) into which are fed a number of underlying meanings (13). But this seems to imply massive polysemy, since a totally unrelated set of meanings could equally well be fed into a single surface form by rules. Either we must say that the explanation is merely historical, an original causal sense (13c) having given rise to many other varieties no longer psychologically related among themselves, or we can agree with traditional wisdom that the varieties of (13) are felt as similar to each other, a partly unified range of contiguous meanings. A decision between such alternatives will often be a matter of degree, but in this example I would not want to say that meaning-split had occurred, except perhaps separating off h32, h29, h26, h21, h27, and h28 from the rest. Even this separation could be the biased intuitions of a speaker of English (myself); but Spanish could also be an accidental exception to the norm here. A typological comparison of many languages plotted on such a chart might show partitions most often excluding just that same list of meanings from the range of the verb most analogous to make/hacer in the particular language, and then we could probably conclude that psychological similarity of meanings within the core area was greater than similarities across that partition-boundary. This is at any rate a program for research.

6. The 'passive'

The grammatical analog to the lexical example (11) through (13) which I wish to discuss is the 'passive', or the range of grammatical categories in various languages which are traditionally covered by that term. This links in neatly with the universal grammatical-space of (20), and with the Spanish-English contrastive partitions of (12). After listing six varieties of 'passive' (14c), (15), (16b), (16d), (16e), and (17b), emphasizing distinctions of meaning among them in a psychological-processing variant of generative semantics, I compare them explicitly in a feature-analysis (18). The similarities among these are then indicated visually in (19) in their appropriate locations as extracted from the fuller (20).

(14) Active vs. impersonal ('narrative') passive without agent.

      (a) A meaning-structure neutral between the two; the choice of which proposition-node to grammaticalize as (main-) clause S-node in processing is indicated by dotted-line additions,

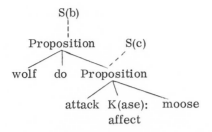

(b) actives by proposition-consolidation into a single clause: ('The wolf attacked the moose')

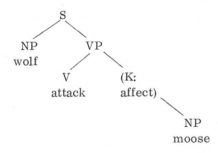

(c) impersonal passive: by addition of auxiliary to mark occurrence of event (without agent, which normally has an agent); and subject-selection: ('The moose was attacked')

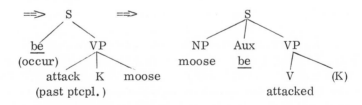

(15) Passive with contrastive agent
    (a) The moose was attacked by <u>the wolf.</u>
    (b) What attacked the moose was <u>the wolf.</u>
    (c) It was <u>the wolf</u> that attacked the moose.
    (d) <u>The wolf</u> attacked the moose.

(I do not attempt to explain the difference between (a), (b), (c), and (d); though I do suspect a gradient in that order! Suffice it that they are more closely related to each other than are any of them to other types of passive.)

(e) Deep-structure
    (meaning-structure)
    for (a), (b), (c), (d):

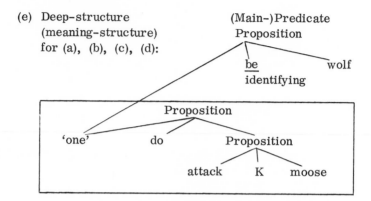

(f) Standard equivalent of the box as relative clause for
    those more conservative in their trees:

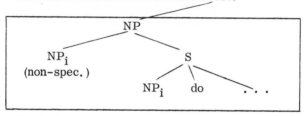

The psychological processing in the production of (15a) from (15e) might well be as follows: First, processing starts for the relative-clause-as-subject (boxed area in (e)), as would be required to produce (b) or (c) (??). Second, the processing mechanism forgets the material outside of the box in (e). We would then expect an impersonal sentence on the order of German man . . . - and French on . . . - constructions, unless the non-specific 'one' here is different from those subjects in some important way. The English equivalent for these is sometimes an impersonal sentence with they ('They say . . .' etc.), but more often an impersonal passive (14c); so it would appear that it is the lowest 'proposition'-node within the box of (e) which has taken control of psychological processing, perhaps for lack of substantive content in the higher of the two (compare the alternatives in (14a)). An English 'Something attacked the moose.' is really existential, not impersonal: 'there was [something which] attacked the moose' is the explicit form of some translations into Tagalog, for example. For further arguments on deep-structure distinctions as between alternatives of (14a), see Anderson (1974; esp. part III).

Without the interference of ongoing processing within the box of (15e), processing now returns to the unfinished business outside the box (this is the third step). To be grammatical, this content can only

be expressed as a superficial adverb by the wolf, despite its main-
predicate status semantically.

(16) Mutative passives

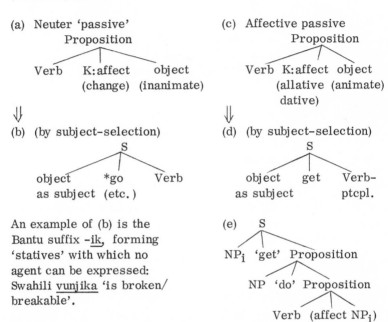

(a) Neuter 'passive'
     Proposition

           Verb   K:affect   object
                  (change)   (inanimate)

(b) (by subject-selection)
                    S

     object   *go   Verb
     as subject (etc.)

An example of (b) is the
Bantu suffix -ik, forming
'statives' with which no
agent can be expressed:
Swahili vunjika 'is broken/
breakable'.

(c) Affective passive
     Proposition

           Verb K:affect object
                 (allative (animate)
                  dative)

(d) (by subject-selection)
                    S

     object   get   Verb-
     as subject   ptcpl.

(e)   S

     NPᵢ   'get'   Proposition

           NP 'do' Proposition

                 Verb (affect NPᵢ)

The structure (16e) may arise from that variant of (14a) which
would normally become (14c), by building of new grammatical structure with a recipient (the NP_i 'get') and a sort of Equi-NP-deletion on
the lower NP_i; further details of this possibility might be as from
(15e) to (15a).

The 'neuter passive' may often have the same surface form as true
inchoatives from intransitive adjectival-verbs (English 'turn red',
'grow red', and 'become red' also do not allow expression of an agent
'by someone').

Bickerton (1975) notes that passives in Guyanese Creole are unmarked if the object is inanimate, but are marked with get if the object is animate. This is the difference between (16b) and (16d): for
an inanimate object, once changed, remains that way since it has
'become' different, whereas an animal 'receiving' (! !) some effect
may usually return to its original condition. Burning a piece of
paper is harder to correct than burning one's hand, as viewed by the
paper and hand. The opposition discussed by Bolinger (1973) within
inchoatives 'become healthy/get well' also shows the non-essential
nature of 'get'-effects.

(17) Mutative affective passives in which the affected entity plays no direct role in the affecting proposition (is not the direct object, etc.)

(17a)

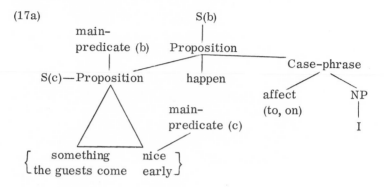

(17b) I had something nice happen to me (today)!
I had the guests come early on me (three times last week)!

(17c) The guests came eárly on me.
Finally something níce happened to me.

In (17) the alternatives are indicated in much the same way as in (14). The general rule seems to be that the main-predicate (new important information) will determine that the proposition within which it is contained becomes the surface main clause. For (17b), the lower proposition is as a whole the predicate, and the upper proposition becomes the grammatical main clause; the occurrence of the event (lower proposition) is in opposition to its lack, or to the occurrence of some other event. For (17c) the main predicate is within the lower proposition, and the lower proposition becomes the grammatical main clause; the opposition is to the guest coming at the proper time, and to something not-so-nice happening.

When we are affected by events beyond our control, we will dislike this more often than we like it, so the passive of type (17) was first called 'adversative passive', and favorable effects were overlooked, within the tradition both of English grammar and of Japanese grammar (Sag 1973 etc.).

(18)   Features of types of passives

	(14c)	(15)	(17)	(16d, e)	(16b)	inchoatives	'middle voice'
original lexical meaning (*) and derived grammatical meaning in use as auxiliary	be, *occur	*occur	*have *get	*get	*go etc.	become, *grow *turn etc.	∅
essential change-of-state?	+/0	+/0	+/0	+/0	+	+	+/0
temporary affect?	+/0	+/0	+	+	+	+	+
transitive verbs allowed?	+	+	+	+	+	0	?+/0
agent (two propos. layers) allowed?	0	+	+	+	0	0	0
voluntary?	0	0	0	0	0	0	+/0

The +/0 entries indicate that the value varies with lexical choice of verb and object: attacking a moose affects the moose, but understanding a book does not affect the book.

It should be clear that the exact boundaries of the 'passive' are hard to define. The types in (18) can be arranged in (19) as they appear in (20).

(19)

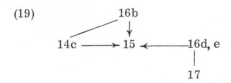

The 'middle voice' includes typical self-moves and body-moves (Diffloth 1974) such as 'I sit down' and 'I close my eyes' (the latter not in the sense allowing '. . . with silver chopsticks' which is "active", but in the sense of French 'Je ferme les yeux'. These are not passivizable, and are perhaps to be regarded as intransitive (similar to (16a) with an actor but no agent. Micronesian languages have what may be a similar distinction between VP like 'drink yagona' (indefinite object, a kind of drinking, object 'incorporated' into the verb) and VP like 'drink-*it the yagona' (def. object). By analogy,

moving one's eyes, in the middle voice, would be a kind of moving,
not moving of an object. For further discussion see Anderson (1974b:
14-15).

7. The space of traditional grammatical categories

From traditional work on grammatical categories, I have abstracted
that part relevant to 'get', 'have', and 'be', which includes much of the
case-system and of verbal tense-aspect. This is presented in (20),
(21), and (22). For perspective, the larger-scale space for part-of-
speech categories is given in (23), from Anderson (1974a:55).

(20) The semantic space of get, have, and be: their use as auxiliaries

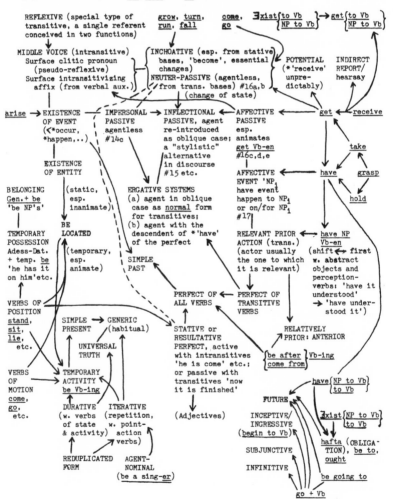

(21) The semantic space of copular be

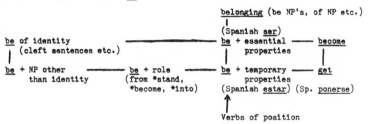

belonging (be NP's, of NP etc.)

(Spanish ser)

be of identity ─────────── be + essential ──── become
| (cleft sentences etc.)   properties

be + NP other ───── be + role ───── be + temporary ──── get
    than identity   (from *stand,   properties
                    *become, *into) (Spanish estar) (Sp. ponerse)

Verbs of position

(22) The semantic space of oblique cases

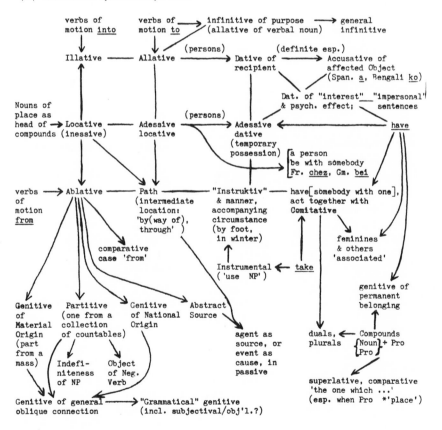

In addition to the maps of universal meaning-space in (20), (21), and (22), the dashed-line enclosures of (23) indicate some common partitions of the space into language-particular part-of-speech categories, in the manner of (11) and (12).

(23)

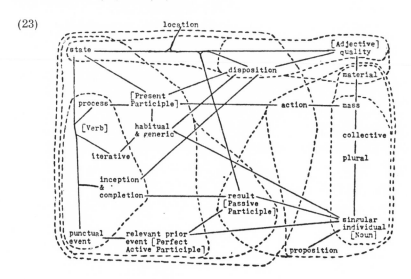

Much of (20) through (23) will be understood in terms of the earlier discussion of subparts. In (20), (21), and (22), I have tried to arrange the more 'lexical' items at the periphery, the more 'grammaticalized' forms in the center. Arrows connect two meanings such that a form having the first meaning tends to shift to use with the second meaning or grammatical function. Thus typically 'I have gotten (= obtained) it' tends to shift to I('ve) got it = 'I have it'. When lines have no arrow-heads, I am not aware of any such common directional shift. Sometimes either form can expand to cover the uses of the other; sometimes two uses have a common origin but different contexts so there is no competition. Thus in (22) verbs of 'motion to' are shown as developing into 'allative' case (with NP), but into 'purposive' verbal infinitive (with verbal noun).

Some shifts are favored by certain contexts. In (22) the allative may shift to dative in the context of persons, and the dative may shift to the accusative uses with definite (person) objects, since the accusative of a person is only indirectly affected in a majority of instances, whereas an inanimate is more often greatly changed. Compare the discussion above just before (17), and the Spanish a of the indirect object used for animate direct objects.

An interesting merger in (20) is English be Vb-ing, from earlier 'be at Vb-ing' and an iterative (?) 'be fight-ende' from 'be a fighter'.

On such iterative-to-actual-present shift, see also (25) through (27).

A similar use of lines with arrowheads, applied to shifts of use of particular words comparing adult with child English, is by Menyuk (1969:54).

8. Some predecessors and related questions

In the area of case-categories, Ferguson (1970) has argued that the traditional view of surface case categories, each uniting a range of case uses, is needed in typological comparison. By contrast, Fillmore (1968) with his fixed list of atomic case-units is more like generative semantics.

Kurylowicz (1964 and elsewhere) has attempted to synthesize traditional knowledge of meaning-shifts in grammatical categories. I have learned much from him. But his formal notation is quite hopelessly abstract. He makes the point (1964:11) that the core of a category may be at one end of the category rather than centrally located within it, as I noted for 'green' in part 2 above, Berlin and Kay's stage IV:

(24) As long as the inherited form [I write] combined both functions, the 'general' present was its primary, the 'actual' present its secondary function. The latter was always conditioned by the speech situation . . . , whereas the former was independent.

He also expresses the typical model for meaning-change with reference to some regular, recurring types (25), (26) (1964:95-96) and the rule-inversion involved in terms of markedness (27) (1964:11-101):

(25) successive chronological layers of iterative formations which replaced the older types first in their secondary functions [imperfective], afterwards also in their primary function.

(26a) Three historical stages:

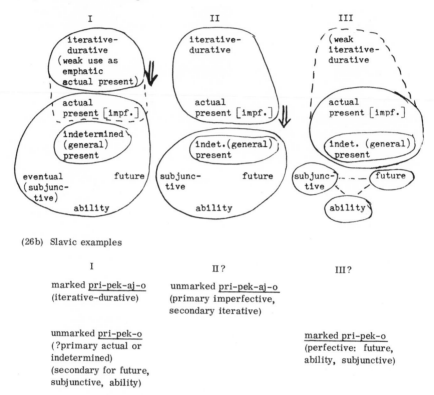

(26b) Slavic examples

I	II ?	III?
marked <u>pri-pek-aj-o</u> (iterative-durative)	unmarked <u>pri-pek-aj-o</u> (primary imperfective, secondary iterative)	
unmarked <u>pri-pek-o</u> (?primary actual or indetermined) (secondary for future, subjunctive, ability)		marked <u>pri-pek-o</u> (perfective: future, ability, subjunctive)

In (26b) I am not certain of the assignments ?II and ?III; I could not match Kuryłowicz's prose description with my (?more precise?) diagrams. But as it stands, (26b) resembles (5).

The example (26-III) brings up a process of category-split again. Kuryłowicz states that there is no direct semantic relation between future and subjunctive, that they are both relics of earlier uses in secondary functions (perhaps as the allative case and purposive infinitive discussed in connection with (22)). The exact historical point at which a category splits, or the degree-of-split at any given time more generally, is obviously not a solved problem.

At least one example in which split seems not to have occurred is discussed by Labov (1973:362-363): <u>mug</u> is used for a special range of containers, non-tapered with a particular ratio of width-to-depth favored; this is surrounded on both sides by the range of use of <u>cup</u>:

(27)   cup #   10   11   12   (increasing depth)

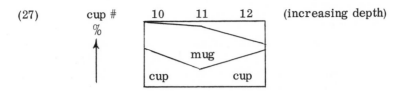

If we represent more dimensions of meaning, the range of cup will not come as close to being cut in two, since mug will recede in other dimensions in which cup remains strong. Schematically (since Labov 1973 does not include the necessary data) we could expect something like (28), where the term listed before the '/' is favored over that following the '/':

(28)

	cup #	10	11	12
Neutral context		cup/mug	mug/(cup)	cup/. . .
Potatoes context		cup/. . .	cup/. . .	cup/. . .
Flowers context		. . ./cup	. . ./cup	. . ./(cup)

9. Some mathematical graphs

For the situation of forced-choice between two categories A and B, different mathematical graphs have been proposed to represent the choice as a function of variation in meaning (29):

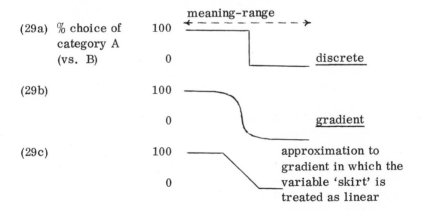

(29a) % choice of category A (vs. B)   100   0   discrete

(29b)   100   0   gradient

(29c)   100   0   approximation to gradient in which the variable 'skirt' is treated as linear

I include treatment (29c) only because it has been recently proposed (Labov 1972:367–368). I suspect it is an example of theoretical formalism which actually interferes with our understanding, even though it may advance our mathematical sophistication in this area; for the graphs based on actual data look more like (29b) above (Labov 1972:356). And (29c) may be a holdover from the discrete view of

linguistics. Witness Labov's desire to 'locate the boundary [!!] between the invariant and variable areas of language with the same
precision that we have learned to use in studying the variable elements themselves' (1973:367-368). It may also be relevant that in
lexical diffusion (the statistically gradual shift of vocabulary from
one phonological or grammatical category into another), Chen (1971:
26) suggests that the shift is slow at first, rapid in the middle, and
slow to include the last few items at the end. Curve (29b) may fit
this phenomenon also if the horizontal dimension is time instead of
meaning.

When two neighboring categories are not in a forced-choice data
structure, we must represent the probability of each category with
its own curve. For phoneme-identification along acoustic space,
with a maximum allowed response-latency, we would obtain graphs
approximately as in (30):

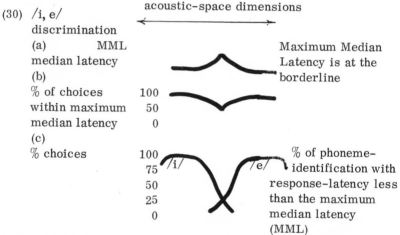

(30) /i, e/   acoustic-space dimensions
     discrimination
     (a)   MML   Maximum Median
     median latency   Latency is at the
     (b)   borderline
     % of choices   100
     within maximum   50
     median latency   0
     (c)
     % choices   100   % of phoneme-
                       75 /i/   /e/   identification with
                       50   response-latency less
                       25   than the maximum
                        0   median latency
                                         (MML)

These are adapted from graphs in Lane (1967). Since only 50 percent
of responses will be quicker than the maximum median latency for
the acoustic stimuli on the category borderline which produce that
maximum median latency, the total responses for such acoustic
stimuli will be 25 percent /i/ plus 25 percent /e/ (50 percent). The
graphs in Lane were forced-choice with no latency limit, so with
sums to 100 percent for all stimuli. In actual perception of speech,
there is no need for all stimuli to be phonemically identified within a
practical length of time, since redundancy will allow the message to
be reconstructed from partial information.

When the question is the willingness of a person to use a given
form (word or grammatical category) for a given referent, more than
one form will be usable at the borderline, with sums greater than

100 percent by definition, without any information on latency, and no forced choice from a fixed list. But defined as willingness to use a term, we might expect graphs like (31):

(31) % willingness
     to use term

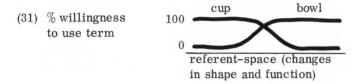

There may be a substantial difference between category borderlines in perception and in production. Although false identification at the borderlines is to be avoided in perception (witness the increased latencies), alternative expressions for the same referent may be desirable since the speaker may view it in different ways. Labov's tests do not actually map forms against psychological meaning directly, since there is little independent evidence for speaker-internal (or 'semantic') meaning. It may be that fluctuating usage at the borderline reflects the speaker's fluctuating points of view toward the referent, and that there is a discrete grammatical rule for use of the forms:

(32) A particular real-world
     shape and function in the
     borderline area:

     Conceptual point-of-view
     (alternative aspects in
     focus):

     surface forms:

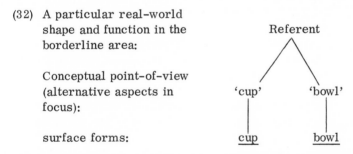

But to finally determine whether the curves in (31) have the same mathematical shape as those in (30c), the types of data will have to be made more comparable than they are at present. There seems at present no reason to assume they will be the same, and some reason to suspect not.

10. Conclusions

The role of a general linguist in the generative tradition has been to devise simple, strong generalizations which can be represented in a formalism with few variables. I feel quite ambivalent about this. Strong claims and assertions of simple patterns do prompt counter-claims, and collection of data to establish the limits on the generalizations. Indeed, we have learned much about language which was not known earlier, and have increased mathematical precision in many areas. But much of the work is rediscovering what was known earlier and neglected because it was not in theoretical vogue. And most recent progress achieved in the area of meaning and grammar has come through rejecting previously proposed transformations, by showing that the 'paraphrases' supposedly related by the transformations in fact differ in meaning. (Much progress in 'constraints on transformations' has of course been independent of that.)

A pendulum-swing which has been of much concern in this paper is between the two views of (33):

(33a) 'one form--one meaning', in its more sophisticated version 'one form--some component of meaning common to all uses'
(33b) 'list all the meanings of a given form--they do not necessarily form a system'

I think true progress here will come by recognizing the gradient squish, from data fitting (33a) to truly ambiguous terms (33b) like bank (for money; of a stream). Only a theory handling the intermediate examples as well as the extremes can hope to account for the dynamics of change and the subtleties of meaning-ranges. I hope I have brought together a set of tools to handle data which can stimulate inquiry, at least allowing important questions to be asked, and reuniting the studies of lexicon and grammar.

Ralph Fasold once said to Charles-James Bailey (according to Bailey) that he felt like the Janitor of Linguistics. C.-J. claims to have replied, 'If you're the Janitor, Andy's the Garbage-Man.' I have the wonderful feeling that one can build an integrated theory with explanatory potential from the remains in neglected garbage cans.

NOTE

I am very grateful to Ralph Fasold, Don Larkin, and Richard J. O'Brien, S.J. at Georgetown University for interactions which led to a great revision from an earlier version. Work of two graduate students at Boulder, Mary Coberly and Robin Mader, has contributed to an expansion of part of (22).

REFERENCES

A. General

Anderson, Lloyd. 1974. Distinct sources of fuzzy data: Ways of integrating relatively discrete and gradient aspects of language, and explaining grammar on the basis of semantic fields. In: Toward tomorrow's linguistics. Edited by Roger W. Shuy and Charles-James Bailey. Washington, D.C., Georgetown University Press. 50-64.
Berlin, Brent and Paul Kay. 1969. Basic color terms. Berkeley, University of California Press.
Binnick, Robert. 1970. Ambiguity and vagueness. Papers from the Sixth Regional Meeting. Chicago, Chicago Linguistic Society. 147-153.
Chen, Matthew. 1971. The time dimension: Contribution toward a theory of sound change. Berkeley, University of California Project on Linguistic Analysis, II, Series No. 12, February.
Chomsky, Carol. 1969. The acquisition of syntax in children from 5 to 10. Cambridge, The MIT Press. [Research Monograph #57].
Closs Traugott, Elizabeth. 1972. The history of English syntax. New York, Holt, Rinehart and Winston.
Ferguson, Charles. 1970. Grammatical categories in data collection. Stanford University Committee on Linguistics, Working Papers on Language Universals No. 4, November. F1-F15.
Fillmore, Charles. 1968. The case for case. In: Universals of linguistic theory. Edited by Emmon Beck and Robert Harms. New York, Holt, Rinehart and Winston. 1-88.
Haas, W. 1973. Rivalry among deep structures. Lg. 49.282-293.
Hagerty, Timothy and J. Donald Bowen. 1973. A contrastive analysis of a lexical split. In: Readings in Spanish-English contrastive linguistics. Edited by Rose Nash. Hato Rey, Puerto Rico, Inter American University Press. 1-71.
Kuryłowicz, Jerzy. 1948. Le sens des mutations consonantiques. Lingua 1.77-85. ['le renversement des termes positif et négatif de l'opposition originaire'].
_____. 1964. The inflectional categories of Indo-European. Heidelberg, Carl Winter.
Labov, William. 1973. The boundaries of words and their meanings. In: New ways of analyzing variation in English. Edited by Charles-Janes N. Bailey and Roger W. Shuy. Washington, D.C., Georgetown University Press. 340-373.
Lakoff, George. 1972. Hedges: A study in meaning criteria and the logic of fuzzy concepts. Papers from the Eighth Regional Meeting. Chicago, Chicago Linguistic Society. 183-228.

Lane, Harlan. 1967. A behavioral basis for the polarity principle in linguistics. Lg. 43.494-511.

Lehrer, Adrienne. 1970. Notes on lexical gaps. Journal of Linguistics 6.257-261.

Menner, Robert. 1945. Multiple meaning and change of meaning in English. Lg. 21.59-76.

Menyuk, Paula. 1969. Sentences children use. Cambridge, The MIT Press. [Research Monograph No. 52].

Smith, Heilson. 1973. The acquisition of phonology. Cambridge, Cambridge University Press.

Vennemann, Theo. 1972. Rule inversion. Lingua 29.209-242.

B. For Charts (12) and (14) through (19), sections 4 and 6

Anderson, Lloyd. 1974b. The part-whole squish: Why grammatical insertion is like lexical insertion. Papers from the Tenth Regional Meeting. Chicago, Chicago Linguistic Society. 1-16.

Bickerton, Derek. 1975 (in press). The dynamics of a Creole system. Cambridge, Cambridge University Press.

Bolinger, Dwight. 1973. Essence and accident: English analogs of Hispanic ser-estar. In: Issues in linguistics: Papers in honor of Henry and Renée Kahane. Edited by Braj Kachru et al. Urbana, University of Illinois Press. 58-69.

Diffloth, Gérard. 1974. Body moves in Semai and French. Papers from the Tenth Regional Meeting. Chicago, Chicago Linguistic Society. 128-138.

Eckman, Fred. 1974. Agentive and agentless passives. Stanford University Committee on Linguistics, Working Papers on Language Universals No. 14, August. 59-74.

Lakoff, Robin. 1970. Passive resistance. Papers from the Seventh Regional Meeting. Chicago, Chicago Linguistic Society. 149-162.

Sag, Ivan. 1973. 'Happenstance' have. Paper presented at LSA summer meeting, Ann Arbor.

Sinha, Anjani. 1974. Roles of underlying structure in historical syntax. University of Chicago, ditto.

SYNCHRONIC LINGUISTICS AND THE PROBLEM OF INTERLINGUAL INFLUENCE

DAVID O. OKẸ

University of Ifẹ, Nigeria

1. The distinction between the diachronic and the synchronic study of language is well known.

> By the diachronic study of a particular language is meant the description of its historical development ('through time') . . . By the synchronic study of a language is meant the description of a particular 'state' of that language (at some 'point' in time). (Lyons 1968:46)

Originally an understandable Saussurean reaction against the Junggrammatiker preoccupation with the historical study of language, the synchronic-diachronic dichotomy almost became a ritual in structuralist linguistics and served as a convenient excuse for ignoring aspects of language that are no less relevant to linguistic theory than other aspects that were accepted as the legitimate concern of synchronic linguistics. The limitations of the synchronic model are serious and, it would seem, insufficiently realised. The usual comparison of the synchronic study of language to the study of a fixed state of the board in a game of chess is an overclaim for synchronic linguistics. At least we can see the entire board at a glance in a game of chess; and we can be sure that the arrangement we see on the board is all the arrangement that is relevant. Until transformational grammar legitimized the use of the linguist's own intuition and power of introspection as a source of data for language study, synchronic linguistics had nothing comparable to the entire openness of the chess board. Even now, the linguist who proceeds to describe

a language other than one in which he has native-like competence is
forced to depend on a source of data far less accessible to him than
is the chess board to the chess strategist.

By focusing attention on the state of language at a given 'point' in
time, the synchronic linguist abstracts from the incontestable fact
that language continues to change all the time. When he seeks homogeneity of data by concentrating on the idiolect of one informant, he
is deliberately suspending his knowledge of one of the elementary
facts about language, namely that language varies from one person
to another and from place to place.

In recent years, scholars concerned with variation in language
have noted the static nature of the synchronic model. We notice,
however, that in the variationist reaction against the static synchronic
view of language, attention has been directed, as far as we know, only
to intralanguage problems--to a study of the knowledge and use of
varieties within the same language. Indeed, most recent variationist
studies would appear to be concerned with the question: in a dynamic
model of linguistic description, how can we integrate the rules of
various idiolects/dialects of one language into the unified description
of that language?

Variationists are certainly right to have put aside the synchronic
straight-jacket and permitted themselves the freedom to begin to
develop a rigorous metatheory that would incorporate variation into
the heart of language study (Bailey and Shuy 1973, Bickerton 1973,
DeCamp 1971, Labov 1969, etc.). We believe, however, that there
is an equally interesting (and probably related) aspect of language
that has been largely set aside, presumably because the synchronic
model could not cope with it. We refer to the large-scale use of the
elements of one language within the system of another, sometimes
without adaptation--a phenomenon that has resulted from the intense
contact of, for example, many West African languages with English
or French in the colonial situation.

Such questions of interlingual influence are by no means new to
linguistics. Indeed, at the 1954 Georgetown University Round Table
on Languages and Linguistics, Einar Haugen and Uriel Weinreich
made a call for the study of similar influences between languages in
contact (Haugen 1954, Weinreich 1954). In his paper, Weinreich
outlined areas in which research was needed while Haugen in his own
paper explored some of the problems involved in describing the interlingual identifications made by Norwegian-English bilinguals. Weinreich (1954:48) noted that 'scholarly interest in the effects of bilingualism on language' was increasing, citing that particular panel
of the 1954 Round Table Meeting as one of its symptoms.

In a number of important ways, the continuing interest in the
effects of bilingualism has borne fruit. It has resulted in

sociolinguistic descriptions of contact situations as well as in the intensified study of pidginization, creolization, decreolization, and even recreolization. The interest has also brought about the development of contrastive analysis of languages and the analysis of errors (presumed to be) due to linguistic interference.

In all these, however, the kind of phenomenon of code-mixing dealt with in this paper has been largely ignored. For instance, of the areas of interest listed in the preceding paragraph, only contrastive analysis seems to be in any way concerned with the issue of how the bilingual individual harnesses his resources of linguistic items and structural patterns in two different languages to produce utterances. Even so, contrastive analysis has not been centrally concerned with the question of what, or how much language, the bilingual knows and how he builds utterances out of this stock of knowledge. The phenomenon of 'code mixing' illustrated in Section 2 below makes it necessary to ask questions such as: how much language does a bilingual know and what kind of competence underlies his use of it? The purpose of this paper is to draw attention to the phenomenon and show that the synchronic model is, by nature, inadequate for the study of this product of language contact. This paper does not discuss the undoubtedly interesting question of how to analyse the phenomenon; such analysis is in preparation. [1]

2. Yoruba is spoken by about 13 million people largely concentrated in Southwestern Nigeria. With more than fifteen years' practice of universal free primary education in the area inhabited by most members of its mother tongue group, a majority of the non-adult Yoruba-speaking population is literate in both Yoruba and English. [2] There are varying degrees of literacy and proficiency in English, ranging from very high to minimal and depending largely on the number of years of exposure to the language in the educational system. For a large number of people with Yoruba as mother tongue, therefore, there is also a second language, English.

The sociolinguistic rules relating to the bilingual's use of these two languages require a much deeper study than we have so far made; but they seem to be of only marginal relevance to the main interest of this paper and therefore need no particularly rigorous statement here. We may say with reasonable certainty that there are hardly any Yoruba-English bilinguals who never have cause to use one of the languages after acquiring them, although most people use one for more purposes, in more situations, and more frequently than the other. All of them are code mixers. The ability to make new forms of the mixed code (i.e. the creativeness of the process) depends to a great extent on the individual's proficiency in both languages; but from preliminary analysis of our data, it appears that the frequency of the mixed code in actual speech does not depend on

this. Even people who are not proficient in English do use complicated English syntax patterns in the mixed code. English expressions
in the mixed code often filter down from the well-educated to little-
educated bilinguals (or totally illiterate imitators). For the less educated, language mixing sometimes constitutes a device for the acquisition of more English expressions; and, this way, it is a potent
disseminator and reinforcer of malaproprisms and doubtful English
syntax. For instance, from the very common sentence-initiator
'being that . . .' of the mixed code, as in:

(1) Being that wọn fẹ́ẹ́ pa á, ó escape,

it is a very short step to the equally common English sentence:

(2) Being that they wanted to kill him, he has escaped,

of Nigerian school English.
Most Yoruba-English bilinguals are capable of constructing the
Yoruba sentence:

(3) Mo fẹ́ẹ́ mọ gbogbo ìtàn náà

as well as its semantic equivalent (4) in English:

(4) I want to know the whole story.

Presented with an individual who is capable of constructing (3) and
(4), and an infinite number of sentences in each of the two languages,
the linguist ought to be asking whether this individual holds exactly
the same interest for him as another one who is capable of constructing or understanding only (3) or (4). If, on account of his own concept of linguistic synchrony, he is interested only in the homogeneous
idiolect of a speaker of Yoruba or English, or is 'concerned primarily with an ideal speaker-listener, in a completely homogeneous
speech community, who knows its language perfectly . . .' (Chomsky
1965:3), he may be denying himself and linguistic theory a deeper
insight into the human faculty for language learning and language use.
The bilingual's knowledge of two languages sometimes raises a type
of problem for linguistic theory which is not raised by monolingualism.
Here we wish to open up one aspect of the problem. We start with two
hypotheses representing two extreme possibilities.

Hypothesis 1. The two languages known by a bilingual (or
by entension the n languages known by a polyglot) are learned,
stored up, and used as completely separate systems by him.

Hypothesis 2. The two languages known by a bilingual (or by extension the n languages known by a polyglot) are learned, stored up, and used as complete variants of each other.

Hypothesis 1 implies that the linguistic experience acquired in the learning and use of one language is irrelevant in the learning and use of another. Anyone who has ever learned a second language or is at least conversant with the phenomenon of linguistic interference can easily see that this view of linguistic experience cannot be sustained. It is conceivable, of course, that sociolinguistic rules may apply in such a way that the two languages are kept functionally apart by the bilingual all the time. But it is a totally different matter whether, and to what extent, this helps to keep the two languages apart in his brain as two separate linguistic systems.

It would seem that if synchronic linguists had ever seriously considered this kind of problem, their position would have been very close to that implied in Hypothesis 1. The synchronist has often ignored the fact that the 'ideal speaker-listener' in certain mother tongue groups is obligatorily bilingual or multilingual;[3] it is arguable whether the linguist can present an adequate description of the mother tongue of such people without including variable rules that draw on, or at least relate to, the rules of the other language.

Hypothesis 2 is not as unreasonable as it may seem. The author of this paper actually began to learn English by a method that must have been based on this or a very similar hypothesis; and many teachers still use the method today. By that method, the Yoruba-speaking pupil learns equations of the following type:

(5a) Yoruba 'mo' (or 'èmi') = English 'I'

(5b) ìtàn = story

(5c) gbogbo = $\begin{bmatrix} \text{all} \\ \text{whole} \end{bmatrix}$

(5d) fẹ́ = $\begin{bmatrix} \text{want} \\ \text{like} \end{bmatrix}$

(5e) fẹ́ẹ́ = $\begin{bmatrix} \text{want to} \\ \text{like to} \end{bmatrix}$

(5f) mọ̀ = know

(5g) náà = the

(3) Yoruba: Mo fẹ́ẹ́ mọ gbogbo ìtàn náà

$$= \text{(4a) English: I} \begin{bmatrix} \text{like to} \\ \text{want to} \end{bmatrix} \text{know} \begin{bmatrix} \text{all the story} \\ \text{the whole story} \end{bmatrix}$$

(Although no one said so in the English-learning workshop, English (4a) is derived from Yoruba (3) via a non-attested English string (4*)

$$\text{I} \begin{bmatrix} \text{like to} \\ \text{wish to} \end{bmatrix} \text{know} * \begin{bmatrix} \text{all story the} \\ \text{whole story the} \end{bmatrix}).$$

All the same, Hypothesis 2 has, among others, the implication that, since any of the Yoruba items (5a)-(5g) is used as a complete variant of the English items listed against it in the equation, the following Yoruba-based forms (6a)-(6v) should be usable. [4] (English items are underlined):

(Recall (3): Mo fẹ́ẹ́ mọ gbogbo ìtàn náà)

(6a) Mo fẹ́ẹ́ mọ gbogbo ìtàn <u>the</u>
(6b)   "   "   "   "   <u>story</u> náà
(6c)   "   "   "   "   <u>story</u> <u>the</u>

$$\text{(6d)} \quad " \quad " \quad " \begin{bmatrix} \text{whole} \\ \text{all} \end{bmatrix} \text{ìtàn náà}$$

(6e)   "   "   "   "   <u>story</u> náà
(6f)   "   "   "   "   ìtàn <u>the</u>
(6g)   "   "   "   "   <u>story</u> <u>the</u>
(6h)   "   "   <u>know</u>** gbogbo ìtàn náà
(6i)   "   "   <u>know</u>** gbogbo ìtàn <u>the</u>
(6j)   "   "   <u>know</u>** gbogbo <u>story</u> <u>the</u>

$$\text{(6k)} \quad " \quad " \quad \underline{\text{know}}** \begin{bmatrix} \text{whole} \\ \text{all} \end{bmatrix} \underline{\text{story}} \; \underline{\text{the}}$$

(6l)   " <u>want</u> <u>to</u> mọ   gbogbo ìtàn náà
(6m) "   "   "   mọ   gbogbo ìtàn <u>the</u>
(6n) "   "   "   mọ   gbogbo <u>story</u> <u>the</u>
(6o) "   "   "   mọ   whole <u>story</u> <u>the</u>

$$\text{(6p)} \quad " \quad " \quad " \; \underline{\text{know}}** \begin{bmatrix} \text{whole} \\ \text{all} \end{bmatrix} \underline{\text{story}} \; \underline{\text{the}}$$

(6q) I*** féé mo gbogbo ìtàn náà

(6r) I*** féé mo gbogbo ìtàn the

(6s) I*** féé mo gbogbo story the

(6t) I*** féé mo $\begin{bmatrix} \text{whole} \\ \text{all} \end{bmatrix}$ story the

(6u) I*** féé know** $\begin{bmatrix} \text{whole} \\ \text{all} \end{bmatrix}$ story the

(6v) I*** want to know** $\begin{bmatrix} \text{whole} \\ \text{all} \end{bmatrix}$ story the

(to derive the final form of the sentences, note the following:

(a) Apply English PS rules to reorder all English items that are dominated by the same node.

(b) At all points marked '**', we have an option between Yoruba and English phonosyntactic rules marking the Transitive Verb + Object-NP juncture.

(c) Similarly, at all points marked '***', we have an option between Yoruba and English phonosyntactic rules marking the Subject NP + VP juncture.)

Although the implication appears rather ludicrous, it is in reality not entirely so. At least one of the twenty-two mixtures listed in (6a)-(6v) would be used by almost any Yoruba-English bilingual. This is the sentence:

(6b) Mo féé mo gbogbo story náà.

Sentence (g), with application of appropriate re-ordering rules in the English portion of it, is just as likely to be encountered in the speech of any Yoruba-English bilingual--and actually occurs in our data as:

Mo féé mo the whole story.

Sentences (6f), (6k), and (6h) are of doubtful acceptability, but they are all less unacceptable than the rest; for instance, in the case of (6h), a substitution of the English word enjoy for know would make the sentence sound normal and acceptable, as in:

(7) Mo féé enjoy gbogbo ìtàn náà.

The conclusion here is that the language-mixing behavior of the Yoruba-English bilingual cannot be correctly predicted by rules based on either of our hypotheses. In other words, the two languages known to the Yoruba-English bilingual are not kept apart by him as completely separate linguistic systems; they are somehow, but not randomly, mixed. Certainly such language-mixing practice has to be rule-governed, otherwise any of the sentences (6a)-(6v) as well as any other mixed arrangement of the Yoruba and English items listed in (5a)-(5g) would be acceptable. By what rules, then does the language-mixing take place? It is certainly part of the business of linguistics to answer this question. If we were to answer the question: what, linguistically speaking, does the Yoruba-English bilingual know?, one reasonable answer would be that what he knows is not really the sum total of two separate systems, it is probably a sum of what is common to both languages and the unshared features of the two languages.

3. Variationists have rightly categorized the structuralist as well as the post-structuralist transformational concept of synchrony as static. They have continued to express concern over the shortcomings of a synchronic model that excludes all types of variation (in space, in time, in function, etc.) from the purview of linguistic analysis (Shuy 1973:1). Their criticisms are by now well known, and, although we consider such criticisms to be largely fair and valid, we do not intend to repeat them. Rather, we should like to draw attention to the language-mixing phenomenon noted in the preceding section and consider the adequacy of the synchronic model in dealing with such a problem.

The exclusion of variation of any sort makes it difficult to cope with the type of phenomenon we are here considering. The emphasis on 'one language' imposes some restrictions right from the start: the linguist is out to describe the Yoruba language or the English language. Notice that it would be a different story if he were simply to pick on any person or persons and record what they are saying, how and where they are saying it, etc. If he did that among the Yoruba-speaking community in Nigeria, he would discover that probably one out of every random choice of two or three informants would provide him with a corpus containing a large number of sentences like (6b) or (6g) above. If he approached such data with objectivity, he would come out with rules of sentence formation (in respect of corpus containing sentences like (6b), (6g), that would turn out to be in many ways identical to the rules employed by a Yoruba monolingual and in some other ways identical to the rules that are peculiar to the grammar of the English monolingual. However, the synchronic model does not permit him that much latitude; in practice, he complies with the demand to describe 'one language', and asks his informant to tell a story or give word-sentence equivalents in language L, the informant's mother-tongue. Some of us who have served as linguists' informants know only too well that the informant simply does as he has been told: partly to satisfy the linguist and partly to preserve his own pride as someone who knows his mother tongue well, he scrupulously refrains from mixing elements of another language with those of his own throughout the session with the linguist.

Let us suppose that, in the process of data gathering, the linguist hears his informant utter sentences of the type (6b) and (6g), [5] what is the linguist to do? If he were to stick to the one-language rule, he would either record such sentences as belonging to the one language in which he is interested or he would simply reject them as non-sentences within the language. If he did the former, he would come up with rules that are well known and used in another language but are unknown to many speakers of his subject language. His synchronic model has no room for this and we may now expect him to do what he did not do earlier--reject this intractable portion of the data. No existing synchronic grammar known to us has in fact incorporated such material; and it is safe to assume that they have (ultimately?) had to reject all such inconvenient data if they ever turned up in the corpus. Notice, however, that when a linguist throws out such data, he is indirectly making a pre-analysis structuring of the nature of linguistic data and the final description reflects his own prejudgment, not the nature of language. We have to draw the same conclusion even when the suppression of this type of sample from his data results only from his demand that the informant tell him something in a given L.

It is, of course, possible to take the view that sentences like (6b) and (6g) contain examples of borrowing which could be handled as instances of language change and dealt with in diachronic linguistics. There can be no valid excuse for so doing. It is, of course, true that self-appointed judges like school teachers and publishing house editors often pronounce on the state of the language and exclude, or otherwise treat as special, items that clearly seem to them not to belong in their language. In the case of Yoruba, for instance, the school teacher bans the use of such sentences as (6b), (6g), or (7) because they contain English words; and the publishing house editor italicises them where the context curtails his power to expunge them from the text altogether. It is to be hoped that the linguist does not intend to subject his data-gathering process to that kind of normativeness or purism which he abandoned long ago. There are good reasons why he should not.

First, the use of lexical and grammatical features of one language within the system of another may be found in the language of the infant monolingual who has acquired it as part of his mother tongue.

Such people are native speakers of this variety. [6] It is beside the point to argue that this type of practice may never become a permanent feature of the sociolinguistic situation or that such code-mixing is probably no more than an unstable feature of one of the bilingual's two languages; what feature is guaranteed to be permanent, anyway?

Secondly, as we saw earlier, there are syntactic restrictions on the occurrence of English items in Yoruba and such restrictions are worth describing in the grammar of the bilingual user of Yoruba. It is not sufficient to state the rules of Yoruba and add that whenever an item is borrowed from English, it is to be inserted in the syntactic position of its Yoruba synonym. Sometimes this will yield well-informed mixtures; sometimes it will not, as can be seen in the unacceptable sentences in the sample (6a)-(6v), or in the following rather different example.

Consider the structure of the following Yoruba sentence:

(8) Ó dára (Ó = he/she/it; dára = good/nice/fine, etc.)

Sentence (8) has the structure

NP + VP

in which VP → V.

V in this case is to be selected from a subclass of attributive verbs or what some people describe as predicative adjectives. This sentence permits the substitution of any of the English synonyms of the attributive verb to form

(9) Ó $\left\{ \begin{array}{l} \underline{good} \\ \underline{nice} \\ \underline{fine} \end{array} \right\}$

and this may appear to vindicate the claim that whenever an item is borrowed from English, it is simply to be inserted in the syntactic position of its Yoruba synonym. [7] However, note what happens when either an expanded form of the same English adjectives (e.g. quite good, very nice) or an English participial form (e.g. interested, disturbed) is to be substituted for a synonymous Yoruba constituent in the same syntactic position. Thus while (9) is well formed and frequently heard in speech, (10) and (11) are badly formed and are not attested:

(10) *Ó <u>very</u> <u>nice</u>
(11) *Ó <u>interested</u>

instead of (10) and (11), the language permits (12) and (13):

(12) Ó wà <u>very nice</u>
(13) Ó wà <u>interested</u>

Now, <u>wà</u> (= English BE) does not occur before attributive verbs in
the rules of monolingual Yoruba grammar; thus (14) and (15) are not
even remotely acceptable Yoruba sentences:

(14) *Ó wà dára   (He is nice)
(15) *Ó wà dára púpò   (He is very nice)

The element <u>wà</u> does occur in Yoruba as a locative or existential
verb, (e.g. Ó wà n'ilé 'he is at home'; Ó wà 'he exists') but never
as a copula. It is under the pressure of the English predicative adjective (or its syntactic equivalent) in the position illustrated above
that <u>wà</u> has come to be used as a copula in Yoruba. From the foregoing, we can see that Yoruba-English language mixing has important
implications for the rules of Yoruba grammar and for a theory of the
bilingual's linguistic competence. The linguist cannot shove all these
facts into the diachronic basket where they are simply ignored and
nothing happens to them.

4. In the foregoing, we have drawn attention to and illustrated a
certain type of interlingual influence which linguistics cannot brush
aside. We have attempted to show that it constitutes a problem which
the synchronic model is not equipped to solve: indeed the structuralist and transformational conception of synchrony in linguistics seems
to have been responsible for keeping data reflecting this aspect of
bilingualism out of the purview of synchronic description. If we are
to make a meaningful study of such data, a more elastic model is
required that permits us within our theory of language to make more
flexible or more penetrable the walls we have solidified by means of
such words as language, dialect, and idiolect. And there will be
reasonable justification for making such walls flexible. For instance,
within many so-called language groups, there are varieties that are
almost mutually unintelligible; whereas in some geographical areas,
there are contiguous or co-territorial so-called separate language
groups whose speech forms are mutually intelligible. Yet, the linguist maintains that in the former case, there is only one language
while in the latter there are two or more. By means only of the
application of items and rules appropriate to his other language, the
user of the Yoruba-English mixed code will be incomprehensible to
the Yoruba monolingual for much of the time, and to the English
monolingual, almost all of the time. Since he is equally capable of

making himself entirely comprehensible to either monolingual, are we
to conclude that he has three distinct languages, one in which he can
confuse both monolinguals and two others in which he can communi-
cate with them? The reality is, of course, more complex than that;
for while his linguistic hybrid has rules as do other linguistic systems,
it is not an autonomous system and may never be one. It would,
therefore, not be accurate to attribute three different languages to
this code-mixing individual.

We are in all probability witnessing the emergence of a new
variety of one of the two languages in contact. By studying the rules
by which absorption of elements of the other language takes place, we
should be in a position to know more about the process of linguistic
change and the development of new language variety.

If, as seems reasonable, we accept the mixed code as a new or
emerging variety of one of the languages in contact, the question
arises: how are we to describe it? By what rules shall we reflect
the 'double source' of the grammar of the mixed code? Can the concept of variability apply in this case? Can we have within a unified
grammar of Yoruba variable rules that involve the structures of
another language? Or could it be that the code-mixing bilingual has
now developed a sort of 'upper case LANGUAGE' (to use the word
'language' for want of a better one) of which his Yoruba and English
now serve as variant forms subject to certain linguistic rules of
structure as well as to usage rules?

That leads to our last question: what does the type of phenomenon
referred to here tell us about the knowledge of language possessed by
a human being? This is, in a way, a more complicated code to
learn and use than a single language; and it seems reasonable to
suggest that this, more than the straight monolingual case of language use, would be an interesting and revealing subject to study in
our effort to refine linguistic theory.

NOTES

1. As a matter of fact, we are only at the beginning of a study of
an extensive recording of the speech of native speakers of Yoruba
who have also achieved varying degrees of proficiency in English.
The overall goal is to describe their code switching patterns.

2. There are quite a few native speakers of English and a considerable number of English-speaking (non-Yoruba-speaking)
Nigerians who learn Yoruba. The former are so few and their use
of Yoruba so restricted that they can be left out of consideration for
the purpose of this paper. The latter usually interact so closely
with native speakers that they soon fall into the usage patterns of the
native speakers of Yoruba.

3. For an example of this type of individual, see Oke (1972).

4. There could also be a similar set of English-based mixtures. The use of these is, in fact, inhibited by a rule that effectively bars these non-native speakers of English from taking such liberties with English. The use of English in its 'purest' or 'most correct' form (outside of phonology) is linked with status and, except in situations where one's personality is not in any way at stake, one does not interfere with what is commonly considered to be 'good' English.

5. Such sentences are normally frequently encountered. The following samples are taken from our data for further use by the reader (the English part of the mixed code is underlined) (i) bàtà méta l' o sáà ní . . . se bí tí ikan báá fún e, wà á wo 'yókù . . . wà á wo one of the others. (You have at least three pairs of shoes . . . if one gets too tight for you, you should wear the rest . . . you should wear one of the others). (ii) Ní time kan, à nso n'pa discipline; pé 'tandard discipline pé ó ń fall; so l' enìkan bá dìde, l'ó bá ní . . . áà . . . vernacular speaking gan-an . . . is one of the factors t' ó ó contribute; so l' a bá dè bi eni yen pé kí l' ó feel pé ó ye kí a se? (Once [at one time] we were discussing discipline, that the standard of discipline that it was falling; so someone got up, he said . . . ah! . . . venacular speaking really . . . is one of the factors that contribute; so we then asked that person that what did he feel that it is fit that we should do?).

6. For instance, before coming to the United States a few months ago, my 4-year-old daughter frequently used English phrases and the clause linkers and, but, and so in her Yoruba speech in spite of the fact that she hardly understood any English at all. · Even now, at the time of writing, she still does not understand more than a few sentences of English; but the incidence of English features in her speech has shot up noticeably. All these are explained by the fact that, from age 30 months to age 45 months (immediately preceding her visit to the United States), she had lived in an exclusively Yoruba-speaking neighborhood and with a grandmother who was a regular Yoruba-English code mixer. After rejoining the rest of the family, she has found that the principal medium of communication in her home is the mixed code and has accordingly learned more of it. There is an increasingly large number of such children who are native speakers of the mixed code.

7. Note that none of the other possible combinations is permissible; e.g. there is no 'It dára'.

REFERENCES

Bailey, C.-J. N. and R. W. Shuy, eds. 1973. New ways of analyz-
ing variation in English. Washington, D.C., Georgetown Uni-
versity Press.
Bickerton, D. 1973. On the nature of the creole continuum. Lg.
49:3.640-669.
Chomsky, N. 1965. Aspects of the theory of syntax. Cambridge,
The MIT Press.
DeCamp, D. 1971. Toward a generative analysis of a post-creole
speech continuum. In: Hymes (1971). 349-370.
Haugen, E. 1954. Problems of bilingual description. In: George-
town University Round Table on Languages and Linguistics 1954
(GURT 1954). Edited by H. J. Mueller. Washington, D.C.,
Georgetown University Press. 9-19.
Hymes, D., ed. 1971. The pidginization and creolization of lan-
guages. Cambridge, Cambridge University Press.
Labov, W. 1969. Contraction, deletion, and inherent variability
of the English copula. Lg. 45:4.715-762.
Lyons, J. 1968. Introduction to theoretical linguistics. Cambridge,
Cambridge University Press.
Okẹ, D. O. 1972. Language choice in the Yoruba-Edo border area.
Odu, Journal of West African Studies 7.
Shuy, R. W. 1973. The concept of gradatum in language learning.
Paper presented at the conference of the American Psychological
Association, Montreal.
Weinreich, Uriel. 1954. Linguistic convergence in immigrant
America. In: GURT 1954. 40-49.

JENEPHER REVISITED:
ADULT LANGUAGE CHANGE

BARBARA ROBSON

University of Wisconsin

Casual observation suggests that adult language--by which we mean the language of an individual after he has passed the initial language-acquisition stage--is capable of changing much more than linguists have been taught to believe. When one goes back to the city in which he spent the first twenty-one years of his life he discovers (a) that his family and friends sound funny, and (b) that he sounds equally funny to them. One catches oneself devoicing 1's after voiceless stops, and on thinking about it, discovers that he is unconsciously mimicking one of his best friends. Or at a cocktail party he observes an acquaintance with a southern background sounding more and more southern with each drink.

While primary language acquisition has been the subject of extensive research, very little work--if any at all--has been devoted to the extent and mechanics of linguistic change in adults. Even in the newly emerging field of variation studies, emphasis has been placed on inter-individual variation at the expense of studies of individual variation, whether across styles or points of time. Although theories have recently been proposed to account for variation within the community, little has been done to incorporate variation and change within the individual into these theories.

Generative linguists seem to view the matter of adult language change as a phenomenon involving superficial aspects of language only, that is, those aspects of language which are amenable to description in terms of low-level rules in a grammar. This view either stems from, or was the basis for, Morris Halle's (1962:344) conjecture that '. . . changes in later life are restricted to the

addition of a few rules in the grammar', and that '. . . the elimination of rules and hence a wholesale restructuring of his grammar
is beyond the capabilities of the average adult'. Halle also comments
in his 1962 article on the connection between the superficiality of
adult language change and the necessity for preserving mutual intelligibility.

With these ideas in mind, it might be interesting to compare
samples of the language of an individual at different points in time,
to analyze these samples, and to compare the analyses, in hopes that
such comparisons might produce some insights into the facts of adult
language change.

In May and November of 1970, sentences, stories, and conversation were elicited from several Jamaican schoolchildren as the
basis for a dissertation on style-shifting. This last spring, one of
the children was located again, and a parallel set of data was collected for comparison with the 1970 data.

Jenepher Campbell was fourteen years old when she was first
interviewed in 1970. She was then a student at Craigton School, a
primary school just outside Irishtown, a village some fifteen miles
up the Blue Mountains from Kingston, Jamaica. Three years later
she was finishing her last year at Craigton, with high hopes of
getting a government scholarship to continue her education.

Jenepher, like other Jamaicans, possesses widely varying spoken
styles of her language. For historical reasons, the English spoken
in Jamaica ranges from something closely resembling Standard
British English to a variety of English which has developed out of
the Creole spoken by slaves brought to the island in the seventeenth
and eighteenth centuries. The average Jamaican speaks a variety of
English somewhere between these poles (his distance from one or
the other of the poles correlating with his social position!), and,
moreover, the style he uses in formal situations is markedly closer
to the Standard end of the continuum than the style he uses in informal situations.

The tape recordings of Jenepher in both 1970 and 1973 consist of
sentences, stories, and free conversation. The sentences we constructed so that it would be possible to guarantee enough occurrences
of the focussed segments. The sentences were read to Jenepher one
by one, and she repeated them twice, first in the 'patois' (her name
for her informal style), and then twice in what she considered
Standard English. The stories were of Jenepher's choosing: fairy
tales of the 'Three Little Pigs' variety in 1970, simple folk tales,
and Anancy stories in 1973; she told her stories first in Standard,
then in patois. The free conversation was in her Standard English
only, as she was talking to the fieldworker and that is the style she
would normally use in such situations.

Before she was recorded in 1970, a great deal of time was spent in getting her used to the tape recorder, and overcoming any shyness she felt in using the patois in the presence of the fieldworker. It has been noticed that Jamaicans in general seem to be far more amenable to style-shifting in inappropriate contexts than most people; after a bit of initial giggling, neither Jenepher nor the other children who were recorded then were the least bit inhibited.

As is inevitable in this sort of work, there are fairly frequent instances of code-switching, i.e. occurrences of Standard features in Patois text, and vice versa. This code-switching is a minor problem at most, because Jenepher corrects herself often enough in both styles to give a quite accurate picture of which features are associated with which style.

Of the many features which changed from 1970 to 1973, two were chosen for discussion in detail: Jenepher's behavior with regard to /h/, and her /θ/ and /ð/ segments.

In 1970, Jenepher consistently pronounced words with Standard English /h/ with [ʔ]'s in her formal style, and with ∅ in her informal style:

Standard	Formal	Informal
house	ʔous	ous
hole	ʔuol	uol
happy	ʔapi	ɑpi
behind	bi ʔɑin	biɑin

In 1973, Jenepher pronounced /h/ words with either an initial glottal stop or an initial [h] in her formal style, and without an initial [ʔ] or [h] in her informal style:

house	ʔous, hous	ous
husband	ʔozbɑn, hozb n	ozban
had	ʔad, had	av
hardly	ʔɑrdli, hɑrdli	ɑːdli

Moreover, in her formal style Jenepher frequently dropped the initial [h] or [ʔ] in unstressed words such as <u>him</u> or <u>her</u>:

Standard	Formal	Informal
saw her	so ɪr	si ɑr
because he	bikɔz hi, bikɔz i	bɪk ^{n} ɪ^n

It seems reasonably clear that Jenepher's original English differed from the Standard in that where the Standard has the segment [h], she had [ʔ], which dropped in her informal style. It also seems clear that sometime between 1970 and 1973 she discovered the correlation between her [ʔ] and Standard [h], as well as the fact that in Standard [h] drops in unstressed words; these discoveries have resulted in changes in her language.

The most reasonable analysis of Jenepher's 1970 [ʔ]'s is one in which the [ʔ]'s are underlying, with a rule deleting them in informal style:[1]

    1970: UF: /ʔ/, e.g. /ʔapi/, /ʔous/
           Rule: ʔ → ∅ / INFORMAL Oblig

Setting up the informal forms (without the [ʔ]'s) as underlying is unsatisfactory from the point of view of simplicity of description, as the rule required to get the [ʔ]'s on the proper words would have to distinguish between ordinary vowel-initial words, which are vowel-initial in both styles, and vowel-initial words in informal style which get [ʔ]'s in formal style.

The best analysis of the 1973 data still has the glottal stop underlying, and the rule deleting /ʔ/ in informal style; but an additional rule is necessary in formal style to either delete the /ʔ/ in unstressed words or to change it to [h]:

    1973: UF: /ʔ/, e.g. /ʔozban', /ʔous/
           Rule 1. ʔ → ∅ / INFORMAL Oblig
           Rule 2. $ʔ → \begin{cases} ∅ / \underline{\quad} \begin{bmatrix} V \\ -sts \end{bmatrix} \\ h \end{cases}$ / FORMAL Opt

Rule 2 cannot be added to the end of the rules in Jenepher's grammar; there is a rule changing stops to glottal stops in certain environments which Rule 2 has to precede, and the stops-to-glottal-stops has in turn to precede other rules.

It would seem, in summary, that the differences in Jenepher's /h/'s from 1970 to 1973 can be characterized, as Halle has suggested, as the addition of a rule to her grammar; the added rule, however, is not a low-level one.

Jenepher's interdental fricatives are another matter. In 1970, [θ] and [ð] occurred only in formal style, and then in quite sporadic alternation with [t], [d], [s], and [z]:

Standard	Formal	Informal
farther	fɑrdɑ, fɑrðɑ	fɑːdɑ
think	tıŋk, θıŋk	tıŋk
some	sɑm, θɑm	sɑm

Standard	Formal	Informal
there's	dɛrz, dɛrd,	***
	dɛrz, dɛrd	

In 1973, on the other hand--surprisingly enough--in her formal style Jenepher consistently produced [θ] and [d] in Standard [θ] and [d] words, and never in Standard [s] and [z] words. Moreover, in 1973 she code-shifted occasionally, producing a [θ] or [d] in informal style, something which never happened in 1970.

Standard	Formal	Informal
thirty	θɨrti	toti
think	θɪŋk	tɪŋk
father	fɑdɑ	fɑdɑ
them	dɛm	dɛn

There seems to be no interpretation of the situation other than that Jenepher has learned a new contrast; she has added two distinct segments, /θ/ and /d/, to her inventory. Her 1970 behavior was suspiciously similar to that of foreigners learning to pronounce [θ] and [d]; her 1973 behavior indicates unequivocally that she has mastered the segments.

This state of affairs is reflected in the different analyses of the 1970 and 1973 data. It is very difficult to justify setting up an underlying /θ/ and /d/ for the 1970 data, as it is impossible to decide which forms should have /θ/ and /d/, and which should have /t/, /d/, /s/, or /z/. An analysis in which Standard [θ] and [d] words have underlying /t/'s and /d/'s and in which there is a rule converting alveolar segments to [θ] and [d] very optionally in formal style seems preferable:

1970: UFs: /t, d, s, z/, e.g. /tɪŋk/, /sam/ /dɛrz/

$$\text{Rule:} \quad \begin{Bmatrix} t, s \\ d, z \end{Bmatrix} \rightarrow \begin{Bmatrix} \theta \\ d \end{Bmatrix} / \text{FORMAL} \quad \text{Opt}$$

For the 1973 data, on the other hand, considerations of simplicity of description require an analysis with underlying /θ/ and /d/, which become [t] and [d] obligatorily in informal style:

1973: UF: /θ/, /d/, e.g. /θɪŋk/, /fɑda/

$$\text{Rule:} \quad \begin{Bmatrix} \theta \\ d \end{Bmatrix} \rightarrow \begin{Bmatrix} t \\ d \end{Bmatrix} / \text{INFORMAL} \quad \text{Oblig}$$

Note that setting up underlying /t/ and /d/ in /θ/ and /ð/ words would necessitate a rule which had to distinguish the /t/ and /d/ words which were /t/ and /d/ in both styles from the /t/ and /d/ words which were /t/ and /d/ in informal, but /θ/ and /ð/ in formal.

Jenepher's incorporation of /θ/ and /ð/ into her language, then, is characterized grammatically as the loss of one rule and the gain of its converse, and as the addition of two new distinct segments, which are reflected in the lexicon as changes in underlying forms. (Think, for example, is underlying /tɪŋk/ in the 1970 analysis, but /θɪŋk/ in the 1973 analysis.) All of which is definitely not in accord with Halle's conjecture that adults cannot radically restructure their grammars: given that underlying forms are commonly thought to be far more stable than rules, any change in them has to be considered restructuring of a fairly fundamental nature.

Two general comments will conclude these observations. First, the changes in Jenepher's language from 1970 to 1973 have all been in her formal style; her informal style is unchanged (except perhaps that the incidence of code-switching from formal to informal is a bit higher in 1973 than in 1970). This seems to suggest that perhaps a better analysis of the whole situation would be one in which the styles were treated in separate grammars altogether; it might be that what Jenepher has been doing is in effect learning a new language. There are two objections that can be made to this proposal from a purely descriptive point of view; first, there are several phonological pro- cesses which occur in both styles: the tensing of lax vowels in stressed position, nasal assimilation, and the stops-to-glottal-stops rule mentioned earlier are examples of such processes. Treating the styles in different grammars would necessitate stating rules for these processes twice, and stating things twice is not the most ele- gant way of doing things.

The second, and more serious, objection is that if the styles are described separately, there is no way to express the fact that there are regular correspondences between segments in one style and seg- ments in the other, say [ʔ] and [θ], or between [θ] and [t]. We would in effect be equating Jenepher's bi-dialectalism with cases of bi- lingualism, in which there are no regular correspondences between segments in one language and segments in the other. But Jenepher is not bilingual; the correspondences are most unequivocally there; and to do oneself out of a way of stating them grammatically is to miss a generalization that must be made.

The last question for observation concerns the wholesale restruc- turing of grammars. To reiterate, Jenepher's learning of the [θ]- [t], [ð]-[d] contrast is a counter-example to the Halle conjecture that changes in adult grammars cannot involve restructuring, presumably because such restructuring would impair intelligibility.

But the restructuring in this case involves only a minor change in surface forms: the switch from an alveolar stop to a dental or interdental fricative--[θŋk] instead of [tɪŋk]--is hardly a change which is going to impair communication.

It might be argued, then, that restructuring is possible only if the resultant surface changes are not drastic: to which one might counter-argue that there is in that case no restriction on restructuring per se; that the no-drastic-surface-change restriction is a particular instance of a constraint which seems to operate on linguistic variation in general. One would characterize this constraint as a requirement that corresponding surface segments from variety to variety of a language must be phonetically similar, and one might cite as evidence for this constraint the lack of languages in which one variety has, say, an [h] which corresponds to, say, an [m] in another variety. There seems to be no reason for this state of affairs: surely it should be no more difficult for an individual, on encountering a dialect different from his own, to take note of the fact that that dialect's [h]'s correspond to his own [m]'s, than to resister the fact that that dialect's [h]'s correspond to his own [ʔ]'s. Why, then, the lack of correspondences between wildly non-similar segments?

It is surely unarguable that a constraint on variation exists; the interesting part of the constraint lies in defining the notion of phonetic similarity among corresponding segments from variety to variety of a language, in asking such questions as 'What is the range of segments which occur, in varieties of English, in correspondence with Standard [h]?' or 'What effect does the existence of distinct /θ/ and /š/ have on the range of possible variants of /s/?'

It would be very nice, indeed, if we could arrive at a clearer notion of the range of possible variation; such a notion would surely allow us more insights not only into problems of restructuring like the one raised in this paper, but also into problems of language acquisition in general.

NOTE

1. The presentation of rules here is not intended to be definitive in any theoretical sense; we are concerned mainly with getting the processes represented in an easily understandable form. The INFORMAL and FORMAL environments designate which style the rule applies in.

REFERENCES

Halle, Morris. 1962. Phonology in a generative grammar.
    Word 18.54-72.

Robson, Barbara. 1972. Community vs. individual competence: English /h/ in Jamaican Creole. In: From soundstream to discourse. Edited by D. G. Hays and D. M. Lance. Topeka, University of Missouri Press.

_____. 1973. Pan-lectal grammars and adult language change. In: New ways of analyzing variation in English. Edited by R. W. Shuy and C.-J. N. Bailey. Washington, D. C., Georgetown University Press. 164-170.

A GOOD RULE OF THUMB:
VARIABLE PHONOLOGY IN
AMERICAN SIGN LANGUAGE

ROBBIN BATTISON, Gallaudet College and University of
    California, San Diego
HARRY MARKOWICZ, Gallaudet College and Georgetown
    University
JAMES WOODWARD, Gallaudet College

Introduction. Knowing that modern linguistics owes much to a
centuries-old tradition of phonology, it may be difficult to understand
why interest in sign languages of the deaf has focussed primarily on
syntax, and has tended to ignore the form of the signs themselves.
There are three principal reasons.

First, superficial examination of these very special languages has
tended to perpetuate the myths that they are auxiliaries to spoken languages, are ideographic, lack duality of patterning, or are even universal. Hence, one would reason that it would be of interest only to
study the order of signs in sentences and make some comparisons
to speech, if the forms of the signs themselves are unconstrained,
and to map isomorphically onto their referents.

Second, the status of sign languages in deaf education is vitally
linked to the question of syntax, since a substantial number of North
American educators advocate the use of some variety of Signed English, a pidgin language (Woodward 1973a) which imposes English word
order and inflectional structure on the morphological system of American Sign Language (ASL). Needless to say, both the natural morphology and natural phonology of ASL are strained by this imposition.
Much of the work on sign languages thus far has been geared to
pointing up the need to appreciate them as the independent systems
they are.

Third, linguists sometimes find it difficult to make the jump from oral languages to manual-visual languages, and bring their theoretical baggage with them at the same time. In encountering language in a different modality, differences appear more important than similarities. However, as more of what is common to all languages is understood, it is found that sign languages are linguistically structured in very familiar ways.

What we shall attempt to show here is (a) that ASL has a level of structure analogous to the phonology of an oral language, (b) that the form of this phonology is in part determined by the articulatory dynamics of the body, and (c) that variation theory offers significant insights into this phonology.

There are those who would balk at our use of the term 'phonology', since, taken literally, it must involve sounds, and sign languages clearly do not. There are others who intuitively grasp what the term means when it is applied to signs. Just what do we mean by phonology?

For sign languages, the phonology systematically separates the set of gestures which may represent meanings in a given sign language from the entire range of gestures which may be produced by the human body. This involves constraints on underlying forms (morpheme structure conditions) and constraints on surface variation, expressed by phonological rules.

In every case, the form of the constraints and P-rules is familiar to generative phonologists of whatever persuasion, while the content of the rules, and their motivations, refer to a different articulatory and perceptual basis. Thus sign phonology will eventually lead to a 'phonetics' of sign, based on the natural dynamics of manual articulation and visual perception. For example, we have one tongue, but two independent hands. This independence is constrained, however, by the need to simplify manual-visual signals in a rapid transmission context.

The importance of this type of motivation cannot be overemphasized, and we will introduce it when relevant to the analysis. While we are far from a theory of naturalness of signs, we have a good idea of some general tendencies based on the constraints and processes we have observed so far.

Lexical description

In attempting to describe and classify both the static and dynamic aspects of signs, we have relied heavily on the seminal work done by Stokoe (1960) and Stokoe, Casterline, and Croneberg (1965). Their success in producing a first dictionary of ASL was due to their insightful classification of signs and their development of a suitable transcription.

Stokoe (1960) first proposed three aspects relevant to the lexical description of signs: (1) the 'tab', or location in space or on the body where the sign is articulated; (2) the 'dez', or hand configuration (shape) of the articulating hands; (3) the 'sig', or movement. All of these are distinctive, since many minimal pairs exist for each of these aspects. In addition, they have been found to be of some explanatory value for the errors made in memory tasks (Bellugi 1972).

More recently, it has become apparent that more information is needed to fully specify signs in the lexicon. This is the 'orientation' aspect, which specifies how the hands spatially relate to each other or to other body parts. Signs such as those for SHORT versus TRAIN and NAME versus SIT are distinguished only by the orientation of the hands.

This establishes the existence of sub-lexical units, but in order to strengthen the claim that ASL displays duality of patterning we can go much further. The elements within each of the four broadly defined aspects compose finite sets, and their combinations into morphemes are severely limited. Depending on the lect and the eventual form of the complete phonological analysis, there are approximately 25 different locations, 45 hand shapes, 10 types of movements, and 10 types of orientation. [1] Not all of these are distinctive at a relatively abstract phonological level. Each of these elements may be further decomposed in a distinctive feature analysis, but the details of this will be introduced only where they are relevant to the rules in the section on variation.

While working with the units of analysis themselves poses some knotty problems, even in a preliminary form they offer insights into the sublexical structure of signs. Predictably, not all combinations of these units are utilized by the signs of ASL. This redundancy can be captured by morpheme structure conditions, both segmental (simultaneous) and sequential.

The 'Symmetry Condition' is an expected feature of an articulator with bilateral symmetry and independently moving arms: if both hands have a movement component for a given sign (as opposed to being static), then specifications for hand configuration, movement, and location must be identical, and therefore symmetrical.

A second segmental constraint on possible signs is the 'Dominance Condition', which reflects the physiological fact of hand preference: if the hand configurations of a given two-handed sign are non-identical, then one hand must remain stationary while the other hand, usually the dominant hand, executes the movement.

In addition, for the signs which meet the Dominance Condition, there are restrictions on which of the 45 different hand configurations may serve as the stationary hand. Only six different hands are allowed in that position, and they are the most unmarked, maximally differentiated six hands, which is just what one would expect in dealing with a true phonological system. These are (1) A -- the closed fist, (2) B -- the flat palm, (3) 5 -- the palm with fingers spread, (4) G -- fist with extended index finger, (5) C -- hand arcs in a semi-circle, and (6) O -- fingertips meet thumb, forming a circle.

These dezes are considered unmarked because they are maximally distinct both in articulatory and perceptual terms, have a high frequency of occurrence, are found in all sign languages which we know of to date, and are among the first handshapes mastered by the child acquiring signs. In addition, both adults and children make errors of substitution which tend toward this small set of handshapes. Another criterion which defines this class is 'point of contact'; these unmarked dezes may contact other body parts in a greater variety of ways than marked dezes, which may be restricted to one or two contact points. There are also other, more detailed criteria.

There are other morpheme structure constraints involving more complex types of signs. The body is divided into four major areas with respect to where a given sign may be articulated. These are (1) the head and neck area, (2) the trunk, from the shoulders to the hips, (3) the arm, from the shoulder to the wrist inclusive, and (4) the hand (we shall exclude from this limited discussion signs made off the body, in space). Although there are no a priori reasons why these particular boundaries have formal significance in ASL, they can be shown to be operative in two types of constraints, the first of these being a set of absolute constraints holding across these major areas.

For signs whose articulation involves contacting the body twice rather than just once, most make both contacts within the same major area. But there are signs whose contact is made first in one area, and then another. Not all sequences of contact are utilized by the ASL lexicon. For example, there are signs which originate in the head area and then contact the trunk, but there are none known which first contact the trunk and then the head. These facts are summarized in Table 1. A+ indicates that there are signs which have the indicated contact sequence. Note that only half the possible sequences are used.

A second constraint related to this same large set of signs involves a neutralization of place distinctions within these major areas. So far we have found that the second contact is constrained to a fixed, neutralized position, so that internal distinctions within a major area are lost. For instance, there is a sign made with the fully open '5' hand which first contacts the chin with the thumb. This is one of the signs for 'woman'. However, there seems to be no possibility of an

TABLE 1. Inter area constraints

		Second contact			
		head	trunk	arm	hand
First contact	head	+	+	+	+
	trunk	–	+	–	+
	arm	–	–	+	–
	hand	+	–	–	+

ASL sign which first contacts the chin and then some more extreme part of the trunk, say the shoulder or any corner of the trunk.

The two types of constraints outlined above show a conspiratorial similarity, in that a relative complexity (double contact as opposed to a simple single contact) is counteracted by an increase in redundancy due to the neutralizing effects of the sequential morpheme structure constraints.

There are two major points to be made on this discussion of sublexical systems. The first is that there is indeed a 'system' to the components of signs, and that every possible gesture is not necessarily a possible sign. General constraints rule on the possible forms of ASL signs. Second, the motivation for these constraints comes directly from a consideration of the articulatory dynamics of the body, thus providing the basis for a discussion of the naturalness of signs and the naturalness of form change. So, although the 'phonetic' basis of signing presents some radically different dynamics, constraints on form manifest themselves in rather familiar ways at the level of lexical description.

Variation and change in ASL phonology

There are many ways in which the form of a given sign may vary, all of them stable in phonological terms. Deletion of one hand of a two-handed sign, deletion of contact, or modification of a movement may occur. Locations of a given class of signs may shift from one part of the body to another. Assimilation of orientation, movement, location, and handshape all occur frequently within compounds and across lexical boundaries.

These changes are motivated by the need to limit the complexity of signs in rapid transmission and to facilitate transitions between signs. We also believe that a theory of natural phonology is possible for signing, which should eventually take into account both articulatory and perceptual complexity.

One striking example of phonological variation we have observed is the addition of an extended thumb to dezes which already have other fingers extended. The 'G' (index finger extended from fist) and 'H' (index and mid fingers extended from fist, contacting) dezes are two good examples. [2]

When G changes to [+thumb], it merges with the dez 'L', which Stokoe (1960) considered a contrastive unit. When H changes to [+thumb], the configuration resembles that of '3' (thumb, fore, and mid fingers extended, and separated), an independent dez. Thus 'G' and 'H' changing to [+thumb] is highly interesting, since it causes a neutralization between distinctive segments in one case and a near-neutralization in the other case.

We believe this variation indicates ongoing historical change in ASL, since some 60-year-old sign films we have seen do not display this variation, and current sign manuals still list citation forms without the thumb. However, in conversation and even occasionally in citation, informants sometimes produce the [+thumb] variants of 'G' and 'H'. Not all signs with 'G' or 'H' dezes allow this variation currently.

Field procedures

We obtained the intuitive responses of 39 signers as to whether they use [+thumb] or [-thumb] variants of eleven 'g' and 'H' signs. The informants vary according to three extralinguistic variables: whether they had deaf parents or not, whether they learned signs before or after the age of six, and sex. The variables [±deaf parents] and [±before age six] have been shown to correlate significantly with grammatical variation in ASL (Woodward 1973b).

We also tested the reliability of the above elicitation by comparing the informants' intuitive responses with the data we obtained by videotaping five of our informants. Three different levels of style were taped for each informant as they signed ten sentences. The eleven signs used in the elicitation were incorporated in these sentences in such a way as to avoid the influence of assimilation from surrounding environments. Style was introduced as an independent variable by requesting our informants to sign first to a deaf friend, and secondly, to a hearing teacher. A third, less formal style was obtained by taping a session without our informants' knowledge.

The informants' signing in the experimental situation closely followed their intuitive responses. For four signers there was a difference of one lect between the intuitive responses and the conversational signing. For one informant there was a difference of two lects (see Woodward 1973b). We also found that the feature [+thumb] remained the same for each informant in the three styles. However, there were striking lexical and grammatical differences in the styles for each of the informants.

Implicational patterns

The eleven signs were found to be implicationally ordered as follows:

ME ⊃ NOSE ⊃ BORING ⊃ RIGHT ⊃ BLACK ⊃
NEGRO ⊃ NAME ⊃ WEIGH ⊃ RED ⊃ CUTE ⊃ FUNNY

Table 2 shows the twelve lects resulting from this implication. With thirty-nine informants there were 429 responses. There were twenty-two expections to the implication, yielding a 5.1 percent rate of exception or a 94.9 percent rate of scalability, a strongly valid implication.

TABLE 2. [+THUMB] Implication

	Lects											
	1	2	3	4	5	6	7	8	9	10	11	12
ME	+	–	–	–	–	–	–	–	–	–	–	–
NOSE	+	+	–	–	–	–	–	–	–	–	–	–
BORING	+	+	+	–	–	–	–	–	–	–	–	–
RIGHT	+	+	+	+	–	–	–	–	–	–	–	–
BLACK	+	+	+	+	+	–	–	–	–	–	–	–
NEGRO	+	+	+	+	+	+	–	–	–	–	–	–
NAME	+	+	+	+	+	+	+	–	–	–	–	–
WEIGH	+	+	+	+	+	+	+	+	–	–	–	–
RED	+	+	+	+	+	+	+	+	+	–	–	–
CUTE	+	+	+	+	+	+	+	+	+	+	–	–
FUNNY	+	+	+	+	+	+	+	+	+	+	+	–

Correlation of lects with social variables

Table 3 shows membership in each of the lects in relation to social variables.

At the present time no correlation between membership in the lects and social variables has been found. This may be due to the fact that the present sample is too small and irregular, especially for phonological variation, which is often not as sharply stratified as grammatical variation (Wolfram 1969).

Features conditioning the variation

Six features (or constellations of features) distinguish the eleven signs:

TABLE 3. Membership in lects

Groups							
Deaf Parents	+	+	–	–	–	–	
Before 6	+	+	+	+	–	–	
Female	+	–	+	–	+	–	
Lects							Total
1	0	0	0	0	0	0	0
2	0	0	0	0	0	0	0
3	0	0	0	0	0	0	0
4	0	1	0	0	0	0	1
5	0	0	0	0	0	0	0
6	1	0	1	0	2	0	4
7	1	0	0	1	0	1	3
8	2	1	0	1	0	1	5
9	1	1	0	2	3	0	7
10	0	1	1	0	2	2	6
11	1	0	1	0	2	1	5
12	1	1	1	0	5	1	9
Total	7	5	4	4	14	6	39

± Indexic	whether or not the sign is contiguous to (index) its referent.
± Bending of fingers	bending movement of the extended fingers from an open to a relatively closed position.
± Mid finger	whether or not the mid finger is extended.
± Twist	whether or not the sign has a twisting movement.
± Face	whether or not the sign is on the face.
± Center	whether or not the sign is made in the center of one of the four major areas of the body.

These features are justified independently on descriptive grounds (Woodward 1973b).

From the features in Table 4 we can determine the most heavily weighted environments and write a rule incorporating the constraints.

Table 5 shows the weightings with A being the most heavily weighted environment and Z being the least heavily weighted environment. The tentative rule which incorporates the weighted environments is given in Figure 1.

TABLE 4. Features of the eleven signs

	Features					
	Indexic	Bending of fingers	Mid finger	Twist	Face	Center
ME	+	–	–	–	–	+
NOSE	+	–	–	–	+	+
BORING	–	–	–	+	+	+
RIGHT	–	–	–	–	–	–
BLACK	–	–	–	–	+	–
NEGRO	–	–	+	+	+	+
NAME[3]	–	–	+	–	–	–
WEIGH[3]	–	–	+	–	–	–
RED	–	+	–	–	+	–
CUTE	–	+	+	–	+	–
FUNNY	–	+	+	–	+	+

TABLE 5. Weighted features of the eleven signs

	Features					
	Indexic	Bending of fingers	Mid finger	Twist	Face	Center
ME				Δ-		Z+
NOSE				Δ-	E+	Z+
BORING	A-				E+	Z+
RIGHT	A-			Δ-		
BLACK	A-			Δ-	E+	
NEGRO	A-		Γ+		E+	Z+
NAME	A-		Γ+	Δ-		
WEIGH	A-		Γ+	Δ-		
RED	A-	B+		Δ-	E+	
CUTE	A-	B+	Γ+	Δ-	E+	
FUNNY	A-	B+	Γ+	Δ-	E+	Z+

FIGURE 1. The rule of thumb

$$\begin{bmatrix} +\text{fore} \\ -\text{ring} \\ -\text{pinky} \end{bmatrix} \rightarrow [+\text{thumb}] \Big/ \begin{bmatrix} E\ (+\text{face}) \\ Z\begin{pmatrix} -\text{high} \\ -\text{low} \end{pmatrix} \end{bmatrix} \begin{bmatrix} \underline{} \\ \Gamma\ (+\text{mid}) \end{bmatrix} \begin{bmatrix} B\ (+\text{bending movement}) \\ \Delta\ (-\text{twist}) \end{bmatrix} \begin{bmatrix} A\ (-\text{indexic}) \end{bmatrix}$$

Environments are simultaneous, not sequential.

There are partial explanations for why these particular weighted features facilitate the operation of the rule, based on the articulatory dynamics of the body.

For the signs which involve a twisting movement, the extended thumb may interfere with a smooth movement by brushing against the body. Since unnecessary contact between body parts must be minimized, [-twist] facilitates the rule, while [+twist] inhibits it.

The presence of the middle finger, which distinguishes between the 'G' and 'h' dezes, facilitates the operation of the rule, since it seems that the more fingers that extend from the closed fist, the more tension is felt in the hand. This tension is subjectively reduced by extending the thumb, and is further reduced by bending the extended fingers.

We have no good explanation for the facilitation effect of [+face] and [+center]. In view of Siple's (1973) proposed perceptual constraints on signs, we should expect that signs made on or near the face should not promote neutralization of segments, as our Rule of Thumb does. Siple found that finer differentiation of movements, dezes, and sublocations are to be found in the facial zone, and that less differentiation is to be found in the areas further away from the face. This is simply because receivers focus their eyes on the signer's face, and visual acuity is thus highest in that area. Our proposed neutralization rule is thus not expected in an environment which supports differentiation of elements. Some other principle may be operating here, and it may explain the facilitation effect of both [+face] and [+center], since they are both relatively unmarked locational (tab) features. In any event, these two features are the least heavily weighted for our rule.

While the definition we have offered so far for [±Indexic] is most easily stated in semantic terms, this should not be regarded as a departure from phonological orthodoxy. Indexic signs can be characterized as a phonological class, though not in terms of existing features in our tentative framework. Indexical signs are those which are primarily defined by their place of contact (as in NOSE) or their orientation (as in YOU). They are unspecified for movement, while the other signs in this study must be specified for movement.

An elegant feature solution for this particular problem remains to be found. [4]

The inhibitory influence of [+Indexic] is perhaps based on the fact that the saliency of the index finger in contacting or pointing must be maintained. The thumb not only adds a visibly ambiguous aspect to the hand, it offers another potential point of contact.

Conclusion

American Sign Language has duality of patterning, that is, it has a level of structure analogous to the phonological component of oral languages. Sign phonological components are describable in terms of feature matrices, morpheme structure constraints, and other constructs in current phonological theory. Like their oral counterparts, sign phonologies are dynamic and require implicational and/or variable rule descriptions. The Rule of Thumb in this paper offers evidence of predictable on-going phonological change in American Sign Language. Observation of such changes is one of the many ways of approaching naturalness in sign phonology.

NOTES

This study was supported in part by NSF Grant GS-31349, NIMH Grant NS-10302, and by NEH Grant AY 8218 73 136.

1. For example, some movements can be described in terms of locations, assuming an unmarked direct movement between the two points.

2. 'G' and 'H' are simply names given to these particular dezes; they should not be confused with fingerspelled letters.

3. At the present time, we are not sure of the best way to distinguish name and weigh.

4. Even NAME and RIGHT, whose saliency seems to involve where they contact rather than how they move, must be specified for movement. This is evident when the stationary hand is deleted from these two-handed signs in certain very informal contexts. With no place to contact, the ordinarily redundant movement of these signs is emphasized.

REFERENCES

Battison, Robbin. 1973a. Phonology in American Sign Language. Paper delivered at the Third Annual California Linguistics Association Meeting, Stanford University, May, 1973.

Battison, Robbin. 1973b. Toward a phonological theory of sign languages. Paper delivered at the Communication Center, NTID-RIT, Rochester, New York, September, 1973.

Bellugi, Ursula. 1972. Studies in sign language. In: Psycholinguistics and total communication: The state of the art. Edited by T. J. O'Rourke. Silver Spring, Maryland, American Annals of the Deaf. 68-84.

Friedman, Lyn and Robbin Battison. 1973. Phonological structures in American Sign Language. NEH Grant Report AY 8218 73 136.

Frishberg, Nancy and Bonnie Gough. 1973a. Morphology in American Sign Language. Working Paper, Salk Institute for Biological Studies.

_____. 1973b. Time on our hands. Paper delivered at the Third Annual California Linguistics Association Meeting, Stanford University, May, 1973.

Siple, Patricia. 1973. Constraints for sign language from visual perception data. Working Paper, Salk Institute for Biological Studies. (To appear in Semiotica.)

Stokoe, William C., Jr. 1960. Sign language structure: An outline of the visual communication system of the American deaf. Studies in Linguistics, Occasional Paper 8.

_____, Dorothy Casterline, and Carl Croneberg. 1965. A dictionary of American Sign Language. Washington, D.C., Gallaudet College Press.

Wolfram, Walter. 1969. A sociolinguistic description of Detroit Negro speech. Washington, D.C., Center for Applied Linguistics.

Woodward, James C., Jr. 1973a. Some characteristics of Pidgin Sign English. Sign Language Studies 3.39-46.

_____. 1973b. Implicational lects on the deaf diglossic continuum. Unpublished Ph.D. dissertation, Georgetown University.

VARIATION IN
AMERICAN SIGN LANGUAGE SYNTAX:
AGENT-BENEFICIARY DIRECTIONALITY

JAMES C. WOODWARD, JR.

Linguistics Research Laboratory, Gallaudet College

1. Introduction. Recent studies of sign language in the United States (Stokoe 1970, 1972; Moores 1972, Woodward 1972, 1973a; Friedman 1973) posit a diglossic continuum between American Sign Language (ASL) and Standard English in the deaf community (as described by Meadow 1972, and Schlesinger and Meadow 1973). This is not the classic diglossic situation described by Ferguson (1959), since the H variety (Standard English) and the L variety (ASL) are two separate languages, but it is a situation that shares much of the attitudinal and social characteristics of typical diglossic situations.

Until this year, however, there had been no attempt to describe this diglossic continuum utilizing variation theory. This paper reports on three recent studies of variation in ASL syntax that utilize variation theory. These studies offer a crucial testing ground for the descriptive and explanatory power of variation theory, since these studies are on visual phenomena that linguists have not normally observed.

The first study, the D. C. study (Woodward 1973a), analyzed data on three ASL rules from 141 informants from the Washington, D. C., Frederick, Maryland, and New York City areas who varied according to four social variables. These variables identified the informants as deaf or hearing, as having deaf or hearing parents, as having learned signs before or after the age of six, and having attended some college or not. The second study, the Montana-Washington study (Woodward 1973b), tested the same three variables using thirty-six informants from Montana and Washington state who were chosen on the basis of the same three social variables as in the D. C. study. The third study, the interrule implication study (Woodward 1973c), took the data from the D. C. study and attempted to show implications between these three ASL rules.

It is impossible to discuss all aspects of each study. Only implications related to one of the rules, Outward-Inward Agent-Beneficiary Directionality, will be discussed in this paper. This rule, although it has the weakest implication of the three rules tested, is in some ways the most interesting.

2. Outward-Inward Agent-Beneficiary directionality

American Sign Language has a number of verbs that express the relationship between agent (actor) and beneficiary (dative) by direction of movement in three-dimensional space. The verb sign begins at the agent (or at a point in his direction) and moves to the beneficiary (or a point in his direction). Although directionality may be used for all three persons, only second-person-as-agent directionality is considered in this study. The following example shows the derivational history of a typical example of second-person-as-agent directionality.

(1) you give me (you and me may be deleted)
    'you give me'

Example 1 can be seen as coming from the underlying structure represented in (1a).

(1a)

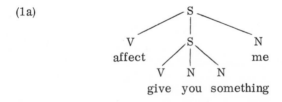

Affect is deleted and me is marked with +benefactive and sister adjoined to the other two noun phrases yielding (1b).

(1b)

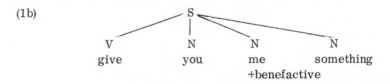

From (1b) we can assign rules that will give the correct order of elements, assign the proper direction to the verb (from agent to beneficiary), and delete all N elements that are +understood (from previous statements).

3. The D. C. study

There is, however, variation in signs as to which verbs can take second person directionality. This study utilized intuitions of informants to test nine verbs that were empirically observed to take this directionality occasionally. These nine verbs were found to be implicationally ordered as follows: 'fingerspell', 'hate', 'hit', 'force', 'say no', 'ask (question)', 'tell', 'show', and 'give'. This implication produced the ten possible lects listed in Table 1. For 141 persons at nine slots a person, there was a total of 1,269 slots. There were 130 exceptions in the responses, yielding a 10.2 percent rate of exception or an 89.8 percent rate of acceptability, a valid implication. (The other two implications, Negative Incorporation and Verb Reduplication showed 97 percent and 90.6 percent rates of acceptability, respectively.)

TABLE 1. Implicational lects for Agent-Beneficiary directionality

	Lects									
	1	2	3	4	5	6	7	8	9	10
'fingerspell'	+	–	–	–	–	–	–	–	–	–
'hate'	+	+	–	–	–	–	–	–	–	–
'hit'	+	+	+	–	–	–	–	–	–	–
'force'	+	+	+	+	–	–	–	–	–	–
'say no'	+	+	+	+	+	–	–	–	–	–
'ask'	+	+	+	+	+	+	–	–	–	–
'tell'	+	+	+	+	+	+	+	–	–	–
'show'	+	+	+	+	+	+	+	+	–	–
'give'	+	+	+	+	+	+	+	+	+	–

3.1 Correlation of Outward-Inward Agent-Beneficiary Directionality with social variation. Most sociolinguists have attempted to correlate social class with linguistic variation. They have generally assumed that social class may be described by an inter-correlation of education, occupation, and income. Other factors such as age and sex have been shown to be correlated with linguistic variation (Wolfram 1969, Trudgill 1972).

For the study of the deaf, four social variables seemed likely to correlate well with variation in sign language. These variables were: $\pm$ deaf, $\pm$ deaf parents, $\pm$ before six, and $\pm$ college.

Basically there are two reasons for choosing these four variables over others. (1) It did not seem justifiable to assume that social class was determined in the same way for both the hearing and the deaf communities. (2) It seems that the first three of these social variables are extremely important criteria for socialization into the deaf community. If a person is deaf, he can much more easily join the deaf community. Very few hearing people can really be considered part of the deaf community. Meadow (1972) pointed out that socialization into the deaf community invariably includes language socialization. With the children of deaf parents this language socialization generally takes place from birth. With children of hearing parents it may take place at other times. However, the age of six seems to be a crucial time in first language acquisition. Quite possibly a person learning signs after the age of six will sign differently from a person who learned signs earlier.

The fourth variable, education, seems to be a universal social variable for those societies having a formal education system, since education tends to preserve and transmit traditional values toward language and society as well as to promote a maintenance of language forms and structures that may not be present in everyday conversation.

As far as variation in Outward-Inward Agent-Beneficiary Directionality is concerned, lects 1 through 5 in Table 1 are the lects that are closest to pure ASL on the deaf diglossic continuum, since they are the lects that accept this ASL rule in the most environments. Conversely, lects 6 through 10 in Table 1 are the lects that are the furthest from ASL on the continuum, since they are the lects that accept this ASL rule in the fewest environments. Thus, it is possible to test dependency relationships between each of the four social variables and membership in lects 1 through 5 (ASL-like lects) and lects 6 through 10 (Non-ASL-like lects) by setting up two by two charts and running Chi-square tests on the data. Tables 2 through 5 show the relationship between lectal membership and each of the social variables.

TABLE 2. Lectal membership vs. deafness

Lects	+Deaf	−Deaf
1– 5	77 (71%)	8 (24%)
6–10	31 (29%)	25 (76%)
$\chi^2 = 21.45$, p < .005		

A Chi-square test of this data shows a very strong dependency relationship (at the .005 level) of $\pm$ deaf and membership in the lects.
One is more likely to find a deaf person in lects 1 through 5 (closer
to ASL) and more likely to find a hearing person in lects 6 through
10 (further from ASL).

TABLE 3. Lectal membership vs. parentage

Lects	+Deaf Parents	−Deaf Parents
1– 5	25 (69%)	60 (57%)
6–10	11 (31%)	45 (43%)
χ^2 = 1.22, p > .25		

A Chi-square test of this data shows no dependency relationship of
$\pm$deaf parents and membership in these lects.

TABLE 4. Lectal membership and age of sign acquisition

Lects	+Before 6	−Before 6
1– 5	50 (77%)	35 (46%)
6–10	15 (23%)	41 (54%)
χ^2 = 12.69, p < .005		

A Chi-square test of the data shows a strong relationship of the
variable $\pm$before six and membership in these lects. One is more
likely to find a person who learned signs before six in lects 1 through
5 (closer to ASL) and more likely to find a person who learned signs
after six in lects 6 through 10 (further from ASL).

TABLE 5. Lectal membership vs. education

Lects	+College	−College
1– 5	37 (84%)	32 (50%)
6–10	7(16%)	32 (50%)
(Hearing informants are not included in this chart.)		
χ^2 = 11.7, p < .005		

A Chi-square test of this data shows a very strong dependency
relationship (at the .005 level) of $\pm$college and membership in these
lects. One is more likely to find a deaf person who has attended
some college in lects 1 through 5 (closer to ASL) and more likely to
find a deaf person who has not attended any college in lects 6 through
10 (further from ASL).

Tables 2 through 5 have demonstrated that there are very strong
dependency relationships between the variables $\pm$deaf, $\pm$before six,

and ±college and membership in Outward-Inward Agent-Beneficiary
lects. As intuitively expected, deaf persons who learned signs before the age of six are more likely to be in lects that approach ASL
more closely. However, there is no dependency relationship between ±deaf parents and membership in these lects.

3.2 Features conditioning the variation. In the first attempt at
describing what factors were conditioning the Outward-Inward Agent-
Beneficiary Directionality implication, I proposed a series of
semantic and cherological features. However, based on Ralph
Fasold's comments and suggestions on the D.C. study, I would like
to propose the arrangement of a continuum of semantic features to
explain the variation. Ignoring the sign 'fingerspell' for a moment,
we can see a gradual change from something that might be called extremely beneficial to something that might be called extremely harmful. From left to right on the implication there is: 'give', 'show',
'tell', 'ask (a question)', 'say no', 'force', 'hit', 'hate'. 'Fingerspell' can now be seen as being outside this system--an extremely
new entry that has not had time to find its way to its proper place in
the already existing system. This is supported by the facts Outward-
Inward Agent-Beneficiary Directionality for 'fingerspell' was earlier
considered to be a child language overgeneralization from (Bellugi
1973) and that only 10 out of 141 informants (7 percent) in this study
and 4 out of 36 informants (11 percent) in the Montana-Washington
study used this form. In the future, it seems likely that 'fingerspell'
will fit in somewhere around 'tell'.

The solution presented here to describe the implicational variation can be fairly easily tested out with certain other verbs that
may take Outward-Inward Agent-Beneficiary Directionality. 'Bawl
out' is an example of such a crucial test case. If 'bawl out' has
entered the system, then it should be towards the harmful end of the
continuum. If it is not, then it could be a lexical exception or else
it could help prove the beneficial-to-harmful feature continuum presented here is not adequate to explain the implicational variation.
A number of other verbs like 'bawl out' need to be tested before any
final conclusion can be made.

4. The Montana-Washington study

The Montana-Washington study was a follow-up study to the D.C.
study to test if the implicational patterns found in D.C. would be the
same as those found in other parts of the country. They were the
same and with generally higher rates of scalability. Outward-
Inward Agent-Beneficiary Directionality was 92.6 percent scalable
according to the implicational pattern in Table 1. (The other two

implications Negative Incorporation and Verb Reduplication, showed a 95 percent and a 97 percent rate of scalability, respectively.)

There were not enough informants in each cell to reliably test for correlation of membership in the lects and social variables.

5. The interrule implication study

The D. C. study revealed six lects for Negative Incorporation, ten lects for Agent-Beneficiary Directionality, and ten lects for Verb Reduplication. It was pointed out that the implicational scales could be divided and that Negative Incorporation lects 1 through 3, Outward-Inward Agent-Beneficiary lects 1 through 5, and Verb Reduplication lects 1 through 5 were the part of the continuum that approached ASL most closely, that is, were the lects that used these three rules in the largest number of environments. These three rules then may be treated as parts of another implicational ordering. Table 6 shows the four lects so determined with '+', indicating membership in the ASL-like lects and '-', indicating membership in the more English-like lects.

TABLE 6. Rule-to-rule implication

Lects	Agent-Beneficiary lects 1-5	Neg-Incorporation lects 1-3	Verb Reduplication lects 1-5
1	+	+	+
2	-	+	+
3	-	-	+
4	-	-	-

There were twenty exceptions to this implication out of 423 responses. This gives a 95.3 percent rate of scalability. By dividing this implication in half, lects 1 and 2 represent the end of the continuum in which most ASL rules are used in the most environments, and lects 3 and 4 represent the end of the continuum in which few ASL rules are used in few environments. Chi-square tests of membership in lects 1 and 2, and 3 and 4, and the social variables used in the D. C. study showed strong dependency relationships between +deaf, +deaf parents, and +before six and membership in lects 1 and 2 and between -deaf, -deaf parents, and -before six and membership in lects 3 and 4. Thus deaf people, people with deaf parents, and people who learned signs before the age of six patterned in lects that approach 'pure' ASL more closely, and hearing people, people with hearing parents, and people who learned signs after the age of six patterned in lects that do not approach ASL closely. [1]

6. Summary and conclusion

These three studies have shown that variation along the ASL to English continuum is regular, rule-governed, and describable in terms of current concepts in variation theory.

One interesting point remains to be discussed, however, and this is the fact that the Outward-Inward Agent-Beneficiary Directionality implication was the weakest implication in both the D.C. and Montana-Washington studies. One possible explanation for this is that this implication is still in flux because it is historically the last one of the three rules tested to develop implicational variation. This explanation can be partially supported by the interrule implication study showing Outward-Inward Agent-Beneficiary Directionality to be the first of the three rules to be rejected by some informants.

Hopefully, there will soon be more research on this problem as well as on other variation in ASL syntax and cherology (for example, Battison, Markowicz, and Woodward 1973). Analysis of the ASL to English continuum not only offers a crucial testing ground for variation theory but also a useful way of describing the complex variation that exists in the languages of the United States deaf community.

NOTES

The production of this paper was supported in part by NSF grant GS-31349 and NIMH grant NS-10302. I want to thank Ralph Fasold for his comments and suggestions on part of this paper.

1. The charts showing membership in these lects are not listed here but can be found in Woodward (1973c).

REFERENCES

Battison, Robbin, Harry Markowicz, and James C. Woodward, Jr. 1973. A good rule of thumb: Variable phonology in American Sign Language. [This volume, pp. 291-302].

Bellugi, Ursula. 1973. Personal communication.

Ferguson, Charles. 1959. Diglossia. Word 15. 325-340.

Friedman, Lyn. 1973. Semantics of space, time and person in sign. Unpublished Master's thesis, University of California, Berkeley

Meadow, Kathryn. 1972. Sociolinguistics, sign language, and the deaf sub-culture. In: O'Rourke 1972. 19-33.

Moores, Donald. 1972. Communication: Some unanswered questions and some unquestioned answers. In: O'Rourke 1972. 1-10.

O'Rourke, T. J., ed. 1972. Psycholinguistics and total communication: The state of the art. Washington, D. C., The American Annals of the Deaf.

Schlesinger, Hilde and Kathryn Meadow. 1973. Sound and sign. Berkeley, University of California Press.

Stokoe, William C., Jr. 1970. Sign language diglossia. Studies in Linguistics 21. 27-41.

_____. 1972. Semiotics and human sign languages. The Hague, Mouton.

Trudgill, Peter. 1972. Sex, covert prestige and linguistic change in the urban British English of Norwich. Language in Society 1. 179-195.

Woodward, James C., Jr. 1972. Implications for sociolinguistic research among the deaf. Sign Language Studies 1. 1-7.

_____. 1973a. Implicational lects on the deaf diglossic continuum. Unpublished Ph. D. dissertation, Georgetown University.

_____. 1973b. Report on Montana-Washington Implicational Research. Sign Language Studies 4. 77-101.

_____. 1973c. Interrule implication in American Sign Language. Sign Language Studies 3. 47-56.

Wolfram, Walter A. 1969. A sociolinguistic description of Detroit Negro speech. Washington, D. C., Center for Applied Linguistics.

WHAT IS THE STUDY
OF VARIATION USEFUL FOR?

ROGER W. SHUY

Georgetown University

A few years ago a group of English professors met in Columbus, Ohio to discuss the value of literary criticism in the academic arena. The basic question put indelicately by one of the participants was, 'What is the point of all this time killing, anyway?'. Despite heroic efforts on the part of many of the participants, the general conclusion was that the major function of literary criticism was to teach graduate students to become literary critics who will then teach other graduate students to become literary critics. As the chairman of one Big Ten University, English Department put it, 'We are all playing an academic game and merely teaching other people to play an academic game.'

One of the inevitable developments in any field of study is the tendency toward narcissism. Academic fields, perhaps even literary criticism, usually originate in a practical need, either in society in general or within an already existing field of study. The social sciences are a case in point. At one time, they were heavily service-oriented. But as social workers began to contemplate the details and complexities of their work, determining what was their territory and what was not, they quite naturally elaborated a theory of the social sciences leading, in some quarters, to an almost total separation of the theoretical phase, sociology, from the practical phase, social work.

In linguistics also there was great concern for practical problems in the forties and fifties, which could be characterized as a time of strong interest in real problems of language teaching, especially in teaching English to foreigners, Bible translation, and interest in relating linguistic theory and research to the concerns of psychology and anthropology. The great period of theoretical concern set in during the sixties and is still with us today. This emphasis on theory parallels what happened in the social sciences and in many aspects of the humanities in earlier days. Many academic fields which once addressed themselves to everyday problems in real life settings grew more and more detached from these problems as the important work of theory-building took place. However necessary and desirable this theory-building was, it led to separations within the disciplines. Thus, sociology split from social work as an academic entity, literature departments frequently developed a caste system which relegated service-oriented or 'how to' courses to graduate assistants, to lower ranked faculty or to another department entirely. It is small wonder then that on college campuses the recent renewal of interest in values, in services, and in relevance has hit the theoretical phases of various disciplines very hard. They are being accused of elitism and of developing elaborate academic games which are to be explained and communicated only to the elite few, who, having scaled the required intellectual heights, can spend the rest of their lives as medical specialists in the third rib on the right, as literary critics with a specialty in George Herbert's later poems or, alas, as linguists who specialize in word-initial semivowel alternation in the Rigveda.

Apparently, there are simultaneous contradictory forces which are at work in the disciplines at all times: the need to solve a real problem versus the need to appear so independent of that problem as to seem to be self-sufficient. These forces provide many of the interesting paradoxes which ultimately embarrass the various fields. The field of linguistics has been embarrassed, for example, many times in recent years. It was embarrassed in the late fifties to be caught with a rather superficial theoretical base, with a focus largely on phonology rather than grammar and a naive view of research design by which it was actually believed that by interviewing in depth one native speaker of a foreign language one could actually write a grammar which would describe the speech of all the native speakers of that language. More recently linguistics has been embarrassed by accusations of elitism.

One of the more exciting things that is happening in the academic world today is the small steps we are beginning to make toward destroying this elitism. Although the trend for many years was toward ever-increasing degrees of specialization with concomitant scorn for all that was not specialized, such a position is less well received in today's world.

In the January, 1971 issue of The Journal of Internal Medicine, for example, C. P. Kimball editorialized that the field of medicine

has too long lived in isolation from the lower socio-economic
bracketed patient. He urged medical training of a sort that starts
with the culture and language of a patient where he is, not where the
physician is. He urged that the medical profession abandon its
elitist, witch-doctor status if it is serious about its lofty aims of
doing good for people who are unlike its members.

The re-discovery that there is a larger world out there somewhere
has been highlighted in recent federal government, management problems. Warren Bemis has observed that most of the younger Water-
gate witnesses look and act alike because they are really spiritual or
ghostly doubles--doppelgangers--of their bosses. But the doppelganger effect is by no means limited to the federal government. Almost any bureaucracy produces it--corporations, universities,
hospitals, even academic fields, where leaders tend to select key
assistants, students, or colleagues who resemble them for they feel
that the verification, analysis, and decision-making of kindred spirits
will do a better job of furthering their own causes.

The major danger of such a practice is that the leader becomes
overprotected as he receives complete loyalty and he develops the
vulnerability that comes from such dependence. The ultimate implication of the doppelganger effect in the federal government has become
widely known and it might serve as an important beacon to those in
academia. It was John Mitchell who unashamedly testified that all of
his effort and concern was on re-electing Mr. Nixon to the neglect, in
fact, of ethics, human dignity and, apparently, the law. Academic
narcissism is certainly a parallel to Mr. Mitchell's loyal single-
mindedness. The President's practice of surrounding himself with
people like Mr. Mitchell and other doppelgangers most certainly
must be questioned. Those of us concerned with language variation
have already taken an important step away from such narcissism, for
our origins are from a diverse set of fields, our concerns are by
definition dynamic and pluralistic, our methodologies partake of the
best aspects of several different fields of study, our unit of measure
is the gradatum rather than an oversimplified polarity-set and our
attitude is at least pointed in the direction of reasonable practicality.
No accusation of the doppelganger effect can be made of a field which
was born in such diversity (linguistic theory, ethnography of communication, creolization, and dialectology, to name a few) and which
continues to bring together people from such broad interests. Contro-
versies over methodology continue to rage, clearly indicating a
healthy state of non-orthodoxy. The framework of static linguistics
is clearly being affected by this recent flurry of interest on variation,
realistic context and the re-examination of our assumptions and this
is clearly one of the things that variation is good for. Linguistic
theory, itself, will be one beneficiary.

Another area to benefit from a focus on variation is that of education. Historically speaking, it is reasonably safe to observe that linguistics has had, at best, only a minor influence on native language education in the United States. To be sure, teaching materials for beginning readers now are beginning to recognize that reading is a language processing operation and texts are beginning to be written in language which approximates more natural speech. Some language arts programs are even beginning to stress linguistic pluralism and place proper value on language variation, but much, if not most, of the focus of the linguist in American education in the past has been negative. That is, he has chosen to address himself to what is wrong with the system as it is rather than to enmesh himself in the question of what constructive contribution he can make to the field. The structural linguists' attack on traditional grammar in the forties and fifties was largely a description of what was wrong with the way traditional teachers were teaching about language. The stance was one of laughing at the atrocities of the stereotyped, old-fashioned, prescriptive school teacher and, however clear and accurate such criticisms were, they most certainly could not be considered tactful.

Teachers concerned with the preservation of traditional values also saw in structural linguistics a threat to the status quo. The linguists were loud in their rhetoric but were generally unable to complement their criticisms with a positive program of replacement. This situation is not unparalleled in the field of educational change. The apparent excessive claims of behavioral psychologists, for example, have been under constant and often convincing attack by advocates of a cognitive approach but the cognitivists have yet to provide a convincing programmatic alternative to all of the idols which they are attempting to destroy. This is not to say that they are wrong in their criticisms--only that the process seems to call for attack and criticism before the development of a viable and tested alternative.

The advent of generative grammar in no way improved the interrelationship of linguistics and educational concerns. Almost before the structuralists had rallied themselves together to produce an alternative strategy for the application of linguistics to school problems, the revolution from within linguistics began to discredit any potential application. To make matters even more difficult, generative theory changed (and continues to change) very rapidly during the sixties and seventies, making a shambles of any effort to relate it to the classroom. This is not to say that nothing from structural or generative grammar has proven useful to the classroom. On the contrary, a great deal has been learned about how language seems to work and about the undertakings and attitudes concerning language which a teacher might develop. In addition to factors such as those

mentioned earlier, however, linguistics tended to focus its potential
usefulness on language universals, deep and surface structure relationships and rules which generally characterized the innateness of
native language. No one can doubt the usefulness of such study to
linguists, psychologists, sociologists, anthropologists, and philo-
sophers, but one might seriously question the usefulness of such
information to elementary and secondary school children. To put it
another way, one might seriously ask what good it will do a child to
learn how to talk about what he has already learned how to do. On
the other hand, the general problems addressed by the teacher are
concerned with helping children learn to write, read, and speak
better. The teacher might seriously question how information which
explains extant competence might contribute answers to these problems. Naturally, a teacher might be expected to know these things,
for it is her responsibility to know many things related to how a
child has acquired his language, how language problems can be
accurately diagnosed as well as the theoretical underpinnings of
language production, but there is little reason to expect children to
improve their writing, reading or speaking by studying how it is they
know what they already know. It may contribute to their general
knowledge of the universe but it is unlikely to have the immediate
impact expected of the schoolroom.

With the relatively recent developments in the study of language
variation we have come a bit closer to the sorts of problems which
also concern the schools. This focus on variability makes a better
match with the setting in which a child can be found than its recent
predecessors did. Most children in the United States are surrounded
by people who speak with variation which stems from differences in
social status, geography, sex, age, and style. They are faced with
conflicting pressures to conform to the norms of their peers, their
parents, their school, and their region. Often they are placed in
conflict with a value system which contrasts to that of the school.
In addition, some children are in conflict with the language and culture of textbooks and instructional strategies and the mismatch between their lifestyles and those of the educational process is too
great for them to overcome. They may be placed in further conflict
by developments of minority awareness which may militate against
school or majority norms in a way in which they may become politically involved to their own disadvantage.

Research on variation which has been done recently in urban lan-
guage in the United States (Labov 1966, 1968; Shuy, Wolfram, and
Riley 1967; Wolfram 1969, 1971; Fasold 1972), in language attitudes
(Frender and Lambert 1972; Fishman 1971; Williams 1970, 1971;
Tucker 1969; Shuy and Fasold 1973), in language planning (DasGupta
1970; Rubin and Jernudd 1972; Rubin and Shuy 1973), in the ethnography

of speaking (Abrahams 1970, Bauman and Sherzer 1974), and in pidginization and creolization (Hymes 1971) is the type of research which bears more closely on the problems faced by the schools. One reason why such studies bear directly is that they all deal with concrete rather than abstract language situations, and that they face squarely the fact of variability and deal with it as a kind of systematic and predictable continuum.

The application of such research appears to be, once again, promising evidence of the applicability of linguistics to educational problems. An enthusiasm and optimism much like that of the early days of structural and generative grammar is once again upon us and now is the time to prepare for a strategy of planned application. We must avoid the overenthusiasm of the friends of linguistics who sometimes promise more than we can offer. We must avoid the temptation to be nasty or arrogant as we face the linguistic ignorance of the education system and we must be careful to build a complete strategy rather than a partial one.

The study of language variability gets to the heart of many problems involving writing, reading, and talking. It is in this area of variability that answers can be found to perplexing questions about how to delimit styles, exactly how to effect acceptability in school writing and talking, how to appreciate the dynamics of variation in the language of others, how to sequence language materials, how people set themselves off from each other through language, or how subtle variation between spoken and written language forms can cause problems in composition or reading. Native language teaching must deal with these and similar issues, but has generally lacked the tools to do so.

Information about language variation may be used to help re-think the education of teachers, the development of instructional materials and techniques and the building of educational programs of various sorts. If linguists really have things to say about pedagogy, and if they can overcome the bad feelings caused by arrogance and over-promise of linguists in the past, they must do it by starting with the teacher's and children's problems, not with a stance of aloofness. Furthermore, they must plan to approach the problems of the classroom in many different ways and at many different levels at the same time.

One might hypothesize, for example, that what linguists should do is to pressure teacher training institutions to re-think their curriculum, placing language at the center rather than as the peripheral stepchild. As fine as this might sound, reality will soon make very clear that it is very difficult for education departments at universities to change even if they know they must.

There are predictable reasons why it is difficult to work for change within the education system. Teacher training institutions, like other institutions, tend to defend against change. Drastic changes in teacher preparation (such as putting language at the core of the education of elementary teachers) suggest drastic staffing problems. How do we incorporate language training (general linguistics, language acquisition, and language variation should provide the bare minimum) without overburdening the training staff and reordering certification requirements? And how do we deal with the buck-passing that ultimately stops with the teacher, who gets blamed for all the failures in her training and her bureaucracy simply because there is no one else to blame the failure on except the children? What do we do about the compensatory education advocates who claim that if children do not learn it is because they have not gotten up to the social and cognitive level of the school? Despite decades of saying that we start with children where they are, the child is usually blamed for his own failure. Changing from within may be a great deal more difficult than even the most optimistic observer might suggest. The system may not admit that it is in trouble. To change it will involve subtlety far beyond anything linguists have suggested to date.

If the preceding analysis is accurate, the tactic for establishing a temper for innovation must be carefully and solidly built. Linguists who are concerned about education must go to education rather than expect education to come to them. But not only must they go to education, they must also become accepted by education. This observation is not a popular one among those linguists who hold education in particular scorn. To be sure, education has displayed many weaknesses and produced many failures. But the simple truth of the matter is that the field of education also has its value systems, its establishment, and its pecking order. An outsider may be treated with dignity, even heeded, but the ultimate success of his suggestion will depend on political factors in education, just as it does in any other field of study.

One obvious strategy for establishing an entry for specialists in language variation in education is for such linguists to become accepted by the educationists as functioning members of their establishment. A linguist on a commission which deals with requirements for teacher certification is in a strategic position to suggest that language courses become central to the training of reading and language arts teachers. A linguist on the evaluation of early childhood education programs being developed by educational laboratories and research and development centers is in a strategic position to effect changes in the staffing and focus of such projects. A linguist in the administration of a city school system is in a strategic position for implementing changes suggested by his field in the humanizing of native language instruction. Not all linguists, of course, will be able or willing to accept such roles, even as a supplementary aspect of their primary activities in linguistics. But if linguistics is to gain influence within the field of education, it is likely that some linguists will need to be so motivated. Such a strategy will involve their going to education with their ideas, presenting these ideas from the viewpoint of education rather than linguistics, expressing these ideas in terms and concepts which will be likely to be understood and valued, developing a tolerance for the naivete of educators about linguistics, and admitting their own naivete about certain understandings and skills held by educators.

In order to engage in effective educational planning it will be necessary for linguists to effect a rather major attitude shift in themselves. It has been popular, especially in the past decade, for linguists to delimit that which and only that which they, as linguists, are qualified to say. Perhaps this has come about as a healthy reaction against the overpromise of linguists in the forties and fifties. Perhaps it developed as a by-product of the attempt by linguistics to establish its own identity and territory. Linguistics as it was known in the fifties was very difficult to describe for it seemed to partake of many other fields and had little identity of its own. With the development of a more sophisticated theory came a natural abstractness which placed a gulf between linguistics and other fields as well as between practical concerns within linguistics. Meanwhile, there are always those who either, with naive altruism or with a more cynical opportunism, try to capitalize on the prestige of a field before its theory is well-enough developed or merely in an effort to make use of the current fads.

Regardless of its origins, however, this tendency of linguists to disqualify themselves from having anything to say about the educational relationships of linguistics has tended to widen the gulf that exists between the schools and linguistic knowledge. One predictable outcome of such a gulf is that the university course usually called introduction to linguistics is almost always set up for linguistics majors only. Those who major in sociology, psychology, or education must approach the field just as linguists do in order to get anything out of it. In this, linguistics departments can be accused of a kind of compensatory education model in which the learner (in this case, the educator) is told that he must adjust to linguistics rather than causing linguistics to adjust to him. Many linguists have argued that educators frequently overlook one of the basic tenets of education--starting with the learner where he is. On the other hand, it appears that linguistics is often quite guilty of the same sort of practice. Likewise, linguists accuse some educators of dealing with

children from different (often minority) cultures as deficient rather
than different. Yet a linguistics which perceives the objectives and
methods of educators as deficient rather than different from the objectives and methods of linguistics is surely deserving of the same
sort of condemnation. The application here is that if linguists are
really concerned about relating their field to other disciplines such
as education, they must set aside old biases against non-linguists
and accept the vulnerabilities and insecurities involved in operating
out of their own depth. For too long linguists have assumed the role
of isolative egotism, sitting in critical judgment of other fields but
not venturing out to them with what linguistics has to offer.

It has been argued that the study of language variation in real
social contexts stands a better chance of being useful to education
than any other focus in linguistics. It has also been noted that major
handicaps to any progress in this area have come from the linguists'
own attitude toward education, from skepticism stemming from past
atrocities and over-promise of linguists and from educational entropy.
An illustration of this entropy may be seen in the current situation
involving standardized tests in reading. A great deal of pressure
has been placed on test manufacturers to change their tests to conform to more modern findings. Certain publishers respond with
mild interest but explain that their tests still sell very well and that
they do not intend to stop producing a good seller. The only strategy
to get these tests changed is to lobby for boycotting the test--an
economic solution to an economic problem. The educational planning
involved in such an issue is that which addresses itself to conscious-
ness raising, organizing, and communication of the problem to the
appropriate opinion leaders. Similarly, vested interests in education
departments will continue to hamper change there. If it is true that
innovation comes either from the realization that one is in trouble or
from the jealousy of neighboring products, the strategy for change
becomes clear. Either we convince the educators that they are in
trouble or we build on their tendency toward jealousy of their neigh-
bors.

Both strategies tend to plan from within the system. An alternative
approach would be to devise a teacher preparation program totally
outside the conventional education department framework. One such
program which stresses language variation is currently being developed at The University of California at San Diego, under the direction of Hugh Mehan. The program is currently in its very beginning
stages and it is still too early to evaluate either its success or its
potential for impact. In essence, a select group of future teachers
is being trained for certification in the content areas most relevant
to elementary teaching in the United States (mathematics, social
studies, language arts, and science), while the more traditional

education courses are brought in as supplementary services. The base is in the content areas, two of which, language and social studies, are heavily sociolinguistic in orientation. Such a program bears careful watching for, if it is successful, it may signal an efficient method of overcoming the educational lock-step in teacher preparation which is caused by the self-perpetuation of vested interests.

Perhaps the more difficult task is one which tries to work for change from within the existing education system. There are predictable reasons why it is difficult to work for change within the education system. In the United States teacher training institutions are just that--institutionalized entities. Drastic changes in teacher preparation (such as putting language at the core of the education of elementary education majors rather than at the periphery) suggest drastic staffing problems.

On the assumption that teacher preparation institutions either do not realize that there is a problem or that their commitment to the status quo is too great to permit changes which would allow easy access to training in sociolinguistics, at least three plans are available for working within the system: infiltration, the jealousy motif, and management control.

(a) Infiltration. This plan puts the major pressure on the linguist. He must utilize his training and manage to fit into an already existing educational system (in this case, a teacher training institution) by adjusting his concerns to the expectations and needs of the department in which he works. This means that a person trained in linguistics may also need to teach courses in educational methods, philosophy, and research for which to this point he has been only marginally prepared. The major problem is in being hired in the first place. A second problem is in deferring his gratification or in waiting for change to come about slowly. In this, linguists as a whole have had little experience, at least until the recent job market decline. In many departments, such as English literature, well trained specialists may have to teach general introductory courses for several years until their departmental seniority allows them the privilege of teaching the area of their specialty. This has not been generally true of linguists until rather recently, largely because the field was expanding as a field and new graduates found little difficulty teaching their specialty almost as soon as they were hired. Today we have a different situation. Like the literature specialists who are forced to teach freshman composition (for which they were poorly prepared, if prepared at all), linguists are forced to teach in fields only marginally relevant to their training. My point here, however, is that training in language variation is closer to educational concerns than apprenticeship early-teaching areas usually are for specialists in other fields. To be sure, the training of linguists might well gear itself to this eventuality.

In terms of long-range planning, however, the strategy of infiltration will be a slow and arduous one. Its success will probably depend on how seriously the task is taken by the linguist, how well he can survive in an 'alien' climate, how well he is accepted by his colleagues, and how well he does his job.

(b) The jealousy motif. One of the major motivations for educational innovation is one in which a system changes primarily because another system which has status has already implemented that change. Innovation in suburban school systems in the United States frequently follows this model. If the schools of Winnetka, Illinois, Shaker Heights, Ohio, or Montgomery County, Maryland innovate in a certain manner, it can be expected that other school systems will be sure to follow. In an effort to test the jealousy motif as a model for educational planning involving sociolinguistic concerns, various sociolinguists at Georgetown University have been working with in-service education in the Norfolk, Virginia public schools. In practice, the project was to assist in the desegregation effort of that school system by providing teachers, especially white teachers who had not previously encountered black children, with knowledge of the communication system of minority children. Less obviously, it was an attempt to build positive attitudes on the part of teachers toward children whose language and culture were foreign to them. For the purposes of educational planning, however, the project served as an experiment in testing the jealousy motif in a new and interesting manner. The question was: Can educational change be brought about in local teacher training institutions by building into a major school system's in-service program features which are seen as desirable, therefore transportable, to the pre-service programs? In other words, the strategy was to provide such an attractive in-service program that the local universities will want to modify their curriculum to keep up with Norfolk's expectations.[1] It is still too early to evaluate the success of this experiment in utilizing the jealousy motif, but there are many early signs that much of our in-service work will be continued by local institutions in the future.[2]

(c) Management control. A third type of planning for educational change in sociolinguistics is one which observes the importance of the well-known principle of innovation which recognized that for successful innovation, the innovator must be protected by those in authority over him. The process of educational innovation may begin at any place in the system, but unless the people in control understand it and at least tolerate it, the innovation is not likely to survive. An example of past error, now rectified, in this matter may be found in much of the United States Office of Education support of Title XI summer workshops to upgrade the knowledge and skills of teachers. Many of these workshops were crash courses in linguistics for teachers who had been trained before the newer findings were made available. Typically, workshop directors selected only those teachers who were the brightest, youngest, most flexible, and daring. In short, they usually selected innovators who absorbed the information, returned to their schools, and were considered wildly radical in every attempt at implementing what they had just learned. They were in no way protected in their innovation and often became discouraged, if not embittered. Efficient planning might have yielded better results. But, as everyone who has labored with educational administrators knows, this is a difficult group with whom to work. For one thing, they are pressured by groups of various sorts, many of whom are political in their concerns for education and are obsessed by a complex with which linguists are thoroughly familiar.

To this point we have addressed ourselves to plans for reaching teachers and plans for changing both pre-service and in-service training. Obviously the planning suggested is only suggestive and is by no means comprehensive or complete. But mention must also be made of strategies to implement sociolinguistic principles at other levels. These strategies for extending the influence of sociolinguistic principles to the schools involve the achievement of power. Occasionally the educational system will look to 'outsiders' for advice but to assume implementation of that advice one must become, as it were, a part of the establishment. The ineffectiveness of the major critics of education who advocate its complete overthrow displays a sharp contrast to the power exerted in the area of consumer rights by Ralph Nader, whose strategy has been to work more or less from within the system. The strategy being suggested here may not be as dramatic as the one generally used by Nader, for there is considerably less public dissatisfaction about quality education than there is about faulty manufacturing; but it is closer to his approach than to out and out revolution.

In addition to the preparation of teachers, linguistics has many things to offer the education process in the area of teaching materials. If the influence of language variation in the schools follows the examples set by its predecessors, structural and generative linguistics, we will soon be seeing a spate of programs labelled the sociolinguistic approach to oral language, etc. It would appear that now is the time to plan the potential usefulness of language variation to the development of educational materials before the field becomes faddish and the opportunists swoop in with still another set of lofty but unrealizable claims.

It would seem obvious that the impact of linguistics on the development of materials geared to improve the written composition of children from various minority groups would hinge on a number of factors: effective and accurate research, selection of an appropriate vehicle for dissemination, an assessment of the potential public reactions to such materials (will they be thought to exploit, single out, or degrade the potential audience?) and a clear estimate of how such materials might differ from or be similar to materials developed for the non-target audience. Fortunately, linguistics has already come to grips with some aspects of these situations both in the teaching of standard English and in the teaching of reading. Although controversy still rages among linguists concerning whether or not the schools should offer to help speakers of nonstandard English or any type (including Vernacular Black English) learn to speak English according to school norms, all indications from research surveys (Cazden 1969, Hayes and Taylor 1971, Taylor 1973) show that minority communities favor such acquisition.

One last area in which language variation can play an important role in education is in the area of evaluation, particularly in standardized testing. The United States is in a national mood which stresses accountability in education and this accountability is frequently determined by measurements such as nationally normed standardized tests. Such tests frequently ignore expertise which linguistics can provide in order to offer a more accurate and fair assessment of the child's skills and cognitive abilities. Several specialists in language variation are currently at work on such concerns and their work will be of great assistance to educational evaluation in the future.

To this point we have stated that the study of variation is good for the field of linguistics itself and for the field of education. The third area of usefulness is one which, though essentially selfish, grows naturally out of the other two. It deals with our very employment and employability.

The interim report of the Manpower Survey conducted for the Linguistic Society of America by the Center for Applied Linguistics set out to determine the present and future needs for linguists. The rather discouraging results of this survey indicate that there will be little or no job market for linguists in established linguistics departments during the next decade. The report points out that over 65 percent of linguists working at colleges and universities teach other subjects in addition to linguistics. Any increase in demand for linguists during the next five years is likely to be highest at institutions offering no degree or concentration in linguistics.

This report concludes with a series of recommendations ranging from the need to restrict the number of linguists being trained to the broadening of training programs in order to provide our students with

versatility as they approach the job market. The latter strategy
seems most helpful to me for it is a natural outgrowth of recent
developments in our field. The restriction on the number of our students, though humanely motivated, is defeatist and possibly unethical.
I can think of few scholars who are more excited about their field than
linguists. We can only speculate what we might be doing if we had
been forced into our second choice and we can only wonder about our
right to make that decision for someone else. A more reasonable
tack would be for us to put our minds to creating the market, a task
which we have hitherto considered demeaning if, indeed, we have
considered it at all. Yet the study of language variation offers the
best opportunity for providing this versatility to our students in that
the study of language in realistic contexts necessarily involves our
knowing at least something about psychology, anthropology, sociology,
mathematics, and philosophy. With only a small gulp more, we can
also be immediately involved in education. Foreign language and
anthropology departments still need linguists, despite our divorce
from these fields in recent years. The market in sociology has been
largely untapped, while psychology has developed its own breed of
linguist--usually a static type. There probably won't be much of a
market for linguists in math or philosophy departments but the fields
of education, English, and speech are certainly ripe for infiltration.
The greatest issues tearing these fields apart today involve the inability of their practitioners to distinguish between pathological and
socially realistic variation in the behavior and language of children.
Likewise, linguists have disgraced themselves in English departments,
offering grammatical theory and Old English structure to future high
school teachers of English whose major concerns will involve problems of systemic interference and the need to develop stylistic variation and appropriate switching.

The question will ultimately be asked, 'Is the sacrifice of curriculum to minors in education or anthropology or French feasible in
light of pressures brought about by the explosion of knowledge in
our field?'. That is, can we trade off technology for such a functional benefit? A brief answer to this question might be seen in a
similar situation in medical schools today. Recent research in the
communication between doctor and patient has revealed shocking
evidence of what happens when a field ignores function at the expense
of technology. Although 95 percent of the potential success of medical treatment depends on obtaining accurate information from the
medical history interview, little or no attention is given in medical
schools to the training of physicians in interviewing techniques or
the language and culture of patients from different socioeconomic,
racial, or ethnic backgrounds. Likewise little or no attention is
paid to the dehumanizing process of women in OB-GYN settings.

The medical profession is undoubtedly the most secure one of all and even here we are seeing the beginnings of a consumer rebellion. Linguistics does not now have, and never has had, security remotely similar to that of medicine. The choice is to refine the curriculum in such a way that our graduates are versatile enough to be hirable in several markets or to restrict our enrollments. I find the latter alternative elitist, if not unethical.

In summary this paper has argued that the study of language variation is our best way of making use of our current natural resources. The study of language variation is, by definition, an avoidance of the doppelganger effect. It is well suited to avoiding the dangers of elitism. It has led us to new vistas in theoretical matters. It makes a good match with current educational concerns and it offers hope for a way out of the increasing job-market problems which the discipline is currently facing. If we play our cards right, have a little patience, and develop a charitable attitude toward the diverse set of ideas that cross-fertilize and feed the field, we stand a good chance of making progress unprecedented in the past.

NOTES

1. A complete description of the Norfolk Project can be found in 'Sociolinguistic Strategies for Teachers in a Southern School System' (R. Shuy, 1972), Proceedings of the Third International Congress on Applied Linguistics (Copenhagen, in press).
2. Norfolk State University and Old Dominion University, for example, are offering similar work. Likewise, the University of Virginia Extension Program is now offering work in educational anthropology and sociolinguistics.

REFERENCES

Abrahams, Roger. 1970. Positively Black. Englewood Cliffs, Prentice-Hall.
Bauman, Richard and Joel Sherzer. 1974. Explorations in the ethnography of speaking. Cambridge, At the University Press.
DasGupta, Jyotirindra. 1970. Language conflict and national development. Berkeley, University of California Press.
Fasold, Ralph. 1972. Tense marking in Black English. Washington, D.C., Center for Applied Linguistics.
Fishman, Joshua A. et al. 1971. Bilingualism in the barrio. The Hague, Mouton.

Frender, Robert and Wallace Lambert. 1972. Speech style and scholastic success: The tentative relationships and possible implications for lower social class children. In: Georgetown University Round Table on Languages and Linguistics (GURT) 1972. Eduted by Roger W. Shuy. Washington, D. C., Georgetown University Press. 237-272.

Hymes, Dell. 1971. Pidginization and creolization of languages. Cambridge, At the University Press.

Kimball, C. P. 1971. Medicine and dialects. Annals of Internal Medicine 74:1.137-138.

Labov, William. 1966. The social stratification of English in New York City. Washington, D. C., Center for Applied Linguistics.

_____ et al. 1968. A study of the non-standard English of Negro and Puerto Rican speakers in New York City. New York, Columbia University.

Rubin, Joan and Bjorn H. Jernudd. 1971. Can language be planned? Honolulu, University of Hawaii Press.

Rubin, Joan and Roger W. Shuy, eds. 1971. Language planning: Current issues and research. Washington, D. C., Georgetown University Press.

Shuy, Roger W. and Ralph Fasold. 1973. Language attitudes: Current trends and prospects. Washington, D. C., Georgetown University Press.

Shuy, Roger W., Walt Wolfram, and William K. Riley. 1969. Field techniques in an urban language study. Washington, D. C., Center for Applied Linguistics.

Tucker, G. Richard et al. 1969. Negro listeners' reactions to various American-English dialects. Social Forces 47.463-468.

Williams, Frederick. 1970. Language, attitude and social change. In: Language and poverty: Perspectives on a theme. Edited by F. Williams. Chicago, Markham Publishing Company. 300-344.

_____, Rita C. Naremore et al. 1971. Attitudinal correlates of children's speech characteristics (technical report). Austin, Center for Communication Research, University of Texas (mimeo).

Wolfram, Walt. 1969. A sociolinguistic description of Detroit Negro speech. Washington, D. C., Center for Applied Linguistics.

_____. 1971. Overlapping influences in English of second generation Puerto Rican teenagers in Harlem. (Final report). Washington, D. C., USOE 3-70-0033(508) mimeo.